# Sister Days

# Sister Days

## 365 Inspired Moments
### in African American Women's History

*Janus Adams*

**John Wiley & Sons, Inc.**
New York • Chichester • Weinheim • Brisbane • Singapore • Toronto

973 A

ISBN  0-471-28361-4

*For my grandmothers and great-grandmothers beyond*
*For my daughters and theirs yet unborn*

# Acknowledgments

In the researching and writing of *Freedom Days*, I came upon a quote by Septima Clark, known in Civil Rights movement lore as "Mother Conscience." A proverbial lightbulb suddenly flared inside my head as I read her words condemning movement leaders for minimizing the role of women. Bearing witness, said she: "The work the women did during the time of civil rights is what really carried the movement along. [It] would never have taken off if some women hadn't started to speak up." What was true then had forever been true; as half the world, women had been no less than half the struggle, no less than half the story, and sometimes a lot more. And, as I read her words, as the lightbulb shone, I knew what book I'd have to write as soon as I could—a celebration of how we, as women of African descent with ancient roots of culture and courage, have fared the flames of racism, colonialism, slavery, and segregation—and yet borne a collective self complete, gentle, and strong.

I called my lawyer and friend, Joan G. Zooper, and tried the idea on for size. After *Glory Days* and *Freedom Days*, what will you call it, she said—*Sister Days*? We giggled with a tickle, and then found ourselves silent. *Sister Days*, she came back, that's the title, yes, that's what it should be. And, so it is—inspired by a mother, reasoned by a sister-friend, forged by family and friends as encouraging as they have been courageous in their time—my mother, Muriel Tuitt; my daughters, Ayo and Dara Roach; and "sisters" Cheryl Hill, Sharon Robinson, and Sonia Sanchez.

Thanks are due to a network of librarians and archivists in Wilton, Westport, Stamford, and Greenwich, Connecticut; at the Beinecke Archives at Yale University; at the Schomburg Collection of the New York Public Library; and at the Indiana and Philadelphia Historical Societies. A thank-you, too, to A'Lelia Bundles for sharing research on her great-great-grandmother, Madam C. J. Walker.

Thanks to the team at John Wiley: Carole Hall, who brought me to shore, my editor, Hana Lane, and production manager, Diane Aronson.

To the Brothers who love the Sisters, thank you, too. And to the Sisters who love life, thank you for the wind at my back.

# Introduction

In the beginning, the story is told, this is how things came to be — the who was who and what was what — between Man and Woman.

What the gods had given Man, the gods had given Woman. What he could do, she could do. What he had in knowledge and strength, she had too. Everything was even, for that was God's plan. Then one day the two got into a terrible row. Maybe it was that snake in the grass thing again, when the gods called Man to account and he blamed Woman for tempting him with her apple pie. Maybe it was something like that. Whatever it was, it went on so long that Man finally walked out, slammed the garden gate, and headed up to Heaven to have a talk with God.

There's got to be a way to put an end to all this commotion, Man said to himself. And all the while he's walking, he's talking to himself, he's remembering the good times when he, Man, was in charge of everything and Woman was just a rib. By the time he got to Heaven he knew what he wanted. Man walked right up to the gods' counsel and stated his case. He said, God, I've got a woman down ther-r-r-re, uh, uh, uh. He said, God grant me strength to deal with that woman. And God did. God gave Man more strength. He knew what was going on. He had given equally to both, but there was something about that Woman that made all that Creating and sun-rising and moon-making a whole lotta fun. But, business was business. With his extra strength, Man could also better tend the fields and the flock. So it was done. And Man was ecstatic. He raced home to tell Woman that he was boss now; with his strength he was *king!*

Well, as you can imagine, Woman was having none of that. Night and day, she said, day and night I work my fingers to the bone and he's the one gets the strength? No, no, no, no, no. Time for a talk. God wouldn't do a thing like that. And, wasn't her God a woman? Out the garden gate she sped and up to Heaven she went. Just like that. Before she knew it, she was there, for once Woman made up her mind to do a thing, the thing got done. She had heard that just before she got to Heaven, she could freshen up a bit at the Pearly Gates, so she would stop off to do that — shake the dust off her feet, you know, out of respect. There at the Gates she spied a set of golden keys, exquisite in construct, stunning in simplicity, ageless in design. But this was no time to admire the decor. At Heaven's Gate she turned right and found the gods waiting for her. From what Man had said, they knew that she would come around in her own time. Now God, she said, with all you've given me, I hate to trouble you. But, she said, God whatever that was you gave my Man you need to give him a little less. But God said no, a gift is a gift, you don't take it back. They could give her more strength too, but keeping Man and Woman even in all things hadn't worked out according to plan. She thought. They thought. Then, she remembered the keys at the gate. So you saw the Keys to the Kingdom, they smiled all-knowing. She could have them if she liked. They knew greater wisdom was a gift she would use well. Thankful, she said her praises and rushed home to Man. He had his strengths, for sure, but she had greater wisdom.

And that's why things are the way they are to this day. Man holds up his end, but Woman holds the power. So it was told by our mother's mothers and so it is to this day true: women hold the Keys to the Kingdom. In her wisdom, the Great Mother has passed on her stories; from them our herstory has come.

"Come, let me tell you 'a Nancy story,'" I would hear my grandmother call, when I seemed in need of a little soothing down. Years later I decoded her Caribbean lilt to learn that "a Nancy" was "Ananci," the trickster-spider who spun a web of African lore. But each story no matter its filigree would have the same moral, the same reason for being told: to share her philosophy of life. All things are one, said Grandma. In this world, everything is related, all things are one. And sometimes in her daily sojourn, the endless struggles with her life and times, she would pause, "situate" herself, and exhale. "I'd write a book, but who would read it," she would say, knowing her vindication would not soon come.

I remember, too, the days my grandfather would walk my cousin and me along the New York harbor to teach us about geography and life with lessons charted by the ports of call of the ships at shore. And then he'd stand at the pier, his figure etched against the sunset, his arm pointing to places we would some day have to go—to see and to be.

Places like Jamestown, Virginia. In August 1619 a Dutch man-of-war sailed into harbor in colonial Jamestown, traded its human cargo for food, and launched an industry so successful that even today—nearly four hundred years later—vast stretches of the African continent remain underpopulated. Slavery in the Americas consumed more than one hundred million African lives—but not their souls.

Visiting that Jamestown site, I marvel at what happened to those first African Americans and what has sustained their descendants—their powerful stories of history, heritage, and hope, a saga I began retelling with *Glory Days*, my first book in what has become a trilogy. From our *Glory Days* (a thirty-five hundred year daily memoir of African Americans in their time) to our *Freedom Days* (a celebration of the extended Civil Rights years at one with the global movement for Pan-African liberation) and now to our *Sister Days*—the story of our sojourn and of our Sojourners: a trailblazer's diary of routes charted by our Harriets and our Hatshesputs, by our Nailahs and our Nefertitis, our Rashidas and our Rosas.

And what a herstory we have made, what stories our lives tell. "And ain't I a woman?" Sojourner Truth is said to have rallied, challenging the narrowed eye of a norm. With higher expectation, we have conjured a womanhood others have dared attempt to deny and made real the worlds we would behold. It's quite a legacy, as you'll read on these pages, these odes to our womanhood.

I remember a conversation with an administrator. Asked why her school district was so reluctant to include African American history and multicultural perspectives in the curriculum, she seemed caught off-guard. "The truth is," she confided, "parents and teachers are afraid that if we tell children the truth, they'll think their ancestors were bad."

And, I couldn't help thinking of all those children so long sacrificed at a blockade of lies that others might be raised isolated from truth. I saw the children and the child within, I heard the voices of the children and those of eighty who remain but a child of God. From them came my inspiration. I knew *why* I wanted to write. But, it was not until I looked in the mirror of memory, that I knew *what* I needed to write.

On the days when my grandmother would tire, her stories used up, her memories dim, I remembered how she would croon to herself, "I'd write a book, but who would read it," and yet go on.

From the collectivity of the stories of our grandmothers untold and for all of their very great- and very grand-children, here, I hope, is the book they would have written. Here is their power, their strength, their pain, their ways, and their better days. Here are their woes and their problem solving, their laughter and their haughty, naughty ways. Here, too, are our stories, the ones we would put in our hope chest, woven into tapestries, knowing that we today are the ancestors of tomorrow. And, as you read of these our *Sister Days*, somewhere beyond our Grandmas smile. Somewhere, our Grandpas glance upon the docks of our day and look to the horizons their dreams helped paint.

For you to read, these are the stories they have told me to keep, the measure of our Sister Days, inspired moments to alter the view on both sides of the blockade. To alter the cadence of one who might not otherwise know that her place in this land was staked in Jamestown; bought and paid for in 1619—long, long years ago; that her source has been channeled from a river called the Nile, her wisdom dredged at Timbuktu. Yes, my Sisterlove, so begin our days. There was Boston, Nicodemus, and Mississippi, always Mississippi; New York and Nantucket and on and on and so we go on. . . .

# January

*Dara and Ayo Roach* (January 8, 1975). Photographer unknown.
Reprinted courtesy of the author.
For more information, see November 2.

"*H*oney, I went to a Negro History meetin' tonight," said the voice on the phone. "Well, they had several speakers. . . . There was one pretty young colored girl who . . . gave a nice talk about Harriet Tubman, Sojourner Truth and *many others* . . . and I noticed that everybody would name a couple of folk and then add 'and many others. . . .' Now I can't think about the *many others* without thinkin' of my grandmother. . . . Toys? She'd pull up a clump of grass, tie it in the middle to make a 'waist line' and then comb the dirt out of the roots so she could braid them in two pigtails, and that would be a 'grass doll' with 'root hair' . . . and the boys got barrel wires for hoops and pebbles and a ball for 'jacks.' Every minute of Grandma's life was struggle. . . . After the kids was off to bed she'd sit in her rockin' chair in the dark kitchen, and that old chair would weep sawdust tears as she rocked back and forth. She'd start off singing real low-like . . . 'I'm so glad trouble don' las' always,' and switch off in the middle and pick up with 'Savior, Savior, hear my humble cry' . . . and she'd keep jumpin' from tune to tune . . . 'I'm gonna tell God all of my troubles when I get home' . . . and she'd pat her feet as she rocked and rassled with death, Jim Crow and starvation. All of a sudden the rockin' would stop and she'd jump up, smack her hands together and say, 'Atcha dratcha!' and she'd come back revived and refreshed and ready to go at them drat troubles. . . . I bet Miss Tubman and Miss Truth would like us to remember and give some time to the *many others.*"

On this New Year's Day, this day of *Imani* (faith), the final day of Kwanzaa, with the words of author Alice Childress from her book *Like One of the Family,* published in 1956, we honor all of our sheroes and sister-griots—our Tubmans, Truths, *and many others*—who have brought us thus far by faith, forging our Sister Days.

Saturday, January 1, 2000

National                                USA

---

**Women and Womanhood**                    **Kwanzaa: Faith**

*M*akeda, Queen of Sheba (Ethiopia), and Solomon, King of Israel . . . theirs was a love story for the ages. So impressed by news of Solomon's deeds was Makeda that she journeyed to Jerusalem to meet him. There, according to the Old Testament and the ancient Ethiopian *Kebra Nagast,* the most powerful woman of her day and the man prized for his wisdom fell in love and had a child. "I am smitten with the love of wisdom and I am constrained by the cords of understanding," wrote Makeda. "For wisdom is far better than treasure of gold and silver, and wisdom is the best of everything that hath been created on earth." But, to Makeda, wisdom was a *woman*—a virtue she extolled with the female pronoun: "I will love her like a mother, and she will embrace me like her child."

> Through wisdom I have dived down into the great sea, and have seized in the place of her depths a pearl whereby I am rich. I went down like the great iron anchor whereby men anchor ships for the night on the high seas, and I received a lamp which lighteth me, and I came up by the ropes of the boat of understanding. I went to sleep in the depths of the sea, and not being overwhelmed with the water I dreamed a dream. And it seemed to me that there was a star in my womb, and I marvelled thereat. . . . I went in through the doors of the treasury of wisdom and I drew for myself the waters of understanding. I went into the blaze of the flame of the sun, and it lighted me with the splendour thereof, and I made of it a shield for myself, and I saved myself by confidence therein, and not myself only but all those who travel in the footprints of wisdom, and not myself only but all the men of my country, the kingdom of Ethiopia, and not only those but those who travel in their ways, the nations that are round about.

Through wisdom, the best of herself as a woman, Makeda had found her love.

Circa tenth century B.C.E.

Ethiopia

---

*T*he library in the diaspora. An ancient African institution, the library dates back to Egypt's King Osymandyas, circa 1240 B.C.E. At a time when most libraries in the United States were private and for the rich, one of the nation's first public libraries was founded by African Americans in 1833—the Philadelphia Library Company of Colored Persons. Then, with growth of the historically black colleges, a new page was added to the story on January 3, 1924, when Sara "Sadie" Delaney opened the Veteran's Library at Tuskegee.

In a unique contribution, Delaney created bibliotherapy—"the treatment of a patient through selected reading"—for which she earned international acclaim. Significantly, Delaney's career had begun in 1920 at Harlem's famed 135th Street branch of the New York Public Library, which, in 1927, acquired the collection and expertise of noted Afro–Puerto Rican bibliophile Arturo A. Schomburg. From that branch, another keeper of the flame, Jean Blackwell Hutson, would emerge. In her thirty-two years there, she guided the collection from its branch library status to a resource of world renown, the Schomburg Center for Research in Black Culture. As a patron once mused, the "branch libraries love people and the research libraries love books." But Hutson was so successful at combining the two that President Kwame Nkrumah invited her to Ghana to replicate, for his newly independent nation, his own youthful quests there as a student.

There are those who would derogate African Americans with trinkets like this one: "If you want to hide something from black folks, put it between the pages of a book." Then there are those who know better. From ancient Egypt to America to Ghana, if you want to find something sacred to black folks, look to how we have built our libraries.

Thursday, January 3, 1924

Alabama                                    USA

---

**Libraries**                          **Zest for Learning**

$\mathcal{A}$fter President Abraham Lincoln signed the Emancipation Proclamation, notifying Congress and the military of his plan to free the slaves, three months would pass before the decree became official, and then only on Rebel soil. For Lincoln, the issue was not the slave, it was the war. But you couldn't prove that by the newly free. On New Year's Day 1863, as news of freedom came down the wires and soldiers spread the word, in first a trickle and then a flood, people broke the dam of slavery. Even for those who were not immediately free, in spirit if in no other recognizable form, there was no turning back. Charlotte Brown recalled her liberation on the first Sunday of 1863, January 4. This was the scene on the Virginia plantation, where she had been enslaved:

> De news come on a Thursday, an' all de slaves been shoutin' an' carryin' on tell ev'rybody was all tired out. 'Member de fust Sunday of freedom. We was all sittin' roun' restin' an' tryin' to think what freedom meant an' ev'rybody was quiet an' peaceful. All at once ole Sister Carrie who was near 'bout a hundred started in to talkin':
>
> *Tain't no mo' sellin' today,*
> *Tain't no mo' hirin' today,*
> *Tain't no pullin' off shirts today,*
> *It's stomp down freedom today.*
> *Stomp it down!*
>
> An' when she says, "Stomp it down," all de slaves commence to shoutin' wid her: *Stomp down Freedom today* — Wasn't no mo' peace dat Sunday. Ev'rybody started in to sing an' shout once mo'. Fust thing you know dey done made up music to Sister Carrie's stomp song an' sang an' shouted dat song all de res' de day. Chile, dat was one glorious time!

Sunday, January 4, 1863

Virginia                    USA

---

**Freedom**                                                    **Joy**

*I*n the 1940s, Estelle Carter was a retired teacher in her late seventies living in New Bedford, Massachusetts. When her great-nephew visited, she would always send him home with a gift—a morsel of history collected over the years. "Did you know that your great-grandfather was a druggist?" she once asked, planting seeds of the state's first African American pharmacist in the soul of the child who would follow her footsteps instead. Grown into an educator and historian, Robert Carter Hayden Jr. would patch together the quilt of Carter family history with pieces bequeathed by his great-aunt.

In the winter of 1971, the sad task of disassembling a deceased cousin's apartment yielded Hayden *Grandpa Carter's notebook!*—a handwritten treasure with its proprietary formulas for such compounds as Carter's Toothache Powder. News of his find unlocked his mother's memory of an old photo: "Robert H. Carter, First Colored Pharmacist in Massachusetts!" His father recalled a brown paper bag in the cellar. In it was a certificate dated January 5, 1886: "This is to certify that Robert H. Carter is a registered Pharmacist . . . hereby vested with the authority to conduct the business of a Pharmacist by law." Then, in 1977, after years of gingerly prodding her for an interview, his ninety-two-year-old grandmother, Parthenia Harris Carter, related the moment that would chart a family's destiny. In 1864 or so, shoveling snow for a local pharmacist after school, young Carter had found a wallet stuffed with money and turned it over to his employer. In reward, the pharmacist apprenticed him. Mastering the science at age twenty, Carter later opened his own store—powering his family for the century to come.

In life, today's family fortune is the snow shovel find a century ago; empowered with the gifts of knowledge and pride, we just never know where our inspired moments will lead. . . .

Tuesday, January 5, 1886

Massachusetts            USA

---

$\mathcal{I}$n 1961, the University of Georgia, then 176 years old, had never admitted a black student. That ended on January 6, when Charlayne Hunter heard a voice on the phone blurt "Congratulations!" The legal suit filed on her behalf had been won. Federal Court Judge William Bootle had ordered her and co-plaintiff Hamilton "Hamp" Holmes admitted to the university. With the 1954 Supreme Court *Brown v. Board of Education* decision upheld (see May 17), white America could no longer presume admissions excluding blacks solely on the basis of color.

In the battle over segregation, the central issue — education — is always lost. So, too, is principle. The fundamental wrong is this: a public institution funded by the tax dollars of people both black and white denies blacks access to their funds for the benefit of whites. That exploitation was at the root of the NAACP Legal Defense Fund's attack on segregation. But how did the students themselves feel? "Even in the best high school in Atlanta, we had hand-me-down textbooks and our labs were certainly not as well equipped," Hunter has said. Credit was due black teachers for the fact that black students were able to compete at all, given the conditions. "We didn't want to go to school with white people — that wasn't it. It was those facilities they had." And how did these pioneers perceive their role? Said Hunter, "I was really much more interested in integrating the place and Hamp was much more interested in desegregation."

Still today, North and South, the nation is divided by objective: segregation versus separation; integration versus desegregation. Perhaps one day we will be united by a common objective — education.

Friday, January 6, 1961

Georgia            USA

*A*lice Walker was closing out a notebook begun eight years earlier—closing out a chapter in her life and beginning a new one as well. "Next month I will be forty," she wrote on January 7, 1984. "In some ways, I feel my early life's work is done, and done completely."

Her first story, "To Hell with Dying," had been published by Langston Hughes in 1967, when she was only twenty-three. Since then, she had returned the favor with a children's biography of the then-often-forgotten Hughes and delivered to our midst three volumes of poetry; two novels; two volumes of short stories; numerous essays; the book that would earn her the Pulitzer Prize, *The Color Purple*, later adapted for film; and the resurrected voice of a literary foremother too long lost to our collective inner ear, Zora Neale Hurston.

How did almost forty feel? "Great spirit, I thank you for the length of my days and the fullness of my work," she wrote, expressing our sentiments as well as ever. "Thank you again. I love you. I love your trees, your sun, your stars and moon and light. Your darkness. Your plums and watermelons and water meadows."

Recalling another writer's words, she thought, "One plum was left for me. One seed becomes an everlasting singing tree!" Thankfully, the gods have kept her waiting and promised her/us more than one. With the mighty fruit fallen from her tree, she has served as host at *The Temple of My Familiar*. There, in the glare and doom, she exposed the practice of female genital mutilation, which had scarred centuries of girls en route to womanhood. The seed she planted raised an international outcry—the sound of women's voices climbing freedom's song.

Saturday, January 7, 1984

California                    USA

---

**Women and Womanhood**                    **Life's Work**

That African Americans have made every sacrifice to build the United States is a fact far deeper than the history of slavery. Indeed, African American men have seen combat in every military campaign from the nation's earliest days. Yet, well into the late twentieth century, no black woman was ever able to join the Daughters of the American Revolution (DAR)—not on the basis of simple racist exclusion but by the manipulation of regulations that would bar blacks by means that spoke more to the history of racism than of patriotism. As recorded in the *New York Times* of January 8, 1978, that changed when Karen Farmer became the first African American woman to produce documents proving her ancestor's participation in the Revolutionary War.

Why would a black woman want to join the DAR—the group that had so flaunted its racism in the face of our great Marian Anderson (see April 9)? The fact that Anderson would later be allowed to perform at Constitution Hall after being snubbed did not absolve the sin. For some, to become a DAR member was to prove a point. For along with a denial of membership came a denial of the sacrifices made by the black men who risked personal freedom to side with the Americans, hoping to free their entire families, when siding with the British would have granted the enslaved immediate personal liberty. To some applicants, the issue was principle. Then, as W. E. B. Du Bois would titter in his June 1929 editorial in *The Crisis*, there were the others. . . .

"My friend, who is in the Record Department of Massachusetts, found a lady's ancestry the other day," wrote Du Bois. "Her colored grandfather was a soldier in the Revolutionary War, and through him she might join the D. A. R. But she asked 'confidentially,' could that matter of 'his—er—color be left out?'"

Sunday, January 8, 1978

National                              USA

---

**Social History**                    **Identity**

*J*n one landmark week of January 9, 1943, *Time, Newsweek,* and *Life* magazines all published features on the same "light-brown, soft-spoken young Negress." That was the way the white press spoke of African Americans back then—and that was when they were being complimentary.

But Lena Horne possessed rare beauty and talent in anyone's book. From her start as a chorus dancer at the Cotton Club at age sixteen—a job she left school to take when her mother was extremely ill—Lena Horne had hit the Hollywood jackpot in ten short years. Added to her own hard work, three strong black men encouraged her film breakthrough. Actor-singer Paul Robeson and the NAACP's Walter White befriended her on the same night, after hearing her sing at the trendy Café Society, the only nonsegregated New York club south of Harlem. If there was an opportunity, she should take it, they said; her style and regal demeanor would do wonders for the image of the race on-screen. Robeson pressured MGM to treat her well from his post inside the industry; White used his NAACP clout on the outside. And walking straight up the steps of MGM with her for contract talks was her father. Teddy Horne looked MGM boss Louis B. Mayer straight in the eye and told him nobody would make a maid or a buffoon of his Lena; she didn't need the job that badly. She was signed to a seven-year contract, and the publicity mills started rolling, leveraging her nightclub appearances into box office capital.

"When Lena sings at dinner and supper, forks are halted in mid-career," wrote *Time.* "She has broken every Savoy-Plaza record," reported *Newsweek.* "Young Negro with haunting voice charms New York," gushed *Life* over a photo spread. Soon every black soldier would paste her picture in his footlocker. The war had been on for a while—on two fronts.

Saturday, January 9, 1943

National                          USA

*L*ucie E. Campbell was one of the most influential music directors in the history of the National Baptist Convention. Elected in 1916 as director and pianist of the youth choir, which sang at services throughout the convention week, "Miss Lucie," as she was called, wrote a new song virtually every year until her death in 1963. Among them, her classic "He Understands, He'll Say 'Well Done,'" written in 1933, kept her status as a living legend growing. Such annual offerings, a tradition begun with "Something Within" in 1919, would place her among the leading composers in the history of African American church music.

On a cold, wet Memphis day in the winter of 1919, perhaps this one, Miss Lucie was shopping at a local fish market in the Beale Street district when she observed an incident between a blind street singer and some men who apparently loved good gin as much as they loved good music. Exiting a local bar, they spied Connie Rosemond, his feet wrapped in rags, and asked the impoverished singer to play some "good ole Southern blues." He refused, explaining that he only sang for the Lord—hymns and spirituals. The "bribe" of a tip rose to five dollars before the men would believe Mr. Rosemond's protestations that he only sang songs that came from "something within." Inspired, Miss Lucie wrote: "Something within me that holdeth the reins, / Something within me that banishes pain, / Something within me. I cannot explain. / All that I know there is something within."

That year, Miss Lucie invited Rosemond to premiere the song he had inspired at the National Baptist Convention. Its story of a true believer was a success. From 1919 on, a new Lucie Campbell song became an annual convention event and an instant addition to the repertoire of church choirs nationwide.

Winter 1919

Tennessee                                        USA

---

**Music**                                        **Inspiration**

On January 11, 1991, Tina Turner was inducted into the Rock and Roll Hall of Fame. It sounds so special. It was.

In 1960, before the act was called the Ike and Tina Turner Revue, she was the lady with the incredible voice and legs. Then, boosted by the adulation of her fans, came the miniskirted frenzy, the wigs, and the whirling dervishness. There was also the private physical and emotional torture by Ike, her husband and partner of fifteen years. Then, on July 1, 1976, her rebirth-day, Tina Turner got tired of being beaten down and lifted herself up from a Dallas hotel room with barely the clothes on her back, walked to the highway, and walked out on Ike Turner. She was shunned by the industry for the next year. Those who condemned her—by walking out on Ike, they declared, she had walked out on the tour—knew better. But with the misplaced priority that protects violent men who beat their wives, they were unlikely to admit it. In need of work, the truth was that she needed to work on herself, needed time to heal. She did both by working small clubs in the United States and solid houses in Europe. In 1980, she relocated. In 1984, with less than two weeks of production, Tina "the pro" recorded *Private Dancer*. That landmark album went super-platinum, winning Tina Turner three Grammy Awards and helping her make the super-comeback of all time. In 1985, she joined in "We Are the World," the record that raised unprecedented funds for famine relief. By 1988, her concert at a Brazilian soccer stadium garnered the largest paid audience for a solo artist in history.

And so, Tina Turner was inducted into the Rock and Roll Hall of Fame. What a story! A personal and professional tribute to a woman of extraordinary character. More than a survivor, Tina Turner was a winner. Not only did the public know it—most important, she had come to that recognition deep within herself.

Friday, January 11, 1991

National                                    USA

---

**Music**                                    **Character**

*J*n the waning months of the Civil War, desperate Southerners scapegoated blacks with a venom so sadistic, even in war, that women and children felt the sting.

At Fort Pillow, Tennessee, surrender of the Union-held fort did not stop the cold-blooded massacre of black soldiers by Confederate troops. Their refusal to honor blacks as prisoners of war was similar to their refusal to allow the families of black enlistees customary protection. So incensed was the owner of Patsey Leach at news of her husband's enlistment that he stripped her naked and whipped her. Fleeing, she could rescue only the youngest of her five children. Jane Kamper's owner "locked my children up so that I could not find them. I afterwards got my children by stealth." So abused were the families of black enlistees that Federal recruiters reported a slack in the number of volunteers. Reporting his "hands & heart full" dealing with refugees from the terror, a Union district commander noted, "I blush for my race . . . when I discover the wicked barbarity of the late Masters & Mistresses." And yet we fought on—black men, women, and children—in the War for Liberation, as we called it back then. "It is with grate joy I take this time to let you know Whare I am." With these few words, John Boston's wife learned of her husband's escape to a New York regiment.

Amid escalating terror, on January 12, 1865, the United States government acted in a manner unheard of before—and rarely since. In the persons of War Secretary Edwin M. Stanton and General William T. Sherman, twenty black men were invited to Union Headquarters to envision their future freedom. Four days later, General Sherman issued Special Field Order Number Fifteen, setting aside a tract of coastal land from the Carolinas to Florida and providing "forty acres of tillable ground" for each family and the legal basis for reparations.

Thursday, January 12, 1865

South Carolina                              USA

---

**Reparations**                                            **Sacrifice**

*O*n January 13, 1994, two thousand women gathered in Boston for a conference co-sponsored by the Massachusetts Institute of Technology (MIT) and Radcliffe College. A national symposium, "Black Women in the Academy: Defending Our Name" could have been called a national referendum.

Because "eighty-six percent of African American women who voted" in 1992 voted to make Bill Clinton president, they represented his strongest constituency. With expertise in diverse scholarly disciplines and experience far beyond their ivied walls, and with their majority holding a master's or a doctorate, they were uniquely qualified to assess the state of the nation—a task President Clinton would officially address later that week. By conference resolution, they issued a letter of concerns and solutions. "This is a crucial moment of challenge and opportunity for learning as well as in public policy," they declared, spotlighting such new forms of social injury as "environmental racism in communities of color." Five actions were urged: to commission a blue ribbon panel on race relations; to extend the "glass ceiling" commission to explore career advancement for and research by women of color in higher education; to increase funding for community-based service to the poor and others in greatest need; to "end the destructive anti-democratic covert actions against Haiti" and restore Jean-Bertrand Aristide as president; and to extend support for the democratic process in post-apartheid South Africa.

Their activism befit the holiday weekend marking what would have been Dr. Martin Luther King Jr.'s sixty-fifth birthday. The results were impressive: Dr. John Hope Franklin, the venerated historian, would head a new race commission; Aristide was restored; and despite the predictable ransacking of her reputation by a hostile congress, the nation would award itself the first sister-secretary of labor, Alexis Herman (see May 9).

Thursday, January 13, 1994

Massachusetts      USA

---

*I*n the annals of the West, few characters are more colorful or less known than Mary Fields, otherwise known as "Stagecoach Mary," of Cascade, Montana.

Six feet tall, two hundred pounds, a crackerjack shot with a .38 Smith & Wesson, she was a legend in her time. The actor Gary Cooper, who knew her when he was a boy, once said, "I remember seeing her in Cascade when I was just a little shaver of nine or so. . . . Each day, never missing a one, she made her triumphant entry into [St. Peter's Mission] seated on top of the mail coach dressed in a man's hat and coat and smoking a huge cigar." There were the stories of how she overcame nature's obstacles en route. Trapped and lost in a blizzard, she avoided freezing to death by walking back and forth all night. Another time, her horses were frightened by a wolf pack and overturned the freight load in fear, but lone Mary stood guard against the pack all night until help came in the morning. Settling down to a simpler life when she was about seventy—because she was born enslaved, her exact age was unknown—she opened a laundry business. There, too, she could stare down danger, and danger would flee. Belting down a beer in the town saloon, a deadbeat customer with a long overdue two-dollar laundry tab made the mistake of crossing her sight. She tapped him on the shoulder; he turned around; she leveled him with a right and announced, "His laundry bill is paid."

She smoked cigars till the day she died in 1914, somewhere near eighty, and it could be said she was *some kinda woman*. A sign at Yellowstone National Park reads TAKE ONLY PICTURES, LEAVE ONLY FOOTPRINTS. Today, the only remnants left of the picturesque Stagecoach Mary are a sketch in the local bank by famed artist Charley Russell, a grave marker at Hillside Cemetery, and footprints staking the trail of her wondrous exploits.

Winter 1899

Montana                    USA

$S$ ince the assassination of Martin Luther King Jr. in 1968, Coretta Scott King had worked to have her late husband's January 15, 1929, birth commemorated as a national holiday.

Aid for Mrs. King's efforts came in many ways. Singer-composer Stevie Wonder donated a Happy Birthday song. Others gave the precious gift of tenacity—among them Harriet Elizabeth Byrd, Wyoming's first African American elected official, who entered the state house in 1981. With four generations of family history etched deep in the rolling ranges of Wyoming and her father the first African American born in Laramie, Liz Byrd's roots were as old as the state, which entered the Union in 1890. She and the plains had shared the wind. Yet each year when she put up the bill for a state holiday, a "silence" swept through. The issue wasn't roots, it was votes. "There're not enough blacks here to qualify for a holiday," fellow lawmakers told her, as if King's vision of freedom was for blacks alone. But by 1983, numbers nationwide added up for President Ronald Reagan to sign the bill into law: as of January 20, 1986, the third Monday of January would be henceforth celebrated as a federal holiday, Martin Luther King Day.

But with the president's jurisdiction in such matters limited to the District of Columbia and federal offices, the push for state legislation continued. Whenever Liz Byrd ran for reelection the question was the same: "Are you going to go back up there with it?" So was the answer: "You can count on this: if I'm there the legislation will be there."

Wednesday, January 15, 1986

Wyoming                    USA

---

It was billed as the Battle of Swing—a midnight rumble at the legendary Savoy Ballroom on January 16, 1938. Ella Fitzgerald with Chick Webb's band taking on Billie Holiday with the Count Basie team.

Billie's spin with "My Man" knocked 'em dead. Ella, in her inimitable way, was scattin' all over "Loch Lomond." Ivie Anderson joined in, with Duke Ellington on the keys. Even Lionel Hampton was there for the bout; Jimmy Rushing, too.

But when the "girl singers," as the press loved to bill them, jumped in, it was Ella Fitzgerald and Billie Holiday for the count. A two-way call on the bands split the decision—*Metronome* magazine went for Webb; *Down Beat* voted Basie victor. But Billie's sonorous "Man" couldn't shake Ella's "Loch." History records a win for Ella. The audience knew otherwise. The real winners were the ones with tickets to this, the last of the great battles of the bands.

Sunday, January 16, 1938

New York                          USA

*T*he exact date is unknown, but this miracle of fact and faith has been well documented in Underground Railroad history and lore (see March 20).

It was the 1840s, winter. A woman and her baby arrived at a Newport, Indiana, station from bondage in Kentucky. Her other two children had died, and upon learning that this two-year-old would soon be sold, she had fled with the child. Late one night, slavecatchers neared the safe house where she hid. As she fled through a back door, the men took quick pursuit. Like so many others, she had heard the Spirituals sung all her life. Now, these ancestral lessons inscribed with their sacred codes resurfaced within—hers to use to stoke her courage. "My lord he calls me, he calls me by the thunder; the trumpet sounds within-a my soul, I ain't got long to stay here." And "Wade in the water, God's gon' trouble the water."

With the thunder of hooves as her trumpet, she propelled herself to the half-frozen Ohio River, determined to be free or drown trying. Daring the water's tenuous edge, she slid her baby and herself from ice patch to breaking ice patch. She trembled at the fates ahead, horror-struck by what lay behind. She had nothing she could call her own, only the precious bundle that was her child. That weight, the responsibility and love of that life, made her light as rain as she slipped along the checkered route. To Eliza, what happened that night must have seemed like that ancient parting of the waters that enslaved preachers promised the faithful would someday come again. For, as the ice parted underfoot, it separated her from her captors, leaving them and slavery behind. "God's gon' trouble the water."

On the other side, an unknown man, awed at the sight, helped her to safety. "See that man with the big hat on. No more working on the cotton farm . . ."

Winter 1846

Indiana                                        USA

---

**Underground Railroad**                              **Human Spirit**

*A*nd so, the voices of women on art and the art of being woman:

"After I decided to be an artist, the first thing that I had to believe was that I, a black woman, could penetrate the art scene and that I could do so without sacrificing one iota of my blackness, or my femaleness, or my humanity."

—Faith Ringgold, 1985

On Afrofemcentrism: "I pay homage, seek comfort, and experience rage . . . in [this] public mourning/reunion place. In [this] 'memory place' whether Gorée, Elmina, or elsewhere, [I] touch the trace of the past which remains [my] very present. [I] romanticize, cry, embrace, and leave renewed through [my] own experience which stimulates [my] consciousness with memories or others' memories."

—Freida High, 1995

"Every time I think about color it's a political statement. It would be a luxury to be white and never to think about it."

—Emma Amos, 1993

"This is not the first thunder but a thousand-year recognition."

—Barbara Chase Riboud, 1987

"We ought to stop thinking we have to do the art of other people. We have to create an art for liberation and for life."

—Elizabeth Catlett, 1971

"I had a dream, its voice spoke to me, 'Why don't you draw or die?' 'Is that it?' I said, 'My, My.'"

—Minnie Evans, circa 1987

1971–1995

National                                    USA

---

**Art**                                                                 **Voice**

*O*n the battlefields of the nation, on the battlefronts of home, the Civil War raged on, and black families waged a War for Liberation, as we called it, all their own.

A husband gone to war, a wife at home with the children, that was the nature of war. But when the husband is a slave and the wife left behind is the property of his enemy, there is a different story to tell. He is a traitor, she his accomplice. Add to this their forced illiteracy and the letters between Ann and Andy are precious indeed. From a plantation in Paris, Missouri, came Ann's letter to Andy, "My Dear Husband," dated January 19, 1864:

> I rec'd your letter dated Jan'y 9th also one dated Jany 1st but have got no one till now to write for me. You do not know how bad I am treated. They are treating me worse and worse every day. Our child cries for you. Send me some money as soon as you can for me and my child are almost naked. My cloth is yet in the loom and there is no telling when it will be out. Do not send any of your letters to Hogsett especially those having money in them as Hogsett will keep the money. . . . Do the best you can and do not fret too much for me for it wont be long before I will be free and then all we make will be ours. . . . P.S. Sind our little girl a string of beads in your next letter to remember you by.

The Civil War lasted four years, our War for Liberation much longer. To keep their love alive the Anns and Andys enlisted a network of accomplices — "spies" and "agents," often free people who endangered their own freedom and their lives — who rallied around the Anns and Andys everywhere. To understate our foes at every turn is to undervalue the lengths to which we have gone to achieve our greatest triumph — ourselves — sheroes within the belly of the beast.

Tuesday, January 19, 1864

Missouri                                          USA

$\mathcal{A}$ drawing on the exterior wall of a home, not far from the old sailors' home, shows a woman kneeling with her hands tied behind her back and a noose hanging from her neck. This Saturday in Togo, January 20, 1979, at four o'clock, a spiritual law court will determine the guilt or innocence of a seamstress accused of stealing cloth from her employer in a "trial by ordeal."

In the "courtroom," benches are arranged between altar-lined walls. The key players are there: the old woman employer, the alleged thief, the priest, the observers. The witness stand in the room's center conjures belief in a judgment day. The accuser sits on a stool in the center of the arena. Her foot rests on an object possessed with the power to effect decisions. It is attached to a cord that rises up through the core of a blood-soaked cowried globe poised between roof and floor, heaven and damnation. The accused takes her seat, denying the charge. How can one know who is telling the truth? A hole in the dirt floor has been filled with whiskey and lemonade. Into it, a palm nut is lowered on a string with a noose at its end. Sand then covers the hole. The accuser kneels before the hole, her hands tied behind her back and the noose around her neck. In one deft move, she extracts the palm nut with ease. It is proof that her heart is pure, her conscience free. Now the accused attempts to repeat the process, but she cannot release the palm nut, proof of her guilt. But maybe not. Collapsing in tears, she protests her innocence—this time. Once before she had stolen something, and the guilt still weighed upon her. That is what the "ordeal" has shown.

Whether an authentic trial or tourist attraction, it is an old story. Truth can be elusive. But guilt weighs heavily upon the soul. That is the lesson of the day. So ends the trial; the priest leaves by taxi—another town, another trial.

Saturday, January 20, 1979

Lomé                                                    Togo

*W*ith the third Mormon migration to the land of the Ute people, renamed Utah, came the Robert Smith family wagon train and their forty slaves—among them Biddy Mason, whom Smith had made the mother of three. To Mason went the tasks of herding cattle, making camp, cooking the day's first meal, caring for her newborn, and breaking camp. Walking the two-thousand-mile trek from Mississippi to Utah and later on to California, because her job had her follow up the rear, "she literally ate the dust of the entire wagon train," as one biographer wrote. But she had not "bit the dust." In Mason's mind, if nowhere else, she was free. Just as she had walked from Mississippi to California for a slavedriver, she would walk anywhere for freedom and for herself. Realizing her plight—a bound woman on free soil—the black community of Los Angeles rallied to her aid and asked that Mason and her three daughters be placed in protective custody. Sheriff Burnside agreed, and in a landmark California case on the legal rights of black settlers, Judge Benjamin Hayes granted her freedom on January 21, 1856.

Mason and her daughters settled in what had certainly been her "city of angels." A midwife and nurse, she bought a homestead; founded a day-care center and nursery; cofounded the First African Methodist Episcopal Church (FAME); tended the needy at home, in hospital, or in jail; and devoted her life to others as a philanthropist.

A century later, people were still singing her praise. Led by the city's first African American mayor, Tom Bradley, and her great-granddaugters, on March 27, 1988, a gathering of three thousand unveiled a headstone at her grave, proclaiming Biddy Mason Day. It was Palm Sunday, a fitting day for tribute. As Jesus had walked for miles bearing a terrible cross, she, too, had achieved her epiphany.

Monday, January 21, 1856

Utah/California                    USA

---

**Pioneers**                                        **Freedom**

*O*n January 22, 1987, public television premiered *Eyes on the Prize*—the landmark documentary chronicling the Civil Rights movement years 1954 to 1965. Unseen but ever-present in the background (in the backbone, as it were) of the saga were three women—Rosa Parks (see December 1), Ella Baker (see June 9), and the *grand* mother of them all, Septima Clark.

Dubbed "Mother Conscience," Septima Clark had begun her teaching career on St. Johns, one of the South Carolina Sea Islands, in 1916. There she realized the need to help people fight the squalor in which they were forced to live and work by teaching citizenship skills along with the Three R's. Returning to college for a graduate degree, she attended NAACP cofounder Dr. W. E. B. Du Bois's lectures on race, and turned conscience into crusade. In 1956, Clark was one of South Carolina's first black public school teachers. When the state banned city employees from joining Civil Rights organizations, she refused to resign from the NAACP at the cost of her job and her retirement benefits. She challenged the decision; it would take her twenty years to win. Joining the staff of Myles Horton's Highlander Folk School, an interracial human rights incubator in Tennessee, she taught literacy and citizenship to poor farmers. Among her students in education programs for SCLC would be Fannie Lou Hamer, Martin Luther King, John Lewis, Rosa Parks, Wyatt Tee Walker, and Andrew Young. For her work, she was harassed by the KKK, white citizens councils, and sheriffs. Where did she get her grit? From her father and mother, of whom she said, "His nonviolence helped me to work with people and her haughtiness helped me stay." After years of activism, before her death at age eighty-nine, "Mother Conscience" had one more lesson to teach. The Civil Rights movement's greatest failure, she said, was not according women like Ella Baker and Rosa Parks—and, we might add, Septima Clark—the credit due.

Thursday, January 22, 1987

South Carolina                    USA

**Leadership**                                        **Initiative**

"*T*he Need of Hospitals and Training Schools for the Colored People of the South," that was the topic of Dr. Daniel Hale Williams's paper and order of the day when the Phillis Wheatley Club gathered in Nashville on January 23, 1900.

In 1891, Williams had founded Provident Hospital, the first African American hospital. Since then, alliances of black doctors and black women's groups had been raising awareness and funds for other teaching hospitals. With Dr. Williams on rounds nationwide, the founding and funding of hospitals made medicine an attractive, attainable profession for aspiring black doctors (see June 13) and nurses—a healthy prescription for black patients. From Provident had come residencies for physicians and surgeons who could train at white medical colleges but could not touch white patients. This at a time when segregated hospitals did not admit blacks, depriving black patients of care and black doctors of vital hands-on experience. With its racially integrated staff, a first for the nation, Provident's school for black nurses similarly overcame the problem at hand. Such was the level of care and commitment, hallmarks of the institution, that Provident and its founder were world renowned. There, in 1893, Dr. Dan, as he was affectionately known, had performed the world's first open-heart surgery.

In 1886, a grant from John D. Rockefeller to Atlanta Baptist Seminary (the future Spelman College) had established the first academic nursing school for blacks with Provident leading the way in 1891 as the first black-hospital-affiliated school. A testament to their success, the number of black nurses was inching upward. In 1908, fifty-two nurses met at St. Mark's Episcopal Church in New York City to found the National Association of Colored Graduate Nurses. Gathered at the call of Martha Franklin, they elected her founding president.

Tuesday, January 23, 1900

Tennessee                                            USA

---

**Medicine**                                    **Better Worlds**

In 1947, Jackie Robinson left the Negro Leagues to join the Brooklyn Dodgers, breaking the color bar in baseball. A stellar athlete (UCLA's first four-letter man) and a man of principle (a soldier who accepted arrest over segregated bus seating), Robinson had been selected by history to score many points on an unlevel playing field. But with his early death in 1972, it was left to his family to turn legend into legacy. In 1973, his widow, Rachel Robinson, founded the Jackie Robinson Foundation. Because of her leadership initiative, students are mentored through full four-year college scholarships. In 1996, Jackie and Rachel's daughter, Sharon, recalled a Connecticut childhood and paid tribute to her father-teacher in her book *Stealing Home*:

> It was Dad's official job to test the ice on the lake to determine its safety. We kids lined up along the shoreline, and shouted . . . encouragement as Dad proceeded out onto the snow-covered ice. Before he placed one big foot in front of the other, he would tap the ice with his broomstick. After what seemed like forever, Dad would reach the deepest part of the lake, give one last tap with his stick, then turn to us and call out: "Go get your skates!" But sometimes . . . a loud rumble would roll across the lake and we would cry out in near hysterics for fear that the lake would open up and swallow Dad. [Given] the possibility, I thought Dad was very brave.
>
> Now I think it even more. . . . It dawned on me only gradually what it had meant for him to break the color line, the courage it took for him to enter uncharted, and dangerous, waters. No one really knew what would happen. He had to feel his way along an uncleared path like a blind man tapping for clues. That was Jackie Robinson. And that was my dad—big, heavy, out there alone on the lake, tapping his way along so the ice would be safe for us.
>
> And he couldn't swim.

January 1959

Connecticut                      USA

---

Mrs Mary Seacole (Late of Kingston, Jamaica), Respectfully announces to her former kind friends, and to the Officers of the Army and Navy generally, That she has taken her passage in the screwsteamer "Hollander" to start from London on the 25th of January (1855), intending on her arrival at Balaclava to establish a mess-table and comfortable quarters for sick and convalescent officers.

So read the card of Mary Seacole: healer, entrepreneur, gold prospector, heroine of the Crimean War. She was born to a free Creole mother and a Scottish army officer father in colonial Jamaica in 1805, when slavery still reigned and Britain had just begun to "rule the waves"—thanks to the godfather of her future husband, Edwin Horatio Seacole. Edwin's godfather was Lord Horatio Nelson, the martyred commander-in-chief of the British fleet. Mary Seacole was widowed at thirty-one, lost her mother soon after, and watched her business burn to the ground. Yet she went on to live the *Wonderful Adventures of Mrs Seacole in Many Lands*, as she would title her 1857 memoir.

A healer like her mother, Seacole had been educated in traditional Creole medicine and by British military doctors stationed in Jamaica. When war broke out in the Crimea, she decided to go as a nurse "with all the ardor of my nature." Twice she applied, twice she was rejected despite her expertise—even Florence Nightingale, the "angel" herself, the founder of modern nursing, was too contaminated by racism to accept her. "Tears streamed down my foolish cheeks, as I stood in the fast thinning streets," Seacole wrote of the "doubts and suspicions [that] arose in my heart for the first and last time, thank Heaven." Founding her own hospital on the front lines, she was awarded the French Legion of Honor. She was bankrupted by her effort, but the book she wrote to repay her debts, full of wit and charm, was so successful that it brought her world acclaim—one more of her *Wonderful Adventures*.

Thursday, January 25, 1855

London                                  England

**Medicine/Nursing**                                  **Enterprise**

*T*he voice that had soared above a thousand cadences, break-ing down the barriers between secular and sacred walls to take gospel music "wherever two or more gather in My name," was still. On January 26, 1973, a "Going Home Service of Praise and Thanksgiving" was celebrated for Clara Ward, the Queen of Gospel Music, at the Shrine Auditorium in Los Angeles, her adopted city.

Ward Singers past, like Marion Williams, raised the roof in praise. Rev. James Cleveland, gospel's king, led the mass choir in a songbook of "Precious Memories." And Gertrude Ward (see May 30) reminisced about her daughter's last days. "On Watch Meeting Night [December 31, 1972] I asked Clara to sing me a song . . . 'My Soul Looks Back and Wonders How I Got Over'"—the hymn Clara Ward had contemporized from its roots as a spiritual. "'Mother, that's not the song I would like to sing for you.' She then sat down at the piano and sang 'When the Storms of Life Are Raging, Stand by Me.'" That was the last song Clara ever sang. Struck by an aneurism, she lapsed into a coma and died a week later.

In her Philadelphia hometown the Sunday before, a "Service of Triumph" had united others, including Rev. C. L. Franklin of Detroit and his daughter, Aretha, who performed the closing solo, "The Day Is Past and Gone." As the *Gospel Gazette* reported, "In the up-tempo shout number 'We Shall Be Changed' . . . the prom-ise of this song [lifted] the family and 7,000 friends out of the depths of gloom and the spirit made many join in the holy dance." In the words of the spiritual, those who once *scandalized her name* for taking gospel music into nightclubs, now forgave. "Each time a voice is lifted in a song that Clara Ward wrote or inspired, each time a singer enters the realm of music once unthought for gospel, we remember 'Though she is dead, yet she speaks.'"

Friday, January 26, 1973

California                                    USA

---

**Music/Events**                                    **Life's Work**

Della's face crumbled and turned ugly, the pure ugliness of a woman who has lost everything, a woman who has offered up all she has and been found wanting. She snarled at him like a cornered dog that had been kicked once too often. . . . Releasing one of Della's hands, Lute hauled back and laid a brutal open-handed slap across her face. She partially blocked the blow, but it still struck her with enough force to send her sprawling to the floor, where she lay, momentarily dazed. . . . Flecks of blood mottled her lips. "I'll see you put in jail for that, chair maker," she hissed, her voice rising to a screech on the last word.

Tina huddled behind her bedroom door, her hands pressed to her ears, her mind blank with fear. This was the way Barby had told her Daddy acted with mothers sooner or later, but before now she had never believed her. . . . Tina did not know what to do, but she knew that she could not stay in the house a minute longer. She had been drawing a picture for next door's mother and could wish no better time to present it. The expected hug and kiss and gentle stroking of her hair would quiet her palpitating heart. Throwing caution to the wind, she opened her bedroom door, and sprinted out onto the lawn. Neither Lute nor Della noticed her run past.

Blind instinct guided Tina down the hill to the safety of next door mother's house. . . .

*I*n January 1995, at age eighty-seven, Dorothy West, the last of the Harlem Renaissance writers, was back with her first novel in forty-seven years—*The Wedding*, from which this excerpt is taken. Set on Martha's Vineyard, where she had vacationed as a child and lived year-round since 1943, it had been championed by her editor and island neighbor, Jacqueline Kennedy Onassis. Oprah Winfrey would send out *The Wedding* invitations via the Internet to view it as a television miniseries in 1998.

January 1995

Massachusetts                    USA

---

O n January 28, 1913, one week after her death, Fannie M. Jackson Coppin (see November 30) was reborn for a new generation, resurrected by the publication of her book, *Reminiscences of School Life, and Hints on Teaching.* A dean among educators, from 1869 to 1902 she was principal of Philadelphia's prestigious Institute for Colored Youth, the collegiate division of which, renamed Cheyney, is one of the nation's oldest historically black colleges. During her tenure, she became legendary for moments like one recalled by a former student:

> I first made Mrs. Coppin's acquaintance while I was . . . contemplating the prospect of a sound trouncing. Mrs. Coppin walked over to me and asked my name. She talked pleasantly to me and won my confidence. . . . Finally she asked me what I intended to be after leaving school. I promptly answered: "A clerk!" . . . In language which was perfectly clear to me at ten years of age, she pictured the great work to be made by specialists in the learned professions, great cures to be made by colored doctors, cases to be won by colored lawyers, books to be made by colored writers. Then she said, "Mr. Venning tells me that you like arithmetic. I think that I'll have to make you a civil engineer." And she did. From that time on, until the day of the conferring of my degree sixteen years later she was my constant advisor.

When John Durham shared that account of his teacher and mentor, he had become an engineer, a journalist, and a diplomat. How Coppin worked her miracles may be found among her "hints" in a section of her book titled "Object of Punishment": "Sometimes if a child is naughty it will do him good to run out in the yard a minute. Remember all the time you are dealing with a human being, whose needs are like your own." Words to the wise teacher—and parent.

Tuesday, January 28, 1913

Pennsylvania USA

---

**Education** **Empowerment**

*Medallion of John Brown:* The subscriber invites the attention of her friends and the public to a number of medallions of John Brown, just completed by her, and which may be seen at room No. 69, Studio Bldg, Tremont St., Boston

On January 29, 1864, that advertisement by sculptor Edmonia Lewis appeared in *The Liberator.* So successful was her invitation, and so elated was the response to her work, that an interview with her by the abolitionist writer Lydia Maria Child appeared in the same pages three weeks later. Born to an African father and a Chippewa mother, Lewis had exhibited her talents early while living among the Chippewa:

"When my mother was dying, she wanted me to promise that I would live three years with her people, and [there] I did as my mother's people did. I made baskets and embroidered moccasins and I went into the cities with my mother's people, to sell them. . . ."

"But . . . you have had some other education . . . for your language indicates it."

"I have a brother who went to California, and dug gold. . . . He placed me at a school in Oberlin. I staid there two years, and then he brought me to Boston, as the best place for me to learn to be a sculptor. I went to Mr. Brackett for advice; for I thought the man who made a bust of John Brown must be a friend to my people. Mr. Brackett has been very kind to me. [Then, inviting Child to view her bust of Voltaire, Lewis went on.] I don't want you to go to praise me . . . for I know praise is not good for me. Some praise me because I am a colored girl, and I don't want that kind of praise. I had rather you would point out my defects, for that will teach me something."

Learning well, Lewis sailed for Italy and further study with the masters of the day.

Friday, January 29, 1864

Massachusetts                    USA

---

$\mathcal{A}$ woman wrote a letter (penned by a friend) and sent it to her husband—a normal enough act. But because the couple was enslaved at the time, the fact of the letter is historic. Plantation slaves in the years of backlash following the Nat Turner Revolt, Hannah and Michael Valentine endured the sale and dispersal of family members and long separations from each other. Hannah managed the house slaves at Montcalm, the home of Virginia's governor, David Campbell. Michael, a carriage driver, was usually away with the Campbells in the capital city. On January 30, 1838, Hannah wrote Michael:

> I begin to feel so anxious to hear from you and my children, and indeed from all the family that I have concluded to write to you altho you have treated me badly in not answering my last letter. I heard through Mr Gibson last week that you were all well, but hearing from you in that way does not satisfy me. I want a letter to tell me what you are doing and all about yourself. . . . There is now a great deal of sickness in town & country. The measles are still spreading, and some that have taken cold after having had them are very sick. Our children are very well and are free from the cough which usually succeeds the measles. Tell Eliza her children grow very fast. They do not talk much about her now, but seem to be very well satisfied without her. I begin to feel anxious to see you all. I am afraid my patience will be quite worn out if you do not come back soon. . . . You must write and tell me when Master talks of returning. . . .

How does a grandmother find the heart to tell a mother that her children no longer pine for her? Such was the nature of slavery when the normal was abnormal and the abnormal good news. Such is the strength of our people that we have lived to tell the tale.

Tuesday, January 30, 1838

Virginia      USA

**Family**                   **Human Spirit**

At sixteen, Charlotte Forten, the daughter of a businessman and abolitionist, had been privileged in all but companionship. Tutored at home to avoid Philadelphia's segregated schools, she was sent to Salem, Massachusetts, to attend a newly integrated school. There, in the spirit of eighteenth-century poet Phillis Wheatley (see May 6), she would find a soul mate. Ten years later, teaching recently freed slaves on St. Helena's Island, South Carolina, she met another of her sheroes, this time in person—Harriet Tubman. On January 31, 1863, traveling through "B" (for Beaufort, as Forten wrote in her diary), she spent time with "Moses" herself when Tubman was a Union nurse and scout:

> She told us that she used to hide [escaping slaves] in the woods during the day and go around to get provisions for them. Once she had with her a man named Joe, for whom a reward of $1500 was offered. . . . At last they reached in safety the Suspension Bridge over [Niagara] Falls and found themselves in Canada. Until then, she said, Joe had been very silent. In vain she called his attention to the glory of the Falls. He sat perfectly still—moody, it seemed, and w'ld not even glance at them. But when she said, "Now we are in Can[ada]" he sprang to his feet with a great shout, and sang and clapped his hand[s] in a perfect delirium of joy. So when they got out, and he first touched *free* soil, he shouted and hurrahed "as if he were crazy"—she said. How exciting it was to hear her tell the story. And to hear her sing the very scraps of jubilant hymns that he sang. She said the ladies crowded around them, and some laughed and some cried.

How exciting, too, it is that Forten preserved the scene for us all. In her account, we share the vision of an elder basking in the light of a young sister's pride.

Saturday, January 31, 1863

South Carolina                    USA

# February

*Jane Van Ter Pool* (circa 1911). Mother of William Landsmark.
Photographer unknown. Reprinted courtesy of the author.
For more information, see September 22, November 2.

$\mathcal{J}$n 1898, herstory's shero, Harriet Tubman, was eking out an existence in Auburn, New York, in a modest two-story home with a bed, dresser, side table, oil lamp, and Bible, which she could not read but acted upon *religiously*.

During the Civil War, the Union had employed her Underground Railroad conductor's skills as an army spy, scout, guerrilla strategist, and the first woman in American history to lead a military expedition (see June 2). For her services, she had been promised a pension, but, like other promises of compensation and reparation to former slaves, that pension had never come to pass. A hero to both the black and women's movements, the widow of a Civil War veteran and a veteran in her own right, at seventy-five-plus years of age, with no regular income, she petitioned the federal government for the two pensions rightfully due her. Her papers were handed from one official to another and ignored; she filed an affidavit and signed her X: "I claim for my services above named the sum of Eighteen hundred dollars." When her claim was finally honored, five dollars had been shaved off the minimal twenty-five dollars awarded her per month until her death in 1913.

As Dr. Martin Delany, Harvard's first black medical student, said at the depth of slavery, "To know the condition of a people, one has only to know that status of its women." From the treatment of this extraordinary woman, the condition of African Americans was dour indeed. What status did we accord ourselves? After her death, the home she had willed to the AME Zion church sank into disrepair and was allowed to close. Thinking better of ourselves by 1953, funds were raised and her home restored as a national landmark. And, on February 1, 1978, when the first "Black Heritage USA" stamp was issued, the nation paid long overdue official tribute to freedom's angel, the "Moses of her people," Harriet Tubman.

Wednesday, February 1, 1978

New York                    USA

---

**Heroes and Sheroes**                    **Self-affirmation**

or the first week of February 1997, public television filled the air with *The Story of Gospel*, from "Father of Gospel" Thomas A. Dorsey to contemporary gospel's Tramaine Hawkins. In the story of the music was a twentieth-century history of a people. In the transition from traditional hymns and spirituals to Dorsey's bluesy "Chicago style" was the parallel story of a people preserving cultural roots while breaking out of the traditional roles in which others had cast them. As Shirley Caesar said of the struggle, "Gospel music is our sunshine and strength."

As the first gospel artist to be nominated for and win a Grammy, in 1972, Caesar had been tested many times. When she was twelve, her father died, leaving her to care for her disabled mother. By fourteen, from necessity, she was singing professionally. In 1958, a business major at North Carolina State College, she dropped out to become an evangelist and join the Caravans, the group credited with launching more soloists than any other. In 1966, she formed the Shirley Caesar Singers, with a sound so endemic to its time it was dubbed "gospel rock." A unique stylist, she was offered a lucrative recording contract to sing rock and roll. The offer came when she could have used the money for her mother's care. She refused with a quip: "The only way I'll sing it is if you'll let me rock for God and roll for Jesus."

Hearing her style copied by others who took it to places she would not go, she still remained true to herself. To traditionalists of an earlier generation, Caesar might have crossed the line of authenticity, but she never crossed over from the sacred to the secular. What attracted the industry and audiences to Shirley Caesar was her dramatic style. Each time she sang the word *running* in the song "I've Been Running for Jesus a Long Time," she would run up and down the aisles—bringing *the word* to the audience and the audience to its feet.

February 2–7, 1997

National                              USA

---

**Music**                                    **Authenticity**

On February 3, 1948, in a one-day trial, Rosa Lee Ingram, a Georgia farmer, and her sons Wallace, seventeen, and Sammy Lee, fourteen, were tried, convicted of murder, and sentenced to die in the electric chair three weeks later. The previous November, John Ed Stratford, a neighboring white farmer, alleged that Mrs. Ingram's farm animals had trespassed his land, and set out to shoot the animals. Confronting Mrs. Ingram at their shared property line, where she and her four sons were repairing their fence, Stratford struck the mother with the butt of his rifle. Wrestling the gun from the assailant, her sons prevented him from shooting their mother with four blows, one of which proved fatal. The court-appointed lawyer entered a plea of self-defense for the Ingrams; the jury discounted the Ingrams' testimony and found them guilty of murder.

In a storm of outrage, word quickly spread around the country. Mass meetings raised funds for an appeal. Sixteen hundred branches of the NAACP nationwide went on active alert. The Civil Rights Congress rallied to the Ingrams' defense. And so many northern newspapers carried the story that the judge in the case charged the "agitation" was "an attack on the court." "When attacks are made upon the court," declared Judge W. M. Harper, "that is anarchy." If anarchy alone could stop the rush to execute the Ingrams, anarchy it would be from their defenders, whose "agitation" stayed the execution pending a new trial. Within weeks, the NAACP took over the defense and a new trial date was set. In April, the death penalty was commuted to life imprisonment. Women from Shirley Graham (the author and future Mrs. W. E. B. Du Bois) to playwright Alice Childress rallied friends and funds worldwide. So vital was the need that, to her dying day at age ninety-six, Mary Church Terrell worked to organize a delegation to the United Nations on the Ingrams' behalf. In 1959, this relentless "anarchy" finally freed the Ingrams.

Tuesday, February 3, 1948

Georgia                                          USA

---

**Social History**                                 **Self-defense**

*I*t had been a year since the impromptu Greensboro lunch counter sit-in by four North Carolina A & T students ignited student protests and fired up the founding of the Student Non-Violent Coordinating Committee (SNCC). Wave upon wave of demonstrators had endured unimaginable acts of bestiality for an ideal that was, as stated, *more than a hamburger.* On February 4, 1961, SNCC's young leaders were meeting at Atlanta's Butler Street YMCA to review the past year and plan the next when a telephone call affixed their commitment to inspired direct action at the grassroots and charted a new strategy — "jail, no bail."

In South Carolina, for the Greensboro anniversary, student sit-in participants had accepted thirty days on a chain gang rather than pay one hundred dollars bail. The call was for reinforcements. Four SNCC members, aware of the arrest and jail term that lay ahead, set out for Rock Hill and history as the "Rock Hill Four": Charles Jones, Charles Sherrod, Diane Nash, and Ruby Doris Smith. For her stand, Nash was appointed to coordinate the Freedom Rides and faced another sentence. Married to fellow activist James Bevel, pregnant with their first child, and devout on "jail, no bail," she decided to give birth in prison. Derailing her planned sacrifice, the judge sentenced her to a shorter term on a lesser charge — refusing to move to the back of the courtroom. Smith, then a seventeen-year-old Spelman student, would die eight years later from health problems that first erupted in the Rock Hill jail-in. But not before making her mark as the only woman (on a short list with Congressman John Lewis and Stokely Carmichael [Kwame Touré]) ever to head SNCC. SNCC Communications Director Julian Bond recalled her direct action when an airline representative told their delegation their flight to Africa was overbooked and suggested they take a later plane: Ruby Doris sat on the runway and refused to move. They made the flight.

Saturday, February 4, 1961

South Carolina                         USA

---

**Leadership**                                    **Respect for One's Power**

*W*ell into the 1960s, black bodies would float to the surface of southern streams, dredged from the muck of history by forces of nature, only to be suppressed, given back to the deep. Better to let the past sleep, said some. Only by confronting the past and its demons can we go on, vowed others. Then there was Myrlie Evers. Her husband, NAACP Field Director Medgar Evers, had been shot down in the driveway of their Jackson, Mississippi, home. Just after midnight, June 12, 1963, he lay bleeding to death before her eyes, a bullet in his back. For the Evers family, Medgar could not be carted off to martyrdom a hero and put to rest like that. He was a man—a son, husband, father, brother, friend—lost to those who loved him. It would take thirty-one years for his widow to crack the armor shielding the guilty, but even in Mississippi justice had to come . . . someday. Come it did—on February 5, 1994.

Byron de la Beckwith, Evers's known killer, had been twice tried and freed by a hung jury. "Killing that nigger gave me no more inner discomfort than our wives endured when they give birth to our children," he bragged. No jury would convict him of "defending our way of life." Still, Mrs. Evers persisted. People began to rethink things. The murder weapon with Beckwith's fingerprints, once "disappeared," resurfaced in the private gun collection of a local judge. So, too, did "lost" photos and the original trial transcript reappear. When it was discovered that Beckwith had been aided by the Mississippi State Sovereignty Commission (see May 28), known for its view that black lives were a small price to pay for "states rights," a biracial male/female jury was impaneled. White women admitted childbearing more painful than they had ever before let on, leaving Beckwith discomforted indeed as Myrlie Evers burst out with "Yeah, Medgar!" Hearing the jury pronounce Beckwith guilty, she said, "I was reborn."

Saturday, February 5, 1994

Mississippi                    USA

---

**Law**                                                    **Tenacity**

*I*sabella White had never known her parents or her age. She wasn't even sure where she had been born or how she had come to be a resident of New Bedford, Massachusetts. She could remember that her birthplace had "a few white folks, lots of 'cullud' people and a big farm" and that, as a child of four or five, she took a trip. That was all she knew of her early life. But with her death on February 6, 1924, people began to talk.

Born enslaved, Mrs. White, it seems, had been secretly "headed up" in a barrel of sweet potatoes and shipped North as a small child. Mrs. White had the idea that her parents crated her, confident that "quality folks in the no'th, regardless of who they were, would care for her." But Miss Agatha Snow added a few details. From an explanation her grandfather, Loum Snow, had given her when she was a child, he seemed the most likely to have claimed the "shipment." A known abolitionist, he had purchased the freedom of others. When young Isabella arrived, fragile from the strenuous journey, his family had nursed her back to health and raised her until she was old enough to work for herself. True to the code of secrecy and survival of the UGRR, Loum Snow never admitted to being involved in Isabella's rescue and removal from the South. But, as G. Leroy Bradford has written, "it is not difficult to imagine he may have been expecting something more animated than sweet potatoes from the south when a barrel was received by him sometime in the 1850s."

A century and a half later, still no one knows. As the ancients have passed the word to us: *Don't say all you see, nor tell all you know.* What we do know is that, in every age, there are those who say little and do much. At nearly eighty Isabella White died, knowing that the truth she didn't know had made her free.

Wednesday, February 6, 1924

Massachusetts USA

---

*D*uring World War I, this was typical of the conditions faced by African American soldiers stationed in France: "While white American soldiers were permitted to go freely about the towns . . . passes for [the great mass of colored American soldiers] were oftener than otherwise as hard to secure as American gold." We know this because Addie W. Hunton and Kathryn M. Johnson, two YWCA volunteers, accompanied the troops to the front, documenting their plight in a book, *Two Colored Women with the American Expeditionary Forces.*

The fact that these women had taken on such a dangerous task speaks volumes about the character of each, both of them crusaders in service to a personal mission. Johnson, a former dean of women at Arkansas's Shorter College, is credited as the NAACP's first field agent. From 1913, by selling branch memberships and *Crisis* magazine subscriptions, she extended the organization's reach throughout the South and West. After the war, determined to disseminate word of our history and culture, she championed her "two foot shelf of Negro literature," for the "Father of Negro History Week," Dr. Carter G. Woodson, and his Association for the Study of Negro Life and History. Hunton, a married mother of two, was a suffragist who held the feet of the National Woman's Party to the flame for its indifference to the lives of black women. In 1921, she orchestrated an "onslaught" of conscience that led party founder Alice Paul to admit that Hunton and her allies were "the most intelligent group of women" who had ever attacked her principles.

On February 7, 1921, as Hunton wrote to her sister-activist Hallie Quinn Brown: "You can count on me to stand close beside you in any effort you make for the rights of our women." Indeed, we could count on Hunton, Johnson, and Brown.

Monday, February 7, 1921

National            France

*Jack and Jill*
*Moved up on a hill*
*To get away from the slaughter*
*And things were going real swell until*
*A minority married their daughter.*
— Ruby Dee, *My One Good Nerve*

O n February 8, 1998, Ruby Dee stood center stage reflecting
the glow of the years that had led to her triumphant one-
woman show, *My One Good Nerve*. A consummate actor and author,
never before had she wedded the two onstage. It was an aspira-
tion long denied even to herself. With her esteemed stage and film
career, numerous books and short stories adapted into teleplays,
one would think her comfortable in the skin of both the actor and
the author. "But I guess I didn't trust myself enough," she would
recall of how being a *serious* actor impacted her appreciation of
her own wit; how the insidiousness of racism damages the psyche
and erodes self-confidence. How she had felt dwarfed by her
actor-writer husband Ossie Davis's abilities; how he had encouraged her to own her talents. "So how do you hold on to your one
good nerve in spite of the contradictions and the dichotomies, the
distance between the promise and the fulfillment?" she pondered.
With *My One Good Nerve*, a show based on her "word worker"
self—complete with revisionist Mother Goose nursery rhymes on
the human comedy—she electrified the stage in a tour de force of
rhythm, humor, experience, and always her passion for life and
the stage, grounded in her roots in the Harlem theater of the
1940s where she had come of age as an actor and met her husband. Together they would make of their December 9, 1998, fifti-
eth wedding anniversary a golden opportunity for others: a gala
celebration to benefit a new era of independent community theaters and lovers and theater-lovers.

Sunday, February 8, 1998

New York/National          USA

---

**Theater**                                    **Self-affirmation**

$\mathcal{T}$n February 1867, Morehouse College opened its doors, one of the first schools founded after the Civil War with aid from the Freedmen's Bureau. Born as the Augusta Institute, the school had an impressive pedigree. It began in the basement of the Springfield Baptist Church, the nation's oldest black Baptist church (founded in 1787) and a direct descendant of the first black congregation, Silver Bluff Baptist on South Carolina's Beech Island (founded in 1773). While today's Morehouse is a men's school, it at first accepted men and women. Of Josephine White, the wife of cofounder Rev. William Jefferson White, this story was told in 1952 by their daughter Claudia White Harreld:

Born enslaved in 1834, by age nine Josephine was allowed into the nursery while the slavemaster's children had their lessons, and so learned to read by listening. Retreating to her little blue-speckled speller, she wrote down remembered words. In her time with the family's elderly blind aunt, she would spell out the words without revealing her actual purpose. As a laundry girl, she practiced her reading in the linen closet, where she could quickly hide her book between the pressed rows. From time to time, friends would sneak books to her—one even dared to give her a copy of the "subversive" *Uncle Tom's Cabin* (see March 20), but it was intercepted, never to be seen again. From then until freedom found her, she honed her skill by stealth. When the institute opened, she registered the very first night. Returning home after class, she saw the sewing work she took in to help support the family where she had left it, undone. Choosing between educating herself and earning the money to educate her children, she never went back. Years later when she said she had never attended school, her children would say, "But, Mama, you went one night." Yes, she would say, yes she had. How many others, to this day, sacrifice as much for their families? As we would see the mending done, let us not leave their heroine-ism unsung!

February 1867

Georgia                                             USA

**Education**                                             **Sacrifice**

On February 10, 1990, a photo was fed over the wires for the world to see the actual face of the man who had spent twenty-seven years in prison for the liberation of South Africa — Nelson Mandela. In 1963, the tall, robust freedom-fighter attorney had been condemned to death, his sentence later commuted to life. Then, on this day, a new image emerged, that of a thin, athletically fit elder.

Who was the Mandela the world refused to forget from 1963 to this day? In our sight, his physical being was that of two women — Winnie Madikizela Mandela, his wife, and their daughter, Zindzi.

As spiritual mother of the dawning nation, and a warrior in her own right, Winnie Mandela had sacrificed her all for freedom and spent many years in solitary confinement, under detention, and under house arrest. In the footsteps of her parents came Zindzi. Well schooled by her father's legacy and her mother's daily counsel, Zindzi had a potential for leadership and greatness in her own right that would be demonstrated on this day, February 10, 1985, when she spoke before a crowd of thousands in the names, and to the honor, of both her parents — five years to the day before her father's walk to freedom. It is said, "What is in the root is in the branches." But to that must be added words of praise for the children throughout the diaspora who have been spared neither the cruelty of terrible times nor the courage of their own conscience.

Sunday, February 10, 1985

South Africa

---

*A* s nearly fifty members of the Episcopal College of Bishops gathered in Boston on February 11, 1989, it was clear that this ordination would be like no other. In an environment electric with controversy, Rev. Barbara Clementine Harris would be the first woman ordained and consecrated bishop of the Episcopal Church, its forebears the Church of England and the Catholic Church from which it had been parsed four hundred years previous by a British king in need of a divorce.

Five months earlier, on September 24, 1988, the second diocesan convention in which a woman's name had been raised had taken eight full ballots to reach a clear majority. Harris won, a symbol of all the women who had peered at the ecclesiastical "glass dome" and found it sealed. A two-thousand-year-old male hierarchy had come to an end—and it showed. "My sister," the presiding bishop said as he began the ritual of Examination with words never before spoken. And the bishop-elect answered, presenting an image never before seen. In vestments of Italian silk and Ghanaian kente, symbols of two worlds—Europe and Africa—had been interwoven and interpreted in the program:

Her mitre—*Nyame Nwu Na M'awu* (Ashanti), meaning "Could God die, I would die," expressing God's eternity and Creation's dependence.

Her stole—*Nyame Bribi Wo Soro, Ma No Mmeka Me Nsa* (Ashanti), which translates, "O God, there is something above, let it reach me."

Her cope morse and back of the chasuble—*Onyamedua* (Ashanti), "God's tree," a forked post found in most courtyards or planted at the entrances of a chief's palace as a sign of the people's dependence on God.

What a new world her presence had wrought.

Saturday, February 11, 1989

Massachusetts          USA

---

*O*n February 12, 1909, the National Association for the Advancement of Colored People (NAACP) was officially founded on the centennial of Abraham Lincoln's birth, a date deliberately chosen to honor his role in ending slavery with the signing of the Emancipation Proclamation.

The idea for the NAACP had come from a white woman, Mary White Ovington, who had been moved by recent headlines of white-on-black race riots in, ironically enough, Lincoln's Springfield, Illinois, hometown. Ovington was already active in the work of Dr. W. E. B. Du Bois and his Niagara Movement (so named for a meeting at Niagara Falls in 1905), and her intent was to respond to growing anti-black violence. But Du Bois's group was small and too poorly funded for a national campaign. Ovington, a woman with powerful connections, thought to expand the group across racial lines—blacks and whites working in concert. In January 1909, she and two white men issued the call to a meeting of those who believed in justice. Of the sixty signators who launched the National Negro Committee (NNC), one third were women, two of whom were African American—Mary Church Terrell and Ida B. Wells-Barnett. Du Bois became the only African American officer named to the board of the newly formed NNC. The world's oldest Civil Rights organization, which began with the Niagara Movement, became the NNC, and was renamed the NAACP in 1910, would lead to the National Urban League, followed by South Africa's African National Congress in 1912.

Since then, among the NAACP's highlights in herstory: Althea T. L. Simmons as chief lobbyist, Elaine R. Jones's tenure as president and director-counsel of the NAACP Legal Defense Fund, and the election of Myrlie Evers (see February 5) in 1995 as the first woman chairperson of the national board of directors.

Friday, February 12, 1909

Washington, D.C.          USA

---

**Organizing**                                    **Vision**

$\mathcal{I}$t was early in February 1998 when a letter from Aisha Bailey, a Brown University student taking a semester abroad, reached her parents in Connecticut. "Hello from Zimbabwe!" she wrote. A student educated in the best public and private American schools, even in 1998, she had to admit, her peers and advisers had probably "accepted my choice of Zimbabwe because it had been colonized and had missionaries 'keeping the peace' and teaching 'humanity' to the people." In contrast to their negative conditioning, she, however, had "absolutely NO EXPECTATIONS" for what she would see except that something was calling her there. "I felt fresh air, saw huge grasslands swaying, people singing and dancing, the enormous sunset reflecting on the Earth below." En route, she stopped in Paris, primed to expect a city of romance. But it was "not until I stepped foot on this soil that I understood my distrust of Paris," she wrote from Africa, with fresh eyes:

> The land was a creamy brown expanse with true green trees. I say true green because I now understand why green is green in the Crayola crayon boxes; it is a true color. The lush grass, the swaying trees, the rich, supple flowers bending from their fruitful, overbearing weight . . . I wanted to cry. . . . It is one thing to be swayed by an object's beauty and to see this beauty as the object's worth. It is quite another thing to see the *Earth* for the first time. . . . Africa is a womb. . . . *Aisha* means life in Swahili, and I was always proud that I had an African name. . . . I not only see where I came from here, I also see where life originated from. From the amoeba to the starry expanse of sky, Africa is Aisha. This is a truly beautiful thought and, if considered by the observer, would bring them to their knees in prayer — crying. This is religion. . . . That is why I say "to deny Africa is to deny oneself life. . . ." This is why I feel proud and happy walking down the streets of Harare. I know the truth.

February 1998

Connecticut    USA/Zimbabwe

---

**Education**                                                      **Understanding**

*I*n 1965, Sue Bailey Thurman was best known as the partner and wife of Dr. Howard Thurman, the respected theologian with whom she organized the Church for the Fellowship of All Peoples. But her independent work was equally remarkable. Joining strengths with the National Council of Negro Women (NCNW), she had founded its official organ, the *Aframerican Woman's Journal.* As the first African American woman granted an audience with Mahatma Gandhi, modern India's liberator and scion of the philosophy of nonviolence, she helped further his doctrine of resistance in the American Civil Rights wars. Through her travels, she gathered around her a circle of sisterhood. From within that spirited nest, she wrote a "love letter" to "Dearest Meta," her sister-friend, the sculptor Meta Warwick Fuller:

> Today, I want to have you know how much joy and happiness your very existence and personal friendship have brought to me. Maybe it is a way of sending you an early "Valentine." Quoting from one rare poet that both of us have loved: "We are never far apart. . . . Have not the fates associated us in a thousand different ways? Is it of no significance that . . . the same fruits have been pleased to refresh us both, and we have never had a thought of different fibre the one from the other!" So you know that I am always in the little room where you live, that *we are never far apart.*

In closing she noted Coretta King's love for Fuller's *Mother and Child*: "Aren't you glad that your hands have so inspired her days? I told Coretta that she should be writing something in a diary every day—significant sentences that measure exact times in the symphony." Good advice for us all, no matter our lives' discords and harmonic progressions.

Sunday, February 14, 1965

California                                    USA

---

**Love**                                                        **Sisterhood**

*I*n 1903, on the streets of Chattanooga, Tennessee, you could hear Bessie Smith sing for nickels and dimes. Twenty years later, you could hear her everywhere. On February 15, 1923 — after failing several auditions, including one for the black-owned Black Swan Records — the self-described "tall and fat and scared to death" singer made her first recordings. With "Down Hearted Blues" by Alberta Hunter (see June 27) on the A side and "Gulf Coast Blues" on the B, she was a hit, and Columbia Records was soon known as *the house that Bessie built!*

If ever an African American artist was called "untrained," it was Bessie Smith. It's time to rethink our terms. Tragically orphaned young, she grew up in mean poverty with an older sister. A hard life was her training ground. At nine, she literally sang for nickels and dimes on street corners. There, she learned to hold an audience, grab a note, and punch a song, and she discovered the rewards of crowd pleasing. In 1912, at sixteen, she was mentored by the best as a member of Ma Rainey's traveling show (see November 18). As a teenager in Atlanta, "hanging around the Eighty-One" with her pal Thomas Dorsey, the "Father of Gospel" (see September 23), she honed her craft before listeners with little cash and less patience for anything but the real thing — their blues, their truths. In touring minstrel shows, in "lowdown dives" on the Chit'lin Circuit, and in small northern theaters (getting her big break at Paradise Gardens in Atlantic City), she learned to work a variety of audiences. By the time her record hit, not only was she "ready," she had built a small following of fans who knew her name. Bessie Smith's records soon sold 100,000 copies *per week,* making her the highest paid black performer of her day. No wonder she was called "Empress of the Blues."

How much better trained can one be! A better "student" would be hard to find.

Thursday, February 15, 1923

Tennessee/New York        USA

---

**Music**                                        **Re-visioning**

*H*er "looks" had always been both asset and liability to Alice Moore Dunbar-Nelson. A light-complexioned woman, she lived her life in black and white. Culturally, professionally, socially, she was black. Then there were the times when she functioned white—at libraries and museums otherwise barred to her, to attend concerts, register in hotels, and to "get the job done" (the job of serving as the eyes and ears of the wider black community in an unyielding color-coded world). Hers was a "job" not unlike that done by her contemporary Walter White, who used his skin color to infiltrate lynching parties and other anti-black atrocities for the NAACP. As a New York author, educator, anti-lynching crusader, child welfare reformer, and cofounder of the White Rose Mission (see December 22) and as a Delaware parole officer-advocate for juvenile ex-offenders, founder of the Industrial School for Colored Girls, and the first black woman to serve on that state's Republican Committee, she had assigned herself many a job to "get done"—many an obstacle to overcome.

Writing in her diary on February 16, 1931, Dunbar-Nelson was *fightin' mad*:

> To the Baptist meeting. A stringy, cluttered, packed in, heterogeneous collection of divines and visitors. Noisy, disorderly. Goodall hostile as soon as he saw me. The usual difficulty with the hearing committee, the usual dumb slowness. Why do ministers *have* to walk slow? When—after delays and obstructions, I got a chance to talk—I railed at them for not answering my letters and a brother from the back piped up, "Sister, we didn't know how you look!"

Such were (are) her (our) *Sister Days*.

Monday, February 16, 1931

Delaware                                    USA

---

**Social History**                                    **Racial Dignity**

*I*n the sixteenth century, Spanish colonizers had founded St. Augustine, Florida, the first city to be built in Europe's New World. Two centuries later, with indigenous peoples vanquished and banished from the map of their ancestors' home, control of the region was split between Spain and the United States. On February 17, 1834, with the Van Ness Treaty, Spain ceded all territorial claims to the southern tip of the new nation, little more than fifty years young. It was the end of an era.

Today, the last surviving plantation of the Spanish colonial period holds court on Fort George Island. Designated a historic national site in 1988, the Kingsley Plantation contains twenty-three of the original thirty-two slave cabins, two houses, one barn, and a secret revealed. From 1813 to 1839, this was the home of the slave trader and planter Zephaniah Kingsley and his family of ten children by three slave women, one of whom was his wife. In his castle by the sea, Kingsley reigned with his queen—Anna Madgigine Jai, born an African princess.

In our time, some have analogized the legal status of women in marriage to slaves under slavery. To that, one might add a phalanx of contradictions from the life of Anna Kingsley. Released from bondage, she married a slave trader and slaveholder in an era when her marriage contract could not be upheld in a court, when would-be claims to her husband's assets could compromise her freedom, when her enslavement was the source of her wealth, when the depth of resentments and plots against her from every quarter can only be imagined. To revisit this past, to trespass this world, is to walk among ghosts in a complex of buildings (and relationships) that haunt the land to this day. Out in the open at Kingsley, how thinly veiled and transparent is the scene.

Monday, February 17, 1834

Florida                    USA

---

*J*n the 1940s, as returning vets left foreign battlefields for the battlefronts of home, on February 18, 1947, Hale Woodruff wrote fellow artist Charles Alston: "In light of the Negro artist's present achievements in the general frame work of American art today, there does not exist the necessity to continue all-Negro exhibitions which tend to isolate him and segregate him from other American artists."

Not so, said venerated artist-sculptor Elizabeth Catlett in her historic Mexico City speech of 1961, when the racial climate seemed better still. Black exhibitions did not mean segregated exhibitions; there was a difference between what one chooses and what one is forced to do. "Let us take our painting and prints and sculpture not only to Atlanta University, to the art galleries, and to patrons of the arts who have money to buy them; let us exhibit where Negro people meet — in the churches, in the schools and universities, in the associations and clubs and trade unions. Then let us seek inspiration in the Negro people — a principal and never-ending source." Art was power; art empowered. It had been so in her own life. As a high school student, she had won, on the merits of a competitive exam, a scholarship to attend Carnegie Institute, only to have the scholarship withdrawn on account of racism. Devastated, she was revived by her mother and acceptance by Howard University in 1932. Thinking herself a designer, she majored in textiles under Lois Mailou Jones (see March 11). Art history professor James Herring introduced her to African sculpture and new insights. Painting teacher James A. Porter ushered in the Mexican muralists, and she knew her major would be painting.

What do you say about a school that rescues one of the desolate, that so exposes her to and enraptures her with the best that she becomes one of them? You say that there is much to be said for our historically black colleges and universities.

Tuesday, February 18, 1947

National                                    USA

---

**Art**                                    **Possibility**

*I*t was "a true and laughable slave story" that Martha Johnson had told about herself. Perhaps it happened on a day like today in 1860, just before the war. But as sure as it happened on a Sunday, which it did, it certainly signaled the end of an era.

Miss Martha had always wished she could wear fine silks and satins like the women of the Old South it was her "cross" to dress and pamper. So one Sunday, when the missus dressed for church and left her, in a Cinderella sort of way, to put away the clothes and clean up the room, Miss Martha took time for herself and a dream. Knowing the woman would be gone for a while, she rigged up a full dress outfit for herself: "a handsome silk dress with the old-style silk dress-bonnet to match." Donning the veil and the gloves, she could only admire how beautiful she looked done up in "madam's finery." Then she heard a thump and a "terrible groan, which frightened [her] dreadfully." Knowing that one of her old masters had died in that room didn't make things better. There she was "between two frights," not knowing whether to flee the room in the dress and risk certain punishment or to stay in the room and risk battling the spirits of this life and the next. Knowing that even spirits cared little for slavemasters, she stayed in the room, undressing as quickly as her racing heart would allow. Hearing a second heavier thump and a more horrendous groan, she reconsidered. As she opened the door to exit, petrified, a hand touched her shoulder. As she reeled around in terror, laughter broke out. A mischievous friend had caught her in the act—and scared her so that she never again dared try on her mistress's finery.

But that did not end her dreams. Her daughter was married in a fine dress and veil with white kid wedding slippers, and her granddaughter sailed to Europe, where she lived free—with dresses and peace of mind galore.

Sunday, circa 1860

Georgia                                    USA

---

**Humor**                                    **Continuity**

*J*n 1820, Harriet Bailey was an enslaved young mother soon to be parted from her infant son. Unable to protect him or herself, she was a woman with nothing to give—except the gift of love. And she so lavished her love upon him that long after she had been sold away from him and died on a nearby plantation, the son still basked in the warmth of her remembered embrace. As a young man, the son escaped. Free himself, he helped free others as an antislavery orator, Underground Railroad conductor, abolitionist newspaper publisher, Civil War strategist, and postwar ambassador to Haiti, the first independent African-diasporan nation in the Americas. With all of his accomplishments, there came a time when the son wanted one thing only—a birthday. Separated from his mother from the age of five, he could not ask her. Because he always suspected his father to be the owner from whom he had escaped, he could not turn to his father, either. So it was that he invented a date as he had invented a new life for himself. He knew he had been born in the teens; he chose 1817 as his birth year. And because he remembered that his mother had always called him her "little valentine," he chose February 14 for his birth date. Armed with his mother's love, the son helped move the mountain of slavery. For that, we still honor Harriet Bailey's "little valentine"—Frederick Douglass.

With this history, is it any wonder that from the birth of the national women's movement in 1848 (see July 19), the most ardent male feminist was Harriet Bailey's son? In his latter years, his health failing, he stopped traveling and accepting speaking invitations. Yet, on February 20, 1895, he rallied for the rights of women at a National Council of Women meeting in Washington, D.C. It was his last speech. That night he had a heart attack and was reunited with his mother, at long last.

Wednesday, February 20, 1895

Washington, D.C.          USA

---

*O*n February 21, 1998, Gayl Jones, the author, playwright, and respected academic, published her first novel since 1977. But instead of tributes came tragedy.

At six o'clock the night before, police had knocked on the door of her Lexington, Kentucky, home, a fifteen-year-old warrant in hand for the arrest of her husband, Bob Jones né Higgins, who had often run afoul of propriety and the law. Once, at a gay rights rally, he chided gays for AIDS, left the scene, and returned to sit in his car with a shotgun. Charged with "assault with intent to frighten," the couple fled to Paris, and Higgins was convicted in absentia. When Jones's mother was diagnosed with cancer, they returned undetected. But with her death, Higgins spiraled out of control, threatening violence, convinced his mother-in-law had been the victim of medical foul play. When *Newsweek* heralded Jones's return to the literary scene, an assistant district attorney realized the newly menacing Bob Jones to be the former Bob Higgins who had avoided capture under his wife's last name. With arrival of the police, the couple bunkered in. Jones made a 911 phone call, threatening to follow her husband to death as she had followed him in life. By morning she had been taken from her home in handcuffs and placed under a suicide watch. Her husband lay dying from a knife wound to the throat, allegedly self-inflicted when Jones's threat led a SWAT team to storm the home.

In her new novel, Jones had written, "I was a turtle before I became a human being, said my grandmother. . . . Then I saw this handsomest young man and took a liking to him, she said. . . . I followed him until I turned into a human being. Is that far enough for you . . . ? But once you's a human being, you hunger for being human." There was poetry, there was beauty, and there was life. Ironically titled *The Healing*, one could only hope that it would be so.

Saturday, February 21, 1998

Kentucky                                            USA

---

**Family**                                                    **Demons**

*A*s a capital of the American shipping industry and a city free of slavery since the Massachusetts state constitution abolished it in 1780, Salem hosted a thriving black community. According to a survey taken by *Freedom's Journal,* in 1827 they were numbered at four hundred and growing—in size and in sense of being a community. From this self-consciousness came the first abolitionist assembly of black women—the Female Anti-Slavery Society, founded on February 22, 1832.

While the African Dorcas Society had been launched by Philadelphians in 1827 and held its first national convention in New York City the following year, its primary purpose was charitable: providing clothes for schoolchildren. With the Female Anti-Slavery Society, here was the political voice of black women rising in union. Building on their mutual aid societies (see December 28) and literary clubs (see September 20), they dared new ground. "We, the undersigned, females of color, of the commonwealth of Massachusetts," their constitution read, "being duly convinced of the importance of union and morality, have associated ourselves together for our mutual improvement, and to promote the welfare of our color. . . . Resolved, That this Society be supported by voluntary contributions, a part to be appropriated for the purchasing of books, &c.: the other to be reserved until a sufficient sum be accumulated, which shall then be deposited in a bank for the relief of the needy"—the needy, newly free slave, that was.

Soft as the voice may sound in our ears, it is as loud as it was in its time. To pro-slavers still reeling from Nat Turner's noble revolt six months earlier, to the conservatives of the black church where men held the pulpit, the "threat" was in the Female Anti-Slavery Society's very existence. Here, leadership abilities of black women would flower, making their *rose,* by its secular name, smell all the more sweet.

Wednesday, February 22, 1832

Massachusetts                    USA

**Organizing**                                    **Self-assertion**

*O*n February 23, 1868, in the Berkshire Mountain resort town of Great Barrington, Mary Silvina Burghardt gave birth to a son, Will. Descended from the "black Burghardts," her roots spread over two hundred years of African subjugation and Dutch prominence in colonial Massachusetts. With her husband's desertion while her son was a toddler came hard times, born of single motherhood, that would consume her life. By 1920, thirty-six years after her death, her son—Harvard University's first black Ph.D., cofounder of the Pan-African Congresses and the NAACP—had earned international reknown as Dr. W. E. B. Du Bois. A witness to his mother's dilemma—or quadrilemma, as he called it—he wrote, poignantly, "I remember four women of my boyhood: my mother, cousin Inez, Emma, and Ide Fuller. They represented the problem of the widow, the wife, the maiden, and the outcast." From his essay "The Damnation of Women":

> For their promise, and for their hard past, I honor the women of my race. Their beauty—their dark and mysterious beauty of midnight eyes, crumpled hair, and soft, full-featured faces—is perhaps more to me . . . because I was born to its warm and subtle spell. . . . No other women on earth could have emerged from the hell of force and temptation which once engulfed and still surrounds black women in America with half the modesty and womanliness that they retain. . . . I have known the women of many lands and nations . . . but none have I known more sweetly feminine, more unswervingly loyal, more desperately earnest, and more instinctively pure in body and in soul than the daughters of my black mothers.

An ardent defender of women's rights, Du Bois would rally others to the cause from the pages of *The Crisis* (see August 2), which he launched in 1910 as the official organ of the NAACP.

Sunday, February 23, 1868

Massachusetts                    USA

---

"*I* had reasoned this out in my mind," said Harriet Tubman. "There were two things I had a right to, liberty or death. If I could not have one, I would have the other. No man would take me alive." A slave mother told her daughter, "Fight, and if you can't fight, kick; if you can't kick, then bite." A former slave recalled a woman "who would not be conquered by her mistress." Threatened with sale, she "took her right hand, laid it down on a meat block and cut off three fingers, and thus made the sale impossible." By escape, putting up one devil of a struggle, self-mutilation, and any number of equally decisive and desperate measures, the "powerless" charted routes to self-empowerment.

A letter dated February 24, 1846, documents another way. "I fear you cannot sell Lucy in her low spirited situation," wrote Alex Fitzhugh to the slave traders, R. H. Dickerson & Brothers of Richmond, Virginia, in whose pens she was being held. To sell a slave, an owner had to provide a warranty that her eyes were clear, her teeth good, and her general condition "sound and healthy"; quality set the price. And the price that Lucy would bring was getting lower by the day. Fitzhugh wanted four hundred fifty dollars and not a penny less, but "her hysterical, low spirited situation" made it impossible for the trader to fetch that amount for her. "I apprehend from Frds. [friends] she will come home," wrote the thwarted owner. "Tell her to bring her child's clothes. . . . Assure her I will keep her myself or sell her in Falmo. But my desire and that of the family is to keep her."

Miss Lucy would not be sold from her child; such was her "mother's love." On the battlefields of generations, our warrior-women have honed resistance in many forms.

Tuesday, February 24, 1846

Virginia                                    USA

---

Slavery                                    **Self-determination**

"Y ou're not fat, you're living in the wrong country," proclaimed an article in the February 1998 issue of the international high fashion trendsetting journal *Marie Claire.* For eighty percent of the women of the world, and those worldly wise, full-figured women set the standard of beauty.

In rural Nigeria, in a ritual *Iria* (a ceremonial coming-of-matrimonial-age), young women take to their "fattening rooms" to eat for four weeks, fattening up to attract a mate. In India, a mother with "three chubby rolls bulging over the folds of her sari" is "proud that she looks prosperous" and only wants the same for her diet-conscious exercise-regimened rail-thin daughter. An artist relates the virtues of being voluptuous: "In my twenties I was really big, and lots of men would tell me that they liked my figure very much. The idea of what is attractive is not only visual. The pleasures go beyond just image. The eyes give way to the touch. A soft belly, chubby knees, fleshy clefts in unexpected places . . . all delicious." So too in Mali, among nomadic peoples, a roving eye rests well on a fleshy woman. To those who ferret out their living moving according to the seasons, a woman sizeably proportioned signals wealth: well-endowed, she can afford to be inactive. And so the story goes, for different reasons in different places.

Then there is this . . . whether purging to be small or gorging to be large, Mother Nature would probably prefer that we appreciate her artistry that is us just the way she planned.

February 1998

International

$\mathcal{T}$he language of the nineteenth century was often flowery and fanciful—especially in the South, where "chivalry" masked a culture of violence. But among the truly chivalrous was a traitor and subversive to his peers, John Fairfield. Fairfield was born to a wealthy Virginia family, and his hatred of the treatment given his childhood friend led him to turn his back on his patrimony, become a conductor on the Underground Railroad, and specialize in the near impossible—freeing entire families. And while the names and dates of Fairfield's rescues were discreetly undocumented, a sister who traces her ancestry to a "package" en route from Virginia to Canada in the mid-1850s might thank him still.

In pursuit of his mission, Fairfield often alienated his pacifist white colleagues by fighting fire with fire. But two of his most successful missions were among the UGRR's most engaging, nonviolent, and creative efforts. A wealthy gentleman accorded every societal privilege, he used the greater likelihood of his being a slaveholder than a "slave-stealer" to better his odds of success.

In the mid-1850s, in response to free people in Detroit and Canada who had asked him to rescue relatives in Virginia, Maryland, and Washington, D.C., he came up with a plan. Knowing them to be light-skinned people, he bought eighty dollars worth of supplies. Using what he had bought, he powdered their faces, crowned them with wigs, boarded his party of well-dressed "whites" on the evening train to Harrisburg, Pennsylvania, and from there on to Canada aboard the UGRR. In this way, Fairfield took special pleasure in helping to undo slavery's greatest tragedy—the destruction of families. Reuniting husbands with wives, children with their long-lost mothers and fathers, he worked to undo the devastation "privilege" had entitled his family to commit and had forced him, as a boy, to witness.

February 1855

Maryland          USA

*A*s the first American woman to lecture in public (see September 21), Maria W. Stewart broke new ground in social conventions for women and for African Americans as a whole. A woman of deep religious convictions, she spoke no secret prayer for deliverance, cryptically whispered behind closed doors. Each life experience, each audience, emboldened her growing abolitionist and feminist consciousness. On February 27, 1833, she spoke at Boston's African Masonic Hall:

> African rights and liberty is a subject that ought to fire the breast of every free man of color in these United States. . . . We have made ourselves appear altogether unqualified to speak in our own defence, and are therefore looked upon as objects of pity and commiseration. We have been imposed upon, insulted . . . on every side; and now, if we complain, it is considered as the height of impertinence. . . .
>
> These things have fired my soul with a holy indignation, and compelled me thus to come forward, and endeavor to turn their attention to knowledge and improvement; for knowledge is power. I would ask, is it blindness of mind, or stupidity of soul, or the want of education that has caused our men who are 60 or 70 years of age, never to let their voices be heard, nor their hands be raised in behalf of their color? Or has it been for the fear of offending the whites? If it has, O ye fearful ones, throw off your fearfulness, and come forth in the name of the Lord, and in the strength of the God of Justice. . . . Have the sons of Africa no souls? Shall the insipid appellation of "clever negroes," or "good creatures," any longer content them? Where is the man that has distinguished himself in these modern days to be acting wholly in the defence of African rights and liberty? There was one [Nat Turner], although he sleeps, his memory lives.

Is it any wonder that Maria Stewart's "brave new world" was feared?

Wednesday, February 27, 1833

Massachusetts                    USA

*A*ll Ruthie Bolton wanted from life was to be loved. Folks had mocked her goals and dreams so badly, she'd become a stutterer. Her "daddy," the grandfather who had literally beaten his wife to death, unpunished and unrepentant, had since made Ruthie his sparring partner. Learning to want more practical things, all she wanted was to stay out of reach. Soon her survival strategy became a way of life.

So it was that when two men drove up to her house in a Mr. Tee Vee truck; knowing she had paid the store what she owed, she hid behind the curtains, hoping the men would go away. "Ruthie in there," Eddie, her elderly neighbor, offered. "I just seen her come from the store. She in there. Just keep on knocking." Betrayed, Ruthie answered from behind the locked door. They had come, yelled the men through her armor, for one man to introduce the new man who would be taking over his route. As Ruthie unlatched the door, there stood "this brown-skinned black guy," looking dead at her, "skinnier than a pencil, and I saw the biggest smile on this man's face." The next day, when they ran into each other at the gas station, he was still smiling. He asked if he could call on her, and came by that very night. The next day, she drove his route with him. Two days later, he confided: it had been love at first sight. Two months later, on February 28, 1980, they made love for the first time. Ruthie wrote the date down in her book.

Fourteen years, a marriage, and four children later, they still kept the promise they made that night: to celebrate this date as their anniversary. "No guy had ever dated me for two months and didn't ask me for nothing," said Ruthie of Ray. "And that's why I really really respected him, because he wasn't after my body. He sure wasn't after my money, because I didn't have no money. . . . It was like he was waiting for me or waiting for the right time."

Thursday, February 28, 1980

South Carolina                    USA

---

**Love**                                              **Aspirations**

*F*or a child with the eye and hand of a sculptor, what could be better than to grow up knee-deep in the red clay earth of Green Cove Springs, Florida? There, where the local industry was brickmaking, Augusta Fells Savage watched adults mold bricks that would build great things. With her tiny hands, she would begin modeling her own vision in clay animals. But she was regularly chastized for "fashioning graven images in a Godly house" by her father, a poor fundamentalist preacher whose greatest poverty was his inability to appreciate his daughter's God-given talent. By the time she married early and left home at age fifteen, she said, her father had "licked me five or six times a week and almost whipped all the art out of me."

Born on February 29, 1892, as evil forces steamrolled oppression across the backs of black people, Augusta Fells was said to have come to the world "at the dark of the moon." But whatever effect the moon had on her life, her pains had come because the sun refused to shine. One of fourteen children, five of whom would not see adulthood, she had been the victim of her parents' desire to raise "good" children who did not "cause trouble" or the eruption of racial violence for the slightest "offense." With best intentions and a loving heart, Rev. Fells would come to regret his heavy-handedness. Rev. Fells was appointed pastor of a church in West Palm Beach; when the family moved to the city, Augusta's poetry brought her acclaim. When a local potter gave her a gift of some clay, she molded a miniature of the Virgin Mary. It was then that her father understood that she was a brilliant artist forged in a cauldron of misunderstanding. Even her admirers would find her work "uneven." How could it be otherwise? The miracle—the genius—of Augusta Fells Savage was that she made art at all. Unevenness, too, has its highs. Among them, her sculpture of a boy, *Gamin,* is on view in the permanent collection of the Schomburg Center for Research in Black Culture (see January 3).

Monday, February 29, 1892

Florida                                    USA

---

**Art**                                    **Responsibility to Youth**

# March

*Guadeloupe woman arrives at Ellis Island aboard S.S.* Korona (April 6, 1911). Photo by Augustus Sherman. Reprinted courtesy National Park Service, Statue of Liberty National Monument and Ellis Island.

*D*eep into the winter of 1692, Tituba, an enslaved twenty-year-old charged with caring for her owner's children, retold the tales of jombies and spirits from her own childhood that sent her charges *wild* and ignited the hysteria that was the Salem Witch Trials.

On March 1, 1692, hearings began with evidence of witchcraft. Because Sarah Good, for example, was seen near the farm of her neighbor whose crop had gone bad, she must be a witch. Faced with the logic of Puritan New England, Tituba—the embodiment of "culture clash"—didn't have a chance. A slave with no interest in upholding such a system, the spectre of mass executions made her a pragmatic enough "witch" to "confess." Still, she was sentenced to death. But with true absurdity, hers was the rare case when being a slave was a protection—because her execution would have deprived her owner of his property. It also deprived her of exoneration. When the governor released those awaiting trial, she was unable to pay the cost of her thirteen months in prison and was sold for costs.

Repenting the excesses of the Frenzy, in October 1697, colonial governors limited the extent of future righteous indignation. In lieu of execution, blasphemers, atheists, and any who denied the Bible as divine would receive time in the pillory or six months in prison, have his/her tongue bored with a hot iron, or be seated on the gallows with a rope around the neck. In the seething cauldron of 1690s society, Tituba's tales were the spark inflaming existing biases against such traditional taboos as the *outsider*, the *outcast*, and the *woman in possession of her faculties*. To study the era is to know that given the temper of the times and the psychology of the zealous, any group of people can justify anything in the name of piety; all it takes is power gone mad.

Saturday, March 1, 1692

Massachusetts                USA

*J*t was Frederick Douglass who sold President Abraham Lincoln on the Emancipation Proclamation as a winning Civil War strategy. His next coup upheld a tradition of every American-fought war before (and since): recruitment of black soldiers. On March 2, 1863, Douglass stirred the troops with an editorial that would become a historic recruitment poster: "Men of Color! To Arms! Action!" "There is no time to delay," he rallied. "Better die free, than to live slaves. This is the sentiment of every brave colored man amongst us." By war's end, nearly two hundred thousand brave men would enlist, as brave women battled the homefront.

Victimized, as were their husbands and brothers, by the violent of every stripe and rank, in and out of uniform, North and South, black women enlisted their own courage. "My Dear Husband[,] I received a letter from you week before last and was glad to hear that you were well and happy," wrote Emily Waters. Unable to pay her eight-dollar-a-month rent when the Union neglected to pay its black troops, she was about to be evicted. Black women fought for family: "Mr abarham lincon I wont to kno sir if you please wether I can have my son relest from the arme he is all the subport I have now his father is Dead," wrote Jane Welcome. When Confederates denied black soldiers respect as prisoners of war, black women fought for their men. "Excellent Sir" wrote Hannah Johnson, demanding that the president fulfill his "responsib's to the soldiers and their families." Her son's regiment (joined by two of Frederick and Anna Murray Douglass's sons) was the Fifty-fourth Massachusetts Colored, whose attack on Fort Wagner was immortalized in the film *Glory* and with statues in Boston and Washington, D.C.

*We also fight who stand and wait!*

Monday, March 2, 1863

Massachusetts                    USA

---

*B*illed as a peaceful demonstration in the nation's capital, the Women's Suffrage Parade of March 3, 1913, attracted five thousand women and scores of white men who were so numerous, disruptive, and violent that one could only wonder at the argument that women didn't need the vote because they had men to protect them.

"Hoodlums, many of them in uniform, leaned forward till their cigarettes almost touched the women's faces while blowing smoke in their eyes" wrote a reporter of the scene. As women inched their way up Pennsylvania Avenue, in step, they were jeered, spat upon, and slapped until a "surging mass" of men overwhelmed police and the cavalry was rushed in from Fort Myer to restore control. Of those who were swamped in the melee more than a hundred were trampled, and with only two ambulances, it took six hours to shuttle the wounded to a nearby hospital.

"Does it not make you burn with shame to be a mere black man when such mighty deeds are done by the Leaders of Civilization?" oozed W. E. B. Du Bois in his editorial in *The Crisis*. "Does it not make you 'want to be white'?" From a white woman came this note: "Not one of [the colored people] was boisterous or rude as with great difficulty we passed along the unprotected avenue. The difference between them and those insolent, bold white men was remarkable. . . . The dignified silence of the colored people . . . was a great contrast to those who should have known better. I thank them in the name of all the women for their kindness." Imbedded in her comment, however, was the very notion against which blacks fought and marched that day: that "women" means "white women." As a sister once said, "All the women are white, all the blacks are men, but some of us are brave." A week later, the bravest of all died at close to ninety-two years of age—Harriet Tubman (see March 10). Exiting one era, we began a new . . . *anew*.

Monday, March 3, 1913

Washington, D.C.  USA

---

*O*n March 4, 1789, the Congress of the United States convened for the first time, empowered by the vote of nine of
the original thirteen states ratifying the Constitution. Emancipation should have been achieved with the Revolutionary War.
Instead slavery was upheld, and with humiliating flourish, an enslaved individual was declared three-fifths a man. Seventy years
later, as the crisis flared into Civil War, author Frances Ellen
Watkins Harper took time to read the Constitution. Moved, she
wrote a letter to the editor of the *National Anti-Slavery Standard*:

> I never saw so clearly the nature and intent of the Constitution
> before. Oh, was it not strangely inconsistent that men, fresh, so fresh,
> from the baptism of the Revolution should make such concessions to
> the foul spirit of Despotism! that, when fresh from gaining their own
> liberty, they could permit the African slave trade—could let their
> national flag hang a sign of death on Guinea's coast and Congo's
> short! Twenty-one years [from independence to abolition of the slave
> trade] the slave-ships of the new Republic could gorge the sea mon-
> sters with their prey; twenty-one years of mourning and desolation
> for their children of the tropics, to gratify the avarice and cupidity of
> men styling themselves free! And then the dark intent of the fugitive
> clause veiled under words so specious that a stranger unacquainted
> with our nefarious government would not know that such a thing was
> meant by it. Alas for these fatal concessions. . . . In the freedom of
> man's will I read the philosophy of his crimes, and the impossibility of
> his actions having a responsible moral character without it; and hence
> the continuance of slavery does not strike me as being so very myste-
> rious.

Her letter appeared in the *National Anti-Slavery Standard* on
April 9, 1859.

Friday, March 4, 1789

Maryland     USA

---

**Law**                     **Perspective**

*J*ust the day before, Abraham Lincoln had been inaugurated President of the United States. Now, on March 5, 1861, in the flush of excitement surrounding the new administration, Mary Todd Lincoln met Elizabeth Keckley—the elegantly attired, statuesque African American designer who would be her official dressmaker and confidante throughout her White House years.

Keckley would tell an interviewer thirty years later, "I dressed Mrs. Lincoln for every levee. I made every stitch of clothing that she wore. I dressed her hair. I put on her skirts and dresses. I fixed her bouquets, saw that her gloves were all right, and remained with her each evening until Mr. Lincoln came for her. My hands were the last to touch her before she took the arm of Mr. Lincoln and went forth to meet the ladies and gentlemen on those great occasions." But that was hardly the measure of the depth of allegiance to which Elizabeth Keckley would go.

A former slave who had purchased her freedom and that of her son in 1855, it was to former slaves that she paid greatest deference. When her son George, the light-skinned product of rape by a former owner, joined a white Union regiment and died in the line of duty, she channeled her energies into helping others. As cofounder of the Contraband Relief Association, she raised funds to assist the thousands of refugees who flooded the capital city seeking food and shelter—an effort to which her friend Mary Lincoln contributed two hundred dollars. Then, in 1868, following the president's assassination, she naively hoped to help ease the former first lady's financial woes with publication of her memoir, *Behind the Scenes; Or, Thirty Years a Slave and Four Years in the White House.* Instead, the book dissolved their friendship. Intimate and controversial, it is, to this day, the best account of the Lincolns' family life.

Tuesday, March 5, 1861

Washington, D.C.          USA

---

**Social History**                                          **Dedication**

𝒫eople often look back upon the twentieth-century women's movement and assume that the conversation on the value of "women's work" and its lack of compensation began in the 1970s. Not so, as Gertrude Bustill Mossell wrote in an illustrative anecdote titled "A Boy's Estimate of His Mother's Work." It appeared in her column in the *New York Freeman* on March 6, 1886:

> "My mother gets me up, builds the fire, and gets my breakfast," said a bright youth. "Then she gets my father up, and gets his breakfast and sends him off. Then she gives the other children their breakfast and sends them to school; and then she and the baby have breakfast."
>
> "How old is the baby?" asked the reporter.
>
> "Oh, she is 'most two."
>
> "Are you well paid?"
>
> "I get $2 a week and father gets $2 a day."
>
> "How much does your mother get?"
>
> With a bewildered look the boy said, "Mother, why, she don't work for anybody."
>
> "I thought you said she worked for all of you."
>
> "Oh, yes, for us she does, but there ain't no money in it."

In the days of Reconstruction, Sojourner Truth warned against according men rights denied women (see May 10), and there were a few men, Frederick Douglass among them, who broke with traditional male dominance to fight for the rights of all women. They well knew that a mother who could not protect herself could not protect her children. And every man is first his mother's child— a point not lost on Mossell's nephew, Paul Robeson.

Saturday, March 6, 1886

New York       USA

---

**Motherhood**                  **Values**

They stood in the middle of the floor, crying, with their arms locked about Bigger. Bigger held his face stiff, hating them and himself, feeling the white people along the wall watching. His mother mumbled a prayer, to which the preacher chanted.

"Lord, here we is, maybe for the last. You gave me these children, Lord, and told me to raise 'em. If I failed, Lord, I did the best I could. (*Ahmen!*) These poor childrens been with me a long time and they's all I got. Lord, please let me see 'em again after the sorrow and suffering of this world! (*Hear her, Lawd!*) Lord, please let me see 'em where I can love 'em in peace. Let me see 'em again beyond the grave! (*Have mercy, Jesus!*) You said You'd heed prayer, Lord, and I'm asking this in the name of Your son."

"Ahman 'n' Gawd bless yuh, Sistah Thomas," the preacher said.

They took their arms from round Bigger, silently, slowly; then turned their faces away, as though their weakness made them ashamed in the presence of powers greater than themselves.

"We leaving you now with God, Bigger," his mother said. "Be sure and pray, son." They kissed him.

*B*igger Thomas wasn't just an archetypal invention of his author, Richard Wright, who lived only in the pages of *Native Son.* As Wright confided on March 7, 1940, in his essay "How Bigger Was Born," he had witnessed Bigger's baptism by fire in the racism of Natchez, Memphis, and Chicago; in his life he had come to know five Biggers. There was Bigger the childhood bully, Bigger the angry teenager, Bigger the dangerous young man, Bigger the "crazy nigga," and Bigger the volcano, whom pain had tricked into believing he had nothing to lose. Five Biggers killed the white girl and robbed his black mother of him. Five demons killed Bigger long before his mother's prayer for all the Biggers she, too, had ever known.

Thursday, March 7, 1940

Mississippi                                    USA

---

*I*n the account book of Philadelphia cobbler Abraham Shadd, halfpence and shillings code his Underground Railroad stationmastery. In the journal of his daughter, Mary Ann Shadd, is the story of the first African American woman newspaper editor and publisher. Emigrating to Canada with a growing number of expatriates and slaves "forwarded" to freedom aboard the UGRR, she extended the family's activism with her paper, the *Provincial Freeman*. The voice of freedom, she was the target of repression. A quarter century after Maria Stewart (see September 21) became the first woman on the lecture podium, Shadd was in Illinois to promote the paper when men "so conservative they [won't] tolerate lectures from women" shut down her speech. In the March 8, 1856, edition of the *Freeman*, she documented the incident and called upon activists in the cause of women's rights to head to Illinois posthaste. Half a century later, coincidentally, March 8 was proclaimed International Women's Day. Today, we honor all our sheroes, like Shadd, who helped to make a better world with this parable:

The story is told of an old blind woman and those who would try to trick her. Known for her insight, she is often asked questions that no one else can answer; to define some of life's greatest mysteries and explain into palpable meaning its sorrows. One day, two youngsters decide to find out just how wise she really is. We're going to trick her, they dare think. And so they go out and catch a bird, a littler life innocent in the scheme. They will go to the woman with a question and plan in mind. Is the bird alive or dead? they will ask, knowing that if she says it is dead, they will let it fly; if she says it is alive, they will kill it. Walking up to the blind old woman, they pose their question. She pauses, smiles, and answers. "Whether the bird is dead or alive," she tells them, "it is in your hands." From Shadd's day to ours, like the life of a fragile little bird, the condition of human rights is *in our hands*.

Saturday, March 8, 1856

Illinois                              USA/Canada

---

**Celebrations**                              **Collective Responsibility**

*A*s quiet as it is kept, the truth of lynching is this: the over-whelming majority of African American men, women, and children killed by white mobs were middle- and upper-class indi-viduals guilty of one crime alone—violating the doctrine of white supremacy. Never was that made more clear than on March 9, 1892, when the owners of the People's Grocery Store in Mem-phis, Tennessee, were lynched—an event that propelled Mary Church Terrell and Ida B. Wells to launch the anti-lynching cam-paign that nearly made them victims.

Threatened by the success of the three businessmen and its portent for black economic independence, a white competitor and his friends in the press, police, and courts fueled the white rage that led to the slaughter, in which one victim's eyes had been gouged out and three of his fingers shot off. In a wave of terror mirroring the increased scapegoating of blacks for the Civil War losses of an unreconstructed South, 255 known lynchings would be committed that year by whites angered by the loss of former prey. Four years later, the Supreme Court would restore total white-over-black dominion with its *Plessy v. Ferguson* decision legalizing segregation and circumventing "freedom amendments" to the Constitution for the next sixty years (see May 17). But what made the lynching of Thomas Moss, Calvin McDowell, and Henry Stewart unique was its effect.

Mary Church Terrell (see May 14), daughter of a wealthy ex-slave who raised her to be "a lady," pregnant wife of the future first black federal judge, would lose her baby to substandard seg-regated hospital care. Ida B. Wells, a seasoned anti-segregationist crusader, was co-owner of the *Memphis Free Speech*. The movement forged by these two very different women (see July 30) would yield a tale of fear in black and white, and legendary courage where *hell hath no fury . . .*

Wednesday, March 9, 1892

Tennessee                                             USA

---

**Lynching**                                   **Respect for One's Power**

*O*n March 10, 1913, Harriet Tubman died at her Auburn, New York, home. Nearing ninety-two years of age, she had been an icon for the African American and women's rights movements, remaining active in both in her later years. As long ago as slavery and her life seem, it is significant that Tubman helped define two human rights agendas across two centuries. In a time of freedom that was not free, when the gains for which she fought were as endangered as most of her life had been, her calls for vigilance and self-determination took on new meaning. On August 28, 1868, Frederick Douglass wrote the testament that well serves as her eulogy:

> The difference between us is very marked. Most that I have done and suffered in the service of our cause has been in public, and I have received much encouragement at every step of the way. You, on the other hand, have labored in a private way. I have wrought in the day — you the night. I have had the applause of the crowd and the satisfaction that comes of being approved by the multitude, while the most that you have done has been witnessed by a few trembling, scared, and foot-sore bondmen and women, whom you have led out of the house of bondage, and whose heartfelt "God bless you" has been your only reward. The midnight sky and the silent stars have been the witness of your devotion to freedom.

Coming one week after women's suffrage marchers in Washington, D.C. (see March 3) had been attacked by irate men along the Pennsylvania Avenue parade route, the timing of her death was significant. For the woman who had seen the best and the worst of valor and ignorance, it must have seemed time to venture to higher ground.

Monday, March 10, 1913

New York                                        USA

---

*O*n March 11, 1973, visitors crossed the threshold of Boston's new Museum of the National Center of Afro-American Artists into a world wrought by two visionary women. In twenty years of building the national center, Elma Lewis, the venerated educator-entrepreneur and future MacArthur "genius" Award recipient, had opened many a door for artists. Now she opened doors for art lovers on the "Reflective Moments" of Lois Mailou Jones. It was a retrospective exhibition of the Boston-born artist's forty-six years as a door opener herself as founder of Charlotte Hawkins Brown's Palmer Institute (see June 17) art department in 1927 and as a member of Howard University's art faculty since 1930.

As museum director Edmund Barry Gaither noted in the show catalog, Mailou Jones was "one of the few figures in American art to achieve a long, exciting and inspiring career in which there is no room for defeat, dullness, or trickery." As a child, summering on Martha's Vineyard while her mother plied her own artistry as a beautician and milliner, Lois met the African American singer-composer Harry T. Burleigh. Generous to the island children, he inspired them with stories of his own success in Europe. He urged them to go abroad—to "try to make something of the importance of your life" away from American racism. Remembering his advice, Jones took a "shackle-free" sabbatical in France, studied Africa's classical art traditions, designed masks for the African choreographer Asadata Dafora. So consumed by art was she that her mother warned her against being singular and single: "Some day you'll wake up and find yourself surrounded with pictures." It was not to be. Mailou Jones was soon influenced by Haitian art and a Haitian artist, Louis Vergniaud Pierre-Noël, to whom Dafora introduced her. "Tall, handsome Pierre reappeared in my life when that reminder from my mother seemed to be true." Married in 1953, they shuttled to Haiti, explored Africa, enriched their art, and made of their love an artful gift to others.

Sunday, March 11, 1973

Massachusetts                    USA

---

**Art**                                                    **Vision**

*O*n the morning of March 12, 1959, basking in opening night reviews, it was official: Lorraine Hansberry's play *A Raisin in the Sun* was a hit! The first black drama to achieve such kudos, it was directed by Lloyd Richards; starred Ruby Dee, Claudia McNeil, Sidney Poitier, and Diana Sands; and took its title from a poem by Langston Hughes: "What happens to a dream deferred? Does it dry up like a raisin in the sun? Or does it explode?" A classic "well-made play" in craft and art, it won the Drama Critics Circle Award for the twenty-nine-year-old Hansberry. With that distinction came the responsibilities of success.

In romantic reflections of the Kennedy era as the "days of Camelot," it is easy to dismiss as incongruous the alter images of the time: police dogs and fire hoses set upon children, fire bombings, and J. Edgar Hoover, an FBI chief obsessed with destroying Martin Luther King. On October 27, 1962, racked by a cancer that would claim her life, Hansberry left a sickbed to issue "A Challenge to Artists" at a Carnegie Hall protest against the dangling McCarthy era threat posed by the House Un-American Activities Committee (HUAC):

> Simply being against life as it is is not enough . . . it is perhaps the task, I should think certainly the joy, of the artist to chisel out some expression of what life can conceivably be. . . . As I stand here I know perfectly well that such institutions as the House Committee, and all the other little committees, have dragged on their particular obscene theatrics for all these years not to expose "Communists" or do anything really in connection with the "security" of the United States, but merely to create an atmosphere where, in the first place, I should be afraid to come here tonight at all and, secondly, to absolutely guarantee that I will not say what I am going to say, which is this: I think that my government is wrong.

Thursday, March 12, 1959

New York                          USA

In the seventeenth and eighteenth centuries, as kidnappers swarmed the African continent seizing bodies for the slave trade and destroying ancient civilizations, a tradition emerged as a means of survival: the secret societies. From culturally specific rituals evolved rites and rituals uniquely female and male.

Among the Baule of contemporary Ivory Coast, such is the sacred nature of the woman's body and its sexuality that boys are allowed to go nude longer than girls, who are usually clothed after their second birthday. When a girl first experiences menstruation, she is given an *atonvle,* a coming-of-age ceremony. Dressed for womanhood in fine clothes and gold jewelry, she is celebrated by her family and friends. Then her courting years begin—symbolically in most regions, actually among the eastern Baule. She is encouraged to have lovers and to marry. For the full community of women, there is the diety of womanhood, *Aδyanun,* in whose dance all women are welcome. Dressed in white, their faces speckled with white paint, they sing and dance through the village, the distinctive African women's shrill "whoop" piercing the air, marking each cadence. For some, it is a sign of crisis, for others it might fulfill a chief's request to ward off potential danger. But in no case are men present. They have their own times and sounds for the protection and perpetuation of the culture. When the women dance, it is a time, as men well know, to remain out of sight, to "hide themselves."

In our time and space, when most Africans in the Americas no longer know our precise lineage, what a revelation it is to hear a Caribbean elder say "Aw, go hide yourself." Our past might be past, but it is not gone.

Circa 1800

Baule region          Ivory Coast

*F*ree at last! Having arrived safely in Toronto, Canada, and having changed her name from Mary Epps, on March 14, 1855, "Emma Bowen" wrote a note of thanks to William Still, Philadelphia's main line Underground Railroad conductor. Upon the sale of her child, she explained, she had been so deeply grieved that violent, convulsive seizures left her unable to speak for a month. When she recovered, inspired by a hope that she would one day "sit under her own vine and fig tree where none dared to molest or make her afraid," she had fled to freedom. But Bowen did not realize that her flight was a disease first diagnosed in 1851 by Dr. Samuel Cartwright, a noted member of the faculty of the University of Louisiana, in his paper "Drapetomania; Or, the Disease Causing Negroes to Run Away":

> Drapetomania is from [the Greek, meaning] a runaway slave and *mad* or *crazy*. It is unknown to our medical authorities, although its diagnostic symptom, the absconding from service, is well known to our planters and overseers. . . . The cause in most of the cases, that induces the Negro to run away from service, is as much a disease of the mind as any other species of mental alienation, and much more curable as a general rule. With the advantages of proper medical advice, strictly followed, this troublesome practice that many Negroes have of running away, can be almost entirely prevented. . . . The experience [of owners is] whipping them out of it, as a preventive measure against absconding, or other bad conduct.
>
> Dysaethesia Aethiopica, or Hebetude of the Mind and Obtuse Sensibility of Body—a Disease Peculiar to Negroes—Called by Overseers, "Rascality" . . .

With medical expertise like this, is it any wonder that blacks held to their own secret remedies? Clearly, someone was *crazy,* but not Mary. Mary was free.

Wednesday, March 14, 1855

Louisiana          USA/Canada

---

**Resistance**                                     **Respect for One's Power**

*B*orn in Toccoa, Georgia, in 1896, Ida Cox had the blues. At fourteen, she ran away from home to put them to music, where they could do her some good. From White & Clark's Black & Tan Minstrels to the studios of Paramount Records, with the bands of Jelly Roll Morton, King Oliver, and her own road shows, she could work the crowd. And work it she did when she sang this song in 1924, her own "Wild Women Don't Have the Blues":

> *I've got a disposition and a way of my own,*
> *When my man starts to kicking I let him find a new home,*
> *I get full of good liquor, walk the street all night,*
> *Go home and put my man out if he don't act right.*
> *Wild women don't worry,*
> *Wild women don't have the blues.*
>
> *You never get nothing by being an angel child,*
> *You'd better change your way an' get real wild.*
> *I wanta' tell you something, I wouldn't tell you no lie,*
> *Wild women are the only kind that ever get by.*
> *Wild women don't worry.*
> *Wild women don't have the blues.*

Always a lady, a tough and demanding professional in every way, Miss Ida could *take care of bizness. Uum Huuummm.*

1924

Georgia                    USA

---

**Music**                                        **Empowerment**

*F*rom newspaper ads come a history of African American businesswomen.

### Boarding & Lodging

The subscriber respectfully informs her friends and the public generally, that she has opened a house for the accommodation of genteel persons of colour with Boarding and Lodging at No. 88 South-Fourth St. . . . Philadelphia. Citizens and strangers in want of Boarding and Lodging may depend upon having every attention paid to them on the most reasonable terms. Gracy Jones, Philadelphia.

### Leghorn Bonnets

Mrs. Sarah Johnson, No. 551 Pearl-Street, respectfully informs her Friends and the Public, that she has commenced Bleaching Pressing and Refitting Leghorn and Straw Hats, in the best manner. Ladies Dresses made, and Plain Sewing done on the most reasonable terms. Mrs. J. begs leave to assure her friends and the public that those who patronize her may depend upon having their work done faithfully, and with punctuality and desptach. New York.

On March 16, 1827, Samuel Cornish and John B. Russworm founded African American journalism with the publication of *Freedom's Journal,* the first black-owned American newspaper. "We wish to plead our own cause," they wrote in their first editorial. "We form a spoke in the human wheel, and it is necessary that we should understand our pendence on the different parts, and theirs on us." Critical to that "pendence" were the paper's advertisers. With print space provided by publishers, ads placed by businesses, and subscriptions from readers, the key to success lay in the support of black business by black business—or, as each sister-advertiser made note, by the patronage of "her friends and the public."

Friday, March 16, 1827

New York                    USA

---

*O*f the portrayal of African American women, author bell hooks has said, "We don't have to be punished . . . we don't have to sacrifice our lives when we invent and realize our complex selves." In *Bone Black*, her memoir of coming-of-age in the 1960s, she writes of the bond of hair in the African American sisterhood.

> We are six girls who live in a house together. We have different textures of hair, short, long, thick, thin. We do not appreciate these differences. We do not celebrate the variety that is ourselves. We do not run our fingers through each other's dry hair after it is washed. We sit in the kitchen and wait our turn for the hot comb, wait to sit in the chair by the stove, smelling grease, feeling the heat warm our scalp like a sticky hot summer sun.
>
> For each of us getting our hair pressed is an important ritual. It is not a sign of our longing to be white. It is not a sign of our quest to be beautiful. We are girls. It is a sign of our desire to be women . . . a rite of passage. Before we reach the appropriate age we wear braids and plaits that are symbols of our innocence, our youth, our childhood. Then we are comforted by the parting hands that comb and braid, comforted by the intimacy and bliss. There is a deeper intimacy in the kitchen on Saturday when hair is pressed, when fish is fried, when sodas are passed around, when soul music drifts over the talk. We are women together. This is our ritual and our time.

Born with "good hair," hooks will wish to share in the rite of the hot comb; wish for its power to transform her "thin good hair into thick nappy hair." That is her child's-eye view. Later, she will want an Afro, "never to get my hair pressed again." Having tasted and tested this ritual of womanhood, she concludes, its "intimacy masks betrayal." Come of age, the girl is a woman now.

Circa 1962

Kentucky                         USA

On March 18, 1895, two hundred pilgrims—men, women, and children—left Savannah, Georgia, emigrating to Liberia. With their journey, they renewed the back-to-Africa exodus of the early 1800s (see August 27, October 24) that had been suspended in the hopeful years following the Civil War and revived in the 1870s, fleeing the terror of the Ku Klux Klan and its allies. In search of peace, some chartered prairie schooners to the western territories, others sailed sea schooners east. In Liberia, the first African nation to emerge from colonial rule, they found what they had been seeking.

In the eternal quest for home and for peace, our journeys across the seas go on, propelled by circumstance. In 1967, Arzu Titus was a child fleeing Honduras for the United States "with nothing but the clothes I was wearing." Years later, still pained by that legacy, she took a course entitled, "You Can Heal Your Life." From it came a work of art, a self-love piece, as she calls it, her story quilt, *She Kisses.* An assignment to look into a mirror each morning and say "I love you" sounded easier than it was. "For three months I did this exercise in front of the bathroom mirror with my eyes closed," said Titus. "One day I looked at myself in the mirror and was able to look into my own eyes. What I saw was a beautiful woman. I said, 'I love you.' I kissed the woman in the mirror, and the woman kissed me back." In dialogue with her inner self, new revelations and new quilts would come. "Take the pain and do something useful with it," said *My Spirit.* "You have exhausted your allotted time for regret in this life. The only time left is for creating value. Eat the pain and make yourself strong. Swallow the tears and nurture me. Take the pressure and use it like a diamond. Make yourself shine."

In Liberia, in the mirror of Arzu Titus a change of destination and of destiny. *This little light of mine, I'm gonna let it shine. Everywhere I go, let it shine. . . .*

Monday, March 18, 1895

Georgia                                    Liberia

---

**Emigration**                                    **Re-visioning**

On March 19, 1935, in Harlem, a seething wound waiting to burst stopped waiting.

As with such things, the inciting incident seemed simple: a boy had shoplifted a ten-cent penknife. But as guards ejected him from the store, a woman screamed—and by midnight, five hundred policemen had been called out to quell the riot that left one dead, one hundred wounded, and scores more arrested for looting and sentenced to months in prison on the spot. The few shopkeepers to escape damage did so by posting notices in boarded windows: "This shop is run by Colored people"; "This shop employs Negro workers." Six years into the Great Depression, half the city's black workforce was unemployed. Anger was turning inward or to despair as even the most menial jobs, once conscribed to blacks, now went to desperate whites. "My purpose is to let the Communists know that they cannot come into this country and upset our laws," a careless, opportunistic district attorney told the press. Four sacrificial Communists—one black man, three whites—were held for the rebellion that left broken shop windows to mirror the shattered lives of most black passersby. The "Communist threat," it seemed, was easier to target than the true cause-and-effect of labor woes.

Above the din, educator Nannie Burroughs charged "Declaration of 1776 Is Cause of Harlem Riot": "The framers of the Declaration . . . prophesied that uprisings would occur 'in the course of human events.'. . . They declared that 'when a long train of abuses and usurpations pursuing, invariably the same object, evinces a design to reduce them under absolute despotism, it is their right, it is their duty to throw off such government, and to provide new guards for their future security.' If that's Red, then the writers of the Declaration of Independence were very Red." "Harlem did not have a 'race' riot," she concluded. "It had a human revolt."

Tuesday, March 19, 1935

New York                    USA

---

**Revolt!**                                    **Perspective**

*O*n March 20, 1852, the book *Uncle Tom's Cabin* was published. A sentimental depiction of slavery, it was so radical in its day that President Abraham Lincoln later greeted its diminutive author, Harriet Beecher Stowe, with the immortal line "So this is the little lady who wrote the book that made this great war!"

First serialized in newspapers, the complete book sold out its five-thousand-copy first printing in just two days. Translated into twenty-five languages, performed onstage continuously from 1853 to 1930, it even launched its own merchandising campaign—the Tomitudes, statuettes of the book's main characters. A cultural icon rarely out of stock and never out of print, it has added two terms to the modern lexicon: *Uncle Tom,* for self-effacing blacks; and *Simon Legree,* for chiseling evildoers. A favorite of teachers, *Uncle Tom's Cabin* has shaped the view of slavery held by most people worldwide—surpassing such authentic African American voices as Margaret Walker's *Jubilee,* based on her own family's odyssey, and even Alex Haley's *Roots,* now more synonymous with genealogy.

Perhaps the book's greatest contribution to American letters, however, was its humanity. Stowe's witness to children being ripped from mothers came from her despair at the deaths of her own children. Uncle Tom, a conflicted man who later helped others escape, was based on Josiah Henson (see October 28). In 1851, a chance meeting in Canada reunited "Poor Eliza" and an Ohio-based Underground Railroad agent. With abolitionists persecuted for causing the Civil War long after its close, not until the 1876 publication of his *Reminiscences* did the UGRR agent divulge his connection to the slave, dubbed "Eliza Harris" by his wife, who slipped across the half-frozen river to his door (see January 17). Eliza's story was real, and Stowe's fictional Quaker couple, Simeon and Rachel Halliday, were the real-life rescuers, Levi and Catherine Coffin.

Saturday, March 20, 1852

Ohio/Connecticut          USA

"*And* before I'll be a slave, I'll be buried in my grave, And go home to my Lord, And be free." That was the decision Margaret Garner had made for herself and her children, as reported in *The Liberator* on March 21, 1856.

In late January 1856, Margaret Garner and her four children had been among a slave party escaping from Kentucky across the frozen river into Ohio. Splitting up on shore, one group boarded the Underground Railroad and found freedom in Canada. Garner's group was less fortunate. Tracked by a posse and surrounded, the slave men fought hard, but to no avail. Determined to kill herself and her children rather than be returned to bondage, Garner seized a butcher knife and slit the throat of her youngest child before being restrained. She was then jailed under the Fugitive Slave Act of 1850, which required the return of escaped slaves and imposed penalties on would-be rescuers. The trial lasted two weeks. When her lawyer could not prevent her return, he made a desperate attempt to have her charged with murder in order to keep her in Ohio and save her life. When that, too, failed, Margaret Garner was shackled and forced aboard the *Henry Lewis*, bound for Louisville. En route, an accident occurred. Whether she fell or jumped into the river with her child was never clear. But all agreed she was overjoyed when her child drowned and bitterly fought her own rescue by a friendly albeit ill-advised cook. She was then put aboard the *Hungarian*, and it is said that Margaret Garner was last seen "crouching like a wild animal near the stove, with a blanket wrapped around her," determined still to avoid further enslavement. Sold in the South, Margaret Garner soon died. "She had escaped at last," her husband wrote.

More than a century after Garner's death, her story inspired Nobel Laureate Toni Morrison to write the 1988 Pulitzer Prize–winning novel *Beloved* (see June 19).

Friday, March 21, 1856

Virginia                                    USA

---

**Revolt!**                                    **Zest for Life**

*O*nly the night before, a young artist had been stag-partying around New York till four in the A.M. with his artist-writer friends. A truly talented—and soon-to-be legendary—group, they were roaring through their twenties, imbibing Harlem's cultural scene, and stirring up their own notable brew—the "New Negro." It was 1925. "We build our temples for tomorrow," one of their number, Langston Hughes, would write. But the "visionary" among them, artist-muralist Aaron Douglas, was turning his eye for painterly detail to matters of the heart. Spring was here! as he wrote to his lady love.

> Sweetheart: I looked at the moon last night. I wondered at it. What a beautiful thing it was. How full of mystery. How full of life. How full of love. It seemed to reek with voluptuousness. What a sensitive thing it seemed last night. How charming. But the most fascinating thing about it was that it seemed to give me an unusual sense of your presence. I could feel you. I lived in the memory of all moons. Last night I saw the happiness and beauty and love of all moons crowded into the memory of that most glorious of all moonlight nights. The night that I shall never forget. The night that we rode from Topeka to K. C. last June. I can see it now. We were one with nature that night as we sped along oblivious of everything except our own happiness and the flood of moonlight that spread over us a soft canopy of love.

Douglas signed his letter "Daddy," in that swinging fashion that would be immortalized by Ella Fitzgerald in her hit song "My Heart Belongs to Daddy." It certainly did for Alta Sawyer, to whom the letter was written. She soon pledged her heart to Douglas as his future bride.

Spring 1925

New York          USA

*J*t was the Roaring Twenties, the temperance years of Prohibition when rum joints for revellers of every hue flourished in backroom parlors after dark. Right out front at the Cotton Club, Ethel Waters was queen, crooning "Am I Blue?" But "being blue" and "having the blues," like city slick to country folk, were worlds apart. Taking sweetness from a honey man could get you to misbehavin'. Better get with the jive talk, a sound all its own:

Bird's-eye maple: a very light skinned woman
Blue: a very dark skinned person
Bolido: gambling on the New York clearinghouse numbers
Buzz cart: a car
Dicty: high-class, a good sport
Dogs: feet
Eight ball: a blue
Honey man: a kept man
Juice joint: an after-hours spot during Prohibition
Lammer: a car
Lap: liquor
Scronch: a dance
Skip: to dance
Snouts: food, as in pickled pig snouts
Speakeasy: a juice joint
Spruce: a sucker
Sweet man: a honey man
Unsheiking: a woman trying to get a divorce
Working moll: a prostitute

1929

New York                         USA

---

It was a Sunday in early spring the first time that Caramel Johnson dawned on the congregation of _____ Church in a populous New England city. The Afro-Americans of that city are well-to-do, being of a frugal nature, and consider it a lasting disgrace for any man among them, desirous of social standing in the community, not to make himself comfortable in this world's goods against the coming time when old age creeps on apace and renders him unfit for active business. . . . Of course, these small Vanderbilts and Astors of a darker hue must have a place of worship in accordance with their worldly prosperity, and so it fell out that _____ Church was the richest plum in the ecclesiastical pudding. . . .

The attendance was unusually large for morning service, and a restless movement was noticeable all through the sermon. How strange a thing is nature; the change of the seasons announces itself in all humanity as well as in the trees and flowers, the grass, and in the atmosphere. Something within us responds instantly to the touch of kinship that dwells in all life. . . . There was a suppressed feeling of expectation, but not the faintest rustle as the minister rose in the pulpit, and after a solemn pause, gave the usual invitation: "If there is anyone in the congregation desiring to unite with this church. . . ." The words had not died upon his lips when a woman started from her seat near the door and passed up the main aisle [and] the men said to one another, "She's a stunner, and make no mistake." The minister whispered to the candidate, coughed . . . and, finally, turned to the expectant congregation: "Sister Chocolate Caramel Johnson—" He was interrupted by a snicker . . . "I'd get the Legislature to change that if it was mine, 'deed I would!"

*T*his passage is from "Bro'r Abr'm Jimson's Wedding," by Pauline E. Hopkins (see April 6), in the December 1901 issue of *Colored American Magazine.*

Spring 1901

Massachusetts                    USA

---

*J*t was the "last great march" of the Civil Rights era: a ribbon of marchers miles long streaming over the crest of the hill and the struggle called Selma, Alabama. The Selma-to-Montgomery march, over a fifty-four-mile course, rallied on March 21, 1965, and culminated at the state capitol building on March 25. What had begun as a voter registration campaign the year before had escalated into a violent assault on marchers crossing the Pettus Bridge, to become a showdown on segregation.

On March 7, state trooper Major John Cloud and Sheriff Jim Clark had launched a violent assault on the Pettus Bridge, beating back demonstrators. So horrid was the spectacle that it was called "Bloody Sunday" and President Lyndon Johnson signed the Voting Rights Act the next day. Two weeks later, demonstrators returned with reinforcements, conquering their dragons in a sweeping tide of four thousand under protection of the National Guard. The date, March 21, had been chosen for its solidarity with South Africa's victims of apartheid and the infamous Sharpeville Massacre of March 21, 1960. With America's swelling casualty list came a swell of conscience as people the nation over headed to Selma. With marchers gathering en route like an avalanche gathers momentum, a streaming ribbon of twenty-five thousand marchers miles long reached Montgomery in five days. In the lead was Dr. King, who had taken up the mantle of Selma at the invitation of a woman too often overlooked in the story of the struggle — Amelia Boynton.

Boynton was one of the few blacks registered in pre–voting rights Selma; for her campaign to register others, Sheriff Clark dragged her off to jail by the collar. Boynton had recruited SNCC to Selma. When a court injunction blocked SNCC, she sought out Dr. King. For her strategic role, as one historian noted, "It would probably not be too much to call her the mother of the Voting Rights Act."

Thursday, March 25, 1965

Alabama                                   USA

---

**Organizing**                                          **Tenacity**

*I*n 1863, at the age of ninety-seven, a woman who had spent fifty years on the road, traveling the United States and Canada as an itinerant preacher, sat down to write the story of her life, *The Memoir of Old Elizabeth, a Coloured Woman.* Enslaved until the age of thirty, she had the stripes of the lash to prove it. She began her career at about the time the slave trade was outlawed in 1808. At first, she was predictably discouraged from her mission on account of gender and of race, and she was made to feel "very unworthy and small." There were times when her "imprudency" was "so much condemned, that I was sorely tempted by the enemy to turn aside into the wilderness." But with her growing confidence came converts from the ranks of her staunchest opponents:

> At one of the meetings . . . a great scripturian, fixed himself behind the door with pen and ink, in order to take down the discourse in short-hand; but the Almighty Being anointed me with such a portion of his Spirit, that he cast away his paper and pen, and heard the discourse with patience, and was much affected, for the Lord wrought powerfully on his heart. After meeting, he came forward and offered me his hand with solemnity on his countenance, and handed me something to pay for my conveyance home. . . . At a meeting which I held in Maryland, I was led to speak from the passage, "Woe to the rebellious city," &c. After the meeting, the people came where I was to take me before the squire; but the Lord delivered me from their hands. [In Virginia] the people did not believe a colored woman could preach. And moreover, as she had no learning, they strove to imprison me because I spoke against slavery.

Venturing on "without purse or scrip," she made her way. An inspiration to her sisters enslaved, she was a *dangerous* woman to the wicked indeed.

1863

Maryland/Virginia                    USA

---

**Religion**                                        **Confidence**

*T*he Africana Studies and Research Center of Cornell University was twenty years old and celebrating. On March 27, 1990, it inaugurated its anniversary with a lecture series by the noted historian in whose honor its library had been named, Dr. John Henrik Clarke. Beginning his talk with his roots in the rural Georgia of 1915, he spoke of growing up poor in a family too often separated by the search for work. "I had to work against all of the odds to succeed, but succeed I did." That success, as a master teacher, he would attribute to three women.

As a young child, he would follow behind his great-grandmother as she tended turkeys on the farm, running up and down the hill after them and telling him her African stories. If he was mischievous, even though she was 108 years old, "She would hit me and her arm would almost go around me as though she was hugging and apologizing at the same time. . . . Then I would go through this fake crying, and when it was all over, I would sit there and she would tell me African stories." Planting the word *Africa* in him, she said her husband was "brave like in Africa" for fighting back; she knew the look and sound of the last Africans from the continent, having witnessed their landing. In a time when only one child per family outside the city limits could attend a city school, of his nine sisters and brothers, John was the chosen one. There, "the dark-skinned kids went to Miss Taylor . . . and the light-skinned kids went to Miss Fontrice." It was Miss Taylor who "raised my face between her hands and looked me dead in the eye . . . and said something that every child needs to be told at least once in his or her lifetime, simply: 'I believe in you. I have confidence in you. I believe you'll make it.'" Said Clarke, "I've had three deities in my life, all women. My great-grandmother; my mother, who died when I saw seven; and Miss Evelina Taylor." No wonder he became a master teacher.

Tuesday, March 27, 1990

New York                              USA

---

**Education**                              **Responsibility to Youth**

$O$n March 28, 1976, the National Conference on the Black Family in the American Economy was meeting in Louisville, Kentucky, when the eminent psychiatrist Dr. Frances Cress Welsing broke the seal on language and the identity crisis it belies. "Blacks ask, 'What's happening,' because we really don't know *what's going on*," led Dr. Welsing, evoking a quandary posed in the song by Marvin Gaye. "The black man's language reflects his powerlessness in the face of white supremacy. The 'man' refers to the white man. The black man revolted against being called 'boy,' and now they call each other 'baby.' The black man calls the black woman 'mama,' he calls his house a 'crib,' and he calls himself a 'motherfucker.'"

Hardly content to leave things on that note, Welsing developed her "Cress Theory of Color Confrontation and Racism" and other healing balms for the wounded. In that, she joined such grassroots pragmatists as Los Angeles organizer Margaret Wright, a married mother of four known, in the 1970s, for her work with Women Against Repression. "Black men have been brainwashed into believing they've been emasculated. I tell them they're nuts," said Wright. "Black women aren't oppressing them. We're helping them get their liberation":

> In black women's liberation we don't want to be equal with the white man, we're fighting for the right to be different and not be punished for it. . . . Equal means sameness. I don't want to be equal with the white community because I don't think it's very groovy. . . . Men are chauvinistic. I don't want to be chauvinistic. Some women run over people in the business world, doing the same thing as men. I don't want to compete on no damned exploitative level. I don't want to exploit nobody. I don't want to be on no firing line, killing people. I want the right to be black and me.

Sunday, March 28, 1976

Kentucky/California          USA

---

$\mathcal{J}$t was spring 1859 when Cordelia Loney approached the Philadelphia Vigilance Committee. Within days she had been rescued from the fashionable boardinghouse where she was staying with the slaveowner-mistress who had warned her about "free niggers." And so, it was of great concern to the woman, left to worry over how she would comb her own hair and dress her own form, that her slave return to the "kindnesses" offered by slavery. A wealthy woman of high standing in the Episcopal church, "a certain Doctor of Divinity" agreed to help relieve her distress by inquiring into the whereabouts of her missing property:

> Hailing on the street a certain colored man with a familiar face, who he thought knew all the colored people about town, he related to him the predicament of his lady friend from the South . . . signified that Cordelia would rue the change . . . quoted Scripture justifying Slavery, and finally suggest[ed] that he (the colored man) would be doing a duty and a kindness to the fugitive by using his influence to "find her and prevail upon her to return. . . ." The colored man thus addressed was Thomas Dorsey, the well-known fashionable caterer of Philadelphia, who had had the experience of quite a number of years as a slave [and had] himself once been pursued as a fugitive . . . felt entirely qualified to reply to the reverend gentleman . . . telling him that Cordelia had as good a right to her liberty as he had, or her mistress either . . . that he would "rather give her a hundred dollars to help her off, than to do aught to make known her whereabouts, if he knew ever so much about her." What further steps were taken by the discomfited divine, the mistress, or her boarding-house sympathizers, the Committee was not informed. [But Cordelia] took her departure for Canada.

As this incident, anonymously reported in the *New York Evening Post*, proves: those who believe the free were indifferent to the enslaved should consider the source.

Spring 1859

Pennsylvania        USA

---

**Freedom**        **Unity**

*T*o hear Gladys Knight sing "Memories" is to find it unbelievable that there had been a time when she actually prayed to lose her voice: "I don't want this voice. . . . It's getting in the way of the things I want to do. It's causing so much trouble. Please, God, just take it away." She was a teenager then, with parties and fun in mind, and that was one prayer she would later "hope he tuned out." But in Las Vegas in 1989—thirty-seven years after she had won national acclaim on the *Original Ted Mack Amateur Hour* and begun singing with the Pips (her brother and their two cousins)—this was different. It was time to move on to new dreams.

From the age of seven, she'd been riding that "Midnight Train to Georgia" and up to New York to compete for Ted Mack. It had been quite a year of commuting and competition, carrying her little shoe box lunch, riding the segregated trains with her mother and siblings, for that was "The Way We Were" back then. Her father wasn't for it, at first, and "Daddy Could Swear, I Declare," but he came around. Indeed, she could say of her voice, "You're the Best Thing That Ever Happened to Me" and "Try to Remember" the great times at Motown before she "Heard It Through the Grapevine" that she hadn't been paid all she was due. Through it all, "There's a Lesson to Be Learned," she thought; "I Can See Clearly Now"—1989 marked "My Time" to "Give Me a Chance." Yes, Gladys Knight had sung a lot of songs in all those years:

> I sang for preachers, parents, princes, and presidents; for drag queens and mob kings; for regal audiences and drunken fools. I sang for my husbands, for my children, for my band members, my managers, my record companies, my debtors, and, of course, my fans. On March 30, 1989, I sang purely for myself. . . . On that night, at the age of forty-four, I made my world premiere as an adult solo artist.

Thursday, March 30, 1989

Nevada                                          USA

**Women and Womanhood**                                          **Growth**

*T*hese were revolutionary days. Abigail Adams declared her own independence of thought. In bold strokes, she linked the plight of the slave, the rights of women, and the hypocrisy of men who would suppress both. In its denial of universal freedom, she knew the plank on which the Founding Fathers teetered was fragile indeed. In a letter dated March 31, 1776, Abigail Adams wrote to her husband, John, co-signer of the yet-undeclared Declaration of Independence and the future nation's second president. Chiding him for coddling slaveholders by denying others the rights he so prized for himself, she wrote:

> I have sometimes been ready to think that the passion for Liberty cannot be Eaquelly Strong in the Breasts of those who have been accustomed to deprive their fellow Creatures of theirs. Of this I am certain, it is not founded upon that generous and christian principal of doing to others as we would that others should do unto us. . . . I desire you would Remember the Ladies. . . . If perticuliar care and attention is not paid to the Ladies we are determined to foment a Rebelion, and will not hold ourselves bound by any Laws in which we have no . . . Representation. That your Sex are Naturally Tyrannical is a Truth so thoroughly established as to admit of no dispute, but such of you as wish to be happy willingly give up the harsh title of Master for the more tender and endearing one of Friend.

In 1935, another revolution loomed as the Great Depression—fiscal and emotional—lumbered on. With most black breadwinners *out of dough* and segregation peppering the stew, predictably, the recipe was a disaster. Again, it was a woman who saw the plight of the oppressed in global terms. As published by *The Afro-American*, activist-educator Nannie Burroughs titled her historic column "Declaration of 1776 Is Cause of Harlem Riot" (see March 19).

Sunday, March 31, 1776

Massachusetts          USA

---

# April

*Three Guadeloupe women arrive at Ellis Island aboard S.S.* Korona (April 6, 1911). Photo by Augustus Sherman. Reprinted courtesy National Park Service, Statue of Liberty National Monument and Ellis Island.

O f her liberation at age fourteen, Susie King Taylor wrote:

On April 1, 1862, about the time the Union soldiers were firing on Ft. Pulaski, I was sent out into the country to my mother. I remember what a roar and din the guns made, they jarred the earth for miles. The fort was at last taken by them. Two days after the taking of Ft. Pulaski my uncle took his family of seven and myself to St. Catherine Island. We landed under the protection of the Union fleet and remained there two weeks when about thirty of us were taken aboard the gunboat P—— to be transferred to St. Simon's Island; at last, to my unbounded joy, I saw 'the Yankee' . . . There were about 600 men and women and children on St. Simon's, the women and children being in the majority and we were afraid to go very far from our own quarters in the daytime, and at night even to go out of the house for a long time, although the men were on the watch all the time; for there were not any soldiers on the island, only the Marines, who were on the gunboats along the coast. The Rebels, knowing this, could steal by them under cover of the night, and getting on the island would capture any persons venturing out alone and carry them to the mainland. Several of the men disappeared. . . . I learned to handle a musket very well . . . and could shoot straight and often hit the target.

Educate a woman, it is said, and you educate a world. At age seven, an enslaved Susie was sent to live with her free grandmother in Savannah, Georgia. There, in an intricate ruse, she was educated by a family friend (see December 5). With her gift of literacy, she penned an autobiography, *Reminiscences of My Life in Camp: With the 33rd United States Colored Troops, late 1st S.C. Volunteers*, published in 1902. Today, it is her account that educates the world on the first days of freedom through the eyes of a newly free African American woman.

Tuesday, April 1, 1862

Georgia                                    USA

---

**Literacy/Freedom**                                    **Legacies**

*J*t was spring in Indiana when Sandy went to the bank to explain that her account couldn't be overdrawn.

I'm hooked, he sed. . . . This time it's different. . . . You see I got out of the joint and looked around and saw those brothers who are my friends all still on the stuff and I cried inside. . . . Baby, I felt so sorry for them and they wuz so turned around that one day over to Tony's crib I got high wid'em. That's all babee. . . . Say you understand it all. Say you forgive me. At least that, babee.

He raised her head from the couch and kissed her. It was a short cooling kiss. Not warm. Not long. A binding kiss. She opened her eyes and looked at him, and the bare room that somehow now complemented their lives, and she started to cry again. And as he grabbed her and rocked her, she spoke for the first time since she had told that wite/collar/man in the bank that the bank was wrong.

*The-the-the-the bab-bab-bab-ies. Ar-ar-ar-are th-th-th-they o-o-okay? Oh my god. I'm stuttering. Stuttering, she thot. Just like when I wuz little. Stop talking. Stop talking, girl. Write what you have to say. Just like you used to when you wuz little and you got tired of people staring at you while you pushed words out of an unaccommodating mouth. Yeh. That was it, she thot. Stop talking and write what you have to say. Nod yo/head to all of this madness. But rest yo/head and use yo/hands till you git it all straight again. . . .*

This passage is from "After Saturday Night Comes Sunday," written in 1971 by poet-author-educator Sonia Sanchez.

Spring 1971

Indiana                                    USA

---

Literature/Drugs                                    Choices

*O*n April 3, 1952, in Washington, D.C., in the presence of friends and members of the press, the three African American alumnae of the Oberlin College Class of 1884 held a class reunion: Dr. Anna J. Cooper, Ida Hunt, and Mary Church Terrell. Each, in her own way, had been freedom's child. Each, from birth, owned a different part of the story. Each, a woman of service, had made her own mark.

Born into slavery in North Carolina in 1858, Anna J. Cooper was freed by the war. At ten, she entered a church school on scholarship and there began her battle for the academic rights of women. A teacher and college cofounder, her motto was "Educate for service," and at times, she sacrificed her salary to do so. An author, she skewered black male sexism in *A View from the South.* A Sorbonne Ph.D. and solo female American Negro Academy think tank member, she lived to be 105. Canadian-born Ida Hunt followed her mother's footsteps to Oberlin. Her father was a businessman and a judge. She earned her B.A. in 1884, then her M.A., taught for a time, married William Henry Hunt in 1892, and traveled to Africa and the Caribbean for his work as a U.S. consul. A human rights crusader, she contributed scholarly papers to the Pan-African Congresses. And then there was the incomparable Mary Church Terrell (see May 14). Daughter of the South's first black millionaire, wife of Washington's first black judge, author and organizer, she put her privilege to work for justice — at ninety, walking the picket line to desegregate the capital's accommodations and launching a UN campaign to free Rosa Lee Ingram (see February 3), a black woman on death row.

Hail to the Class of 1884! Reporting the story of their reunion, the *Washington Post* wrote, "They agreed that the difficulties they encountered as mere female members of a recently freed race only made their triumphs sweeter."

Thursday, April 3, 1952

Washington, D.C.        USA

---

**Sisterhood**          **Empowerment/Excellence**

During the Vietnam War, the first war fought by desegregated troops, black men were sent to the front in disproportionate numbers as black women continued the struggle at home. These were the sounds of the times:

> I get down and scrub all day. I'm tired of giving people my money. Just filled to the brim. Tired of being walked over. Tired of being mistreated. Thank God you came here, Rev. King. My house, just now the kitchen is falling in. I'm not going to pay no rent where there are rats and nobody going to throw me out.
>
> —*Millie Thompson, Chicago, January 26, 1966*

> We, the poor people of Mississippi is tired. We're tired of it so we're going to build ourselves, because we don't have a government that represents us.
>
> —*Unita Blackwell, Greenwood, January 31, 1966*

> A few years ago there was a shining moment in the struggle. . . . Then came the buildup in Vietnam, and I watched the [anti-poverty] program broken and eviscerated as if it were some idle political plaything of a society gone made on war, and I knew that America would never invest the necessary funds or energies in . . . its poor so long as adventures like Vietnam continued to draw men and skills and money like some demoniacal destructive suction tube.
>
> —*Martin Luther King, April 4, 1967*
> *(assassinated a year later to the day)*

Little wonder Muhammad Ali, hero to a generation, would refuse induction into the army with these words, "I am not going ten thousand miles to help murder and kill and burn other people simply to help continue the domination of white slavemasters over the dark people the world over. This is the day . . . when such evil injustice must come to an end."

Tuesday, April 4, 1967

National             USA

---

**Social History**             **Priorities**

*I*n 1987, Spelman College was as radical as it was conservative on the status of women. Its record for molding black girls into women fit to climb to the top of their professions was impeccable in every field but one. In its then-106-year history, its board had never considered any alumna or other black woman fit to reach the top of Spelman itself. The contradiction was not lost on students. How could it be that with an alumna like NAACP Legal Defense Fund attorney and Children's Defense Fund president Marian Wright Edelman on the board, that neither she nor a peer could head the college? In 1976, as the board replaced one exemplary black male with another, student and faculty protest resulted in a volatile and embarrassing lock-in. Eleven years later, the college braced itself again as the board sought a new president. When votes were cast on April 5, 1987, it wasn't "the right thing to do," it was the best thing that could have happened. A whole new era would begin in women's education and for *herstorically* black colleges with the selection of Dr. Johnnetta Betsch Cole as the first African American female president of Spelman — its "Sister-President," as she delighted in being called.

In just over a century of African American college history, only one other women's institution survived — Bennett College, which had led the way in naming a woman, Dr. Willa Player, president in 1955. In 1987, the then-114-year-old institution named its second woman president — Dr. Gloria Dean Randle Scott, whose résumé included election in 1975 as the first African American national president of the Girl Scouts. Also in this banner year of 1987, the nation's oldest historically black college, Lincoln University, named its first woman president — Dr. Niara Sudarkasa, former vice-president of academic affairs at the University of Michigan in Ann Arbor and that school's first black woman tenured professor. Cole, Scott, Sudarkasa: 1987 was a vintage year for education.

Sunday, April 5, 1987

Georgia       USA

---

**Education**           **Empowerment**

*I*n a letter to the editor of the *Boston Observer* dated April 6, 1906, author-editor-historian Pauline E. Hopkins (see March 24) wrote, "I have argued the union of the Negro and labor for a number of years, but being only a woman have received very little notice." The validity of her argument would take more than a decade to realize, but denial of her wisdom on account of gender would be immediate.

Hopkins's 1900 novel, *Contending Forces,* has been named among the "most powerful protest novel[s] authored by a black woman." With the success of her novel, published by the Colored Co-Operative Publishing Company of Boston, she became an editor of the company's *Colored American Magazine* that same year. Serialization of her novels and her profiles of historic figures from Toussaint L'Ouverture to Harriet Tubman made her creative output and her influence as the magazine's literary editor unequalled until the "second Renaissance" of the 1960s and 1970s. But just as her public anti-lynching and pro-feminist stance built circulation, it was also grounds for termination when the company was purchased with backing from Booker T. Washington. A decade earlier, his "Atlanta Compromise" speech accommodating segregation had made him white America's "most celebrated Negro" of the day.

Losing the battle but winning the war, Pauline Hopkins was insistent that blacks must tell their own stories. To "faithfully portray the innermost thoughts and feelings of the Negro with all the fire and romance which lie dormant in our history," she wrote, "fiction is of great value to any people as a preserver of manners and customs—religious, political and social. It is a record of growth and development from generation to generation. No one will do this for us."

Friday, April 6, 1906

Massachusetts          USA

---

**Historiography**                                    **Perspective**

*I*n the April 7, 1974, edition of the *Des Moines Sunday Register,* women's movement activist-attorney Florynce Kennedy was quoted as saying, "If it's a movement, I sometimes think it needs a laxative."

If ever a mother gave birth to a daughter, Zella Kennedy was the atom that split to power Florynce Kennedy (see September 7). Born in Missouri in 1916, a girl come-of-age in the Great Depression, Flo Kennedy had paid hefty dues to graduate from law school in 1951 at age thirty-five. Her intellect and courage were tributes to both of her parents. But she was clearly her mother's child.

The story is told of the day Mrs. Kennedy's employer had the audacity to accuse the proud young woman of theft. Affronted beyond words, her tantrum turned boiling into outrage; she stripped naked to the skin and then, dislodging one last article—her "feminine hygiene protection"—she flashed it in the woman's face. And that was the end of that.

With a legacy like that to live up to, Flo Kennedy's later notoriety for her "mouth" and her attention-grabbing garb seems mild-mannered indeed. On matters of principle, no Kennedy girl took any nonsense from anybody. From the start, Zella Kennedy told her daughters they were "precious." Believing their mother, how could they do other than believe in themselves? Believing in herself, Flo Kennedy believed in the rights and potential of every woman.

Sunday, April 7, 1974

Missouri/Iowa                    USA

---

For thirty-eight years, since the retirement of baseball great Babe Ruth in 1935, no one had beaten his career record of 714 home runs. Then came Hank Aaron of the Atlanta Braves. As the 1973 baseball season progressed, it became clear that Aaron was set to do the unthinkable: tie Ruth's record. For far too many white Americans, it was just too much to take. Letters began to pour in from all over the country. "Dear Nigger," went one typical tome: "You black animal, I hope you never live long enough to hit more home runs than the great Babe Ruth." Hammerin' Hank just kept hitting them out of the park; home run number 705, 706, 707 . . . "Dear Nigger Henry: I will be going to the rest of your games and if you hit one more home run it will be your last. My gun will be watching your every black move." Security guards now followed everywhere Aaron went, on and off the field. . . . Number 710, 711, 712 . . . right up to the clincher . . . 714! He did it! Through all the insanity, Aaron kept focused, and each home run told a brave tale.

Then came the next season's opener, April 8, 1974. No one in the park thought it "just a game." Aaron stepped up to the plate and hit home run 715. The crowd went wild, and breaking all restraint, his mother came running, running to reach her son—to shield his body with hers should the bullet come.

In 1998, when Mark McGwire, a white player, beat Ruth's long-standing record for the most home runs in a single season, African American Hall of Famer Joe Morgan recalled the story of mother and son. It moved newspaper editor Gregory Bartlett to write, "I shivered when I heard that; but what a testimony to motherhood! One could see where Aaron got his bravery."

Monday, April 8, 1974

Georgia                                      USA

---

**Motherhood**                                      **Sacrifice**

*I*t was a defining moment of the era: Marian Anderson's concert on the steps of the Lincoln Memorial on Easter Sunday, April 9, 1939.

A world-renowned contralto, Ms. Anderson had performed in Washington to such acclaim that her audience had outgrown the segregated city's largest black venues. Her promoters and her host, Howard University, chose the logical and suitable alternative—Constitution Hall. When the Daughters of the American Revolution (DAR), the hall's owner, refused to rent the hall on racial grounds and the school board followed suit, sixty-five black and thirty-two white groups formed the Marian Anderson Citizens Committee. A similar insult had throttled baritone Roland Hayes years earlier. Never again. The committee seeded the press with letters, petitioned Congress, rallied teachers in support, and picketed the DAR's annual convention. Six hundred press clippings focused the world's gaze on Washington. Finally, a tardy First Lady Eleanor Roosevelt resigned her DAR membership and Secretary of the Interior Harold Ickes offered the Lincoln Memorial. Carloads of the faithful, 75,000 strong, braved the morning snow from states north and south. Millions more attended via radio as Anderson sang a program of arias, spirituals, and her closing volley, "God Bless America."

That night, a young Dr. Charles Drew wrote his bride-to-be, Lenore Robbins: "I sat silent and pondered on the power that lies in a smile to change the course of a life; the magic in the tilt of a head, the beauty of your carriage and the gentleness that struck so deeply. . . . A sigh rises as an evening prayer to ask whatever gods there be to keep you safe for me." It had been quite a day for love. In one man's garland was the sentiment of millions for whom the soaring voice of Marian Anderson that Easter sounded a lasting note of resurrected pride and possibility.

Sunday, April 9, 1939

Washington, D.C.    USA

---

*O*n April 10, 1928, history, culture, and spirituality were joined as one. So were the daughter of Dr. and Mrs. W. E. B. Du Bois, NAACP cofounder and editor of *The Crisis,* and the adopted son of Rev. and Mrs. Frederick A. Cullen, pastor of Salem Methodist Episcopal Church, one of the nation's largest and most influential black congregations—Nina Du Bois and Countée Cullen, her poet-beau. Among the bridesmaids and groomsmen were Langston Hughes and other such luminaries of the glitterati (cynically but cleverly dubbed the "Niggerati"). For "Mecca," in that heyday known as the Harlem Renaissance, it was the event of the decade. The guest list, a Who's Who of Black America, was so comprehensive that had the event been hosted in the South, folk would have declined the invitation for fear of making things too easy for "good ole boys" out for a "good ole time" to pluck too many successful African American thorns in one place at one time.

With hardly humble pride, the father of the bride reflected upon the difficulties he had "scented" as his daughter grew from a "round little bunch of Joy: plump and jolly, full of smiles and fun—a flash of twinkling legs and bubbling mischief" into the independent-minded young woman to whom he would steer "the Boy [who] came to me somewhat breathlessly one Christmas eve with a ring in his pocket." In the thrill of it all, a daughter pled her case for sixteen bridesmaids: "But Papa, there are eleven Moles, and five indespensables and Margaret—" Added to that, there were the obligations of a father pondering the fate of the race— the whole race. "Thirteen hundred were bidden to the marriage and no human being has one thousand three hundred friends!" wrote the befuddled dad, impoverished, and all the better for wear. "The soul wants color with bursting chords and scores of smiling eyes in happy raiment. It must be as this soul wills. The Girl wills this. So the Girl marries."

Tuesday, April 10, 1928

New York       USA

---

**Events**                **Joy**

*O*n April 11, 1987, for the annual Founder's Day ceremony, a celebration of the 106th year of Spelman College—Alice Walker, Pulitzer Prize winner and former student, delivered the address. "I do not intend to speak of war and peace, the economy, racism or sexism, or the triumphs and tribulations of black people or of women," she led, although a discerning ear would note her obvious concern with those topics. She had come to discuss an issue much more profound: hair.

Beyond academic prowess, the mark of the Spelman woman had always been the ability to acquit herself as a lady in demeanor, appearance, and grooming. That meant confronting one's hair; the fact is, alone among the world's minions, people of African descent have hair that does not lay down on the job. Our hair spirals up for the sun—only we rarely express it quite so positively. "I stood in front of the mirror and looked at myself and laughed," said Walker. "My hair was one of those odd, amazing, unbelievable, stop-you-in-your-tracks creations—not unlike a zebra's stripes, an armadillo's ears, or the feet of the electric-blue-footed boobie—that the Universe makes for no reason other than to express its own limitless imagination. I realized I had never been given the opportunity to appreciate hair for its true self. That it did, in fact, have one. I remembered years of enduring hairdressers—from my mother onward—doing missionary work on my hair. They dominated, suppressed, controlled. Now, more or less free, it stood this way and that. . . . Eventually I knew *precisely* what hair wanted: It wanted to grow, to be itself, to attract lint, if that was its destiny. . . . What do you think happened? The ceiling at the top of my brain lifted."

With a revelation graciously shared, the author gave her tome a title and her audience a heads-up on life: "Oppressed Hair Puts a Ceiling on the Brain."

Saturday, April 11, 1987

Georgia                                    USA

---

**Turning Points**                                    **Self-affirmation**

*S*uch were the times. With the free and the enslaved denied citizenship, blacks prized their identity as Africans. Then, in 1835, at the fifth annual meeting of the National Convention—an all-black assembly first launched by Hezekiah Grice in 1830 with support from Bishop Richard Allen—it was "Resolved [that we] remove the title of 'African' from their institutions, the marbles of churches, and etc." With their identity "removed," the organization collapsed, and it was a century before the next secular conference, the Negro Congress of 1936, resurfaced.

In the years post-1835, the black anti-slavery crusade was subsumed into—rather than allied with—the white abolitionist campaign. In 1838, this critical change derailed the twin goals of ending bondage for the slave and ending segregation for the slave's next-of-kin, free blacks. The Female Anti-Slavery Society, begun by black women (see February 22), became a group of predominantly white women, shifted its agenda to getting women "accepted" into the white male American Anti-Slavery Society (see December 4), diluted the strength of women leaders black and white, splintered the movement between those for and against the inclusion of women in the mid-1840s, forged the Women's Rights Convention of 1848 (see July 19), refactionalized the groups when passage of the Fugitive Slave Act of 1850 refocused the spotlight on the life-and-death plight of the slave, and convinced more black anti-slavists than white abolitionists that the route to freedom and the "crimes of this guilty land" would be "purged with blood" as John Brown would say (and ultimately do) in his multiracial assault on the arsenal at Harpers Ferry in 1859 (see October 16). A frustrated attempt at direct action, his new twist on the old slave revolt would be immortalized as "the opening shot of the Civil War," which officially began with the attack on Fort Sumter, South Carolina, on this date, April 12, 1861. It's really quite a story.

Friday, April 12, 1861

South Carolina                    USA

---

**Turning Points**                                **Cause and Effect**

*I*n its report of an event—derogated as an "Abolition Riot" by foes—which rescued a fugitive from slave catchers, the April 13, 1837, edition of the *Colored American* was clearly more impressed with its own sexism than with the courage of African American women. "Everlasting shame and remorse seize upon those females that so degraded themselves yesterday," wrote the editors. "We beg their husbands to keep them at home and find some better occupation for them."

Mercifully, this was neither the first time nor the last time African American women would take such matters in hand. In 1836, they rescued two women from a Boston courtroom. In 1847, an eyewitness to a rescue by Nancy Prince (see April 14) reported, "Only for an instance did [her] fiery eyes rest upon the form of the villain, as if to be fully assured that it was he, for the next moment she had grappled with him, and before he could fully realize his position she, with the assistance of the colored women that had accompanied her, had dragged him to the door and thrust him out of the house." By the time the Fugitive Slave Act of 1850 was enacted (see September 6), such rescues were in frequent need. And in 1855, Jane Johnson arrived for her New York court hearing completely surrounded by members of the Female Anti-Slavery Society (see July 19). As slaveholders acted to increase their grip, one could only hope for such women at the ready.

Reading the *Colored American,* subscribers must have wondered whose side the editors were on. With priorities like theirs, few doubted why freedom seemed so elusive. As Jessie Fauset would note ninety years later in the title of her first book, often quoted as social commentary, *There Is Confusion. . . .*

Thursday, April 13, 1837

New York/National          USA

---

**Revolt!**                                          **Self-worth**

Nancy Gardner was born in Massachusetts in 1799 to free parents. There were happy times when her seaman father was still alive and when her stepfather regaled the children with tales of his escape from bondage. Then he too died, and her mother was so destitute that, on occasion, Nancy had to retrieve her sister from a brothel. Now she was newly wed to Nero Prince, a seaman, cofounder with Prince Hall of the first African American order of Freemasons and servant of the Russian imperial court. On board the *Romulus* with her husband on April 14, 1824, en route to Russia, Mrs. Prince embarked on the journey of a lifetime.

In mid-May, they came ashore in the Danish seaport town of Elsinore and headed to Copenhagen, where they shared a twelve-day sight-seeing honeymoon. Two weeks later they arrived in St. Petersburg, "happy to find ourselves at our place of destination . . . and soon made welcome from all quarters." Lodging with another African American, she spent "six weeks very pleasantly, visiting and receiving friends, in the manner of the country" and was presented at court:

> The Emperor Alexander, stood on his throne, in his royal apparel. The throne is circular, elevated two steps from the floor, and covered with scarlet velvet, tasseled with gold; as I entered, the Emperor stepped forward with great politeness . . . and welcomed me, and asked several questions; he then accompanied us to the Empress Elizabeth; she stood in her dignity, and received me in the same manner the Emperor had. They presented me with a watch, &c. It was customary in those days, when any one married, belonging to the court, to present them with gifts, according to their standard; there was no prejudice against color; there were there all casts, and the people of all nations, each in their place.

And this was only the start of her many adventures in Europe and the Caribbean.

Wednesday, April 14, 1824

Massachusetts          USA/Europe

*H*istorically, April 15 had been known for the sinking of the *Titanic.* But on April 15, 1998, as seventy-five guests, give or take a friend, sailed at the invitation of Oprah Winfrey to honor Maya Angelou's seventy-fifth birthday, it was a high time on the high seas.

The family was out! From elder stateswoman Dorothy Height to Spelman College president-emeritus Dr. Johnnetta Cole, *Essence* magazine editor Susan Taylor to husband-and-wife composer-performers Nick Ashford and Valerie Simpson, author Louise Meriwether, and broadcaster Gayle King, the luminous list of friends and spouses went on.

There was even a treasure hunt as the search went on for a case to hold majestic Maya's broadest broad-brimmed hat. In the end, a professional drum case was cut down to order—in a creative solution worthy of these sisters of creativity. Each in her own way had invented herself, forged great dreams, made a better world with her caring and daring, and could still dance a mean limbo—for fun, not metaphor. With no end to creativity, with neither limits nor boundaries between their resources and their source, in a deckside Easter Sunday sunrise service, they took time to give thanks.

Wednesday, April 15, 1998

Caribbean

*O*n April 16, 1963, as demonstrators carried out an SCLC-led attack on segregation in Birmingham, Martin Luther King was in jail for leading a Good Friday protest. Harsh as his confinement was, what rocked him to the core, as a man of the cloth and of conscience, was a letter by eight white clergymen to the editor of the *Birmingham News* calling the campaign "untimely and unwise" and urging blacks to wait. There, behind the bars of his tiny, narrow cell, King wrote the 6,500-word missive that would become one of the world's most treasured pieces of protest literature, "Letter from a Birmingham Jail." In its most stunning sentence, containing thirteen clauses and several hundred words, King tells "why we can't wait." Among the recitations of violence and brutality, one reason was this:

> . . . when your first name becomes "nigger," your middle name becomes "boy" (however old you are) and your last name becomes "John," and your wife and mother are never given the respected title "Mrs." . . . then you will understand why we find it difficult to wait.

In another part of the city was a young woman who had participated in the demonstration, been jailed for it, and found it not just "difficult to wait" but impossible—Mary Hamilton. When her trial date came, she demanded the respect due her. The prosecutor refused. Knowing his case to be fraudulent, he made an issue of her refusal to answer to her first name alone. The judge found her in contempt of court and sentenced her to five days and a $50 fine. Literally making a federal case of it, Miss Mary Hamilton fought her case up to the U.S. Supreme Court. A year later, on March 30, 1964, she won—so did we. "Mary" was "Miss Hamilton," at last, in the eyes of the law.

Tuesday, April 16, 1963

National                                          USA

---

**Women and Womanhood**                                          **Racial Dignity**

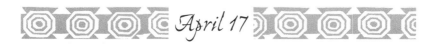 

To meet or read Alice Walker is to be aware that Walker is a woman who knows how to dream. Asleep on April 17, 1984, she was awake as ever to life's possibilities. "The universe sends me fabulous dreams!" she wrote in her journal. "Early this morning I dreamed of a two-headed woman. Literally." A "stout, graying, caramel-colored" wise woman with "blue-gray eyes" was dispensing advice. "Her knowledge was for everyone and it was all striking. While one head talked, the other seemed to doze. I was so astonished!" Seeing the woman, she realized that two-headed people must have existed in fact. But "it is only among blacks (to my knowledge) that a trace of their existence is left in the language. Rootworkers, healers, wise people with 'second sight' are called 'two-headed' people."

Her mother, Minnie Tallulah Walker, was just such a woman of two minds and ability. Working miracles with eight children and twenty dollars in salary, she somehow gave her daughter an abundance of gifts—three of them material: a sewing machine with which to be independent and to make real her own beautiful things, a suitcase loaded with her expectation and appreciation of her daughter's journeys to come, and a typewriter with which to write both of their stories.

As she would urge all women to ask the mothers who made of their lives a bridge to better days, Alice Walker asked the two-headed woman "whether the world would survive, and she said, No; and her expression seemed to say, The way it is going there's no need for it to. When I asked her what I/we could/should do, she took up her walking stick and walked expressively and purposefully across the room. Dipping a bit from side to side. She said: Live by the Word and keep walking." Live by one's word, upon whatever road we are called to travel.

Tuesday, April 17, 1984

California                                   USA

---

**Ideals/Literature**                    **Responsibility to Self**

O n April 18, 1838, Lethe Jackson wrote a letter to her mistress:

My dear and much respected Miss Virginia—I was much pleased at receiving your letter and was very highly flattered to think that you in the gay metropolis so much admired and caressed should still condescend to remember old Aunt Lethe on the retired hill of Montcalm and be assured my sweet young mistress that old Aunt Lethe still remembers you with feelings of the utmost respect and esteem—And my Mistress too I am glad to hear she is getting better and that she has not forgotten lowly me. . . . *Everything is going on finely and prosper in my hands*—The flowers in the garden are putting out and it begins to look like a little paradise and the Calves and the Chickens and the children are all fine and lively—just waiting your return to complete their happiness—I am sorry that Masters' cow has so little manners as to eat Onions—in the City of Richmond too—well what a disgrace! I wish you to tell her that our Mountain Cows are better trained than that—and that if she will come up here we will learn her to be more genteel and not spoil the Governers milk—Tell My Master I think all the world of him and long once more to see his dignified steps up our hill—*Tell Mistress I hope I shall soon hear of her recovery and that we long for the time when she will be again here to give her directions. . . .* We have all done the best we could since she went away but still there is nothing like hav[ing] a person of sense to dictate and then if we are obedient every thing goes on smoothly and happy. [Italics added]

To read this letter, written only six years after Nat Turner's landmark revolt, is to know the value of a "dutiful slave" disguise. Lethe Jackson's master might have been governor, but she was the master politician!

Wednesday, April 18, 1838

Virginia              USA

---

**Strategy**                                   **Self-affirmation**

"*H* ow we got ovah. My soul looks back in wonder, how we got ovah." So asks the beloved refrain. How did we make it through? To flee aboard the Underground Railroad, to be delivered to freedom's door; those were miracles indeed. But how did the fortunate survive their first weeks, build new lives, and live to tell the tale? A "Stock Certificate" issued to "Shareholders" of the UGRR on April 19, 1853, yields answers:

> **Stockholders of the Underground Railroad Company, Hold on to your Stock!!** The market has an upward tendency. By the express train which arrived this morning at 3 o'clock, $15,000 worth of human merchandise, consisting of twenty-nine able-bodied men and women fresh and sound, from the Carolina and Kentucky plantations, have arrived safe at the depot on the other side where all our sympathising colonization friends may have an opportunity of expressing their sympathy by bringing forward donations of ploughs etc., farming utensils, pick axes and hoes, and not old clothes; as these emigrants all can till the soil. N.B. Stockholders don't forget the meeting today at 2 o'clock at the ferry on the Canada side.* All persons desiring to take stock in this prosperous company, be sure to be on hand.
> **Detroit, April 19, 1853**
> **By Order of the BOARD OF DIRECTORS**

To slaveowners and government agents with the force of the 1850 U.S. Fugitive Slave Law on their side, this handbill was a subversive instrument passed among insurrectionists and outlaws. But to the *weary travelers* bound for *glory*, this document held the keys to *heaven* — Canada, peace, justice, friends — dividends of a new life reinvested by those who had escaped before them.

---

*"N.B." stands for North Buxton, Ontario, a refugee settlement of self-emancipated ex-slaves.

Tuesday, April 19, 1853

Michigan             USA/Canada

---

**Underground Railroad**                    **Creative Thinking**

*C* leansing the space in a cloud of incense, she takes the stage in her trademark twelve-inch gélé turned urban crown. An altar, bearing a white candle, is a tableau set for her peace. Sipping from a wooden bowl, in her spiritual incarnation, her get-down conversation, she speaks of ancient Egypt and men. With each you feel, She has *been there.* So who is this Erykah Badu?

On April 20, 1998, working the cavernous stage of the landmark Radio City Music Hall, she is the million-seller recording artist exuding talent built to last. Her sound evokes the "womanist" poets of the 1960s and 1970s (to use a phrase coined by Alice Walker, a poet Badu admires). Resurrecting the seventies in pure *Baduizm,* there is nostalgia—an ironic mood for a black woman, notes one writer. For, as jazz great, composer-drummer Max Roach has argued, black culture doesn't romanticize the past, because the past is pain and injustice; the music, like the driving motivation of black life itself, must push on in search of racial progress.

On this night in concert, Badu will pass over the near past, going back, way back, to reach for the eternal. Words like *afrocentric* will be heard in the writings of those who will observe her. Continuity will be the feeling electrifying the room, connecting other bright African American lights to a past that bounds them into the future. *Badu. Badu.* There is music in the name and in the air.

Monday, April 20, 1998

New York                               USA

---

*J*n the 1930s and 1940s, historians swarmed the South collecting oral histories from the last living slaves. Those with illusions of "happy darkies" and the good ole plantation days had only to hear Martha Harrison's account of her childhood to be disavowed. Gone were the days . . .

When she recorded her childhood experiences for a Fisk University oral history project in the mid-1940s, Miss Martha didn't exactly know her age, but she knew that at twelve or so she had been "crazy about white bread." Adults might get white bread on Sundays. During the week, corn bread and "shorts" would do. Knowing how much Martha liked white bread, in it the mistress had a perfect lure. The promise of a mere crust could coax Martha through her chores in a flash. So special was her treat that when ole Missus died, "it like to killed me," said Miss Martha. In deep mourning she cried, "Ole Miss is dead and I won't get no more white bread." With that, her mother shushed her quick, for fear an overseer might take offense and beat her good. "I thought when she died she carried all the white bread with her," the elderly Miss Martha mused at her innocence. "Folks was saying, 'Look at that po' little nigger cryin' 'bout her Mistress,' but I wasn't cryin' 'bout Mistress, I was cryin' 'cause the white bread was gone."

Certainly, Miss Martha had other tales to tell—tales about how overseers blared horns to tell slave mothers when they could nurse their babies, about the care given black babies by slaveowners "'cause that's where they got their profit," about her father's being sold away from the family and somehow making his way back. "Someday somebody'll stand up and write about me," wrote Langston Hughes. "I reckon it'll be me myself!" And it was.

Circa 1863

Tennessee        USA

---

**Social History**          **Self-affirmation**

"Dear Mrs. Lawrence," a bride wrote her future mother-in-law on April 22, 1938:

Just a note to confess that I love your son Charles and that I have promised to become his bride on June fifth at 4:30 P.M. There is also something else I felt the need of explaining since first I knew, long years ago in 1935. You and I had just met and you were sitting one day on the bank of Cherry Street School talking about the evils of the "younger generation"—when I said that being bored and weary of the young men of my acquaintance, I was so happy to meet Charles because at last I thought here was a young man that I could be friends and pals with; play tennis, go on bikes and swimming and play music and never feel that he would spoil all that by making love to me in the usual "boy-girl" manner. And I remember quite well that you said, "Do you know he said the same thing about you?" And so what I've wanted to explain is that I said that in all good faith and had no idea that this would happen at all. We have been and still are such good pals and friends, and we find so many interesting things and such good fun in life, that I cannot but see great happiness in store for us. And besides I love Charles and think him the most wonderful man ever . . . this I trust to you to keep a secret.

Reading the words of a hopeful bride to her future mother-in-law, how precious their bond seems. How sad for girls who become mothers before they become women and miss so much, forgoing the joyous roller coaster ride from friendship to ecstasy. How can we brighten their way? As to the letter's outcome: it was written by the pioneering child psychiatrist Dr. Margaret Morgan Lawrence, who did, indeed, marry Charles. The letter appears in a biography of her life written by her daughter, the distinguished educator Sara Lawrence Lightfoot, and dedicated to Sara's daughter and son.

Friday, April 22, 1938

New York/Mississippi    USA

---

**Love**                                **Sharing**

*O*n April 23, 1872, Charlotte E. Ray made history as the first woman admitted to the Washington, D.C., bar and the first African American woman admitted to practice nationwide. On April 23, 1951, Barbara Johns's high school rebellion against racism would make new law as one of the three cases consolidated in the Supreme Court's historic *Brown v. Board of Education* decision, which desegregated public schools in 1954.

Ray had applied to the Howard University School of Law as "C. E. Ray"; even at this law school founded to overcome bias, her acceptance had come at the expense of her gender. Once admitted, her gender revealed, to the school's credit, she was enrolled and allowed to complete the course. But although she was qualified and gifted in corporate law, gender and racial bias would deny her sufficient clients to build a practice. Her legacy would instead come from her "daughters-in-the-law."

At mid-century, there were fewer than sixty black women attorneys. Among them, Florence Lucas specialized in general law and supported such enterprises as the groundbreaking Ebony Oil Company. Carmel Carrington Marr was legal affairs adviser for the U.S. Mission to the United Nations. Juanita Kidd Stout, an Oklahoma music teacher turned Philadelphia lawyer, became Pennsylvania's first black female judge in 1956; Constance Baker Motley (see June 24) became the first black female federal judge in 1966; and Carol Moseley-Braun became the first black female U.S. senator in 1992. For her part, Barbara Johns's rebellious youth impacted the lives of every public school child to this day.

What a day for women and the law this has been, in practice and in promise.

Tuesday, April 23, 1872

Washington, D.C.                    USA

---

*E*liza Lyman was a white woman whose husband, Amasa, had left Utah for California to earn a living. Her diary from April 1849 records how destitute she and their children were, and how she was rescued when "Jane James, the colored woman, let me have two pounds of flour, it being half of what she had."

Little is written of the black women who emigrated to the Valley of the Great Salt Lake of Utah as slaves with the sect of which Henry Chase wrote, "Only in their racial perspective could the founders and early adherents of the Church of Jesus Christ of Latter-day Saints (the Mormons) be called orthodox." Because members left most of their possessions behind as they fled religious persecution, slaves were the most valuable "assets" brought through the land they renamed "Emigration Canyon" to where their "This Is the Place" monument would be erected in the state's centennial year. One founding member bequeathed the church $775 in real estate, livestock, farm implements, equipment, and an "African Servant Girl" worth $1,000. Wholly orthodox in their persecution of and bias against blacks, in more than a century from their arrival until 1970, when the church reconsidered an earlier "revelation," only one black man, Elijah Abel, was ordained a Mormon minister.

Considering this history, with emancipation came black freedom from allegiance to the Mormon church. Significantly, the state's first black congregation—Trinity AME Church—was founded in the late 1880s, shortly after Abel's death. And in 1907, a generous contribution by Mary Bright finally gave Trinity a permanent home. An ex-slave who made her fortune as a Colorado mining camp cook-turned-restauranteur, her recipe for success would be shared by all.

April 1849

Utah                    USA

---

**Social History**                    **Collective Responsibility**

*I*n 1956, graduate student Autherine Lucy made headlines for her unsuccessful attempt to desegregate the University of Alabama. On April 25, 1992, she was in the news again—this time as a graduating student from that school with a master's degree in elementary education and the added bonus of seeing her daughter, Grazia, graduate with a bachelor's in corporate finance.

After college, Lucy had hoped to continue her education. Expecting a difficult, but not impossible, journey, she asked the NAACP Legal Defense Fund (LDF) to help. As a graduate school candidate, she was perfect for the LDF assault on segregation. Called the "Houston Strategy" for Charles Houston, its prime strategist, the plan targeted the "soft underbelly" of segregation—the "separate but equal" underpinnings requiring the state to duplicate training for blacks or pay a black student's out-of-state tuition, an expensive proposition. The state of Alabama would not erect a library school just for Lucy, and no nearby state offered the equivalent. She was assigned an incomparable legal team headed by future Supreme Court Justice Thurgood Marshall, hero of the 1954 *Brown v. Board of Education* order desegregating public schools (see May 17), and Constance Baker Motley (see June 24), future first African American female federal district judge. A June 1955 restraining order was secured barring the university from rejecting Lucy on race, a decision the court amended to include all black applicants. But within days of her enrollment on February 3, 1956, campus riots erupted. When the NAACP charged official complicity, the school retaliated by expelling her. Tainted with the brush of "controversy," Lucy had difficulty finding professional work, but she would lecture on her historic role. Invited to speak at her would-be alma mater in 1988, a student's query whether she had ever reapplied led the university to overturn her expulsion, opening the door for her welcome return the next year.

Saturday, April 25, 1992

Alabama          USA

---

*U*.S. Patent Office records dated April 26, 1892, note a patent in the name of Sarah Boone for the invention of an ironing board with collapsible legs. Before her, a plain wooden board would be stretched like a bridge across two chairbacks. Creating her proverbial *better mousetrap*, Boone joined such African American female inventors as Miriam E. Benjamin, whose gong-and-signal chair was adapted for members of the House of Representatives to call their pages, and Sarah Goode, whose folding cabinet was the concept behind the hideaway bed.

In honoring our little-known inventors, it is essential to note that just because we didn't get the credit doesn't mean we haven't joined the rest of the world's peoples in inventing better worlds. Instead, what distinguishes Boone and other late nineteenth- and twentieth-century blacks from their inventive kin of the past are the Thirteenth and Fourteenth Amendments to the U.S. Constitution, abolishing slavery and granting citizenship to African Americans. Prior to the Civil War and the "freedom" amendments of 1865 and 1868, even free blacks were adjudged to have no constitutional rights of protection as noncitizens and, in most cases, could not testify in their own behalf. Hence, while no such shackle was placed on white noncitizens, under a race-based legal system, while the slave had no right to her person or her mind, the free could have her body and little more.

With this tribute to our "mothers of invention," we add those who fashioned the ball gowns, made extravagant the parties, handstitched the quilts, and handed down the greatest invention of all—how to dare dream better worlds, in spite of it all.

Tuesday, April 26, 1892

National                                            USA

*H*arriet Jacobs was tying up loose ends. On April 27, 1867, after thirty-two years away, she was home again in Edenton, North Carolina—in her grandmother's house, where for seven years she had taken refuge from the sexual assaults of her owner by hiding in a cabinet until she could escape. Her grandmother had bequeathed her the house and left it filled with memories. The war was over, freedom had been won, and there was so much to be done, as she wrote a friend and New England Freedmen's Aid Society colleague, Ednah Dow Cheney:

> I am sitting under the old roof, twelve feet from the spot where I suffered all the crushing weight of slavery. Thank God, the bitter cup is drained of its last dreg. There is no more need of hiding places to conceal slave mothers. I had long thought I had no attachment to my old home. As I sit here and think of those I loved, of their hard struggle in life, their unfaltering love and devotion toward myself and children, I love to think of them. They have made the few sunny spots in that dark life sacred to me.
>
> I cannot tell you how I feel in this place. The change is so great, I can hardly take it all in. I was born here, and amid all these new born blessings, the old dark cloud comes over me, and I find it hard to have faith in rebels. . . .
>
> I have hunted up all the old people, done what I could for them. I love to work for these old people. Many of them I have known from childhood. . . .
>
> My love to Miss Daisy. I send her some jasmine blossoms. Tell her they bear the fragrance of freedom.

Saturday, April 27, 1867

North Carolina    USA

"There were always people around reminding me that I was a symbol of certain Negro aspirations," Lena Horne once said. "I'm a symbol. But I'm a person, too." For the person seen as a symbol, being a role model is a privilege, albeit a hard row to hoe. But for an impressionable young person, having a role model and shero can be the greatest gift—as sixteen-year-old Charlotte Forten revealed in her diary on April 28, 1854, when she discovered Phillis Wheatley:

> This evening read "Poems of Phillis Wheatley," an African slave, who lived in Boston at the time of the Revolution. Her character and genius afford a striking proof of the falseness of the assertion made by some that hers is an inferior race.

Wheatley had been born free then enslaved (see May 6); Forten had born free during the years of slavery (see May 24). Wheatley was a child ripped from her mother by slave traders; Forten, too, had lost her mother, to death, when she was young. Wheatley, a child prodigy and acclaimed poet, died a pauper; Forten, who had a comfortable but lonely childhood in a charmed existence, was sent away to school by her successful businessman-abolitionist father to broaden her education. Through Wheatley's words and Forten's need, the two formed a special bond—Wheatley lighting a path for her young mentee across the century's divide.

Friday, April 28, 1854

Pennsylvania/Massachusetts      USA

*I*t was 1946. Daisy Bates's fight for freedom of her press, her person, and her people reached a turning point with a knock on her door by two sheriffs. For the *Arkansas State Press*, a newspaper Daisy Bates co-published with her husband, L. C. Bates, she had written a story on the railroading into prison of three strikers and the unfair treatment of labor in the state. The article appeared in late March, the knock on her door came shortly thereafter, and the warrant called for the Bateses to be arrested immediately and held in custody for a delayed court appearance weeks later, on April 29, 1946. The judge whose miscarriage of justice had led to the story issued the warrant for her arrest, thinking he could silence her. He didn't know what she knew. And what she knew had been given her by her father on his deathbed, as she recalled in her book, *Long Shadow of Little Rock*:

> I haven't much to leave you, Daisy, so come close and listen and remember what I have to say to you. . . . Hate can destroy you, Daisy. Don't hate white people just because they're white. If you hate, make it count for something. Hate the humiliations we are living under in the South. Hate the discrimination that eats away at the soul of every black man and woman. Hate the insults hurled at us by white scum — and then try to do something about it, or your hate won't spell a thing.

"Oh if I had wings that I could fly," the ancestors would sing. Daisy Bates could fly. In fact, she was the only woman pilot in the Arkansas Civil Air Patrol during World War II. As Arkansas state president of the NAACP, counselor, and comforter to the Little Rock Nine (see September 4), she would help others soar.

Monday, April 29, 1946

Arkansas                  USA

Y ou've heard of "Deadwood Dick," otherwise known by his real name, Nat Love. "I roped, threw, tied, bridled, saddled, and mounted my mustang in exactly nine minutes from the crack of the gun," said he of how he won his cowboy title and made a name for himself in Deadwood City, Dakota Territory. But have you heard of "Dakota Dick"?

In the 1930s, with his tales of the "wild and wooly west," Dakota Dick kept readers of the *Chicago Defender* enthralled with his daring exploits. But, as ravenous as his readers were for his every line, they would never have swallowed this one: he was a she — Era Bell Thompson, one of the slickest running track star desperadoes in all of North Dakota. Later, as an editor, her skills would, for thirty years, help build the Johnson Publishing Company.

Hired as managing editor for John H. Johnson's flagship magazine, *Negro Digest* (later, *Black World*), in 1951, Thompson was named co-managing editor of Johnson's new magazine, *Ebony*, becoming its international editor in 1964. The sense of adventure that had first spurred Dakota Dick served her well as she traveled the world filing stories about her experiences. She was the author of several books, including *Africa, Land of My Fathers*. It was her first book, *American Daughter*, about her early years in North Dakota and Iowa, that led to her induction into the Iowa Hall of Fame.

Saturday, April 30, 1932

Iowa/North Dakota          USA

# May

*"Mustered Out: Colored volunteers at Little Rock, Arkansas."* Etching from the drawing by A. R. Waud. Etching published by *Harper's Weekly* (May 19, 1866). Reprinted courtesy of the author.
For more information, see May 19.

$\mathcal{I}$t was 1925. Home from "the war to end all wars," black folks who had helped win freedom abroad bustled with new resolve to experience freedom at home. With the decade of the Harlem Renaissance had come the age of the New Negro—a cultural movement of those who openly shunned notions of white supremacy. In large measure, the wind at the back of this movement came from Charles S. Johnson, editor of the National Urban League magazine, *Opportunity.* To honor the voice of the New Negro, he devised an annual contest and awards dinner— one of the most fortuitous of which occurred on May 1, 1925.

For honorees and newcomers featured in the magazine, attendance at the dinner gave impetus to works in progress—the careers of the up-and-coming. With New York's liberal literati in full flush, those able to make a memorable first impression came away with key invitations and introductions, as that year's winner—"busboy poet" Langston Hughes—would soon find. Joining him this night were Zora Neale Hurston and Dorothy West, who tied for top honors in 1926 and went on that same year to collaborate with Hughes on *Fire!,* a literary magazine that set a milestone for art and culture with its one and only issue.

From these *opportunities,* Hurston would be offered a scholarship to Barnard College, where she studied anthropology and laid important research groundwork for such later culturally devout works as *Jonah's Gourd Vine* (see October 2), *Mules and Men,* and the book beloved as her masterpiece, *Their Eyes Were Watching God* (see September 18). Dorothy West (see January 27) would move to New York, hobnob with the glitterati "when Harlem was in vogue," and find herself en route to London with the original stage production of *Porgy.* For the writers, for the culture, it is amazing what a little Opportunity could do.

Friday, May 1, 1925

New York                    USA

---

*I*n her ninety-eight years, Audley "Queen Mother" Moore had *been there.* And what she had not seen firsthand had been deposited into her marrow by those to whom she was closest: a grandfather had been lynched; an enslaved grandmother had been raped by a white man.

In her time, she worked with Back-to-Africa movement hero Marcus Garvey; she also was an anti-lynching crusader active in campaigns for reparations, tenants' rights, and school reform. And because of what Queen Mother had seen, when she died on May 2, 1997, one would have wished for the end of an era. It was not yet so, but what had changed for the better had happened because she was one of the people who made it better. That's how she got the "Queen Mother" in her name.

It was 1972, and she had been invited to Ghana for the funeral of Dr. Kwame Nkrumah, who had led the nation from colonial rule to independence. Arriving on the continent for the first time, "everything just came down" on her when the ship landed. She said, "I cried, I cried, I cried. I felt the lash on the backs of my people. Just looking at the land, it looked like it had been there forever. I thought, 'Lord, look what they've robbed us of. . . .' I never cried so much in my life." From that experience, she was asked to remain, offered a home in which to stay, honored at the All-African Women's Conference in Dar Es Salaam, and given a name with which to return to the States, her work renewed: Queen Mother. So deeply had she felt the connection, people knew she would use it well. Upon her return, armed with knowledge gained in her tours of farms and industries, she founded the Queen Mother Moore Research Institute to empower Africans in the Americas.

Friday, May 2, 1997

New York　　　　　　USA

---

It was one of those misunderstandings that lead lovers to quarrel in spring. Nature sends the senses aflutter. The eager but slow-to-pollinate among us whiff hinting scents as breezes blow confusion into profusion.

"Frankly, I'm not sure a wife would help you," Lenore Robbins wrote her fiancé, Charles Drew. What he had last written to provoke this reaction he was not sure, but he would immediately write to take back whatever it was. "Man at his best is an odd creature, and I as the least of men am the oddest of creatures at best," he tried. As he thought about it, perhaps he had been acting strangely, what with the pressure of "making myself a good doctor." But, "darn it all Lenore," he would write, "I'm supposed to be here [Columbia University School of Medicine] working, but work is the farthest thing from my mind." Could $100 a month support two as well as one? Flitting between frazzled emotions, on May 3, 1939, he wrote:

> I've ducked, dodged and squirmed away from would-be wives for a long time, it's become almost an art. I don't need a wife just to have a woman. . . . When I think of you Lenore I think more largely in terms of the things I'd freely give what love there is in me unstintedly. . . . More than the things you'd bring to me and the small measure in which I'd be able to repay you [in devotion], are the things we could do, build, dream together. . . . When you were a little girl you must have thought of growing up some day and meeting some guy and marrying him, etc. What was he like, what did you want to be, what did you want him to be. . . . I almost dread your next letter but I'll await it with trembling knees.

With Nature having her way and love at play, the doctor would next write a prescription: they would have to marry *very* soon.

Wednesday, May 3, 1939

New York USA

*I*t was spring 1905, four-year-old Cleora Butler was getting a cold, and all the tears in the world would not induce her mother to let her go to school that day. But it was school picture day—the most important day of the year for the students in Mrs. Ida B. Ayers's one-room schoolhouse in Muskogee, Oklahoma.

Alone in her front yard, disconsolate, Cleora could see her classmates, all thirty-four of them, arriving for school, playing in the yard, waiting for the coming of the picture-man. Just over a block away, there they all were in their Sunday best. Not only could she see them, but they could see her, too, perched on the swinging gate, hoping against hope, her baby-fat hands clutching the rails. Every now and again a classmate would wave in her direction and she would return the favor with a plaintive stare. From eight A.M., when the children arrived, until ten A.M., when the picture-man's trolley car slowed to a halt on Fondulac Street, the torture continued: Cleora in the front yard, her mother some-where in the house engaged in chores, the children running and laughing, the teacher trying to keep them clean for the big mo-ment. Then the picture-man began staging the scene, setting up his tripod and camera. Time was running out for the four-year-old in the front yard just over a block away, where her mother, cau-tioning obedience and expecting too much, had left her. As the picture-man unfolded his black hood—the one he would drape over himself and his camera—there, tugging on her teacher's heart, was Cleora—shoes on the wrong feet, hair undone, out of breath. Mrs. Ayers knew Mrs. Butler would not have sent Cleora to school that way and late on picture-day. She knew, too, that there would always be a missing piece of their little history where Cleora should have been: squeezed into the front row in the photo printed in a book the child would publish eighty years later: *Cleora's Kitchens: The Memoir of a Cook and Eight Decades of Great American Food.*

Spring 1905

Oklahoma                    USA

---

**Children and Youth**                    **Ambition**

"*I* am where I am today because I must work and give for others," said Jane Smith, president of the National Council of Negro Women. Named in 1998 as the fifth president since the organization's founding in 1935, she seemed destined to follow in the notable footsteps of founder Mary McLeod Bethune (see May 18) and Dorothy I. Height (see July 14), whose forty-year tenure led the group to international renown. But Smith's contributions as a leader were almost denied us by the social mores in which she achieved her womanhood:

> I have a brother who is one year younger than I am who was absolutely powerful in high school. And I can remember having dreams and visions of being a civil rights leader when I was in the 10th grade and never vocalizing them because I thought that he should be the one because he was the boy-child. . . . Daddy and Mama have never verbalized that to me, but [it's] the world I'm living in. It was the cultural context of it all that made me have those private thoughts.

The moment that changed her view of her potential came in the spring of 1972. A Spelman College alumna with impeccable credentials, she was earning a doctorate from Harvard University's Graduate School of Education when Shirley Chisholm—the first black U.S. congresswoman in history—declared her candidacy for president of the United States (see July 13). Smith volunteered to work with the campaign. "Not again in my life," said Smith, "did I think that being a woman and being an African-American would keep me from doing what I wanted to do. I had been completely and totally empowered by Shirley Chisholm's race. It has done more for me as a woman than any other thing in my lifetime for being a woman." A woman never knows where her inspired moments will lead or where she, in turn, may lead others.

Friday, May 5, 1972

Washington, D.C.                    USA

---

**Turning Points**                    **Respect for One's Power**

*I*n 1761, a child kidnapped in West Africa was delivered to Boston for purchase from a harbor slaver. Traumatized, unable to speak English, losing her first baby tooth and thus assumed to be seven years old, she was "a pitiful sight." Drawn to her plight, John and Susannah Wheatley bought her. She was given her own room in the main house away from the slave quarters, tutored in reading and writing, and taught the social graces. As John Wheatley would write, "Without any assistance from school education . . . she, in sixteen months' time from her arrival, attained the English language, to which she was an utter stranger before, to such a degree, as to read any, the most difficult parts of the Sacred Writings, to the great astonishment of all who heard her." She would also master Latin and read Roman classics in their original texts. Given the rhetoric used to justify slavery, young Phillis Wheatley—talented poet and one of the colonies' first child prodigies—was a curiosity. Her work was well received but barred from publication by prejudice. Determined to see her poetry in print, in May 1773 she went to London and there achieved her dream. Among her *Poems on Various Subjects,* a verse "To the Right Honourable WILLIAM, Earl of Dartmouth" contained these autobiographical lines:

*I, young in life, by seeming cruel fate*
*Was snatch'd from Afric's fancy'd happy seat:*
*What pangs excruciating must molest,*
*What sorrows labour in my parent's breast?*
*That from a father seiz'd his babe belov'd*
*Such, such my case. And can I then but pray*
*Others may never feel tyrannic sway?*

With this publication, Phillis Wheatley (see October 26) became the second American woman, and the first African American woman, to author a book.

Thursday, May 6, 1773

Massachusetts USA

---

Literature Beginnings

*I*n 1962, after forty years spent in the cotton fields from the age of six, without a promise of better days in sight, Fannie Lou Hamer charted her future. In a state where children suffered from the highest incidence of malnutrition, where the richest 5,800 acres of soil were worked by blacks but owned by one of the nation's most ardent defenders of racial exploitation, U.S. Senator James Eastland, she decided to register to vote. For that, she lost her job, was arrested and tortured by sheriffs' deputies, and was shot at. It did not stop her. She co-founded the Mississippi Freedom Democratic Party (MFDP) and, in 1964, elevated the debate with a televised challenge to the segregated state delegation, the Party's Credentials Committee, and the nation.

"I question America," said Hamer, documenting the lawlessness that had kept the power but not the peace in Mississippi. "Is this America where we have to sleep with our telephones off the hooks because our lives be threatened daily because we want to live as decent human beings in America?" The MFDP was offered two seats. "Do you think I came here to compromise and sit in a back seat at the convention?" Hamer replied, eloquently representing her party. Why not leave the area, asked a reporter? "Why should I leave Ruleville? I go to the big city and with the kind of education they give us in Mississippi I got problems. I'd wind up in a soup line there. That's why I want to change things in Mississippi. You don't run away from problems—you just face them."

On May 7, 1971, Fannie Lou Hamer addressed the NAACP Legal Defense Fund Institute on "The Special Plight and the Role of Black Women." She had changed the view of many who saw themselves as powerless, founded the Freedom Farm Co-op, purchased 680 acres, and built sixty-eight homes for people who once lived in shacks. "We have a job as black women to support whatever is right," said Mrs. Hamer, "and to bring in justice where we've had so much injustice."

Friday, May 7, 1971

New York                    USA

---

**Leadership**                                    **Self-assertion**

*D*ateline: May 8, 1963. Birmingham, Alabama.

Makeshift jails already overflowing with teenage Civil Rights demonstrators, hundreds more were arrested for "parading without a permit." The *New York Times* underscored the magnitude of the situation for its readers with this note: "There were 594 girls there just after the arrests Monday. . . . Girls arrested last Monday outnumbered boys by almost two to one." Among the girls was Anita Woods, a twelve-year-old locked in at the Jefferson County Detention Home with 110 others, all below the age of thirteen. As the girls stood crushed together, twenty to a locked steamy second-floor pen above air-conditioned public main-floor rooms, a reporter asked, "Do you want to go home?" "Yes!" came the answer in unison. "But I'd do it again," said the young Miss Woods. "I'll keep on marching till I get freedom."

As waves of children flocked to jail, Juvenile Court Judge Talbot Ellis changed the terms of their arrest for the "benefit" of all concerned. With a shortage of beds, some of the children were sleeping on floors; the home had never fed so many at one time. The judge declared that instead of a $500 cash bond, he would release the children into parents' custody. Not good enough, protested the children. This was not about their release from jail, this was about their release from the bonds of segregation. What about the parents, wouldn't they insist on their coming home? Said Anita Woods, "My mother told me I had to serve my time."

*Soldiers in the army of the Lord,* these were the children of the struggle, 1963.

Wednesday, May 8, 1963

Alabama                                    USA

---

$O$ n May 9, 1997, Alexis Herman was sworn in as the first African American secretary of labor. One of the few black women ever to achieve the inner circle of presidential authority, she had not done it alone; she did not have to. With her character and commitment, she had made many friends among people of conscience, and they had rallied to her side. In a take-no-prisoners congressional backlash of no less fury than the ones which had removed every black elected official from office a century earlier, foes had marshalled for her defeat. Every dirty trick in the book had been used, every conceivable lie told, yet she was there.

What did those who set out to destroy her know about her? Did they know:

- that she had been born to a father who once sued the Democratic Party for discrimination and later became the first black ward leader in Mobile, Alabama;
- that she had been expelled from her Catholic girls' high school for challenging the racism of the local archbishop;
- that she had far too much integrity and humanity to cower over rumors of lesbianism picked up in the press;
- that among her mentors was Dr. Dorothy I. Height of the NCNW, among whose sister-mentors had been Mary McLeod Bethune, member of President Franklin D. Roosevelt's "Kitchen Cabinet," whose foes had attempted her destruction by branding her a communist;
- that when Klan thugs attempted to run a five-year-old Alexis and her father off the road one Christmas Eve, her father had placed her on the floor with a gun and this instruction: "If anybody opens that door, I want you to pull the trigger."

What did they know of Alexis Herman if they did not know that? What do they know of the sisterhood of women who know *there is no crystal stair.* . . .

Friday, May 9, 1997

Washington, D.C. USA

---

**Leadership** **Heritage**

*O*n May 10, 1866, the American Equal Rights Association was founded in New York City. Daughter to the Women's Rights Conventions of 1848 and 1851, it was a direct descendant of the anti-slavery movement (see April 12) and the result of ostracism meted out to abolitionist women by abolitionist men. One year after liberation, Reconstruction of the South had begun. Black men would soon vote, but women of every hue remained disfranchised. At the Equal Rights convention of 1867, Sojourner Truth spoke for herself—and millions of others:

> My friends. . . . There is a great stir about colored men getting their rights, but not a word about the colored women; and if colored men get their rights, and not colored women theirs, you see the colored men will be masters over the women, and it will be just as bad as it was before. So I am for keeping the thing going while things are stirring. . . . In the courts women have no rights, no voice. . . . I wish woman to have her voice there among the pettifoggers. If it is not a fit place for women, it is unfit for men to be there. I am above [seventy] years old; it is about time for me to be going. . . . I suppose I am kept here because something remains for me to do; I suppose I am yet to help to break the chain. . . . I suppose I am about the only colored woman that goes about to speak for the rights of the colored women . . . to keep the thing stirring, now that the ice is cracked. I am sometimes told that "Women ain't fit to vote. Why, don't you know that a woman had seven devils in her: and do you suppose a woman is fit to rule the nation?" Seven devils ain't no account; a man had a legion in him . . . and yet he won't give women their rights. He keeps them all to himself. . . .

Then, practically enough, she added, "What we want is a little money." And for Miss Truth, that was that.

Friday, May 10, 1866

New York                              USA

---

*O*n May 11, 1968, caravans of the downtrodden, distressed, and dispossessed descended on Washington, D.C.—broke down, fixed up, but there. Five weeks earlier, the man who had set the plan in motion—Dr. Martin Luther King Jr.—had been assassinated. It was felt by many that one of the last straws that broke the camel's back of segregationists was his ability to unite people on higher ground across the plateaus of race, creed, caste, and class. For that—and one more reason—they had come: they were poor Americans in pursuit of their right to life. And this was the Poor People's Campaign.

In December 1967, Congress had enacted anti-poverty legislation harder on the poor than on the causes of their poverty. When President Lyndon Johnson, general in the "war society," signed the bill into law, King swung into action, but he was killed on April 4. In his name and in dire need, grassroots leaders of the poor nationwide met with and were rebuffed by congressional leaders. As King had said of the Vietnam War, a year to the day before his murder: slaughtering Asia's poor was superceding saving America's poor. Wagons rolled on Washington.

As a sixteen-acre shantytown of tents and shacks called "Resurrection City" was erected, the press would duly note the poignant arrival of Coretta King, Dr. King's widow, and the symbolic presence of Rosa Parks (see December 1). But the voices of three unheralded women would bring the agenda center stage: Johnnie Tillmon, Beulah Sanders, and Etta Horn of the National Welfare Rights movement. Within a decade, Bertha Knox Gilkey of Missouri would emerge to bring creative solutions to the need for welfare and tenant rights—cooperative ownership, management, and renovation of deteriorated housing projects. New voices were meeting the challenge of a brand-new day.

Saturday, May 11, 1968

Washington, D.C.                    USA

---

In his Civil War report of May 12, 1864, to Maj. Robert S. Davis, Brig. Gen. Edward A. Wild described the scene when Confederate planter William H. Clopton was brought into camp at Wilson's Wharf in James River, Virginia.

By the firsthand accounts of slaves, Clopton was no minor brute. Indeed, he exhibited the kind of sadistic brutality that would, eighty years later, be echoed in some of the most horrific World War II–era testimony by concentration camp prisoners against their Nazi captors. No war tribunal would mete out justice on behalf of African Americans. But one sympathetic Union soldier delivered Clopton to a "tribunal" of his former victims, ex-slave women, "three of Whom took turns in settling some old scores on their master's back."

Such scenes were rare, but a similar story was told by Armacie Adams:

> Guess I was 'bout 15 years ole when Marse come back from de fightin', mean as ever. Never did say nothin' 'bout de war, an' I didn't even know ef it's over or not. But one day Marse Bob, his son, was switchin' me in de woods playful like an' he say, "Whyn't you strike me back, Mici? You's free. Dat's what de war was fo', to free de niggers." I took dat switch away an' beat him hard as I could 'cross de haid tell it busted. Den I run 'cross de fields to some colored folks 'bout six miles away. Dey name was Foremans, an' dey was free sho' 'nough. Dey tole me dat was right. I been free mo'n a year. Ain't never been back to dat place since.

With the cruel and the callous taking every opportunity, years would pass after the war before many slaves got word of their freedom.

Thursday, May 12, 1864

Virginia            USA

---

**Freedom**            **Passion**

*O*h, the stories we can tell about the hair; about how, historically and into our modern times, "deep penetrating conditioning" has done little for our hair and a major job of conditioning our minds.

In the Freedom Days of the 1960s, members of the Student Non-Violent Coordinating Committee (SNCC) could be counted upon to do more than provide food for thought; they were known for teaching people how to harvest ideas. So it was that SNCC's Jean Wiley, a faculty member at Tuskegee Institute, began the re-education of her students. Among the lessons she deemed critical to impart were living one's philosophy, speaking truth to power, and challenging authority in pursuit of one's convictions.

In the early days of student activism, when wearing one's hair natural was considered anything but, Wiley arrived to teach her class sporting an "afro." It was an unintended test that every student passed, to her shock and dismay. So upset were her students—a proper young group, many of whom were the first in centuries of family history to attend college—that they walked out, boycotting her class. Recalled Wiley, "Well, at least I was successful in teaching them to challenge authority—even though it was mine."

Not every lesson goes by the book.

Late 1960s

Alabama                                   USA

"*D*ear Sir, Please stop using the word 'Negro,'" wrote Mary Church Terrell in a letter to the editor of the *Washington Post* dated May 14, 1949.

> The word is a misnomer. . . . It does not represent a country or anything else except one single, solitary color. And no one color can describe the various and varied complexions in our group. . . . When I studied abroad and was introduced as an 'American' . . . occasionally somebody would say, 'You are rather dark to be an American, aren't you?' 'Yes,' I would reply, 'I am dark, because some of my ancestors were African.' I was proud of having the continent of Africa part of my ancestral background. 'I am an African-American,' I would explain. I am not ashamed of my African descent. Africa had great universities before there were any in England and the African was the first man industrious and skillful enough to work in iron. If our group must have a special name setting it apart, the sensible way to settle it would be to refer to our ancestors, the Africans, from whom our swarthy complexions come.

A warrior if ever there was one, Terrell launched this campaign at age eighty-six. At eighty-seven she initiated and, for the next two years, walked a picket line with cane in one hand and placard in the other. Stooped with age, she was unbowed in determination. Her campaign ended segregated public accommodations in the nation's capital. Her assault on segregation in the D.C. chapter of the American Association of University Women (AAUW) led to the chapter's temporary expulsion and the national association's adoption of an "education only" membership policy. Taking the motto "never give up" to new heights, at the time of her death in 1954, nearing ninety-one, she was crusading to free Rosa Lee Ingram and her sons (see February 3) from a Georgia prison—a victory posthumously won.

Saturday, May 14, 1949

Washington, D.C.          USA

---

**Human Rights**                                        Identity

*A* little-known fact in the world of classical music is that, even as slaves, African Americans had been performing European classical music for centuries. It was our freedom as men and women that whites refused to accept, not our talents as musicians.

On May 15, 1946, the history of African American women in American opera began when Camilla Williams stepped onstage with the New York City Opera to perform the title role in *Madame Butterfly*. With her triumphant debut, she became the first singer signed to a major opera contract, and broke important ground for others in the classical field. Four years later, prima ballerina Janet Collins became the first African American artist in any of the contributing art forms to perform with the Metropolitan Opera. Like many a black diva to come, in 1951, this diva-dancer debuted in *Aida* and remained with the Metropolitan's corps de ballet through 1954. With no opportunities to train with smaller companies, how did these star performers get their training in the United States? Camilla Williams's star rose as a soloist because Mary Lucinda Cardwell Dawson (former president of the National Association of Negro Musicians) founded the National Negro Opera Company in 1941. Janet Collins had her own unique turn with her audition for the Ballet Russe de Monte Carlo in the 1930s. So fine was her performance that her fellow dancers applauded, and she was offered a contract on one condition: that she paint her skin white. She refused. Her solo training came when dance legend Katherine Dunham (see October 20) began her troupe.

Said Collins of her Metropolitan debut, speaking for herself and the other firsts who overcame equality in pursuit of *better than,* "The reason I became ballerina of the Metropolitan Opera was because I couldn't be topped."

Wednesday, May 15, 1946

National USA

---

**Music/Dance** **Opportunity**

*A* diploma in the name of Anna L. James from the Brooklyn College of Pharmacy dated the "sixteenth day of May in the year nineteen hundred and eight" ushers in the stories of two Connecticut legends—the bearer, the state's first woman pharmacist, and her niece and namesake, born six months later in 1908, novelist Ann Petry.

The daughter of a runaway slave from Virginia, Anna James had followed a family tradition as a pharmacist—as would her niece, Ann. James's brother-in-law, Ann's father, Peter Lane, was among the state's first licensed pharmacists. Even James's sister, Ann's mother, Bertha Lane, worked in an allied profession, as a state-licensed barber and chiropodist. Graduating, the only woman in her class, James was first denied her Connecticut license on the grounds of gender, not race. But her membership in the Connecticut Pharmaceutical Association was later accepted, and her license was granted in 1911.

Today, on the town green at 2 Pennywise Lane in Old Saybrook, Connecticut, Anna James's home and authentic early twentieth-century country-style pharmacy still stands, complete with old glass and birch wood display cases and the original soda fountain—a registered national historic landmark.

Precipitously, the relationship between Anna James and her niece, author Ann Petry, inspired the fictionalized story of Aunt Sophronia, the druggist, and her twelve-year-old niece, the narrator in Petry's "Miss Muriel" (see November 1).

Saturday, May 16, 1908

Connecticut/New York      USA

*W*ith a school four blocks from her home, each day seven-year-old Linda Brown took a mile-long bus ride, crossed a busy railroad switching yard, and walked six blocks to her school, reversing the process in the afternoon. Such was the nature of school segregation, which was legally struck down on May 17, 1954.

In *Oliver Brown, et al. v. Board of Education of Topeka, Kansas, et al.* — a suit brought by Linda's father in a twenty-year strategy waged by the NAACP Legal Defense Fund and argued by Thurgood Marshall—the Supreme Court issued its landmark desegregation order. At last, the 1896 *Plessy v. Ferguson* decision had been nullified, vindicating its only dissenting voice, that of a former slaveholder from Kentucky, Justice John Marshall Harlan, who wrote: "The judgment this day rendered will, in time, prove to be quite as pernicious as the decision made by this tribunal in the Dred Scott case [see November 4]. The thin disguise of equal accommodations . . . will not lead anyone nor atone for the wrong this day done." It had not, as shown in the case of lead plaintiff Oliver Brown's daughter and all the children in the four cases collectively known as *Brown v. Board of Education.* Each was as imperiled as Linda by what racial separation perpetrated: disregard for citizens of color and their children—physically, emotionally, and educationally. As Chief Justice Earl Warren wrote in the unanimous Brown decision: "It is doubtful that any child may reasonably be expected to succeed in life if he is denied the opportunity of an education. . . . We conclude that in the field of public education the doctrine of 'separate but equal' has no place. Separate educational facilities are inherently unequal."

Today, Topeka's Sumner Elementary School, to which Linda Brown was denied enrollment, and Monroe Elementary, the school to which she traveled, are both registered national historic landmarks.

Monday, May 17, 1954

Kansas                    USA

---

**Education**                    **Responsibility to Youth**

*I*n an ironic arc of fate, the date May 18 felled human rights in 1896, and in 1955 claimed the life of its ardent defender, Mary McLeod Bethune.

As the nineteenth century drew to an end, the U.S. Supreme Court's May 18, 1896, *Plessy v. Ferguson* decision to legalize "separate but equal" segregation validated a racist reign of terror, undermined human rights, and fired the spirit of the indomitable Mrs. Bethune, one of the century's noblest warrior women. In 1904 she founded Florida's first school to educate blacks beyond the elementary grades, Daytona Educational and Industrial Institute, now Bethune-Cookman College. In 1935 she founded the National Council of Negro Women, her "organization of organizations" to represent the combined clout of over one million women. By the time Death called her name on May 18, 1955, she had served as adviser to Presidents Franklin Roosevelt and Harry Truman, and helped draft the United Nations charter. Bethune's was a life well lived educating, challenging, and inspiring others. Never one to leave a job unfinished, as Death neared in her eightieth year, she prepared a final legacy for generations to come.

"My worldly possessions are few. Yet my experiences have been rich." So began her Last Will and Testament. "From them I have distilled principles and policies in which I believe firmly, for they represent the meaning of my life's work." For the disposition of her assets, she wrote, "I leave you love," then came hope, the challenge of developing confidence in one another, a thirst for education, a respect for the use of power, faith, racial dignity, a desire to live harmoniously with your fellow men, and finally, "a responsibility to our young people."

May Mrs. Bethune's "Will" reap dividends through all your *Sister Days*.

Wednesday, May 18, 1955

Florida                                    USA

*A*n etching in the May 19, 1866, issue of *Harper's Weekly* — *Mustered Out: Colored Volunteers at Little Rock, Arkansas* — captures the homecoming of African American soldiers from the War for Freedom (Civil War) and opens the story of a love that yet endures. Robert Anderson was only there in spirit that symbolic day — he would be mustered out the following year. But he had joined the Union Army, lived, and married Miss Daisy in Arkansas. With her death in September 1998 came the end of an era. Daisy Graham Anderson was the last surviving widow of an African American Civil War veteran and of a former slave.

His youth stolen for slavery, Robert Anderson took what was left of his life and made the most of it. After the war, he tried and failed at farming a few times before buying the two-thousand-acre Nebraska spread that made him a wealthy man. On a visit to his brother in Arkansas in 1922, Robert Anderson met Miss Daisy. For him, it was love at first sight — not so for her. She laughed at his bushy white beard. But when he told her about the fiery years of slavery he had survived to yet stand before her, she could not help loving him. He was seventy-nine and she was twenty-one. Captivated and overwhelmed by the stories he told of his enslaved childhood, in 1927 she turned his recollections into a book, *From Slavery to Affluence: Memoirs of Robert Anderson, Ex-Slave.* In the book, she retraced his years as she had traced the scars on his back — some as thick as the fingers with which she tried to soothe the memories. The "tree" of scars had been delivered in a rawhide lashing by a slave mistress who then rubbed salt and pepper into his wounds. Miss Daisy vowed those scars and the man who overcame them would never be forgotten. Keeping that vow till death claimed her fifty-eight years after his death, she never remarried. With this page in our *Sister Days*, we carry on her promise.

Saturday, May 19, 1866

Arkansas                                    USA

---

**Love**                                              **Memory**

*O*n May 20, 1949, as an electric charge of excitement filled New York's Town Hall, this was the news: Valaida Snow was back! The show-stopping band leader–trumpeter–pianist–violinist–vocalist–linguist and producer was back! Where she had been was the greater story. Valaida Snow, an African American woman, was back from the door of death—the death camps of Nazi Germany.

The multitalented Valaida Snow was a phenomenon by every standard and well rewarded for it—even during the Depression, when she shuttled about in her chauffeur-driven purple Mercedes to avert segregated transport. A command performance for Queen Wilhelmina of the Netherlands was met with the gift of a gold trumpet. A stunning beauty, Snow had a sense of humor to match that made her gifts both boon and bane. In 1941, as the United States entered World War II with the bombing of Pearl Harbor, Snow had just completed a successful Paris run with legendary French vaudevillian Maurice Chevalier. En route to an engagement in Copenhagen, she was arrested by the Nazis as a "non-Aryan" and sent to the Wester-Faengle concentration camp. Interred for nearly twenty months, she was released in a prisoner exchange arranged by a Danish police chief and jazz fan. In 1943, emaciated, weighing only sixty-eight pounds, Snow returned to the United States. It would take years before she was "back."

In this saga of an African American Holocaust survivor is a tale of death camps not usually told. In all, eleven million people were killed for a myriad of pretexts beyond the bounds of caste, class, race, religion, reason, or sanity. To forget that is to forget that no one is immune when the hateful and powerful dance as one.

Friday, May 20, 1949

New York          USA/Germany

---

**Social History**                                         **Truth**

*T*he more things changed, the more they stayed the same. Painful as it was, that was the depressing fact of everyday segregated life—especially in public transportation, where the difference between the expectations of blacks and whites charged the same fare was anything but fair as blacks were shortchanged again and again.

Shortly after slavery's defeat, hadn't our shero Sojourner Truth been forced off a Washington, D.C., streetcar (see September 13)? In 1865, she took the case to court and won. In California three years later, didn't Mary Ellen Pleasant have to fight and win the same battle? Yet during Christmas of 1949, when Jo Ann Robinson, an English professor at Alabama State College, was humiliated on a bus for not giving up her seat swiftly enough for the driver's whim, she probably didn't know the history of her streetcar fight forebears. Nor did her co-sufferers who had decided not to pick the bus battle over other struggles which loomed so large. But Robinson did know the story, in the way that knowing gets deep down in the marrow. That was why she couldn't let that last straw slide from her back.

On May 21, 1954, just days after the Supreme Court handed down its *Brown v. Board of Education* school desegregation decision (see May 17), Robinson, as head of the local Women's Political Council, challenged bus segregation in a bold letter to the mayor of Montgomery: "Three-fifths of the [bus] riders . . . are Negroes. If Negroes did not patronize them, they could not possibly operate." Eighteen months later, when Rosa Parks was arrested for refusing to move to the back of the bus, Jo Ann Robinson was ready. She stayed up all that night mimeographing the thirty-five thousand flyers her students would distribute the next day calling for the historic Montgomery Bus Boycott of 1955 (see December 1) that sparked a national movement and brought a young Dr. Martin Luther King world renown.

Friday, May 21, 1954

Alabama        USA

---

**Travel and Transportation**        **Continuity**

"It is so pure, so womanly—positively agreeable in every feature as reading for private home, instruction, and guidance," enthused Victoria Earle Matthews on May 22, 1892, wishing publisher Julia Ringwood Coston "positive and permanent success" in her new venture—the world's first fashion magazine for women of African descent, *Ringwood's Afro-American Journal of Fashion.*

In the not-so-Gay Nineties, as Jim Crow custom became law, Julia Ringwood was distressed that images of black women were as excised as black concerns in the "ladies' pages." In 1891, she founded her journal, written and edited by and for black women, believing that women writers could best express issues of concern to women of the race and provide girls with intellectual role models. Among the editors of the very first edition was Mary Church Terrell (see May 14), whose human rights activism and leadership would span the first half of the coming century. With illustrations of Paris style, features on prominent women, love stories, and a column called "Plain Talk to Our Girls," the journal was a success. Just $1.25 bought a year's subscription and helped underwrite the next venture—*Ringwood's Home Magazine,* which flourished from 1893 to 1895.

Seventy-five years later, another pioneering women's journal would premiere in May 1970—*Essence,* launched by the four black men of the Hollingsworth Group with photographer Gordon Parks (see August 19) as editorial director. In its first year, three editors-in-chief—including author and journalist Ida Lewis—would come and go before Marcia Gillespie settled in as visionary for the next ten years. In 1981, Susan L. Taylor took the helm. Ironically, Taylor had been the magazine's fashion and beauty editor. From Ringwood's days of leveraging fashion to celebrate every facet of black womanhood, we had come full circle.

Sunday, May 22, 1892

Ohio                                              USA

---

*W*e know that Southerners criminalized teaching slaves to read, but those who opposed educating blacks north of the Mason-Dixon line were no less adamant. In one infamous Connecticut case, Prudence Crandall, headmistress of an elite school, was jailed for admitting black girls under a law passed on May 23, 1833.

In 1832, Crandall enrolled Sarah Harris (see September 9) in the Canterbury Female Boarding School as a day student, prompting many of her white students to withdraw. With counsel from abolitionist friends, Crandall opted to teach "Young Ladies and little Misses of Color" exclusively. Despite the cost of tuition, twenty families from Philadelphia to Boston enrolled their daughters. Enraged, local shopkeepers refused Crandall's business. Vandals tainted her well. Doctors refused care. Clerics barred their sanctums. State Senator Andrew Judson (who would later judge the case of the *Amistad* captives in 1839) ramrodded a "Black Law" through the legislature that made it illegal to enroll out-of-state blacks without the permission of town fathers. As news reached the school, "the bell rang, and a cannon was fired for half an hour," wrote one student in a letter to the *Hartford Intelligencer.* Yet, the teacher and her young ladies persevered with food and water provided by her father and a Quaker friend.

Convicted of breaking the law specifically enacted to create a crime of which she could be found guilty, Crandall went to jail for a night in lieu of bail. "Where is justice?" asked her student. Even with the verdict overturned on a technicality, justice did not come. What a corrupt law could not achieve, violence would. Crandall shut what remained of her doors when a late-night assault with clubs and iron bars threatened the lives of her students—martyrs all in the ongoing crusade for the freedom of education.

Thursday, May 23, 1833

Connecticut                              USA

---

**Education/Law**                              **Responsibility to Youth**

*O*n May 24, 1854, seventeen-year-old Charlotte Forten began writing the journal that, more than a century after her birth, would make hers the voice of nineteenth-century African American girlhood bursting into womanhood.

In four journals dating from 1854 to 1864 and a fifth from 1885 to 1892, she is a Salem normal school student, Philadelphia abolitionist, teacher on St. Helena's Island, and Jacksonville social reformer. On September 12, 1855, Forten returns to "the companionship of my studies—ever my most valued friends." Wounded by duplicitous classmates who act friendly in school and shun her in public, she writes: "Oh! it is hard to go through life meeting contempt with contempt, hatred with hatred, fearing, with too good reason, to love and trust hardly any one whose skin is white. . . . In the bitter, passionate feelings of my soul again and again there rises the question 'When oh! when shall this cease?'" July 4, 1857, is no celebration; it is a "mockery." On August 10, 1857, she meets the poet John Greenleaf Whittier. January 2, 1858, is anointed in doubt: "I wonder why it is that I have this strange feeling of not *living out myself.*" On February 15, 1858, she realizes she does not enjoy chess. Four years later, on October 28, 1862, now a teacher en route to her next assignment at Hilton Head, she is met by a "motley assemblage—soldiers, officers, and 'contrabands' [slaves freed by the war] of every hue and size." Their singing voices are "so sweet and strange and solemn" as she sails to the island. Classes begin and "to you and you only friend beloved, will I acknowledge it was *not* a very pleasant [experience]." But she soon thrills the children with tales of Haiti's liberator, Toussaint L'Ouverture. And, on May 18, 1863, just between friends, her and the page, she mulls over interracial dating: "although he is very good and liberal he is still an *American.*" Our girl is a woman now.

Sunday, May 24, 1854

Eastern States               USA

---

**Social History**              **Perspective**

*I*n 1979, at age sixty-one, Pearl Bailey kept a lifetime promise to herself to return to school. Six years later, on May 25, 1985, the world-renowned actor-singer, five-time author, United Nations delegate, and honorary Ph.D. graduated from Georgetown University with a bachelor's degree in theology. But one of the best lessons learned in her remarkable lifetime and which she passed on in the closing pages of her memoir, *Between You and Me,* came from this course, taken on a stroll with her husband, Louie Bellson, through New York's Central Park:

> In our path, bent over, busy as all hell, was a handsome, young, bearded man scrounging in the wastebasket for anything edible. The sight of a human being digging in that trash among the dog poop and every other filthy thing sickens me.
>
> It was a gorgeous day, sunbeams bathed everyone, even my food-seeking friend. . . . I approached him and asked, "May I give you something with which to buy a meal?" "No," he said sharply, "go away." My head rattled at the sharpness of his tone. . . . "Come on, honey," Louie said, "he obviously doesn't want help." Looking back at him, I noticed he kept peering after me. Suddenly he discovered a goody in a bag. He looked it over, made his choice, and started shuffling off, probably to enjoy some leftover french fries. Everyone else kept eating as if he never existed. . . . We walked back home without saying a word; humanity's pain hurt us. Later that night I said to Louie, "Now I understand. . . . That young man did not mean to be cruel to us. He was not trying to insult me. He was trying with all the decency he had left to save the one thing left: his *pride.*" Without saying a word, he was telling the world, "Leave me something, lady, leave me something."

Said Bailey: "That young man left all of us something to think about, to do something about, that day. God help us if we don't."

Saturday, May 25, 1985

National                       USA

---

**Social History**                             **Understanding**

Thirty years after Emancipation, days after the Supreme Court had legalized neo-slavery in the guise of Jim Crow, the most effective Underground Railroad conductor of all, the "Moses of her People," was still about the business of rescue. As Harriet Tubman neared eighty years of age, the soldier in her rallied for another extraordinary campaign—to expand her house into a home for refugee adults. On May 26, 1896, she was battling to purchase a twenty-five-acre site adjacent to her own home that she had envisioned as the collective farm that would support her mission.

With the pension due her as a scout for the Union Army denied her in a wash of politics, with her meager survivor's benefit as the widow of a Civil War veteran shaved to $20 per month, just as she had in her nineteen Underground Railroad missions and three years as a spy for the Union found a way "in the wilderness," she made "a way out of no way" to reach her goal. Dictating her autobiography, she leveraged her future proceeds. Borrowing fifty dollars from anti-slavery friends, she used the books as collateral until she could repay them with advance sales. At the land auction three weeks later, she bid on her dream crouched down at the back of the hall, so that "like a blackberry in a pail of milk" she would not be expelled. When the bid was won and her identity was revealed, those who doubted that she had $1,450 did not know her. True to her motto, "Keep Going," the "General," as she'd been dubbed on earlier missions, had led the charge to a bank where she mortgaged her good name and future title to the land.

As she would tell her passengers on the line as she led the way from bondage, "Children if you are tired, keep going; if you are scared, keep going; if you are hungry, keep going; if you want a taste of freedom, keep going."

Tuesday, May 26, 1896

New York                                    USA

---

**Heroes and Sheroes**                                    **Determination**

*T*here are those who think this incident has little to do with the history of African American women—and then there are those who know better. It was May 1835 in New York. The Democratic National Convention had just nominated Martin Van Buren to the presidency during which he would hound the case of the *Amistad* captives up to the Supreme Court. The American Antislavery Society was also convening at the Houston Street Presbyterian Church with Rev. Samuel May, Prudence Crandall's (see May 23) loyal advocate, among its leaders. While seated on the dais, he was called outside for this economics lesson by a prominent businessman:

> Mr. May, we are not fools as not to know that slavery is a great evil. But it was consented to by the founders of our Republic. It was provided for in the Constitution of our Union. A great portion of the property of the Southerners is invested under its sanction; and the business of the North, as well as the South, has become adjusted to it. There are millions upon millions of dollars due from Southerners to the merchants and mechanics of this city alone, the payment of which would be jeopardized by any rupture between the North and South. We cannot afford, sir, to let you and your associates succeed in your endeavor to overthrow slavery. . . . It is a matter of business necessity. . . . And I have called you out to let you know, and to let your fellow laborers know, that we do not mean to allow you to succeed. We mean, sir," said he, with increased emphasis, "to put you Abolitionists down—by fair means if we can, but foul means if we must.

There are times when we know what we know because *we just know it*; then there are times when we have proof. In 1869, when Reverend May published *Some Recollections of Our Antislavery Conflict*, proof stepped forward.

Wednesday, May 27, 1835

New York            USA

---

**Business**           **Truth**

*A*uthor William Faulkner, son of the South and its demons, once observed, "The past is never dead; it's not even past." On May 28, 1998, as a voting rights debate raged in Mississippi between a white governor and black elected officials, the past poured forth like kerosene, each word a lighted match. That day, too, the past fueled passions in a court case thirty-two years old — and centuries more — as Ellie Dahmer sought justice in the 1966 murder of her husband, Vernon Dahmer.

In the 1960s, the Dahmers had volunteered their grocery store as a voter registration site. To protect their rights and their family, Ellie and Vernon Dahmer even slept in shifts. Then, on the night of January 10, 1966, two carloads of nightriders led by Sam Bowers, former Imperial Wizard of the KKK, firebombed the store and set the Dahmer home ablaze, tossing Molotov cocktails through the windows and onto the roof. At the cost of his life, Dahmer saved his family. For years, a succession of hung juries set Bowers free. Then, in March 1998, by court order, 124,000 embattled pages of documents generated by a network of informants and state law enforcement agencies offered proof of the state's war on the Civil Rights movement. In 1956, Mississippi had empowered a Sovereignty Commission, which operated through 1977, to maintain segregation at all cost — costs paid by heroes like Vernon Dahmer and Medgar Evers, whose widow, Myrlie Evers, had finally seen his assassin convicted in 1994 (see February 5). As commission records revealed Bowers's guilt, shaming the past and present, some argued the past should remain past. "It may be the past for them, but it's not the past for us," said Mrs. Dahmer. "I still wake up and see the house on fire. I still wake up hearing Vernon yell to get the children out. It'll never be the past for us." As skeletons in the closets of the past rose from the pages of history, one could almost hear the ancestors in refrain, "Bones of the dead tell no lie."

Thursday, May 28, 1998

Mississippi          USA

From the canvas of *La Parisienne*, a young woman, erect in Victorian black, casts a sideward glance. Wiser than her years should allow, her look is tinged with a cynicism schooled by the ways of the world. A product of the brush of nineteenth-century portrait artist Annie E. Anderson Walker, how could she be otherwise?

On May 29, 1895, Walker graduated from New York's famed Cooper Union. But, unlike her fellow students, she was not a young talent of limited means; she was a forty-year-old woman married to a successful lawyer. In her young adult years, when Emancipation fueled the dreams of former slaves and free persons of color alike, she had left New York to teach in the South. In 1875, marriage brought her to Washington, D.C., and a sphere of comfort where she could explore her talents. Then, in 1890, on the strength of her portfolio, she was accepted to study at the Corcoran Gallery of Art, only to be told on the first day of class, "If we had known that you were colored, the committee would not have examined your work." For help, she approached Frederick Douglass. The most venerated African American of his day wrote a letter requesting reconsideration. But in the days when the arc of freedom was on its descent, he too was dismissed—and she was again rejected.

Walker applied to Cooper Union, graduated, traveled to Europe for further study, painted *La Parisienne*, was honored with its inclusion in the Paris Salon of 1896, and returned home that December as the world fell apart with the legalization of Jim Crow. In a three-year burst of promise, she struggled to perfect her art until the art of survival led to a nervous breakdown from which she never recovered. "What happens to a dream deferred?" Langston Hughes would ask in a poem years later. "Does it dry up like a raisin in the sun? Or does it explode?" What has happened to many a woman's dream deferred?

Wednesday, May 29, 1895

Washington, D.C.          USA

---

**Art**                                      **Aspirations**

$\mathcal{J}$t was the deep Depression years of the 1930s. To say that the Wards were poor is to minimize the situation. Their two girls had known twenty-four addresses before adulthood, each "stretched to the last hour before the landlord deposited our belongings on the sidewalk." Once, the elder child was "dispatched to borrow fifteen cents' car fare from one woman in order to go borrow seventy-five cents from another [to] use fifteen cents of that loan to get back home. It took me two hours of waiting and riding time to bring home sixty cents—and to put us ninety cents in debt." Hauling pain in place of groceries, who wouldn't talk to herself? That day in 1931 in the cleaning and dye shop, when the next presser said, "Gert, who are you talking to?" Gertrude Ward had to admit, she was hearing voices:

> I heard a voice that spoke to me so plain. It said, "Go sing my Gospel and help save dying and lost men and women." I answered saying, "Lord, I can't sing that good." The lady working at the next presser [asked who I was speaking to.] I told her what I'd heard. . . . Later, standing on the corner . . . with other dayworkers, I heard the same voice say, "Gertrude, sing My Gospel." The voice added, "Why look for a job when I've already given you one?" Well, I turned around, crossed the street, and used six of the eight cents I had for a trolley ride back home. With the other two cents I bought a few white potatoes. . . . From that day on, I've had no other job but to sing for the Lord.

From that day came the Ward Singers, with Gertrude and her two daughters, Willa and Clara Ward (see January 26). Begun in 1934 at Philadelphia's Mutchmore Baptist Church, Gert's annual May 30 anniversary concerts would become the place to be for legends, among them Mahalia Jackson, and the Drinkard Singers featuring Sissy Houston (the mother of Whitney) and Dionne Warwick.

Wednesday, May 30, 1934

Pennsylvania     USA

---

**Music**                **Voice**

*I*n the lexicon of art critics, certain artists are branded "naive," "primitive," or "untrained," their works labeled "Outsider Art," "Art Brut," or "Compulsive Visionary." Phrases are invoked to impose the not-so-subtle message that some people make art and some don't. Minnie Evans was one such artist, branded from birth by definition and whim, whose work compelled the mythmakers of the art establishment to reconsider what (or who) makes art and what that art can tell us about ourselves. As art critic Barbara J. Bloemink has written:

> During the past 500 years, Western art historians and critics have promulgated the belief that the whole of global culture must be understood and appreciated in light of the European-American visual experience. As a result, any creative work that does not fit neatly within accepted aesthetic canons becomes the battleground for conferring hierarchies of value, often by adopting pejorative categorizations.

Minnie Evans was an easy target for such categorizations. Born in Long Creek, North Carolina, in 1892, unschooled past the sixth grade, a coastal sounder (oyster and clam seller house-to-house) and domestic worker with her husband, her first drawing came on Good Friday 1935 after a voice called to her in a dream: "Why don't you draw or die?" In the 1940s, turning dreams into visions, she perfected her craft. "My dreams are in brilliant colors and I paint the way I remember the dreams," she would say of the creative streams she sailed from Africa to America and up the isthmus of personal truth. Working on May 31, 1962, Minnie Evans completed and signed her drawing, *The Eye of God*, a medallion of lush floral-colored pencil motifs. From her garden, multiple eyes—added insight—peek out, speaking to the viewer. And what they tell us is this: in Minnie Evans's world, God is definitely a woman.

Thursday, May 31, 1962

North Carolina/Delaware     USA

# June

*Graduation day at Cookman Institute: Regennia Cooper, Satsuma Heights, Florida* (May 10, 1895). Cookman Institute is now Bethune-Cookman College. Photographer unknown. Reprinted courtesy of the author. For more information, see May 18.

*I*sabella Baumfree was a woman of faith so strong that she knew her God could withstand a little talking to when her soul could be soothed by nothing less. As an enslaved child, living in New York's Hudson River Valley, she would take to a special island rest where she and her God communed. Over the years, these conversations with God increased in frequency and in vehemence. And it is said that from these talks a powerful, sonorous voice emerged.

Isabella and God discussed the promise of freedom on which her slaveowner had reneged. She decided that she would have to free herself. She walked away from bondage, never to return again. They talked about her son's being sold away. "Oh, God, you know how much I am distressed, for I have told you again and again," she had begun. "Now, God, help me get my son. If you were in trouble, as I am, and I could help you, as you can me, think I wouldn't do it? Yes, God, you know I would do it. Oh, God, you know I have no money, but you can make the people do for me, and you must make the people do for me. I will never give you peace till you do, God. Oh, God, make the people hear me — don't let them turn me off, without hearing and helping me." Together they went to court, sued for her son's return, made the people hear her, and reunited her with her son. They even won a court case over a vicious rumor that she had poisoned the head of the utopian commune in which she had found work and a home for a time. But soon thereafter, her beloved son disappeared at sea.

On June 1, 1843, it was time for a serious talk like none they'd had before. They settled on a mission for her life. She would preach against the evils of slavery, a traveler in the cause of justice. For this, they would assign her a new name: Sojourner Truth.

Thursday, June 1, 1843

New York                           USA

---

**Prayer**                                    **Empowerment**

On June 2, 1863, engaging skills she had honed as an Underground Railroad conductor and Union scout, Harriet Tubman led a regiment in a raid on South Carolina. The *Boston Commonwealth* reported the scene: "Col. Montgomery and his gallant band of 300 black soldiers, under the guidance of a black woman, dashed into the enemy's country, struck a bold and effective blow, destroying millions of dollars' worth of [supplies], striking terror into the heart of rebeldom, brought off near 800 slaves . . . without losing a man or receiving a scratch."

In centuries of military history, Tubman was the first and only woman to lead American troops in battle—that is, until another Maryland-born warrior, Gloria Richardson, succeeded Tubman's Civil War role in the fight for Civil Rights. As disarming and petite as her predecessor, Richardson commandeered SNCC forces in the Battle of Cambridge, Maryland. She too was a first— the first woman in the Civil Rights movement to lead a major campaign. Ironically, it was one of the bloodiest, as SNCC's Cleveland Sellers confirmed: "We marched about three blocks before we saw the national guardsmen. I noticed that they were armed with rifles. Each of the rifles had a bayonet attached to the end of its muzzle . . . I looked at Gloria. We still had time to turn around. . . . We all understood that Gloria was the only one who could decide its outcome." Charging forward, Richardson led the line with "I'm going through." Demonstrators followed her into battle, always outnumbered but not outdone.

Like Tubman, Richardson was not a pacifist, she was a pragmatist. Faced with a violent foe, she practiced self-defense.

Tuesday, June 2, 1863

South Carolina                  USA

*W*hile wedding day jitters have greeted the soon-to-be-newlyweds of every time and place, some have been set aflutter with better cause than most—the mail-order brides, women whose wedding proposals had appeared in newspaper advertisements and church bulletins.

In late nineteenth- to early twentieth-century Arizona, the migration of men seeking their fortunes in the mining camps of the Southwest created an overabundance of available bachelors and of "concern" for their well-being in such notorious places as Tombstone, "the town too tough to die." In this rough-hewn world of too many saloons and too few home-cooked meals, the specter of too many men could give a town a reputation as good only for those with a mind to be bad. To the rescue came the women of the Busy Bee Club. Approaching lonely widowers and rambunctious bachelors (or vice versa), they offered to broker marriages by mail. To qualify, a man had to be employed, able to provide a home, and willing to pay the cost of transportation from the East. Women who answered the call had to head to Arizona on a one-way ticket and marry the men who paid their fare. As prospects poured in, the men chose their brides in order of seniority. It was neither unusual for a woman to find herself less wife than mother to a large brood, nor for the oldest man to marry the most vulnerable bride—a girl in her teens who had, almost always, fled a life of hardship, even abuse, back home.

Regardless of age, what made these marriages work was need. In a harsh world and hard times, companionship was the engine driving the deal.

Circa 1900

Arizona                                      USA

---

*O*n June 4, 1972, in the case of *The People of the State of California v. Davis*, a jury decided what the press, public, prosecutors, police, and FBI had known from the start: Angela Davis was not guilty of murder. Reviewing the events leading up to this moment, one knew what Mark Twain meant when he said, "Of course truth is stranger than fiction. Fiction has to make sense."

In 1969, Angela Davis was the brilliant new-philosophy-professor-on-the-block at the University of California at Los Angeles. Born in Birmingham, raised in the Civil Rights movement, she had graduated from Brandeis University, studied at the Sorbonne in Paris and Goethe University in Frankfort, and was en route to a Ph.D. when an old McCarthy-era loyalty oath in the faculty hiring process spun out of control. Within a year, she would have a warrant for her arrest and a spot among the "Ten Most Wanted" for a murder she was known not to have committed.

For her activism for academic and constitutional freedoms, she received death threats that led her to legally purchase and license a weapon for her own protection. Her later support for prisoners' rights introduced her to Jonathan Jackson, brother of George Jackson, who was then serving a one-year-to-life sentence for a $70 heist he had always denied committing. In August 1970, with a weapon taken from Davis, seventeen-year-old Jonathan, desperate for his brother, led a courthouse raid that left him, a judge, and two prisoners dead. With Davis already a political target and the gun traced to her, a warrant was issued for her arrest. Innocent, she went underground, afraid she would never get a fair trial.

Acquitted, released, two years later she had been captured, imprisoned, tried, but would she ever be *free?* Said Davis, "I will never cease to criticize the judicial system for the cavalier way they argue that once a person is found not guilty, that is a vindication . . . and an indication that the system works."

Sunday, June 4, 1972

California                              USA

---

Law                                    Demons

*R*eaders of the June 1984 issue of *Isaac Asimov's Science Fiction Magazine* were in for a literary and philosophical revelation. In Octavia Butler's award-winning novelette, *Bloodchild*, men were the ones having babies. Human male slaves were charged with incubating the eggs of their alien masters.

Inventive and well-crafted as *Bloodchild* is, Butler was not the only one to have seriously contemplated a reversal of birthing roles. Josephine Riley Matthews (see October 3), the fourth generation in a family of midwives, had been a practitioner for fifty years when she made this keen observation:

> Well, the Bible says the strong should bear the infirmities of the weak. So the woman is supposed to be the weaker sex, but they sure have to stand up for the men a lot of times. I'll bet you one thing, if the man had to have the first baby there wouldn't be but two in the family. Yes sir, let him have the first one and the woman have the next one, and his time wouldn't come around no more.

Butler, the voice of eloquence, and Matthews, the voice of experience, had come to a similar conclusion: the idea of men giving birth was fantastic indeed.

June 1984

California/South Carolina    USA

*J*n June 1920, the second African American Methodist bishop had just baptized the three-month-old daughter of a minister in his flock when he looked at the baby, passed her to her mother, and sighed, "How I wish you were a boy, so that my mantle could fall on you."

His wish was partially granted. In 1970, the baby was fifty and a newly ordained minister in the United Methodist Church — Leontine T. C. Kelly. Getting to that point and beyond, Kelly's would be an amazing trajectory. She had left college in her junior year to marry. Later divorced, she remarried, returned to college, was certified a lay speaker in the church, and, as a forty-year-old mother of four, earned her bachelor's degree in 1960. A decade later, recently widowed, she joined the ministry, enrolled in graduate school, and earned her master of divinity degree at age fifty-six. A pastor of two congregations and active in outreach ministries, she soon achieved two firsts. In 1983, she was ordained the first African American woman bishop of a major religious denomination, and in 1984 she was the first woman to preach from a national radio pulpit.

Asked what the minister who'd baptized her would have thought of her role in the church hierarchy, she said, "He'd probably turn over in his grave at the idea."

Sunday, June 6, 1920

California                                    USA

---

**Religion**                                    **Impossibility**

"*B*lack Patti's Troubadours," blared ads for the week of June 7, 1913. "Greatest Colored Show on Earth!" "Better than a Circus!" With flourish and fanfare, Sissieretta Jones, the first internationally renowned African American operatic soprano, brought her all-black troupe to the New Star Theatre for a limited New York engagement—"The very incarnation of mirth, melody, music and darkey fun!"

Just think of it: her parents' rise from slavery to freedom, her 1869 birth into the first post-Emancipation generation, her pioneering years of voice training at the Providence Academy of Music and Boston's New England Conservatory of Music, her White House concert for President William Harrison, her command performance for the Prince of Wales in London, triumphs on three continents. Yet, for all her success, Jones had to hoe the theatrical cotton field—as a "refined colored fun-maker" of good "darkey fun." Retiring in 1916, she died in obscurity in 1933. Such were the times when, to her chagrin, an admiring critic dubbed her "Black Patti"—a nod to soprano Adelina Patti. Her manager and the press loved the reference, but all comparisons ended there. Unlike the white Patti, the black Patti was racially restricted to the vaudeville stage and her Metropolitan Opera House debut was posthumously sung by her daughters *in the spirit*. Contralto Marian Anderson broke the Met's color bar in 1955 (see December 30), and soprano Leontyne Price opened the new Met in 1966 (see September 16). As the world's first black *prima donna assoluta*, Price would perform *Aida*, the role promised but denied Sissieretta Jones in 1892.

With Anderson's historic Easter concert for an audience of seventy-five thousand in 1939 (see April 9), with the forty-two-minute standing ovation given Price's Metropolitan debut in 1961, history was heard to give Jones a round of applause.

Saturday, June 7, 1913

International                         USA

---

**Music**                                              **Continuity**

Nella Larsen's second novel, *Passing*, was a hit, more so now that Dr. W. E. B. Du Bois had chosen to review it and to recommend it to readers of *The Crisis*, meaning to the NAACP, the largest secular African American membership organization of the day via its widely circulated and highly influential magazine. With titles like *Quicksand* (her first book) and *Passing* (her latest), there was little doubt as to her subject matter or the story of her life. On the page and in the proof, hers was the classic story of the mulatto, doomed but refusing to be tragic, in American society.

But Larsen's personal saga had added intrigue. She was born to a Danish mother and a Danish Afri-Caribbean father who died when she was two. When her mother remarried, to a white man with whom she had a daughter, as a black child in an otherwise all-white family, and given racial taboos, Nella always felt an outsider. She attended Fisk University, then the University of Denmark, but it was not until her tenure as a children's librarian in the Harlem Renaissance years that she found a home among the black literati who squired her into the writer's life.

As Du Bois proclaimed in his June 1929 review in *The Crisis*, *Passing* was "one of the finest novels of the year. If it did not treat a forbidden subject—the intermarriage of a stodgy middle-class white man to a very beautiful and selfish octoroon—it would have an excellent chance to be hailed, selected and recommended. As it is, it will probably be given the 'silence,' with only the commendation of word of mouth. But what of that?" Du Bois was right, but what was made of that was, in 1930, the first Guggenheim Foundation creative writing fellowship awarded an African American woman. With it, Nella Larsen made plans to sail to France and Spain for research on her next work.

June 1929

Illinois          USA

---

**Literature**          **Transcendence**

*T*rans-Africa: an organization founded by Randall Robinson that has come to mean the highest standards of commitment to Pan-African liberation. In 1990, Robinson's hunger strike for Haiti kept him from being in South Africa when Nelson Mandela walked free after twenty-seven years—thanks, in part, to sanctions Robinson helped win. On June 9, 1984, this Trans-Africa had presented its Freedom Award to Ella Baker, shero of the Civil Rights movement too long unsung.

A field secretary for the NAACP in 1941, later on staff at the Urban League, in 1958 "pressed into a job for which she had not applied," as her biographer, Joanne Grant, would write, Baker would give structure and discipline to the fledgling Southern Christian Leadership Conference (SCLC) as acting executive director. When the historic February 1, 1960, lunch counter sit-in by four North Carolina A & T students burst forth in a spontaneous youth movement, Baker raised funds from SCLC coffers to host the April 17 conference that gave birth to the Student Non-Violent Coordinating Committee (SNCC). It was Baker, too, as "godmother," who stepped back from the spotlight to nurture SNCC's raw energy into an unparalleled leadership training ground that yet bears fruit in every field. From politics (Congresswoman Eleanor Holmes Norton) to cause célèbre (Angela Davis), law (Professor Kathleen Cleaver), organizing (Mississippi Freedom Democratic Party co-founder Fannie Lou Hamer), women's rights (the Black Women's Liberation Committee and its co-founder Frances Beal), historiography (biographer Joanne Grant), music (Sweet Honey in the Rock founder Bernice Johnson Reagon), to television (producer Jennifer Lawson), in the work of these daughters and many more, Ella Baker lives. As she would say, "The struggle is eternal. The tribe increases. Somebody else carries on." As Reagon would quote in the refrain of "Ella's Song," "we who believe in freedom cannot rest. . . ."

Saturday, June 9, 1984

North Carolina               USA

**Organizing**                                        **Understanding**

*S*even months had passed since the stock market crash of 1929 officially plunged the nation into the Great Depression. With families who had recently migrated to the factory cities of the North now displaced and out of work, with Jim Crow scapegoating blacks for the powerlessness of destitute whites, the last thing blacks could afford was despair. Needed were: mutual aid, the economic nationalism of Marcus Garvey's UNIA (see July 20), and confidence born of self-determination. Building on the "club movement" of the post-Reconstruction era (see July 30) with roots in the early nineteenth century "societies" (see December 28), fifty women founded the Detroit Housewives' League on June 10, 1930.

They had come together at the call of Fannie B. Peck, wife of Rev. William H. Peck and first lady of a large AME congregation. The idea had come to her after a lecture by M. A. L. Holsey, secretary of the Booker T. Washington–powered National Negro Business League. Holsey reported that Harlem women had pooled their resources as consumers to their buying advantage. From that kernel, Peck eked her philosophy on the "Spending Power of Women." At the core of the idea was building collective wealth. That meant "turning" a dollar three times before it left the community by supporting black-owned businesses, buying black products, and patronizing black professionals. A pledge to do so was the only requirement for membership in the league that, in four scant years, would grow from fifty to ten thousand members. Neighborhood chapters approached local businesses demanding the marketing of black products and hiring of blacks. Citywide events included tactical lectures on picketing and boycotting. As the movement spread to major northern cities, the league was second only to the federal government in securing new jobs for African Americans and building organizing skills that would sustain the coming Civil Rights movement of the 1950s and 1960s.

Tuesday, June 10, 1930

Michigan                                          USA

**Business**                                    **Self-determination**

$\mathcal{F}$or their third New York recital, tickets priced at one dollar, sixty-five cents, and thirty-five cents had been sold at Reckling's Music Shop on 125th Street, heart of Harlem's shopping thoroughfare. Then, at precisely three o'clock on Sunday, June 11, 1939, the lights dimmed on the auditorium of the old Harlem YWCA at 138th Street, and Bernice and Dolores Calvin, aged fourteen and eleven, entered the spotlight and the eye of the storm of applause awaiting them.

With their bright eager faces identically framed in masses of Shirley Temple curls swept slightly off their faces by deftly positioned bows, their careful, stylish look and prim demeanor forecast the performance to come. With top honors in the National Piano Playing Tournament and other awards to their credit, the girls' "musical event extraordinaire" met the highest expectations. A Steinway concert grand piano center stage poised for their gifts, the girls settled themselves and launched into a two-hour program of works by the European classical masters and two new American composers—Bernice and Dolores. In planning the program, their parents and teachers had remembered to celebrate the girls' own sense of self and need for expression.

However unique the talents of Bernice and Dolores might have been, their recital was not unusual. A major part of the cultural life of our communities in a time when the prevailing racial climate was cold and raw, young people somehow seemed more confident and hopeful. These Sunday musicales built the armor that would prepare us for the Civil Rights era, soon to come. Perhaps our rituals of the past should be redeemed as current events.

Sunday, June 11, 1939

New York                    USA

---

*W*hat could be more important than the bond between a father and daughter, a husband and wife? For too many years, the answer has been race. As two events demonstrate, under codes of law and custom, de facto and de jure segregation, a white man could do anything to a black woman except the honorable thing.

In 1885, David Dickson's will gave the bachelor's family a shock: seven-eighths of his $600,000 estate was bequeathed to his biracial daughter and her black mother, and only one-eighth to his already wealthy white heirs. The *New York Times* of June 12, 1886, named Amanda Dickson Eubanks America's richest black woman — a multimillionaire in contemporary dollars. "Disgusted as well as disappointed," the former profiteers of slavery pursued their darker cousin in Georgia's state supreme court. But, *gone were the days.* Empowered by her father's love, Amanda Eubanks stood her ground and won her case.

In 1958, the state of Virginia indicted Mildred and Richard Loving for violating its laws against interracial marriage. Pleading guilty, the aptly named Loving couple was sentenced to one year, suspended on condition that they leave the state and not return together for twenty-five years. Relocated but unhappy in Washington, D.C., they returned to Virginia and fought the court order. On June 12, 1967, a unanimous decision overturned the lower court, anti-miscegenation laws in sixteen states, and three hundred years of history (see November 9). In Chief Justice Earl Warren's majority opinion, such "measures designed to maintain white supremacy" were unconstitutional — violations of the equal protection clause of the Fourteenth Amendment, a post–Civil War "freedom amendment." This note: the Lovings' daughter's married name was Peggy *Loving Fortune.* How appropriate to these struggles for human rights and the right to be human.

Thursday, June 12, 1886

Georgia/Virginia USA

Family Transcendence

*J*n June 1990, Dr. Jewel Plummer Cobb retired as president of California State University at Fullerton. From her first love—cancer research with a specialty in cell biology—she had built a prestigious career. But how did it happen that an African American girl born in 1924 could make such a future for herself?

An answer begins with the frustration and courage of Dr. Daniel Hale Williams, who, in 1891, founded the first teaching hospital for black physicians and nurses, Provident Hospital in Chicago (see January 23). When Cobb's parents graduated in the early 1920s—her mother in physical education from Harvard University–affiliated Sargeants College, her father from Rush Medical College—they headed to Chicago, where her father could complete his studies thanks to "Dr. Dan." Before Provident, segregation thwarted African Americans, who could intern at white hospitals but could neither touch white patients nor treat black patients because hospitals would not admit them. With opportunities for her parents, her family's dinner chat was electrified by a mutual love of physiology. With that ear-training, a high school biology teacher recognized a gem. When other blacks were steered into industrial and commercial courses, her parents' influence and her teachers' inspiration got her into college prep. As a sophomore, she looked into a laboratory microscope and saw her future—biology. When college-bound southern blacks headed north, racially barred from their own state colleges, the University of Michigan at Ann Arbor seemed a logical choice for a northerner. But there, racially barred from the dormitory, she encountered the racism southern students had attempted to flee. In 1942, for scientific excellence and peace of mind, her parents sent her to all-black Talladega College and she was on her way. Dr. Jewel Plummer Cobb's scientific research career benefiting cancer patients everywhere would be nurtured because, despite all, black folks had made a way.

June 1990

Michigan                                    USA

---

**Science**                                    **Possibility**

Threatened with three hundred paddle blows, John Little and his wife (her first name is unknown) fled slavery. With a sense of geography gained from being frequently sold, for three months they slept in shifts and walked from Tennessee to Chicago, where they boarded the Underground Railroad to Canada. In 1855, Mrs. Little told their story:

My shoes gave out before many days—then I wore my husband's old shoes till they were used up. Then we came on barefooted all the way to Chicago. My feet were blistered and sore and my ankles swollen but I had to keep on. . . . At the first water we came to I was frightened. It was a swift but shallow stream. I felt afraid at getting into a boat to cross the Ohio River. I had never been in any boat. . . .

At Cairo, the gallinippers [mosquitoes] were so bad, we made a smoke to keep them off. Soon after I heard a steamboat bell tolling. Presently there she was, a great boat full of white men [who] saw our fire and hailed, "Boat ashore! runaway niggers!" We put out our fire and . . . at last hid in a thicket of briers, where we were almost devoured by mosquitoes for want of a little smoke.

One morning, being on a prairie where we could see no house, we ventured to travel by day. . . . I undertook to make some corn bread. I got it mixed, and put it on the fire,—when I saw a party of men and boys on horseback. . . . I put out the fire; they turned a little away and did not appear to perceive us. I rekindled the fire and baked our bread. John managed to keep us well-supplied with pies and bread. We used to laugh to think how people would puzzle over who drank the milk and left the pitchers and who hooked the dough.

Achievement comes by many names. To know the story of the Littles is to know why James Brown would sing, "Say it loud, I'm Black and I'm proud!"

1855

Illinois                                    USA

---

*W*hen Bessie Coleman saw her route to the skies blocked by biased flight schools that refused to teach her, she did what millions before had done—she became "better than." In a route charted with her brother's teasing on the superiority of French women, who could even fly, she sailed for Paris, trained at the Fédération Aeronautique Internationale, and, on June 15, 1921, became the first American—male, female, black, or white— to achieve an international pilot's license.

At the dawn of the century, in 1903, the Wright brothers had made history with their twelve-second flight at Kitty Hawk. By 1918, World War I made their newfangled new-age contraption a star and its dashing pilot—courageous, heroic—an icon for fearless young men. The sight of Bessie Coleman's barnstorming was passed across the generations (as this author's grandfather would do) with relish. Tragically, in 1926, Coleman was killed in an exhibition accident. A year would pass before Charles Lindbergh soloed, New York to Paris, in a plane with no need for front windows because the transatlantic skies were his alone. And not until 1928 did the world meet Amelia Earhart. It was in this brave new world of aviation that Bessie Coleman made her name, when every flight was a test flight and every pilot a pioneer trespassing the limits of innovation and endurance.

In a tradition begun in 1935, African American pilots still honor Coleman with an annual flight over her grave. For the history she launched, we also honor the publishing pioneer Robert Abbott of the *Chicago Defender*, who sponsored Coleman to Paris, her successor Willa Brown, and the publicity tours of later aviators who would inspire and enlist future generations for flight. Among them, Ida Van Smith realized Coleman's dreams for a flight school, Jill Brown became the first commercial pilot, and in 1992 Mae Jemison was our first astronaut in space.

Wednesday, June 15, 1921

Texas                    USA

---

**Heroes and Sheroes**                    **Opportunity**

On the night of June 16, 1975, two black women were hitch-hiking a lonely stretch through Lyons, Georgia, from nearby Reidsville Prison, where the brother of one of the women was incarcerated. Coming upon them, local officers beat the two, then held them overnight on charges of vagrancy and public drunkenness when one of the women fainted, overcome by heat and stress. The next day, with no bus route from where they had been taken to their home, they were on foot and vulnerable again when a white man posing as a police officer offered them a ride. After stopping to make a phone call, he drove deep into the woods, intending to rape them at gunpoint. This was not the first time he had attempted to force a black woman to "service" him, but it would be the last. When he stopped the car, one woman ran. The other, seeing him take aim at her fleeing friend, wrestled for the gun. It went off, killing the man. Charged with his murder, the woman who tried to flee was sentenced to five years and served under two. The woman who saved their lives — Dessie Woods — was sentenced to twenty-two years and became an international cause célèbre. Held in solitary confinement, physically attacked by a warden incensed at her self-defense, she was kept naked in her cell. Indeed, her plight would be echoed in the martyrdom of Stephen Biko after the June 16, 1976, Soweto uprising of twenty thousand unarmed schoolchildren led to his arrest and murder by police at the height of South African apartheid.

On July 9, 1981, Dessie Woods was released from prison at last. But where is the morsel of good in her tragedy? Perhaps it is in the telling, the writing, the reading, the remembering, the repeating . . . the repeating . . . the repeating . . . lest we forget. Perhaps it is in the knowledge, when we find ourselves in a situation we would never have made, that we are neither crazy nor alone; we are the women who know.

Monday, June 16, 1975

Georgia                USA

*C*harlotte Hawkins Brown had a way with money. You could say that. In the founding years of her Palmer Institute in North Carolina, she raised money by recitations and voice concerts at Massachusetts summer resorts. As her school grew, contributions came from benefactors, black and white, including her friend Madame C. J. Walker (see August 30). As with today's public school funding, but unusual for segregated black schools of the period, she had gotten the state to line-item a per capita tax for each Palmer student in the county. Enduring every inspection imaginable, her school was acknowledged the state's best managed institution of its size. So devoted were her teachers that they went without pay, at times, to keep the school afloat. Then there was a fire; a few checks paid to the school were returned for insufficient funds; they had "neither meat or sugar"; and June 17, 1921, as she confessed to a Boston benefactor, was "the darkest hour I have ever known. . . . Please don't turn me down. . . . I'm at my wit's end—everything looks dark, but I am bound to believe that help must soon [come]."

Help did come—a $10,000 donation when most needed and least expected. She recalled "beating my breast and ejaculating in quick succession saying with all my soul these words, 'God, God, why have you done this for me?'" Clearly, it had been done for her because she had done so much for others. Faced with segregation, she fought back and sued. Livid over lynching, she spoke against it and risked becoming its victim. She felt etiquette would help her charges succeed and wrote the book *The Correct Thing to Do, Say, to Wear.* When "men who occupy high places [thought] that no negro woman whether she be cook, criminal or principal of a school" should ever be addressed as "Mrs.," she fought that, too. At every step, Mrs. Brown stood the test and remained at the helm for fifty years!

Friday, June 17, 1921

North Carolina            USA

---

**Education**                                    **Tenacity**

*A*s the Female Anti-Slavery Society evolved from an all-black group into an integrated one, annual conventions challenged the resolve of participants to live what they preached: abolition of slavery *and* of segregation. So vehement were pro-slavery opponents to the integrated 1838 Philadelphia gathering that rioters, emboldened by the blind eye of the law, stoned the Pennsylvania Hall convention site. When the women refused to refrain from walking through the streets in racially mixed groups, rioters torched the hall. As the terror escalated, the women soon found themselves fighting off not only their enemies but also their allies among the leaders of the all-male Pennsylvania Abolition Society. Seeking to assuage the violent, society president Dr. Joseph Parrish encouraged the women to retract their condemnation of racial prejudice. On June 18, 1838, the noted abolitionist and feminist Lucretia Mott expressed her outrage in a letter to her son-in-law:

> Our proceedings tho' not yet published have greatly aroused our pseudo-abolitionists [and] such timid ones as our good Dr. Parrish who has left no means untried to induce us to expunge from our minutes a resolution relating to social intercourse with our colored brethren . . . and when he failed in this effort, he called some of the respectable part of the colored people together . . . and advised them not to accept such intercourse . . . and to issue a disclaimer of any such wish. This they have not yet done—but it has caused not a little excitement among us.

In Boston, where freedom's first martyrs fell for the new republic, an abolitionist had been mobbed and nearly killed for applying the "all men are created equal" clause of the Declaration of Independence to the slave. In Philadelphia—the birthplace of freedom and the Constitution—patriots demonstrated their hypocrisy against abolitionist women. But then, the Liberty Bell was already cracked.

Monday, June 18, 1838

Pennsylvania                    USA

**Ideals**                                              **Conscience**

$\mathcal{V}$eteran actor Beah Richards has said, "There are a lot of movies out there that I would hate to be paid to do, some real demeaning, real woman-denigrating stuff. It is up to women to change their roles. They are going to have to write the stuff and do it. And they will."

On June 19, 1997, we did just that. Oprah Winfrey had bought the screen rights to Toni Morrison's novel *Beloved* and had taken on a new role as executive producer as well as actor in the film adaptation. It was a dream come true. As chief executive, Winfrey was guardian to the dream. As actor, giving flesh to the role of Sethe meant uttering a praise-song to the ancestors. On this day, she joined her fellow actors for the first read through of the first novel to reach the screen written by the first African American woman awarded the Nobel Prize for Literature. In her journal, she wrote: "One incredible day. . . . We realized what an incredible journey this is we're undertaking"—a journey of which she would later write, "I never felt so free and so joyful as when I was working on *Beloved*."

How poignant, how appropriate, that when *Beloved* reached the screen eighteen months later, Morrison's words and Winfrey's work were graced by Beah Richards's performance as Baby Suggs, elder to a clan that escapes slavery in Kentucky for Ohio. In the post-Emancipation years of the story, Baby Suggs calls her people to a clearing in the woods. Healer of their awesome wounds, she binds them in strength as a people and as individuals. Raising her arms to heaven, she exhorts, "Love your hands, love your black hands." The audience feels the embrace. So, too, must the ancestors who on this day, this Juneteenth, June 19, 1865, first tasted freedom in the year of Jubilee. On their sacred day of joyous celebration, Happy Juneteenth! Happy Freedom Day to us all!

Monday, June 19, 1865

National                                    USA

---

**Celebrations**                          **Collective Responsibility**

"*Let* the women keep silence in the church." While the black church has been no stranger to that sexist "Pauline Doctrine," from the founding days of the AME, pragmatism has dictated that women who suffered the lash and shouldered the freedom fight with men be accorded a place of respect in the heavenly sight. As the church's first woman preacher, Jarena Lee heard the call in 1811. But not until 1819, when she interrupted a sermon by Bishop Richard Allen, did she receive the attention due her. Years would pass before women preachers like Lee and Zilpha Elaw (see July 1) received formal recognition, but that didn't stop the need for a woman's hand in church affairs. As the first annual conference on June 20, 1821, neared, Sarah Allen, wife of the bishop, chose the role of "first mother."

As her husband and the other ministers shuttled the route from New York to Philadelphia, Wilmington, and Baltimore, organizing congregations and the first conference, Sarah Allen was struck by their unmet human needs. She rallied women to support their institution-building efforts. These were not prosperous, settled men. Richard Allen had bought his freedom and worked as a master shoemaker supervising other journeymen and apprentices. From his earnings, he bought a lot and built the first Bethel Church from an abandoned blacksmith's workshop. Set in the context of the time, therefore, the woman who could aid the church was the rare "privileged" woman of color, a *free* woman, happy to prioritize her self-interest in family and community.

When an exhausted, ill-fed, threadbare AME pastor appeared, Sarah Allen's teams fed him, cleaned and darned his suit, and nurtured his spirit and his image as a leader. In 1827, her initiative was formally honored as the Daughters of Conference—the mother society of today's AME Zion women's organizations.

Wednesday, June 20, 1821

National                                    USA

---

Leadership                                  **Building Dreams**

On June 21, 1851, the Women's Rights Convention in Akron, Ohio, was astir as anti-rightist men wagged on in self-congratulation. The "superiority of men" mandated the denial of women. With "superior intellect," the men claimed Christ's "manhood" on their side. And, still smarting from Adam's inability to resist Eve's cooking, the "sin of the first mother" was called to account. As the women offered freedom of speech to men who sentenced them to silence, one rose to the stature of which her six-foot height could not take full measure. As she neared the platform, white women who had sat mute for the rubble of men found the voice to insist a black woman sit down. Undeterred, Sojourner Truth (see June 1, May 10) delivered her now-historic speech, "And Ain't I a Woman?":

> Well, children, where there is so much racket, there must be something out of kilter. I think between the Negroes of the South and the women of the North, all talking about rights, the white men will be in a fix pretty soon. . . . That man over there says that women need to be helped into carriages and lifted over ditches, and to have the best place everywhere. Nobody helps me any best place. And ain't I a woman? I could work as much, and eat as much as man—when I could get it—and bear the lash as well! And ain't I a woman? I have borne children and seen most of them sold into slavery, and when I cried out with a mother's grief, none but Jesus heard me. And ain't I a woman? What's intellect got to do with women's rights or black folks' rights? If my cup won't hold but a pint and yours holds a quart, wouldn't you be mean not to let me have my little half-measure full? That little man in black there, he says women can't have as much rights as men "cause Christ wasn't a woman." Where did your Christ come from? From God and a woman. Man had nothing to do with him. . . .

Having rallied her foes to thunderous applause, she left the platform and a legacy that resonates still.

Saturday, June 21, 1851

Ohio USA

---

**Speeches** **Wisdom**

*A* s the first day of summer appears, heating up our northern days, we are reminded that in our tradition are ways to stave the heat and the chill of romance. In the Swahili language and the tradition of what is now modern Kenya, a *utendi* is an epic poem. Written by Mwana Kupona binti Msham, circa 1858, "Utendi wa Mwana Kupona" reveals an epic secret—the art of being a wife and a lover:

*My child, do not be slovenly, do as you know best;*
*but sweeping and washing out the bathroom, do not neglect it even once;*
*Nor washing and scenting yourself, and plaiting your hair,*
*nor stringing jasmine blossoms and placing them on the coverlet.*
*And adorn yourself with garments like a bride—*
*put anklets on your legs and bracelets on your arms.*
*Take not from your neck the necklace and clasp,*
*nor cease perfuming your body with rosewater and dahlia.*
*Take not the rings off your fingers nor cease dyeing your nails with henna;*
*do not remove the antimony from your eyes nor refrain from putting it on*
*    your eyebrows. . . .*

The advice of a mother to her daughter in the ancient Moslem tradition, this *utendi* counseling total obedience to one's husband begins with a pragmatic view of life: "If he wishes you to go to Paradise, you will forthwith be brought there: if he says you are to go to the fire, there is no escape, you will be placed there"; "Keep faith with him always; what he wishes do not withhold; let not you and him quarrel: the quarreller gets hurt." As the wife of a sheikh, Mwana Kupona binti Msham knew a thing or two about love and war.

1858

Kenya

---

In 1850, seventy-year-old Robert Newsom bought fourteen-year-old Celia at auction. En route to his farm, he raped her, and he continued to do so until June 23, 1855, when, pregnant by him for the third time, she killed him in self-defense. While Missouri law made it illegal for a man to force sex on "any woman," the court ruled that, as a slave, Celia was outside protection of the law. Found guilty of first-degree murder, she appealed. The superior court found that because a slave woman had no right to her own body, she could not be raped and had no legal grounds for self-defense. The guilty verdict was upheld. Celia was hung.

Because stories like Celia's are often dismissed from our her-story as too painful to tell, generations of wounded women have suffered our disbelief, as if their truths were an aberration. Those who argue for change are dismissed as if their fears are ground-less. In 1913, many argued against laws barring intermarriage, mindful that a white woman sexually violated by a white man would have legal recourse to compel support for herself and her child, but a black woman would go unprotected. Others found it easier (and safer) to blame the victim for the crime. In 1948, when Rosa Lee Ingram was attacked and her sons came to her aid, inadvertently killing her attacker, prosecutors denied her the right to self-defense and a jury sentenced the three Ingrams to death (see February 3). Many seemed shocked. In 1975, Joanne Little must have felt terribly alone when charged with murder after defending herself against her jailer-rapist. And the list goes on.

However painful the tale, we must tell our stories. For in the telling and in the memory, even when we cannot protect our bodies, we can protect our truths and our minds. Knowing *the troubles they've seen*, we can tell our sisters that they are within sight, that each sister's burden is worthy of our love and our defense.

Saturday, June 23, 1855

Missouri                                  USA

---

**Revolt!**                                          **Self-defense**

On June 24, 1998, with a civil class action suit against the Wall Street brokerage firm of Smith Barney, Inc., moving forward, the federal district court judge hearing the case rejected the company's settlement offer. It was another landmark decision for the rights of women—a decision made by the first African American woman to become a federal judge, Constance Baker Motley.

As a young attorney, Motley had *been there* in the trenches of the NAACP Legal Defense Fund when Thurgood Marshall argued and won the milestone *Brown v. Board of Education* Supreme Court decision desegregating schools in 1954 (see May 17). In Marshall, the future first African American Supreme Court justice, it would be hard to imagine a better mentor. Even as he interviewed Motley for the job, he began encouraging her with the first of many stories he would tell her about "every successful African American woman he encountered" and began prodding her past many a land mine erected in her path. Arguing ten and winning nine of her own Civil Rights cases before the Supreme Court made her a prime candidate for nomination to the court of appeals by President Lyndon Johnson. But, as she recalled, "the opposition to my appointment was so great, apparently because I was a woman, that Johnson had to withdraw my name." In 1966, when Johnson named her to the federal bench, another sturdy challenge was raised, but this time the wagons had already been circled in her defense.

Now, with the Smith Barney case in her court, in a decision for the rights of women, Judge Motley, intimate with both the law and the practice, put corporate boards on notice. "Not good enough," Judge Motley found, in all good faith. As with school boards in 1954 and industry since, the time had come for brokerage boards to end all manner of *board games.*

Wednesday, June 24, 1998

New York                    USA

---

*I*n 1935, *The Crisis* published "The Bronx Slave Market," a landmark exposé on the plight of domestic workers during the Depression. As Ella Baker and Marvel Cooke observed: "Paradoxically, the crash of 1929 brought to the domestic labor market . . . the lower middle-class housewife, who, having dreamed on the luxury of a maid, found opportunity staring her in the face in the form of the Negro women pressed to the wall by poverty, starvation, and discrimination." Isolated at work and in society, most domestics could only resort to their own wits for help or hope, as Naomi Ward wrote in "I Am a Domestic," published in *New Masses* on June 25, 1940.

"Tie my shoes—I hate leaning over!" was the demand of a woman who insisted on calling her "Naomi Noble" because "Down South we always call our niggers by our own last name, so here we'll call you 'Naomi Noble.'" Another eked out extra work hours from her each day; although she'd been hired to work from noon until after dinner for a flat fee, the dinner hour was then inched from seven to nine. Fired for objecting to having only five minutes' time to eat after a full night's work, she offered her address to the maid. "I am not interested!" Lucille cried dramatically. "I felt suddenly slapped," wrote Ward. "But from the pleading look in Lucille's eyes, I understood. Mrs. B— was still in the pantry, and Lucille was thinking that she would get no references after ten months' work. . . . For a petty whim, they can withhold that precious bit of paper without which it is hard for us to obtain another ticket to slavery. I knew . . . that I would never get a reference from Mrs. B—. So I did not ask for one, but rode on down for the last time with the garbage. Jobless, and with only $15 between [my daughter and me] and starvation, I still felt a wild sense of joy. For just a few days I should be free and self-respecting!" *How we got ovah.* . . . How can we forget our sisters still conscripted into domestic service?

Tuesday, June 25, 1940

National/New York          USA

---

**Labor**                                              **Human Spirit**

O n an island off the eastern coast of Africa, the Malagasy Republic—formerly called Madagascar—with its compote of languages, customs, and cultures Arab, Asian, and sub-Saharan provides perspective on the continent and its women leaders.

To ancient northern and southern Africans were added Asians, sailing due west across the Indian Ocean perhaps as early as the seventh century. Europeans came and went, making the island a popular pirate retreat, luring the likes of the legendary Captain Kidd. Then, in the late 1700s, from within the mix arose the Hova dynasty, with its Indonesian roots, which banned the slave trade, banned Christianity (a frequent precursor to European colonization), and brought Queen Ranavalona III to the throne. A photo of the handsome young queen dressed in the manner of Queen Victoria tells a story. By 1885, as France attempted to claim her nation, she must have thought Britain her ally. But by resisting France and letting down her guard to Britain, the nation was doomed. In 1890, the two European powers struck a deal: Britain recognized French rule over Madagascar, the French recognized British rule over Zanzibar (modern Tanzania). In 1897, Queen Ranavalona was deposed and exiled to Réunion, and it was not until June 26, 1960, that Madagascar retook its independence as the modern Malagasy Republic.

Interestingly, in Mozambique fifteen years later, June 26 would mark that nation's first day of independence since fifteenth-century Portuguese incursions brought the slave trade to its coast and soon decimated the region. Worth noting: Mozambique's liberation force, Frelimo, won victory over Portugal with the aid of Chinese soldiers and its own elite army corps of women volunteers.

Sunday, June 26, 1960

Malagasy

"*C*ome on up some night my castle's rocking," she would revel in song—and it was. On June 27, 1978, performing her Carnegie Hall debut at age eighty-two, Alberta Hunter was back on top and singing the blues. And when Alberta sang the blues, she sang of having *been there* and back, triumphant over all.

Born in 1895, she had been a blues/jazz cabaret singer (she used the terms interchangeably) from the age of nineteen. Her career had taken her around the world with such greats as Louis Armstrong, Fletcher Henderson, Fats Waller, and Paul Robeson in the London production of *Showboat*. Then, in 1954, after her mother's death, she decided to pursue a long-deferred passion— nursing. Earning her license as a practical nurse in August 1957, she worked for the next twenty years, until the mandatory retirement age of seventy forced that second career to end. But Hunter was actually eighty-two. In order to pursue her dream, she had set back the clock twelve years on her applications and was doing just fine.

From 1922, when she composed her "Downhearted Blues," a classical blues tune made famous by Bessie Smith, to 1978, when she was proclaimed a "national treasure" in the press, the self-proclaimed pinnacle of her career would come on December 3, 1978, with a performance for President and Mrs. Jimmy Carter at the White House. From then until shortly before her death in 1984, you could find her holding court in song—snapping and tapping slender red-tipped fingers to the delight of audiences at the Cookery, a New York hot spot made hotter still by her reign supreme.

Tuesday, June 27, 1978

New York                                    USA

---

**Music**                                                    **Joy**

*O*n June 1988, in Cambridge, Massachusetts, ninety-three-year-old Ruth Veletta Jones shared her wealth with an oral history project researcher: her great-aunt and great-uncle's escape from an Albemarle County, Virginia, plantation to a Yankee camp; kinship to Frederick Douglass; and "the day the stars fell" (see November 13). Documenting the provenance of her inheritance, she said, "My grandmother told me that story. It wasn't in her life-time but it was handed down. You know the slaves had long memories because they didn't have a written history.

It is because of our griots in a long African tradition—those oral historians like Ruth Veletta Jones and her grandmother Hardenia White who "archive" our history, listen, and recount it anew—that we have documented our sojourn. How else would we know the spirituals as codes of the Underground Railroad, songs of faith, secret recipes with which to enrich our days? From the front-porch stories of his grandmother, Alex Haley retraced his *Roots* (see September 29) and sparked a national passion for genealogy. Accused of telling her granddaughter "tall tales," Margaret Walker's griot-grandmother replied, "I'm not telling her tales; I'm telling her the naked truth." As novelist Walker later learned, her grandmother was right. Visiting Georgia, Walker came upon an eerily familiar place she recognized from the kitchen tales of her childhood—remnants of the smithy and gristmill her great-grandfather had owned a century earlier. A rich oral tradition sustained, her grandmother had inspired Walker's masterpiece of historical fiction, *Jubilee*.

Snapping beans, shaving carrots, and stirring stew fix more than dinner. Preserving legacies, these techniques shape futures. How sad that so many of us go undernourished—our stories forsaken, possibilities thwarted, and growth stunted by fad diets and fast food.

June 1988

Massachusetts                   USA

---

**Historiography**                                        **Memory**

*A* terrible thing had happened. Dr. Betty Shabazz, widow of slain leader Malcolm X, was dead. She, too, had been slain—but her violent, painful, lingering death had come at the hands of her own twelve-year-old grandson. For weeks friends and strangers lined up to give blood, to give skin to graft onto her charred frame if the hospital would allow it, to do anything that could be done when there was nothing to be done but grieve for a child who would come to know guilt. Consumed with a passion too big for his little boy soul, he had doused a hall with gasoline and lit it aflame, angered by some momentary slight. She lingered near death as long as she could to keep the boy from bearing the scar of his deed and the weight of the word *matricide*. After three weeks she could fight no more and was gone. On June 29, 1997, millions watched on television as thousands packed the Riverside Church in her memory.

Kneeling beside her husband's body on the floor of Harlem's Audubon Ballroom on February 21, 1965, she had seen him fall in a hail of bullets before her eyes, leaving her to raise six daughters aged seven, five, three, three months, and twins in her womb. Two women knew too well her life as widow to a martyred hero, icon in her own right, single mother with meager financial assets, and a woman alone—Medgar's widow, Myrlie Evers, and Martin's widow, Coretta King. Together in the pulpit, a trinity of sister-hood with one now-missing limb, their image was indelible. So too was the final tableau when the six Shabazz daughters shared the tight pulpit space. Betty Shabazz was more than a shero; Attallah, the eldest, reminded stunned listeners, when she called her mother by name: Mommy.

In the shock of tragedy, there was music in that name. "Find the good and praise it," Shabazz would tell her girls. A real person was gone. She would be missed.

Sunday, June 29, 1997

New York                              USA

---

**Heroes and Sheroes**                              Images

O h, to be a June bride!
In the June 30, 1866, edition of *Harper's Weekly,* an etching captured the scene: "Marriage ceremony of a black soldier and a freedwoman at Vicksburg, Mississippi." In joining their spirits as one, their union will give birth to freedom's first generation and define a people. Six months after ratification of the Thirteenth Amendment to the Constitution, abolishing slavery, they know the meaning of freedom. But it will be another two years before they know citizenship. Here, suspended in the moment, they are yet Africans, when politely put. What they make of their lives will define the meaning of African + American for them and for us. You can already see it in their manner and dress as they adopt and adapt the fashion of the day, signs of the times.

A tall figure—in stature, beard, and resolve, every inch the image of Frederick Douglass, man of the people and hero—conducts the marriage ceremony of a bride so blushing that she literally holds a gloved hand to her face. With her love at her side, elegant in his full-dress coat with military flair, they take their vows before a formal wedding party complete with a little flower girl.

A curious sight, in its way, it is a prophetic scene as they pose adorned in the very trappings of those who had oppressed them. Then there is this worthy note on the dresses of the bride and bridesmaids. As slaves, as designers and dressmakers enslaved, these were the women behind the fabled party gowns. It was their vision aglow all along. Who better to wear their creations than they themselves!

Saturday, June 30, 1866

Mississippi          USA

# July

*Cousins: Edna and Muriel* (July 25, 1940). Photographer unknown.
Reprinted courtesy of Muriel Landsmark Tuitt. Edna and Muriel are
daughters of twin sisters, Mabel and Myra, respectively.
For more information, see August 23.

*L*ike her sisters of the cloth—from Jarena Lee, the first woman AME preacher (see June 20), to Barbara Harris, the first woman Episcopal bishop (see February 11)—Zilpha Elaw dared to think her God would call a woman to the pulpit. This so outraged the pious that her loved ones pleaded with her to quit for her own good. Becoming an itinerant minister, in 1839 she headed from Burlington, New Jersey, where she had begun a school, south through the slave states. Hearing a call to go to London but doubting herself, she "argued the matter before the Lord" until a verse came to mind: "say not, I cannot speak; for thou shalt go to all to whom I send thee, and what I command thee, thou shalt speak." Bidding good-bye to her daughter and two grandsons, on July 1, 1840, Zilpha Elaw sailed from New York to London and embarked upon her new life's journey.

Six weeks later, the city that inspired Charles Dickens to write *Oliver Twist* still reeked of the culture that had once peopled the States and Australia with "convicts" guilty of poverty. She would be shocked to see businesses open and vendors hawking their wares on Sunday, "the Lord's day." Some would be skeptical of her. Of them she would write, "Instead of having little faith, they discover none at all." As a preacher, she would indeed be quite busy.

But there on the deck in that summer of 1840, those days stretched ahead like the vast sea before her. Now surveying "the broad canopy above and the rolling ocean beneath, gently moving wave after wave as we glided over its tremulous surface, I observed the birds of the air flying over our heads, and wondered, at such a distance from land, that they were able to take such excursions without resting." How similar her mission was to theirs as she, too, ventured so far from her land. "Oh Lord, how manifold are thy works!" she thought, sailing ahead.

Wednesday, July 1, 1840

New Jersey                           USA

On July 2, 1937, Zora Neale Hurston was in Haiti, where she had gone to research Caribbean lore and to write *Their Eyes Were Watching God* in a seven-week sweat of inspiration. In Port-au-Prince, a change of scene had not brought about a change of heart as she thought of home and began a new essay. Of people and plight, "My People, My People," she wrote. Even the title fumed exasperation.

"Wait until you see a congregation of more than two dark-complected people. If they can't agree on a single, solitary thing, then you can go off satisfied. Those are My People. . . . Study the man and watch his ways. See if all of him fits into today. If he has no memory of yesterday, nor no concept of tomorrow, then he is My People." Zora had a way of seeing things and picking fights. When President Roosevelt referred to America as the "arsenal of democracy" in World War II, she wrote, "I don't know for myself" but perhaps what he said was "arse-and-all." For the "ass-and-all of Democracy has shouldered the load of subjugating the darker world completely." As her biographer, Robert E. Hemenway, would note, "Zora Hurston was a complex woman with a high tolerance for contradiction"—"flamboyant and yet vulnerable, self-centered and yet kind, a Republican conservative and yet an early black nationalist . . . she came to delight in the chaos she left behind."

Then, too, there were moments of peace and of grace. In 1943, she moved to Daytona Beach and bought a houseboat, the *Wanago*. Packing the thirty-two-foot craft with her books and treasures, she found the "solitude I love." Even Florida had not bothered to segregate its shipyards, nor had it found a way to segregate the sea. In the middle of a war, the sea was a strange place to be—but, then, the war for the rights of Africans in the Americas had been going on far too long.

Friday, July 2, 1937

Haiti

---

**Literature**                                   **Attitude**

*O*n July 3, 1960, Alma Thomas was fresh from school with a whole new life ahead of her. At sixty-nine, she had just retired from thirty-five years of teaching to embark upon a new full-time career as a painter.

An artist all her life, she first gained notice as a young architect. Then fascination with marionettes to express feelings otherwise suppressed led to a graduate thesis in puppetry. In 1952, mastery of representational still life yielded work she dubbed her "serious paintings." With retirement, her titles became more realistic, her paintings more abstract, and her signature an impassioned mosaic of geometric color swatches evocative of the intricate Byzantine tile work known as tessera.

She had been taught the art of moving on by her parents. On one terrifying night when her mother was pregnant with her, a lynching party with eager dogs had surrounded their home before recognizing her father, one of the town's most respected men. In 1906, when white riots raged through Atlanta, her parents knew it was only a matter of time before lynchers would come up their hill and, enraged by the family's middle-class life, stop at their door. In 1907, they moved on. As they crossed the Potomac en route to the Washington house Alma would call home for the rest of her life, the senior Thomases told their daughters to remove their shoes—to shake off the dust and sand of Georgia and begin their new life.

Recalling that time on the brink of postretirement artist days, Thomas said: "I have always enjoyed the progressive creativeness of the artist as he releases himself from the past." Like time itself, in an era destined to leave behind the old days of acquiescence to injustice, Alma Thomas—a woman, an elder, black—was moving on, and it showed.

Sunday, July 3, 1960

Washington, D.C.          USA

---

On July 4, 1827, slavery would be legally abolished for African American adults in the state of New York. With that news, for their years of loyal service, Isabella Baumfree and her husband had been promised their freedom one year earlier to the day, July 4, 1826. But when the moment arrived, her slaveowner reneged on the agreement, arguing that the baby to whom Isabella had given birth that year had taken some of her time. The child, like her other four children, was subject to additional years of bondage even after statewide emancipation.

This woman, symbolic of the many, could remember being taken from her parents at just nine years old and sold at auction. The scars of beatings were still etched into her flesh. She determined she would not stay—no matter the choice her husband made. Nor would she run, for that would be wrong, she thought. After one of the many conversations she and her God would have over the years, she picked up her newborn and quietly walked away. Years later, from this habit of talking and walking would come her life's mission—and a new name: she was a sojourner in the service of truth, and so she became Sojourner Truth.

Her story has crisscrossed time, and in it countless people have found inspiration—from schoolchildren to scientists of the National Aeronautics and Space Administration (NASA). On July 4, 1997, after seven months of hurtling through the stratosphere, a landing probe named in her honor—the Sojourner Rover—reached Mars aboard the Pathfinder. How prescient Truth was about many things. She had long said that when she departed this earth, she would not die; rather, she was "going home like a shooting star." As ever, she was as good as her word (see September 13).

Friday, July 4, 1997

New York                    USA/Mars

---

**Freedom**                                    **Defining Ourselves**

On July 5, 1883, Jacob Walker Harris, son of Rev. James Harris and Mrs. Henrietta Dent Harris, and Elizabeth Johnson, daughter of Isaac and Martha Crawford Johnson, were wed at the Church of the Good Shepherd at Walton Way in Augusta, Georgia. Because she was the first free-born daughter in her family, the event took on special significance as the once-enslaved Peter Stewart walked down the aisle with his grand-daughter on his arm, to give her in marriage to a man of her own choosing in a bond no man's slavery could tear asunder. Not only was she the first bride to be wed in the new brick edifice, but the Episcopal congregation was white. The couple's wedding there had been arranged by the rector, Rev. E. G. Weed, as a thank-you for the grandfather's years there as sexton.

Her wedding veil and wreath attached "Virginia style" by Mrs. Mary Owens, the bride was ready. At the head of the church stood Rev. William B. Walker, officiating; there were Dr. Edward Barry and Paul Langdon as ushers, Mrs. Emma Jones as brides-maid, and a church "filled to capacity by colored and white Friends." Down the aisle came the wedding party as Miss Helen Connley played Mendelssohn's "Wedding March" on the organ.

Elizabeth had fallen in love with Jacob one summer's afternoon when he passed her at the well, said "Howdy, little girl," and kept on his way. Six years later here they were, he twenty-five and she sixteen, pledging a life as one. Their wedding gifts "of more than two hundred" included "a handsome parlor lamp, from Rev. E. G. Weed, two large handsome pictures, Mrs. E. G. Weed," a feath-ered satin fan, gilded cups and saucers, silver teaspoons, white kid wedding slippers, and a framed motto: "What is home without a mother." That, too, would come. In thirty-three years of marriage, until Jacob's death in 1916, they had nine children.

Thursday, July 5, 1883

Georgia                              USA

---

**Family**                              **Re-visioning**

*O*n July 6, 1847, this flyer was circulated about town in Frankfort, Michigan.

**FAIR.** The Ladies (of color) of the town of Frankfort propose giving a FAIR, at the house of Mrs. RILLA HARRIS (alias, Simpson,) on Thursday evening next, for benevolent purposes, under the superintendence of Mrs. Rilla Harris. All the delicacies of the season will be served up in the most palatable style—such as Ice Creams, Cakes, Lemonades, Jellies, Fruits, Nuts, &c. &c. It is hoped, as the proceeds are to be applied to benevolent purposes, that the citizens generally will turn out and aid in the enterprise.

One of a series of fund-raising events women sponsored throughout the period, the fair was the means of support for local needs and a step in developing the leadership skills that sustained their growing political acumen. Such events were the core that built congregations in the expansion days of the AME Zion and black Baptist Churches, launched African Free Schools, funded family purchases of loved ones out of bondage, and built businesses. After the demise of *Freedom's Journal,* William Lloyd Garrison, a prominent white abolitionist, launched *The Liberator* on January 1, 1831, with funds raised by black women. The Woman's Association of Philadelphia was founded to help finance the launch of Frederick Douglass's and Martin Delany's *North Star* press on December 3, 1847. So successful was this fund-raising approach that Douglass published the group's constitution in March 1849, acknowledging their contribution to the founding of the press and soliciting others to do the same to ensure the paper's growth and resurrections after assaults and burnings by pro-slavery forces. The fact that there were no banks offering loans to black women, no financiers, no Small Business Administration did not mean that there was no hope, that the will could not find a way.

Tuesday, July 6, 1847

Michigan                                    USA

---

**Business**                              **Cooperative Economics**

The 1952 presidential campaign was under way and the Progressive Party had just unanimously nominated Charlotta Bass, editor and publisher of the oldest black newspaper in the West, the *California Eagle*, as its vice-presidential candidate; Bass was the first African American woman to run on a national ticket. In the words that were to become her campaign slogan: "Win or lose, we win by raising the issues!"

It is a great honor to be chosen a pioneer, and a great responsibility. . . . I cannot but hark back to the thirty years I spent in the Republican Party [where] I could not see the light of hope shining in the distance. . . . Here no one handed me a ready made program from the back door. Here I could . . . write [a] program for me and my people. . . . In that great founding convention in Philadelphia in 1948 we had crossed the Jordan. . . . Now perhaps I could retire. But could I retire when I saw that slavery had been abolished but not destroyed. . . ? To retire meant to leave this world to these people who made profits from oppression in my own land. . . .

This is what we fight against. We fight to live. We want the $65 billion that goes for death to go to build a new life. . . . The $8 billion being spent to rearm Europe and crush Asia could rehouse all my people living in the ghettos of . . . every large city in the nation. We fight that all people shall live. We fight to . . . end colonialism for the colored peoples of the world. . . . I am proud that I am the choice of the leaders of . . . all those who understand how deeply the fight for peace is one and indivisible with the fight for Negro equality. . . . I give you as my slogan in this campaign—"Let my people go."

Monday, July 7, 1952

California                              USA

---

*V*isiting Paris in the 1930s and writing of life there, Eslanda Goode Robeson could report "the average French Negro has no idea that there are important men and important work in Negro art in America." But in London, she was "startled" to find how censored her own view of Africa had been. "In England . . . there is news of Africa everywhere," she wrote in the summer of 1936. And while her husband, singer-actor Paul Robeson, was working in London, she took her young son on an *African Journey,* as the diary of their trip would be titled for publication. A London School of Economics–trained anthropologist in her own right, Essie Robeson was a world traveler for sure, not a fellow traveler as alleged.

"I am a very loyal American," said Mrs. Robeson on July 8, 1953. In the red-scare days of the 1950s, it was amazing how many "very loyal Americans" were being hauled before the House Un-American Activities Committee (HUAC) and its chairman, Sen. Joseph A. McCarthy, and charged with disloyalty. Happiest outside the spotlight trained on her husband, Essie Robeson now faced the glare of scrutiny for her human rights work in the cause of the world's colonized peoples. A perfect target, she was well bred, well educated, well heeled, and well traveled—a definite "threat" to "white supremacy." Even before her husband's renown, she had broken Columbia Presbyterial Hospital's color bar as a surgical pathology chemist. As a photojournalist, she had published numerous essays and a book. Neither "aggressive" nor "meek," she said, "I am convinced that meekness invites pushing around, and brings out the worst in people"—the kind of "worst" that would eventually bring the HUAC down, but not before it had run the ruinous course that forced the Robesons to choose between their commitment to career or to conscience. Essie and Paul Robeson chose conscience.

Wednesday, July 8, 1953

Washington, D.C.          USA

---

**Ideals**                                    **Conscience**

*A* woman had gone for months without a real paycheck — working as she could but earning nothing approximating her income before her business had failed, having been defrauded by an employee. In a slump, she walked for days, seeking an answer to her problem. In the streets, watching others bustle about made her feel not only isolated but useless — unnecessary to life's daily goings-on. What should she do? Where should she turn next? No matter how hard she fought it off, as she later confided, suicide loomed as her best option.

One day, tired of walking, the slump weighing her down, she entered a bookstore in search of a title that would lift her. Some books came close, but what she needed wasn't there. Wandering into a nearby café, an angel came to her. Not a mystical angel, just a woman she had passed in the aisle of the bookstore but hadn't noticed. Somehow, the stranger felt her need. She smiled and the woman, quite uncharacteristically, found herself having tea with a stranger. The stranger spoke of her son and her life. And then she said, "There are good things coming to you. I feel it. Accept your goods. Expect the best."

The woman did not know what the stranger knew or what she saw in her. All she knew was that on that stranger's wings of faith, she felt herself ready to soar. In the stranger's hope, a needy woman was swooped up and carried aloft, just when she needed it most. Some, hearing this story, have interpreted it as religious experience; others speak of coincidence — of being in the right place at the right time. Whatever we call it, there is a bond of sisterhood — a blanket that warms us when we are least aware. Our job is to know when to share it and how to come in from the cold.

Sunday, July 9, 1995

California                    USA

---

**Sisterhood**                                        **Human Spirit**

*J*n 1912, in Washington, D.C., a city with more than its share of monuments to victory and villainy, a statue was proposed to commemorate a heroine over whom many a battle had been won and lost—Mammy. In an editorial in *The Crisis*, Dr. W. E. B. Du Bois was characteristically on point:

> This appreciation of the black mammy is always of the foster mammy, not of the mother in her home, attending to her own babies. . . . And as the colored mother has retreated to her own home, the master class has cried out against her. [The white mother says,] "She is bringing her daughter up beyond her station when she trains her to be a teacher instead of sending her into my home to act as nursemaid to my little boy and girl. . . ." Let us hope that the black mammy, for whom so many sentimental tears have been shed, has disappeared from American life. She existed under a false social system that deprived her of husband and child. . . . In the midst of immense difficulties, surrounded by caste, and hemmed in by restricted economic opportunity, let the colored mother of today build her own statue. . . .

On July 10, 1974, women of another day did just that. Choosing a more suitable shero, the National Council of Negro Women unveiled the Mary McLeod Bethune Memorial—the first such honor to an African American woman in the nation's capital. In bronze likeness, rimmed by skipping children, stands the NCNW founder and educator (see May 18) in Lincoln Park. A tribute to Bethune and to her mentee and successor, Dr. Dorothy Height, whose determination made the monument possible, the memorial was dedicated on what would have been Bethune's ninety-ninth birthday.

Wednesday, July 10, 1974

Washington, D.C.　　　　　USA

In 1921, Lucy Diggs Slowe—a woman best known as the Howard University dean who changed the nature of college life for African American women and an organizer of the National Council of Negro Women in 1935—was actually our first tennis champ. Under the banner of the Monumental Tennis Club of Baltimore, she first ventured to the National Tennis Championships in 1917 to three successive trouncings. Then, in 1921, she won her first of seventeen silver loving cups. For years, African American women attempted further sports breakthroughs to no avail. Then came Althea Gibson—our "First Lady of Tennis" and, from a public standpoint, our "First Lady of Sports."

In 1950—after years of wrangling, politicking, and stalling by tennis officials and aficionados; after notable leadership by Alice Marble, a white former singles champion—Althea Gibson got the nod as the first African American player to enter the National Tennis Championships at Forest Hills, New York. The next year she was invited to play at Wimbledon, England, another breakthrough. And by 1957 she had won both the singles and doubles at Wimbledon and the singles at Forest Hills—a champion on two shores. What more could be said than the message she herself had sent with her victory? What more could be said of the power of second chances than what the child said whose address as a Harlem student had been a home for troubled girls?

On July 11, 1957, a way was found to express the pride people felt in her achievement when her motorcade slowly edged up Broadway in the Wall Street financial district of old New York, the fabled "Canyon of Champions" near City Hall, for the ultimate people's tribute—the ticker tape parade.

Thursday, July 11, 1957

New York    USA/International

---

*W*RITING SCHOOL MARM: ALABAMA TEACHER FINDS LITERARY, MOVIE SUCCESS WITH FIRST SHORT STORY, read a headline in the July 1952 issue of *Ebony*. And the story it told would set in motion a Cinderella dream come true for two women, who would make their marks as firsts in the film industry.

Mary Elizabeth Vroman, born in Buffalo, New York, but a schoolteacher in Alabama, had written a story about a rural teacher's efforts to educate poor children in the segregated South. Based in real life, the story, "See How They Run," was published by the *Ladies Home Journal*. The response was so strong that the story was optioned and Vroman was given the opportunity to adapt her story to film. With that successful script, retitled *Bright Road*, she became the first African American eligible for membership in the Screen Writers Guild. And that was just the first of the firsts.

As the story unfolded, a slender young woman standing prim at a blackboard in a proper 1950s suit wrote in a neat script, "I am the new teacher. My name is Miss Richards." In fact, she was Dorothy Dandridge in her first major screen role. Emitting nary a hint of the vixenesque fire of which she was capable on screen, she was so appropriate in the part that she nearly missed out on another role, the one that would make her a star. Too "regal," too dignified, the casting director remarked, rejecting her upon a first impression. Staging a callback reading, Dandridge entered with tousled hair and a sizzlingly low-cut blouse, every inch the siren. She got the role: *Carmen Jones*. Another first for black women in film, she would receive an Academy Award nomination as Best Actress.

July 1952

Alabama/California             USA

---

*A*nd they said it couldn't be done. On July 13, 1971, three hundred women from twenty-six states met in Washington, D.C., linking forces across the demographic spectrum to found the National Women's Political Caucus. Among them were: Shirley Chisholm of New York, the first African American congresswoman; Myrlie Evers, activist and widow of Civil Rights martyr Medgar Evers; Fannie Lou Hamer, co-founder of the Mississippi Freedom Democratic Party; Dorothy Height, president of the National Council of Negro Women; and Beulah Sanders, vice-president of the National Welfare Rights Organization.

Addressing racial and cultural divides, Hamer set the tone and the limits of many black women when she said, "I got a black husband, six feet three, two hundred and forty pounds, with a fourteen shoe, that I don't *want* to be liberated from." The black man was her partner, not her enemy, in the fight "to bring liberation to all people." From Congresswoman Bella Abzug: "Women have been and are prejudiced, narrow-minded, reactionary, even violent. *Some* women. . . . I will defend that right [to be so], but I will not support or vote for them."

From this coalition would come the first black woman presidential candidate — Shirley Chisholm — whose speech on the floor of the Congress in March 1969, "The Business of America Is War, and It Is Time for a Change," gave stature to the antiwar movement. On July 13, 1972, when the Democratic Convention met in Miami Beach, Chisholm won 10 percent of the first ballot vote. Four years later, another African American woman, Barbara Jordan, would deliver that party's keynote address before a national audience. It was a beginning. Carrying the momentum still further, in 1984, Shirley Chisholm and Pennsylvania's secretary of state, C. DeLores Tucker, would found the National Political Congress of Black Women.

Thursday, July 13, 1972

Florida/Washington, D.C.   USA

---

**Politics**                                                    **Beginnings**

The African American Olympic gold medalists—among them, we celebrate Florence "FloJo" Griffith Joyner, Jackie Joyner-Kersee, Wilma Rudolph, Debi Thomas, Wyomia Tyus. Yet, seventy years after Jesse Owens achieved world renown as a gold medalist in 1936, few realize that Olympic events for women began in 1908 and that two African American women—Tydie Pickett and Louise Stokes—cleared Olympic trials for women's track and field in 1932.

What made their ascent to the Olympics possible was a gradual opening up of opportunity that began in the 1920s in northern city clubs. In 1927, Tuskegee Institute made women's sports a priority—even including two women's events in that year's Tuskegee Relays. With a growing reputation for women's sports among the historically black colleges, Tuskegee developed the competitive model that would earn the first gold medal.

On July 14, 1944, Alice Coachman broke the record for the fifty-meter run. A portent of things to come, four years later at the London Olympics, she broke the record for the Olympic high jump, becoming the first African American gold medalist. In an era when few young women engaged in competitive sports, her talent literally created opportunities for her. She had come to love the sport by watching a boys' meet. With no facility or coach, she created her own high jump with a taut rope. When she entered a Tuskegee meet, the coach watched aghast as she broke the high school record, *without shoes,* and he invited her to train with his collegians in the summer of 1939. Said Coachman, "I've always believed that I could do whatever I set my mind to do. . . . I've had that strong will, that oneness of purpose, all my life."

Friday, July 14, 1944

Alabama/National                    USA

---

**Sports**                                         **Confidence**

With the death of Nina Gomer Du Bois, his wife of fifty-five years, Dr. W. E. B. Du Bois made pilgrimage to his Great Barrington boyhood home, bearing her body for interment. Two weeks later, on July 15, 1950, the *Chicago Globe* published his essay, "I Bury My Wife."

He had admitted to a 1938 Atlanta University convocation, delighted to raise a few eyebrows with a seventieth birthday address, "I have loved wine, women and song." He had not been ever-faithful to Nina. Something in their relationship had dimmed with the death of the infant son he had mourned in his essay "Of the Passing of the Firstborn." Yet, in their fifty-five years, "I do not think it once occurred to either of us as probable or possible that we should ever be separated or the family tie broken." Even when they could not believe in a full life together, they believed in the vow "till death do us part." Now, finally parted, he wrote:

> At the age of only a year and a half, suddenly he died. And in a sense my wife died too. Never after that was she quite the same in her attitude toward life and the world. Down below was all this great ocean dark bitterness. It seemed all so unfair. I too, felt the blow. Something was gone from my life which would not come back. But after all Life was left and the World and I could plunge back into it as she could not. Even when our little girl came two years later, she could not altogether replace the One. So it seemed fitting that at the end of her life, she should go back to the hills of Berkshire, where the boy had been born and be buried beside him, in soil where my fathers for more than two centuries lived and died. I feel that here she will lie in peace.

Burying the grief, he found solace in knowing she had died "in honor and love."

Saturday, July 15, 1950

Massachusetts          USA

---

**Family**                                              **Grief**

*F*AMOUS GRANDMA WALKER WAS 'FULL OF FUN,' read a headline in the *Richmond News Leader* of July 16, 1979, recalling Maggie Lena Walker forty-five years posthumously. Of course Walker had been "full of fun." It was fun to be free of crippling debt born of humiliating racism and sexism, and to know that you had helped free thousands, maybe even millions, of others in your brave new world of empowerment through African American banking.

In 1903, as the first American woman to found a bank, Walker had founded Saint Luke Penny Savings. Said she in 1905, "The Negro is so wedded to those who oppress him that he carries to their bank every dollar he can get his hands upon and then goes back the next day, borrows and pays the white man to lend him his own money." And it could be worse, as the founding of New York's Dunbar Savings Bank illustrates. On its first day of business in 1928, Harlem flocked to its doors, five thousand strong, and most opened new accounts. This despite the Rockefeller-owned bank's unfulfilled promises to appoint black directors to the bank's board and to offer 50 percent of its stock in small lots to potential black shareholders.

Impossible in the land of Maggie Lena Walker! When the Order of Saint Luke, a mutual aid society she had joined in 1883 at age sixteen, fell on hard times, Walker's 1899 initiative saved it and built a community. With $31.61 in the treasury and $400 in debt, she recruited "1,400 new soldiers" with a message so powerful that some listeners wept. It was this: pool your wealth; save yourself. Thirty years later, with membership topping 100,000, the order owned a newspaper, a printing press, a department store, and had issued hundreds of education loans and mortgaged a thousand black homes—all, as Walker noted, "entirely paid for through our bank's help."

Monday, July 16, 1979

Virginia                                      USA

---

**Business**                          **Collective Responsibility**

*B*lacks are "traveling at high speed, materially," Nannie Burroughs noted in the July 1927 issue of *The Southern Workman.* But "With All They Getting," as she titled her article, "preachers, teachers, leaders, welfare workers [must] address themselves to the supreme task of teaching the entire race to glorify what it has—its face (its color); its place (its homes and communities); its grace (its spiritual endowment). If the Negro does it there is no earthly force that can stay him."

It was the Roaring Twenties. African Americans of means were enjoying the high-life high style of the Harlem Renaissance years. All things cultural were abloom for the "New Negro." Despite the fact that the reins of power and segregation were being tightly held to contain the independent economic strivings of blacks, one could even conclude that change for the race really would come. Come it did within two brief years, but not for the best. A careless nation, giddy in its triumph over the "war to end all wars," soon plunged into the Great Depression. Burroughs had been rightly unimpressed by "progress." She had come of teen-age in 1896, when the end of Reconstruction shocked the hopeful to near despair as Jim Crow became law and custom, North and South. An honor student with top scores, she had been barred from teaching in the Washington, D.C., schools for being "too black." Pained but undaunted, by age twenty-six she had founded that city's National Training School for Girls (see October 19). "When the Negro learns what manner of [wo]man *she* is spiritually, *she* will wake up all over," Burroughs argued. "*She* will rise in the majesty of *her* own soul. *She* will glorify the beauty of *her* own brown skin."

The female gender emphasis added here is wholly appropriate to the Burroughs tradition. No shrinking vine, this woman; the snub she suffered did not clip her wings, it powered them. With that power, she taught young women to soar.

Sunday, July 17, 1927

National                              USA

---

**Lifestyles**                                        **Priorities**

*B*y court decree, Jane Johnson was a person, a woman of sound character, able to testify in an American court of law. In 1855, it was rare that law so accurately reflected fact for any black person, enslaved or free. But Johnson wanted to give a special affidavit. Even if it did not save her life, it would set free her soul.

In July 1855, still in the possession of her owner, Col. John H. Wheeler of North Carolina—a U.S. ambassador en route to Nicaragua with Jane Johnson and her two children as his captives— her party stopped in Philadelphia. There, Wheeler instructed her not to speak with any other blacks and, if asked, to tell them she was free—which, of course, she was not. Detecting from the instruction the key to her liberty, Johnson did exactly the opposite of what she had been told. With the help of the Vigilance Committee—a black porter and a white friend—she soon effected her own escape. When her white accomplice was jailed, she risked her own safety in his defense. Arriving at court surrounded by members of the Female Antislavery Society, she told her story. In retribution, two whites were briefly sentenced for "contempt of court," but Johnson went free.

Significantly, Johnson's story was preserved by William Still, a journalist living in Philadelphia who became that city's main line conductor. Each UGRR agent's story was often as compelling as his or her passengers'. Still was no exception. New Jersey– freeborn due to his parents' successful escapes, he became active as a young man. Then, in 1850, came a revelation: an Alabama "package" in his care was actually his own brother, a child his parents had been forced to leave behind enslaved. From that moment, Still and the UGRR were synonymous. In 1872, he documented the accounts of Johnson and others in *The Underground Railroad*, a chronicle based on secret ledgers he compiled for over a decade.

July 1855

Pennsylvania                                    USA

---

**Underground Railroad**                                    **Spirit**

The distance that African American women have traditionally given white feminists is often noted. Rooted in the crisis of race, the story of the women's movement in black and white is one of betrayal dating back to the first Women's Rights Convention in Seneca Falls, New York, on July 19, 1848.

The women's movement was founded by white women active in the abolitionist movement. The founding of the Female Anti-Slavery Society by black women in 1832 (see February 22) grew into an integrated national society with Lucretia Mott, a white feminist and abolitionist, at the helm. In 1840, Mott attended the World's Anti-Slavery Convention in London, where she met Elizabeth Cady Stanton, co-mother of the women's movement. Outraged by slavery and their own ill treatment as females segregated in a curtained gallery at one end of the convention hall, they were particularly moved by testimony on the torture of enslaved women—especially the slaves who could not add to a slaveholder's wealth by producing more slaves. That experience led to the 1848 meeting on women's rights. Women of their times, even the independent-minded Mott and Stanton, ceded the gavel of their own meeting to Mott's husband, James. Stanton's lawyer-husband, Henry, helped with their "Declaration of Sentiments" but balked at its voting rights clause. One man alone, Frederick Douglass (see February 20), supported them as a matter of human rights. But Stanton betrayed his loyalty and black women with her racism. And, in the end, her racism won out over Mott's humanism. "You, like myself, belong to a disfranchised class," Mott wrote Douglass. "We prefer Bridget and Dinah at the ballot box to Patrick and Sambo," mused Stanton, derogating black men in deference to white women. Across time, black women have not shunned the fight for their rights as women, they have shunned the daughters of Elizabeth Cady Stanton.

Wednesday, July 19, 1848

New York                                    USA

---

**Women and Womanhood**                                    **Legacies**

*W*hether a Ghanaian princess, as she asserted, or a Georgia-born preacher, as some alleged, Laura Adorkor Kofey was the greatest organizer for the United Negro Improvement Association (UNIA), second only to Marcus Garvey, who founded the Pan-Africanist organization in Jamaica, West Indies, on July 20, 1914.

In 1915, Garvey had attracted the attention of the Tuskegee Institute's founder, Booker T. Washington, whose untimely death left Garvey without a sponsor for his planned visit to the United States. Undeterred, he arrived in New York in March 1916 and soon built a cooperative international empire rooted in "Africa for the Africans." His first international convention, on August 2, 1920, would be the largest gathering of the diaspora well into the 1950s. "Up you mighty race, you may do what you will!" said Garvey. Whether longitudinally risen from Georgia or from Ghana, Kofey answered his challenge when he needed it most—when jealous leaders became allied with a segregationist government to bring about his imprisonment. Into the fields she headed in 1926, a master organizer, using skill and charisma at camp meetings throughout the South to rally fresh blood and funds to the UNIA. In 1927, she visited the imprisoned Garvey, who, whether motivated by jealousy or "creative differences," denounced her. Undaunted, she launched her own African Universal Church and Commercial League. Extremely successful, she attracted detractors among UNIA friends and foes alike and was assassinated on March 8, 1928. Ironically, it was International Women's Day, a day of homage for women *his-storically* denied. In a slaying foreshadowing that of Malcolm X (a son of Garveyite parents), Kofey was shot down before supporters' eyes. Her murder remains unsolved. After lying in state for days, she was placed in a cortege and was borne through the streets of several cities as mourners lined the route.

Monday, July 20, 1914

International          USA/Jamaica/Africa

**Organizing/Leadership**          **Creative Thinking**

*T*he lady was already a star. But, on July 21, 1983, when Diana Ross stepped before a crowd of 400,000 on the Great Lawn of New York's Central Park, the events of that evening's concert would make her a legend—not a paste-up public relations job, the real thing.

For nearly two years, she'd planned this moment. "I'd picked a dream, a goal, and then imagined all the details, drew it up like a blueprint, designed it, and then I knew it would happen," she said. Life being what it is—glorious and unpredictable—things did not happen as planned. Diana's being what she is—dedicated and tenacious—saved the day. Just as she stepped on her dream stage, a gust of wind brought on a sudden torrent of rain. It was a life-threatening scene. The wind could have sent a light or scaffold flying, killing anyone in its path. The musicians and technicians working electrical equipment could have been electrocuted. The crowd could have stampeded, trampling each other. Friends urged her to leave the stage. She refused. Soaked to the skin, a borrowed jacket over her costume, the "captain" of her dream, she would not "abandon ship." She stood center stage to calm the audience until the last few exited the scene.

Her concert had been washed out by rain, but her dream would never, never be washed up. Her costume had been ruined, the stage set soaked; the souvenirs were drenched and gone. But Diana, her audience, and the sun all came out the next night. At her own expense, she kept her promise to build a playground for the children of New York City. Today, when children romp the playground in Central Park at West Eighty-first Street, they might not know that Diana Ross put it there, but the giggles they share are the words to a song she wrote from a dream she had many years ago.

Thursday, July 21, 1983

New York USA

---

**Music** **Dedication**

*S*arah Breedlove McWilliams was born in Delta, Louisiana, just two years after the Civil War's end, orphaned at age seven when a yellow fever epidemic claimed both of her parents, married at fourteen, and widowed with a two-year-old daughter at twenty. No wonder her hair began to drop. Believing in better days, she headed for Denver, her daughter and $1.50 in hand. July 22, 1905, was her first better day.

Joining Shorter Chapel AME Church, she settled in with her widowed sister-in-law and found work as a cook in the home of the region's best-equipped druggist. It was fortuitous. At night, she tested formulas to repair her hair. What worked for her she tried on her nieces, then offered to others. The response to three innovative products — Vegetable Shampoo, Wonderful Hair Grower, and Glossine — was only the beginning for her fast-growing business. When she was given an opportunity to offer a free demonstration, the products recommended themselves. Washing the future customer's hair with her special shampoo, conditioning it with the "grower," and applying the light oil Glossine before combing the hair with a heated metal comb became her patented trademark. So too was her appearance. She had not yet coined her motto, "Dress your best for success," but her demeanor epitomized it. Wearing a long dark skirt and a crisp white blouse, she carried a sleek black case, and every strand of hair was in place. Mail-order ads in the *Colorado Statesman,* a black newspaper, and product labels featured a dark-skinned woman with thick, long hair — Sarah herself, a woman in whom customers saw themselves.

Within only six months, Sarah was happier still. Remarrying, to a man named Charles Joseph Walker, she took her husband's name, but the "Mrs." sounded dull. Something with a little style was called for as she looked to the horizon — something with flair, like "Madam": *Madam C. J. Walker* (see August 30).

Saturday, July 22, 1905

Colorado                    USA

---

**Business**                                    **Empowerment**

*I*n July 1995 at the University of Virginia, rare book librarians—miners of many an untapped vein of gold—extracted a poem long-forgotten since its anonymous publication two centuries before. In its saga of slavery, "The Sorrows of Yamba; or, The Negro Woman's Lamentation" was the *shero-ic* Everywoman.

"In St. Lucie's distant Isle, Still with Afric's love I burn," Yamba's ode begins. "Mangled my poor flesh with whipping," she prays for death to set her free. Born into a loving family on "Afric's Golden Coast" (modern-day Ghana), she was a married woman with children when one night into her home "rush'd the fierce man-stealing Crew," seizing her and her three children "for love of filthy Gold"—a "Deed of shame for Britons brave." On the Middle Passage to the Caribbean, her baby died at her side in the slave ship's hold. "At the savage Captain's beck," the crew exercised the captives by making them dance on the deck to the "smack" of a cat-o'-nine-tails. Her other children were sold away. Her Massa forced her to eat tainted food, to work when sick, and whipped her into submission. One day she fled "tow'rds the roaring sea to fly" and met a missionary who told her that, like her Massa, she too had sinned and that she must forgive him; her "cruel capture" was "Grace divine." Yamba would allow that it was God's way, but no more. "Let not man the glory share, Sinner, still the guilt is thine." In the missionary's instructions were seeds of self-hatred rooted in African Americans to this day as he analogized everyday human frailty with the greed of the slavetrader and slaveowner; equated being brought to slavery with being brought to God. But what saves Yamba is her memory of home. A stranger in a strange land, she adapts the creed of her new faith, charging "ye British Sons of murder!" to "Mock your Saviour's name no further." In Yamba's truth is the rock upon which theologian Delores Williams stands to observe, "Your Christ is not my Jesus!"

July 1795

St. Lucia

---

**Slavery/Literature**                                   **Rising from Defeat**

*W*ith all that has been done to black women, there are some things we just don't have to tolerate. As those who have internalized this concept would say, "Accept your crown; it has been bought and paid for." Such was the case for Grace Bumbry, a classic diva. Accepting her crown, she has worn it well.

In 1954, no less a legend than Marian Anderson (see April 9), whose struggles had bought and paid for many a crown, heard the seventeen-year-old soprano and proclaimed, "She has a magnificent voice of great beauty." Anointed by her "diety," Bumbry entered a local radio contest and won the top prize: a $1,000 war bond, a trip to New York, and a $1,000 scholarship to the St. Louis Institute of Music. But the institute had never anticipated an African American child with talent profound enough to challenge its racial policies. Reneging on the scholarship promised, it offered a consolation prize of a few segregated private lessons. Said Melzia Bumbry: "It may be *your* school, but it's *my* daughter." Refusing the indignity, mother and daughter declined. And so it was years later, wearing the crown of "Marian and Melzia" that Bumbry was prepared to remain above the fray when news broke on July 24, 1961, that of all the voices from which Wieland Wagner could choose for the role of Venus, the mythic goddess of love, in *Tannhäuser*, his grandfather Maestro Richard Wagner's masterpiece, only one prima donna would do for the new Bayreuth Festival production: Grace Bumbry.

From the tumult raised, it seemed that the nation responsible for the Holocaust was yet experiencing aftershocks. Asked to comment, Bumbry said: "I have a job to do. I can't let myself down." She would not be distracted. At the opening night performance, in a thirty-minute ovation with forty-two curtain calls, great and grateful kudos went to the woman in the "crown," Grace Bumbry.

Monday, July 24, 1961

Missouri/Bayreuth     USA/Germany/Lebanon

---

**Music**                                                    **Self-concept**

*T*hanks to the monument at Fort Leavenworth, Kansas, dedicated on July 25, 1992, by Gen. Colin Powell, and the made-for-television movie produced by actor Danny Glover, the legendary Buffalo Soldiers have been given new life.

Back in the days when the cavalry patrolled the western plains, two units of black soldiers—the Ninth and Tenth Cavalries—became known as the "Buffalo Soldiers." But a century later, when then–Brigadier General Powell strolled the old graveled walkways where they had headquartered at Fort Leavenworth, there was no visible sign of the glory days of the black soldier in the story of the West. True, it was a complicated history. Blacks had participated in the removal of indigenous Americans from their homelands, a feat no less tragic than the loss of indigenous black control of hallowed African ground during the colonial era. That was a part of the history that would have to be analyzed in years and stories to come. But in order to do that, the story of the soldiers themselves would have to be revived. As the history becomes known in its growing complexity, the story of one soldier, William Cathy, is uniquely complex. For this proud warrior was a woman—Cathy Williams. A decorated soldier, she served with distinction from 1868 to 1870. Like one Revolutionary War forebear (see December 26), she had kept her gender a secret.

As we savor the herstory of our own "war for independence" as women of African descent, what shines over all is this: *some women will stop at nothing to achieve their destinies and our collective goal.*

Saturday, July 25, 1992

Kansas                                             USA

---

**Adventure**                                    **Self-determination**

*I*n the wake of the Emancipation Proclamation, the first step was to free the slaves in Rebel states, the second was to enlist those men in the Union army. To avoid "seizure," some owners "warehoused" their "property." In other words, to thwart Emancipation, enslaved men, women, and children were held in the draconian jails of states loyal to the Union where the proclamation was not in effect. On July 26, 1863, pursuant to the intent of the proclamation, orders were given to liberate the slaves of Gen. J. E. B. Stuart and other Confederate Rebels held at Camlin's Slave Pen on Pratt Street in Baltimore. On July 27, Union Col. William Birney wrote, "I have the honor to report that immediately on the receipt of Special Order No. 202, of this date, I proceeded to Camlin's. . . . I found 26 men 1 boy 29 women and 3 infants." In the interests of our humanity and our genealogy, among those liberated that day (the length of time at Camlin's, the slaveowner's name, and county of residence) were:

*Martha Clark* (twelve months, Thomas E. Berry, Prince George); *Susan Collins* and her four-month-old infant *Willie*, born in prison (twenty-four months, Hammond Dorsey, Ellicott's Mills); *James Dent* (twenty-two months, Alfred Osborne, Prince George); *Charles Foote* (fifteen months, Thomas Ristar, Lime Kiln Bottom); *George Hammond* (twenty-four months, Reese Hammond, Ann Arbor); *Lena Harrod* and six-year-old *Rachel* (fifteen months, Dr. Lewis Makel, Georgetown); *Ellen Roberson* (fifteen months, Eriah Hassett, Washington); *Sophia Simmons* (twelve months, William B. Hill, Malbern); *William Sims* (seventeen months, Nancy Counter, Prince George); *John Francis Toodles* (three years, James Mulligan, Prince George); *Betsey Ward* (twenty-three months, Dr. Snyder, Georgetown); *Martha Wells* (twelve months, William B. Hill, Malbern); *Virginia West* (seven months, William Cleggett, Prince George).

*Free at last, free at last, thank God Almighty, they were free at last. . . .*

Sunday, July 26, 1863

Maryland                    USA

---

Freedom                                    **Beginnings**

*J*n 1992, Katie Brown Bennett crossed the threshold of the Family History Center in Colorado Springs and entered a labyrinth of corridors—people, places, time, events—that, once charted, led to her heritage, to her very self. Lured on by a receipt dated July 27, 1843—a bill of sale for the life of her great-great-grandfather, Squire Cheshier—she burrowed deep until her painstaking excavation revealed her family's buried past of two hundred and fifty years.

Throughout her search, Bennett's guiding beacon was her willingness to pursue clues wherever they led. Because both her mother, Cora Cheshier, and her father, Casey Brown, were born in 1907, she began her research with the census of 1910. There, she found her mother listed as a three-year-old. While earlier censuses proved less encouraging, such public records as property ledgers and tax records from her family's North Carolina and Tennessee slaveowners revealed the names of relatives sold away. She interviewed the heirs of slaveholders, tracked bills of sale from plantation to plantation, and was reunited with descendants of those relatives, so long lost.

"I was on an emotional roller coaster," she said of her archaeological dig through the dusky microfilmed and cartoned years. While her discoveries evoked pain, when her work was done she had written a book, *Soaking the Yule Log*, and revealed an ancestral secret. For her enslaved family, the days of Christmas lasted only as long as the log's embers smoldered. To keep the yule log burning, they would select a good sturdy log early in the year, soak it in a creek, and let it dry thoroughly. When lit for Christmas, the yule log burned extra slow, extra long. In those worst of times, her family ignited its spirit, savoring joy from the simplest of resources.

Thursday, July 27, 1843

Colorado                                     USA

---

**Family**                                     **Reclamation**

*L*ynching was no isolated act of a few lawless men, it was the shame of the nation. That was the message African American women had placed before the nation since the lynchings of the People's Grocery Store owner (see March 9) inspired Mary Church Terrell to nationalize and Ida B. Wells to internationalize the anti-lynching crusade.

By Wells's count, between the years 1878 to 1898 no fewer than ten thousand had been lynched. Presidents from Rutherford B. Hayes to Woodrow Wilson had turned a blind eye to the problem. The "Mississippi Plan" of 1890 to disfranchise blacks and consolidate Jim Crow had spread to every southern state. And by 1901, with every black congressman and senator by then forced out through nefarious plots and threats, the subject was no longer raised in Congress. Then came the summer of 1917, when white mobs swarmed the black community of East St. Louis, torching homes and shooting fleeing victims. Then Chicago erupted in fourteen days of terror. This transpired even as black soldiers were fighting and dying for America on foreign shores during World War I. Enough was enough.

On July 28, 1917, people took to the streets of New York City for the Negro Silent Protest Parade. An estimated twenty thousand stood stunned on the sidelines as ten thousand African American men, women, and children walked to the beat of muffled drums down historic Fifth Avenue. Unwilling to wait for the favor of notice in a semisympathetic press, the event was organized by James Weldon Johnson, then executive secretary of the NAACP, and promoted and funded, in large part, through the network established by Madam C. J. Walker and her agents. Maximizing our networks, foreshadowing the Civil Rights era, a powerful image was telegraphed worldwide. *What power is in our midst!*

Saturday, July 28, 1917

New York      USA

---

**Events**                 **Conscience**

*T*hose who speak of the correlation between high intellectual ability and listening to complex forms of classical and jazz music, take note.

In 1934, three-year-old Philippa Schuyler was introduced to the typewriter and the piano. With total creative freedom, she explored both with ease, composing songs, writing and typing stories at will. By four, she was on to bigger things—like spelling *pneumonoultramicroscopicsilicovolcanoconiosis*—a word as commonly used and familiar as its meaning: a lung infection contracted by inhaling volcanic rock dust. It was a word her mother had happened across while reading the morning papers—a word Philippa spelled with ease, as was reported in the *New York Herald Tribune* on July 29, 1935. Making history as the smallest and youngest American child to spell the biggest and longest word in the English language, her spelling was just the first of many accomplishments to come. There was one problem, however, in that the newspapers might have difficulty keeping up with her progress. In reporting the story, the *Tribune* misspelled the key word. No harm done, a month later she was in the news again, the only African American child among four white children featured by *Time* magazine in its story on whiz kids. By age seven, she was touring as a pianist. At ten, she'd finished elementary school. By thirteen, she had composed more than one hundred works, including her first symphonic piece, *Manhattan Nocturne,* performed by the New York Philharmonic in 1944.

To what could her achievements be attributed? Who knew. Her mother said it was fresh, raw food and Philippa's own insatiable curiosity. What George and Josephine Schuyler had done was to answer as best they could.

Monday, July 29, 1935

New York                              USA

---

**Children and Youth**                              **Excellence**

S uch was the magnitude of lynching that, as Ida B. Wells reported, "during the year 1894, there were 132 persons executed in the United States by due form of law, while in the same year, 197 persons were put to death by mobs." Challenging the mobs and those whose silence empowered the violent, she toured England and Scotland to raise international awareness and outrage. Proving correct her accusations of complicity by those whose tolerance fueled the terror, the president of the Missouri Press Association published a letter that smeared Wells and all black women as "having no sense of virtue and altogether without character." Whatever his intent, the letter enlisted local and regional clubs in a national "club movement" with a common agenda.

In Boston from July 29 to 31, 1895, one hundred women from twenty-six states and Washington, D.C., met to strategize a united front as the National Federation of Afro-American Women. Within weeks, the National League of Colored Women would also meet. Pooling their resources, the two groups merged and the National Association of Colored Women was born with Mary Church Terrell (see May 14) as president. In the names of those attending the NACW's first national convention in July 1896 was a people's history. Among them were Ellen Craft, known for her daring and creative UGRR escape (see December 17); Harriet Tubman, the UGRR conductor who had saved thousands (see May 26); Frances Ellen Watkins Harper, our first novelist (see March 4); and Ida B. Wells-Barnett, whose courage had sparked the movement itself. Two moments crowned the moment: Harriet Tubman's entrance into the hall brought the body to a standing ovation; Wells-Barnett's arrival with her newborn son provided the perfect emblem of hope—*and still we go on.* Adopting a motto and an agenda, in the face of those who would attempt to destroy, they would "Lift As We Climb."

Tuesday, July 30, 1895

Massachusetts                    USA

**Organizing**                                              **Purpose**

*J*n the definition of segregation as the "separation of the races" is a key omission—power, the weaponry that turns separation to subjugation. Such is the impact of segregation on music that a white group imitating blacks, the Original Dixieland Band, is credited for making the first jazz recording in 1917, and a white man ironically named Paul Whiteman was hailed "King of Jazz."

Years after slavery's demise, for blacks laboring in the fields of cotton or culture, the Supreme Court's Dred Scott decision (see November 4) still reigned: black men and women "had no rights which the white man was bound to respect." So empowered, the record industry cranked out white images to own black music. Thankfully, greater forces prevented white vaudevillian Sophie Tucker from becoming blues's queen. In 1918, a young Mamie Smith got her first big break singing for black songsmith-producer Perry Bradford, who tapped her to break the record business's color line. Okeh Records had signed Bradford but insisted that Sophie Tucker sing his songs. When scheduling difficulties blocked Tucker, Mamie Smith got the nod. Her first record with Bradford for Okeh worked well, but lightning struck twice with the second, another history maker.

In a testament to the African American press, an ad in the July 31, 1920, edition of the *Chicago Defender* kept the blues black. Boosted by the first ad and its repeat placement, Smith's recording of "Crazy Blues" was so successful that it sold a phenomenal one million copies, granting black women their due as history's authentic blues queens!

Saturday, July 31, 1920

Illinois                                    USA

---

# August

*White Breeze,* 1995 oil on canvas, 48″ × 60″, by Jonathan Green,
Collection of Gilbert and Elizabeth Ney.

On August 1, 1838, thirty years after the slave trade ended, Britain abolished slavery throughout its isles. Galvanizing African American hope, pride in the moment underscored a sad state of affairs. With King Cotton ruling the agricultural South and the industrial North, America's monarch would not soon abdicate its throne, that was for sure. Slavery, that "peculiar institution," would continue to make every black life, enslaved or free, a precarious one. Some, like Zilpha Elaw (see July 1), headed to England. Others, like Nancy Prince, chose the West Indies (see April 14). Ann Plato (see November 25), a teacher at the Colored Congregational Church School in Hartford, Connecticut, memorialized the joy and the quandry of the time in her poem "To the First of August":

> *And when on Britain's isles remote*
> *We're then in freedom's bounds,*
> *And while we stand on British ground,*
> *"You're free — you're free!" resounds.*
> *And, oh, when the youth's ecstatic hour*
> *When winds and torrents foam,*
> *And passion's glowing noon are past*
> *To bless that free-born home;*
> *Then let us celebrate the day*
> *And lay the thought to heart*
> *And teach the rising race the way*
> *That they may not depart.*

To those for whom the griots had so long died, whose memories rose and set in the years of crisis, the decision to stay, to go, and whom to leave behind was a wrenching one. "I told Jesus, be all right if he changed my name. . . ." they moaned in ancestral tones. And in freedom's name, fought on.

Wednesday, August 1, 1838

Connecticut                                    USA

---

*I*n the story of voting rights in the sixties—the 1860s post–Civil War push for the Fifteenth Amendment to the Constitution and the 1960s push for voting rights in the South—a third major voting rights struggle is often overlooked: the crusade for women's suffrage. With the August 2, 1915, edition of *The Crisis*, "Votes for Women: A Symposium by Leading Thinkers of Colored America" was the hot topic of the day.

With men off to World War I, women's work assumed new range and meaning on the homefront—especially black women's work. As the war effort reduced the pool of black male farmhands, "work or fight" rules would be enacted to force black women to the cotton fields whether or not they needed money. Oblivious to their plight, some men were as sexist as their white counterparts, prompting James Weldon Johnson to write: "There is one thing very annoying about the cause of Woman Suffrage and that is the absurdity of the arguments against it which one is called to combat. . . . It takes only a glance to see the striking analogy [to] the old pro-slavery arguments."

From Mary Church Terrell, president of the NACW (see July 30), came this: "What could be more absurd . . . than that one group of individuals who are trying to throw off the yoke of oppression themselves . . . should favor laws and customs which impede the progress of another unfortunate group and hinder them in every conceivable way."

With the growing strength of women as organizers, the Nineteenth Amendment, granting women's suffrage, was ratified on August 26, 1920.

Monday, August 2, 1915

New York    USA

*I*n the August 1938 issue of *The Forum and Century*, Cecelia Eggleston—a Howard University graduate teaching in the Washington, D.C., public schools—posed a question: Given the state of the world, should she have a child? At the pit of segregation, with the doctrine of "white supremacy" contaminating every aspect of life, her problem was not economics, her problem was hope.

> We Negroes teach our youth that the salvation of the Negro lies within the race itself; that, as soon as we become economically independent, educated, cultured, and skillful, we shall arrive. But wealth, education, culture, and technological advancement did not save the Jew in Germany. . . . The Negro child of today, then, must be imbued with more than a normal share of courage, for he has to clear the road before he starts on the journey. . . . The Negro woman who asks her inner self, *Should I have a baby?* will find no ready-made answer. Before she responds to the question irrevocably, she might put it another way: *Will my child rise up to call me blessed or curse the day that he was born?*

With all that has been heaped upon us, all that has been taken from us, should we give up on life itself? "Let no one contaminate your mind," our laborer-prophet William Landsmark (see September 22) would say and ancestors rejoice: *"This little light of mine, I'm gonna let it shine—Everywhere I go, I'm gonna let it shine—Let it shine, let it shine, let it shine. . . ."*

Wednesday, August 3, 1938

Washington, D.C.                    USA

*J*n the summer of 1964, the National Council of Negro Women (NCNW) gave unique meaning to its long-held philosophy, "Leave no one out," with a project that brought white women in—the aptly named "Wednesdays in Mississippi."

Like the teams of women who would participate, the idea had also generated itself in black and white. NCNW president Dorothy I. Height had teamed with Polly Cowan, heiress to the Spiegel fortune, who put her socialite life to work for social action. Setting the local agenda was grassroots organizer and Mississippi Freedom Democratic Party co-founder Fannie Lou Hamer (see May 7). In that Freedom Summer of 1964, forays of young northerners from student teachers to resident physicians had been heading south. On Tuesdays like this August 4, women of privilege boarded planes in the Northeast and Midwest bound for Jackson, Mississippi. On Wednesdays, they would meet with their less fortunate sisters of the Delta and visit Freedom Schools and clinics. And on Thursday mornings, they returned home. For both groups, nurturing a trust in one another constituted a "ministry of presence" as white pilgrims headed down to meet black soldiers opened up their doors, hearts, and hopes. What united them was a concern for children—especially those, barely into their teens, who were going to jail for freedom. But there was more. On June 21, 1964, as the project was about to begin, three young Civil Rights volunteers disappeared—Chaney, Goodman, and Schwerner. On August 4, 1964, their bodies were found murdered; Ben Chaney, the only black, had been mutilated as well.

Uniting in theory was one thing, uniting in the face of harsh fact quite another. A tribute to all who participated, "Wednesdays in Mississippi" continued through the summer of 1965.

Tuesday, August 4, 1964

Mississippi     USA

---

**Organizing**         **Mutual Responsibility**

He was looking at me and talking to someone else, and his mouth grew wide and narrow, small and large, and I wanted him to notice me, but there was so much noise: all the people standing in the gallery, sheltering themselves from the strong rain, had something they wanted to say, something not about the weather (that was by now beyond comment) but about their lives, their disappointments most likely, for joy is so short-lived there isn't enough time to dwell on its occurrence. The noise, which started as a hum, grew to a loud din, and the loud din had an unpleasant taste of metal and vinegar, but I knew his mouth could take it away if only I could get to it . . . so I had to call out my name again and again . . . and by that time my name was like a chain around him, as the sight of his mouth was like a chain around me. And when our eyes met, we laughed, because we were happy, but it was frightening, for that gaze asked everything: who would betray whom, who would be captive, who would be captor, who would give and who would take, what would I do. And when our eyes met and we laughed at the same time, I said, "I love you, I love you," and he said, "I know." He did not say it out of vanity, he did not say it out of conceit, he only said it because it was true.

*T*his passage is from the story "Song of Roland," written in 1993 by novelist-essayist Jamaica Kincaid.

1993

Antigua/USA

---

Our mother, weeping as she went, called me away with the children Hannah and Dinah, and we took the road that led to Hamble Town, which we reached about four o-clock in the afternoon. We followed my mother to the marketplace, where she placed us in a row against a large house, with our backs to the wall and our arms folded across our breasts. I, as the eldest, stood first, Hannah next to me, then Dinah; and our mother stood beside, crying over us. My heart throbbed with grief and terror so violently, that I pressed my hands quite tightly across my breast, but I could not keep it still, and it continued to leap as though it would burst out of my body. But who cared for that? Did one of the many bystanders, who were looking at us so carelessly, think of the pain that wrung the hearts of the negro woman and her young ones? No, no! They were all not bad, I dare say, but slavery hardens white people's hearts towards the blacks; and many of them were not slow to make their remarks upon us aloud, without regard to our grief—though their light words fell like cayenne on the fresh wounds of our hearts. . . . I then saw my sisters led forth, and sold to different owners . . . It was a sad parting; one went one way, one another, and our poor mammy went home with nothing.

*A*s the mother dressed her children for the last time before they were sold apart, she grieved, "See, I am shrouding my poor children," then told her owner, "I am going to carry my little chickens to market." Years later, on a trip to London in 1828 with her owners, Mary Prince became the first African British woman to escape slavery. Three years later she published *The History of Mary Prince, a West Indian Slave, Related by Herself.* Why retell her painful story? Do we not owe it to our ancestral mothers to remember and to bear witness in their names? Do we not owe it to our children to know that Africans were "en-slaved" not "born slaves"? And, in the telling, do we not free ourselves?

1828

Bermuda/England

---

**Slavery**                                                          **Rising from Defeat**

*M*andy and Jourdon Anderson had fled Big Spring, Tennessee, and dear old Colonel Anderson, who would later spare no expense to track them down and get them back. Finding them among the free in Dayton, Ohio, and feeling distressed, he begged them to return to him. This passage is from the reply Jourdon Anderson dictated on August 7, 1865:

> Mandy says she would be afraid to go back without some proof that you are disposed to treat us justly and kindly—and we have concluded to test your sincerity by asking you to send us our wages for the times we served you. . . . I served you faithfully for 32 years and Mandy 20 years. At $25 a month for me and $2 a week for Mandy, our earnings would amount to $11,680. Add to this the interest for the time our wages have been kept back and deduct what you paid for our clothing and three doctor's visits to me and pulling a tooth for Mandy, and the balance will show that we are in justice entitled to. . . . If you fail to pay us for the faithful labors in the past, we can have little faith in your promises in the future. . . . Say howdy to George Carter, and thank him for taking the pistol from you when you were shooting at me. From your old servant, Jourdon Anderson

From this rare letter comes unique documentation of the pay scale for free people of color and the standard of living for the enslaved. As a woman, Mandy worked for, and literally labored for, the colonel by giving birth and adding to his slaveholding assets. Yet her value was only one-third that of her husband, and Jourdon, upon whose back the colonel had prospered, was but "three-fifths a man." With slavery came high profitability! And for Mandy and Jourdon themselves, although "equal pay for equal work" might have been a foreign concept at the time, self-worth was a notion with which they could feel right at home.

Monday, August 7, 1865

Ohio/Tennessee                    USA

---

**Labor**                                    **Self-worth**

*H*aving chronicled a life of achievement, awards, and adventures, Gwendolyn Brooks closed her memoir, *Report from Part One*, with an ode to Fluffy—born September 22, 1961; died August 8, 1971.

Fluffy was the first of Our Family to die. The little dog is gone. We cannot bring him back. His fur was off-gold that edged vaguely into off-white. Fluffy is the name he came with, and it suited him. Nora chose him, at the Animal Welfare Shelter. When Nora chose him, his beautiful tail was wagging excitedly, and his dear puppy head was jerking happily from left to right and back again, and his front paws were planted firmly on the backs of little twin black dogs—one paw on the unprotesting back of a sleepy-eyed little creature, and the other paw on the back of his twin.

He liked to lie in the sun patterns on the living room rug in the early morning.

He liked to race, or saunter, or trot around the back yard, which was *his*, utterly.

We rubbed him off with radiator-warmed towels when he came in from the snow or rain! How he loved it; would stand, sit, or lie down to accommodate his helper. "Now—SHAKE, Fluffy!" And he shoo-oo-k.

He knew how to love without criticism; with acceptance of flaws *and* goodnesses. He knew how to express affection, tenderly, frequently, and how to receive affection, too. He made us all kinder.

How like Gwendolyn Brooks to sum the chapters of her life with a tribute to a friend.

Sunday, August 8, 1971

Illinois                                          USA

---

On August 9, 1942, the army and navy sounded the alarm on the liberty of troops—liberty as governed by personal constitution, that is. HARLEM BARRED TO SERVICEMEN, the *New York World-Telegram* headlined its story on venereal disease on the rise. The police commissioner declared Harlem the source and vowed to wage war on vice. Army and navy officials, on active duty in their war-within-a-war to maintain a segregated military, were hardly objective. Were black men who might or might not have fraternized with white women not routinely charged and even executed for rape? Were white men not given a pass for the same "offense" with a woman of color? With power and bias on their side, restricting white liberty constricted the legal, legitimate black entertainment industry. But the real vice was the power of men to scapegoat women.

Nightlife, the stock-in-trade of every entertainment-driven economy, flourished when the fleet sailed into harbor on leave. Harlem's nightlife—largely white-owned and black-employed— had been a major industry since the 1920s Harlem Renaissance years. Nightclubs had created an influx of entertainment and tourist dollars, providing a steady source of jobs. Prostitutes were the ploy, not the problem. Were downtown's white prostitutes better than uptown's blacks? The attack on vice was a tactic: stigmatizing the black community exported uptown dollars and jobs downtown. It was an old story, told by white feminist labor leader Emma Goldman as early as 1910. "Whether our reformers admit it or not, the economic and social inferiority of woman is responsible for prostitution," she wrote. "Whenever the public mind is to be diverted from a great social wrong, a crusade is inaugurated against indecency, gambling and saloons."

Clearly, Liberty has its price and its vice.

Sunday, August 9, 1942

National                                USA

---

**Social History**                                **Precedents**

*I*n step with the times and tomes of white male presses, *Freedom's Journal* published articles of equivalent bias on the "women's sphere." "Women are not formed for great cares themselves, but to soften ours," went one such tract. "They are confined within the narrow limits of domestic assiduity. . . . Employ yourself in household affairs." As the first African American newspaper (see March 16), the *Journal* had begun its first editorial with the phrase "We wish to plead our own cause." In like manner, Matilda, as she simply and prudently identified herself in one of the earliest documented feminist statements by a black woman, reclaimed title to that "we." Her letter was published in the August 10, 1827, edition:

> Will you allow a female to offer a few remarks upon a subject that you must allow to be all-important? . . . I hope you are not to be classed with those, who think that our mathematical knowledge should be limited to "fathoming the dish-kettle," and that we have acquired enough of history, if we know that our grandfather's father lived and died. 'Tis true the time has been, when to darn a stocking, and cook a pudding well, was considered the end and aim of a woman's being. But those were the days when ignorance blinded men's eyes. . . . The influence that we have over the male sex demands, that our minds should be instructed and improved with the principles of education. . . . Ignorant ourselves, how can we be expected to form the minds of our youth, and conduct them in the paths of knowledge? How can we "teach the young idea to shoot" if we have [not been taught] ourselves? I would address myself to all mothers, and say to them, that while it is necessary to possess a knowledge of cookery, and the various mysteries of pudding-making, something more is requisite. It is their bounden duty to store their daughters' minds with useful learning. They should be made to devote their leisure time to reading books, whence they would derive valuable information, which could never be taken from them.

Friday, August 10, 1827

New York              USA

---

*C*larissa had fled slavery in Virginia and hid out, a $1,000 bounty on her head. By August 11, 1855, she'd reached Philadelphia UGRR stationmaster William Still, who recorded her testimony in his secret ledger of rescues:

Clarissa remained secluded "waiting for the storm to subside." Keeping up courage, day by day for seventy-five days, with the fear of being detected and severely punished, and then sold, after all her hopes and struggles, required the faith of a martyr. Time after time . . . ill luck seemed to disappoint her. . . . In this state of mind, one day, word was conveyed to her that the steamship, *City of Richmond,* had arrived from Philadelphia, and that the steward on board had consented to secrete her this trip, if she could manage to reach the ship safely, which was to start the next day. . . . She had been "praying all the time waiting," but now she felt "that if it would only rain right hard the next morning about three o'clock, to drive the police officers off the street, then she could safely make her way to the boat." Therefore she prayed anxiously all that day that it would rain, "but no sign of rain appeared till towards midnight." The prospect looked horribly discouraging; but she prayed on, and at the appointed hour (three o'clock—before day), the rain descended in torrents. Dressed in male attire, Clarissa left the miserable coop where she had been almost without light or air for two and a half months, and unmolested, reached the boat safely, and was secreted in a box by Wm. Bagnal, a young man who sympathized with the slave, having a wife in slavery himself. . . .

Clarissa "was straightway christened 'Mary D. Armstead,'" given her UGRR passport, and forwarded to her siblings in New Bedford. What's in a name? History is in a name. How many descendants of the Mary D. Armsteads have lost trace of their courageous Clarissa Davises—the once Nailahs and Rashidas? For this, she is all our mothers and we are all her daughters.

Saturday, August 11, 1855

Virginia                                      USA

---

**Underground Railroad**                              **Identity/Memory**

*I*n the late eighteenth century, when city life still nestled near the city's southern tip, free black churches purchased uptown Manhattan sites for burial grounds. When land ownership was made a condition of black male suffrage, families bought land in the area near their cemeteries, the only land available to them. So began Seneca Village, a thriving community stabilized by a high percentage of home ownership and anchored by its churches and its schools. The records of All Angels Church document midwife Margaret Geery's handiwork and growing clientele. From the basement of African Union Methodist Church, Catherine Thomas taught Colored School #3. With her roster of fifty-eight students in 467 sessions, she earned two hundred dollars in 1857—a school year cut short and a bustling community forced to an abrupt demise as the building of Central Park began on August 12, 1857.

As wheelbarrows rolled, twenty thousand men cleared the land; the *way* having been cleared by mighty forces whose palaces rimmed its core. Sullying the magnificent creation of landscape architect Frederick Law Olmsted, the powerful shoveled a bit of dirt themselves, condemning thriving farms as "nuisances" and their owners as "insects." A sketch of crews at work bore the caption "Behind them, huts of disreputable squatters, living among diseased cattle in stench, lawlessness and filth." Like the park itself, this image was carefully cultivated. Truth lay in the story of Seneca Village, a community of African Americans, later joined by European immigrants, living and prospering together in peace. Where did Seneca Villagers go? In the days when free blacks were imperiled by slave catchers who kidnapped them with impunity, with their life savings seized by the devaluation of their property, many are thought to have headed to Canada—and to have returned as volunteers to fight their "War for Liberation," the Civil War.

Wednesday, August 12, 1857

New York                                    USA

---

**Cities and Towns**                                    **Values**

*F*rom the Maroon communities of Jamaica in the early 1700s came a woman of supernatural powers known simply as Nanny—or Granny Nanny—hero of the people in their fight for freedom.

In British Council documents dated August 13, 1670, Jamaica's imperial governor complains of "the Insults of those slaves who begin to grow both numerous and powerfull." These people, powerful enough to escape slavery, were known as the Maroons, meaning the "fierce" ones—a name given them by the Spanish from whom Britain had seized the island first inhabited by the indigenous Caribs. Into the sheltering lush hills of Jamaica enslaved Africans would escape. From there, as Maroons, they sustained a resistance against British rule for the next 150 years—with Nanny as their leader from 1720 to 1739.

Granny Nanny could keep a pot of water boiling without live fire; she could catch enemy bullets and direct them back; she could cast spells with broken glass and blood. So it was said. Whatever the source of her mythic power, it was her unimpeachable skill as a war strategist that saved her people. Striking at night, conch shell horns alerted Maroons and other blacks of a coming raid. From the hills, her warriors would swoop down on British soldiers in attack upon attack and counterattack. To the British she was relentless, to Jamaican slaves she was invincible. As was true for the later betrayal of Gabriel Prosser in his 1800 revolt against Virginia planters, a house slave was the eventual undoing of the Maroons. The exact date and cause of Nanny's death are unknown, but it is said that she was killed by a "quashee," a traitor among the slaves. Today, Maroon descendants still live on land won in their war against Britain. And Nanny, her story retained in folklore and song, remains a proud symbol of Jamaican unity and courage.

Wednesday, August 13, 1670

Jamaica

---

**Heroes and Sheroes**                                             **Power**

*O*n August 14, 1993, author Jill Nelson was vacationing on Martha's Vineyard as she had every summer since childhood. Like other African American families who summer on similar shores, her family exemplified the difference between being an exception and being exceptional. At cottages around the Inkwell, as the island's historically black section (and populace) is known, they have learned to turn the other good-time cheek on the power of a slur. There, in a splendid normality of family and heritage, hard work, accomplishment, making lunch, and putting out life's trash, in all its varied forms, she relaxed in the joy of being herself, undeterred by the way others chose to define or to limit black life. These were the good times. Of life, this day, and of those precious summers, she wrote:

> In the yard of my mother's house, we celebrated her seventy-fifth birthday. We pitched a tent, hung balloons, and, since seven in the morning, made trays of canapés. By twilight the lawn was filled with laughing, talking people, champagne glasses in hand. My mother held forth, a diminutive diva in black and silver. Miles Davis' "So What" floated through the particular air of twilight. We waited until dark to pass out sparklers, lighting them on cue. My niece, Olivia, and the other children raced around the yard, squealing as white sparks flew, delighting in that remembered time when the adults, slightly high and talking intently, forgot all about them. The faces of friends and family, ages three to eighty-three, glowed and became childish as sparklers sprouted from fingertips, lighting up the night and their peaceful faces. Whirling our torches in the air, we sang "Happy Birthday," cradled by the ocean on one side, the island on the other, roots firmly sunk. Someone called out "And many more," and I smiled, knowing that there will be. We are here, we have roots. We are not Halley's Comet, visible only every seventy-five years.

Saturday, August 14, 1993

Massachusetts USA

---

$\mathcal{I}$n 1954, as the Supreme Court rendered its historic decision desegregating public schools and legal scholars debated the intent of the "builders and framers" of the Constitution vis-à-vis race, a woman passed the professional test that would make her a "builder and framer" of brave new-world vision—Norma Merrick Sklarek became the first African American female licensed architect.

Over the years, she would receive such major commissions as the American Embassy in Tokyo, the Pacific Design Center in Los Angeles, and Terminal One of Los Angeles International Airport. She would also realize her vision on a more intimate scale—design that improves the quality of life. Commissioned to design a low-cost housing complex, she knew that altering attitudes toward its planning could change the way future inhabitants would literally view the world and their place in it. But those supervising the project refused. Low-cost housing was as much a way of life as a state of mind. Nothing should be done, city planners demanded, to alter those elements that remind the poor that they are poor—however cost-conscious an improvement, however much it would do for the inhabitants, no matter its dividends in well-being to the wider community. Instead, housing authorities argued for a standard, stagnant plan with rooms in a straight line—rooms that kept residents boxed in with few exceptions and few options. A true "builder and framer," Sklarek dared to design better worlds.

"Architecture" she said, "should be working on improving the environment of people." As with so many dreams in need of a nod, altering the environment with a little (political) climate control could go a long way.

Summer 1954

California                                    USA

---

**Architecture**                                    **Values**

O n August 16, 1914, Dr. Susan Smith McKinney Steward addressed the National Association of Colored Women's Clubs convention in Wilberforce, Ohio. Her paper, "Women in Medicine," provided one of the most complete histories to date of her sister-physicians.

First, there was Rebecca Lee of Virginia, who enrolled in Boston's New England Female Medical College in 1859. She was begrudgingly graduated in 1864 and, with her "Doctoress of Medicine," treated the newly freed slaves of her native Richmond. Next came Rebecca J. Cole, who graduated from the Woman's Medical College of Pennsylvania in 1867. Joining the staff of the New York Infirmary for Women and Children, and making the rounds of the city's poorest and most vulnerable mothers, she was a lifelong crusader for public health education along with its correlative need, civil rights. Then came Dr. Steward herself, the nation's third African American woman to earn a medical degree. Graduating from Long Island Medical College in 1888, she cofounded the Brooklyn Woman's Homeopathic Hospital and Dispensary.

Nearly thirty years a physician, she had begun detecting ills to which her sister-healers were falling victim. "Fortunate are the men who marry these women," she wrote. "From an economic standpoint at least they are blessed threefold measure, in that they take unto themselves a wife, a trained nurse, and a doctor. Unfortunate, however is the woman physician who finds herself unevenly yoked, for such a companion will prove to be a millstone hanged around her neck. But the medically educated women are general good diagnosticians in this direction also." *Physician, heal thyself,* it is said. And they did, with a widely prescribed treatment, divorce. Among the newer doctors, most were marrying twice.

Sunday, August 16, 1914

Ohio                                   USA

"Two days after V-Day," wrote Maya Angelou, "I stood with the San Francisco Summer School class at Mission High School and received my diploma. That evening, in the bosom of the now-dear family home I uncoiled my fearful secret and in a brave gesture left a note on Daddy Clidell's bed. It read, 'Dear Parents, I am sorry to bring this disgrace on the family, but I am pregnant. Marguerite.'"

Worse than the fact that Maya (born Marguerite Johnson) was pregnant was that she had not told her family until three weeks before the baby was due. Nor had she had proper prenatal care. "Who is the boy?" asked her mother. Marguerite told her. "Do you want to marry him?" No, came the answer. "Does he want to marry you?" Sad to say, the baby's father and she had not spoken in months. "Well, that's that. No use ruining three lives." Just over two weeks later, after a "whirl" of doctors, vitamin shots, and shopping for the baby's layette, she gave birth to her son.

Where once these were the stories no one dared tell, the very fact that this day—August 17, 1945—was a day in the life of the people's poet laureate makes it all the more important to be told. For all the frightened young girls and their babies, let it be known: Not only would Maya raise her son, she would learn to make a fabulous quiche! With substance and style, she made a way.

Friday, August 17, 1945

California                                        USA

**Women and Womanhood**                                        **Character**

*I*n her book *Beloved*, Toni Morrison resurrected an African proverb, "It takes a village to raise a child." In *Paradise*, she resurrected the village itself—the story of the long-forgotten all-black towns.

"Ho for Kansas!" Pap Singleton's posters called out in 1878 to those "in pursuit of homes" and peace of mind in the booming all-black towns of the West. From this exodus, African American wagon trains headed out and staked roots on what had once been sacred land for indigenous peoples of the Americas. A tragedy for the Chippewa, the Creek, the Cherokee, and other conquered native peoples, it was a blessing to the victims of ongoing waves of Klan terror.

On August 18, 1886, the town of Eatonville, Florida, would be incorporated. It was just one of a number of all-black towns that sprang up in the South, the West, and the heartland states from the late 1860s into the early twentieth century. But this town—the one a Mr. Joe Clarke dreamed; the one Mrs. Whipple, the bishop's wife, had seen fit to elevate by hauling the old little church across the street to become the new town library—this Eatonville, on January 7, 1891, would give birth to one of her-story's most unique spirits, as independent as her hometown.

From this town of better days would come a woman who believed anything was possible for those who dared believe in magic and dreams. From this town's belief that it could build itself would flow the imagination of an audacious, bodacious author-anthropologist who believed she could create herself and went on to create the line "I love myself . . . when I am laughing . . . and then again when I am looking mean and impressive." From this town would come Zora Neale Hurston.

Wednesday, August 18, 1886

Florida                                    USA

---

*I*n August 1942, Gordon Parks, a rising young photographer, was in Washington, D.C., studying the photos of the masters who had preceded him to the Historical Section of the Farm Security Administration (FSA). With its haunting documentary photos of migrant workers in the dust bowl 1930s, the FSA had been key to President Franklin D. Roosevelt's New Deal plan to rescue the nation from the clutches of the Great Depression. Seeing was believing, and believing was critical to relieving the suffering of millions; so went the president's plan—a success Parks hoped to emulate. "I was impressed by the power of a good picture," said Parks. "More than anything else I wanted to strike at the evil of poverty." His chance came when he met Ella Watson, a charwoman at FSA. With Watson as the subject and Parks as the documentarian, the two created an indelible image of African American womanhood—the photo *American Gothic.*

A woman stands before an American flag that consumes the background of the story. Thin-faced and gaunt; serious, not sour; she pauses. An upturned broom in one hand, a shag mop in the other, she looks directly into the camera—directly into the eyes of her viewer. With half of her face expunged in the shadows, watching us from behind wire-rimmed glasses, her gaze is unrelenting.

In Ella Watson was a portrait of "bigotry and despair." Her father had been killed by a lynch mob, her husband was accidentally shot to death two days before her daughter's birth—she was a hardworking mother and grandmother, suffering in the margins of a government plan to end suffering. Parks presented his portrait to the mentor who had courageously encouraged him to photograph his truths. The verdict: "Well, you're catching on, but that picture could get us all fired."

August 1942

Washington, D.C.          USA

---

**Photography**                                        **Truth**

*T*he Old Testament tells the story of Hagar, an Egyptian slave maiden to Sarah, the wife of Abraham. Unable to conceive a child, Sarah gave Hagar to her husband as a concubine. With Hagar impregnated, Sarah grew so bitter that she forced Hagar to flee into the wilderness. There, by a spring, an angel told Hagar to return to Abraham's home; from her son, Ishmael, would come a nation of men (today's Arab peoples, whose historical sources identify them as descendants of Ishmael). Not long after Ishmael's birth, Sarah conceived a son of her own, Isaac. Fearing that Abraham would favor his firstborn son as his heir, again Sarah cast Hagar out. So Hagar was three times exploited and betrayed—as a woman enslaved, forced to bear a son for her master, and suffering the contempt of her mistress. In her story many have seen the general plight of enslaved blacks, African American womanhood in particular.

In 1862, Mary Edmonia Lewis, a young Oberlin College student, had reason to identify with Hagar. When two white students accused her of poisoning their glasses of mulled wine with "Spanish fly," a supposed aphrodisiac, sexual overtones stirred racial hatreds in the repressive, temperance-minded college town. Lewis was dragged into the night, severely beaten, and left for dead in the snow.

Years later, on August 20, 1870, Edmonia Lewis and her *Hagar* were in Chicago, where she had rented Farwell Hall and advertised an exhibition of *Hagar* in the *Chicago Tribune:* "A beautiful statue representing Hagar as she appeared in the desert [by] the young and gifted Colored Sculptor, of Rome, Italy." Admission for adults was twenty-five cents; fifteen cents for children. Each ticket was a raffle for the statue, which then "sold" for $6,000—a respectable sum in its time. Today, *Hagar,* a work synonymous with the artist, is in the collection of the National Museum of Art.

Saturday, August 20, 1870

Illinois                                        USA

---

**Art**                                        **Self-concept**

*D*uke Ellington, the dean of musicians, loved to tell stories. He told this one about Ole Rastus and some white men in the Civil Rights days, when the glare of television exposed the "race problem." One day, some local white businessmen decided to fix their camera problem: to round up Ole Rastus, put him on TV, and let him tell folks how good the *culluds* had it down there; how segregation was *guud fuh evabody*. They said, "Rastus, when you see that light, the camera is on. You just tell 'em how good we are to you." And Rastus said, "Yassir, boss." They said, "Now, Rastus, just look for the light." And Rastus said, "That light? That red one, boss?" The men said, "Yes." And Rastus said, "The red one that's on now, boss?" They said, "Yes." And Rastus said, "It's my time to tell 'em now, boss?" And, weary of his ways, the men said, "Now, Rastus, now!" Ole Rastus looked the camera dead in the lens, threw out his arms, and yelled, *"HELLLPPP!"*

A century earlier, during the Civil War, it was no laughing matter when Rastus's ancestral spirits, Mill and Jule, saw a Yankee gunboat near their Mississippi River plantation. As it was reported in *The Liberator* in August 1862, their mistress had said, "Now, if the Yankees do stop you all run and hide, won't you?" The closer the boat got, the more wild-eyed became the mistress. "Mill an' Jule, run," she yelled. "Tell all the niggers in the quarters to run to the woods an' hide; quick, for they kills niggers." But Mill and Jule just watched and waited. "Now, 'member I brought you up. You won't take your children away from me, will you, Mill?" Four soldiers, "swords hangin' to their sides," walked up to Mill and Jule and asked if they wanted to leave on the boat. Prophetically, they made the incisive decision to carpe diem (seize the day) that would pour through the veins of generations to infuse Rastus with their sacred wisdom a century later. Mill and Jule looked at Ole Mistress, looked at her beloved "Tara," yelled *"Helllppp!"* got on the boat, and were *gone with the wind!*

August 1862

Slave States                    USA

---

**Humor/Social History**                                **Pragmatism**

*I*n the 1950s, a strategy had evolved to deter blacks from rallying behind (and benefitting from) the Civil Rights movement. Potential voters lining up to register found deputies taking pictures and asking if their white employers knew that they were attempting to vote. A decade later, as women rallied for their rights, similar tactics divided, conquered, and dissuaded supporters. To line up under the banner of women's rights was to imperil their financial and emotional support from their men. The irony was not lost on black women, who equated "high-class" women who could "afford" feminism with the bane of our historic existence, the Miss Annes who had long exploited black women. The very women wielding the lash of racism were now pleading power-poverty.

Hadn't rage against school desegregation by white mothers ignited the August 22, 1957, assault on the home of the NAACP's Daisy Bates for her support of the Little Rock Nine? As Toni Morrison wrote in the *New York Times Magazine* on August 22, 1971: "The faces of those white women hovering behind that black girl at the Little Rock school . . . do not soon leave the retina of the mind." On August 22, 1964, when Fannie Lou Hamer petitioned the Democratic Convention to seat her Mississippi Freedom Party over a delegation of those whose deputies had beaten her to near death for voter registration, hadn't white women joined with white men to expel Hamer from the convention? If any women needed rights, it was black women. Deeper still, wrote Morrison, "Black women . . . could fear them and even love them; but black women have found it impossible to respect white women. I mean they never had what black men have had for white men—a feeling of awe at their accomplishments."

At the pearly gates of herstory, August 22 was *judgment day*.

Sunday, August 22, 1971

National                                        USA

---

*I*n the passport issued on this day, August 23, 1917, to Myra Helena Carlisle, a story of sisterhood emerges. Myra, called "Lena," was born two months prematurely on the island of St. Kitts in 1891, along with her identical twin sister, Mabel. The two seemed so fragile that they were given last rites and round-the-clock care by maids. That was the way things were done then by the Afri-Caribbean elite—those whose lives their mother, Mary Cartey, would more accurately depict as genteel poverty. But living there in Victoria, the section of the island named for England's monarch, reflecting its status as a jewel, albeit a minor jewel, in the British colonial crown, the twins did have a distinct advantage, and survived.

Raised with every available privilege, the sisters and their siblings thrived until their father's sudden death forced their mother to fall back on her inherited land and carriage trade. But there could be little insulation against the general ebbing of prosperity, drip by drip, and the children left home one by one. Among them, in 1912, was Mabel. Her older brothers had already headed to the States, one sending for the next, then the two for her. But once in America! America!—as they called their promised land—the problems of caste and class, like nothing they had experienced at home, took their toll. From having a maid to being a maid herself, Mabel found that her life was drastically different from before. Then came the Great War—a boon for a limited few, but not for Mabel. Nor for Lena, who used every dollar she earned to help raise her younger siblings. Twice, Mabel had thought she had enough; twice, fare increases had put the goal just beyond her grasp. Finally, she made it. She wrote Lena and told her to come. On August 23, the passport was in hand, but not the cash. A ten-dollar increase had gone into effect. In all, five years would elapse before Lena stepped on shore and into her twin sister's arms. Five years to save eighty dollars. *Oh, the power of sisterlove.*

Thursday, August 23, 1917

Basseterre         St. Kitts/USA

---

**Family**                                          **Sisterhood**

*A* mother's pain, a mother's courage, tell the story of Mamie Till Bradley, whose son, fourteen-year-old Emmett Till, had gone to Mississippi to visit relatives and came home a martyr, an international poster child in the fight against lynching.

Arriving in the town of Money on August 24, 1955, Emmett was having fun with some local boys, sharing pictures of his school friends, identifying a white child as his girlfriend. Kidding around, one of the boys dared him to speak to a white woman in a store nearby. Uninitiated in the ways of the South, Emmett took the challenge. Some say he "sassed" the white woman; some say he said only "Howdy." Whatever the fourteen-year-old boy did in the split second when he skipped in and out of the store, giggling, it cost him his life. Days later, at around four A.M. on Sunday, intruders broke into the home of the boy's grandaunt and granduncle, knocked her in the head with the butt of a rifle, and dragged Emmett away before his granduncle's helpless eyes. Three days later Emmett's body was found in the Tallahatchie River. So gruesome was the sight of the child's body that the local sheriff tried to have him buried over the objections of his family. Pressured by the governor, the sheriff shipped the coffin to Chicago with orders that it remain sealed. Mamie Bradley allowed no such thing. There, inside, her child was so mutilated that only his ring identified him: his eye gouged out, his forehead crushed, he'd been shot.

Grieved beyond words, Mrs. Bradley did not crawl inside herself and die, as well she might have. Delaying the funeral four days, she allowed a photo to be published in *Jet* magazine and opened the casket for thousands to pay respects. The world had to know what she knew. Lynching had a face, the face of her child.

Wednesday, August 24, 1955

Mississippi/Illinois            USA

---

**Motherhood**                                    **Courage**

$\mathcal{I}$t was the colonial period, thirty years before the Revolutionary War, when the struggle of indigenous peoples to retain their homelands against French and British incursion erupted in frequent battles and raids. Of those, one at Deerfield, Massachusetts, on August 25, 1746, was immortalized in "Bars Fight," a poem by the first known African American poet—Lucy Terry, a slave.

> *August 'twas the twenty-fifth*
> *Seventeen hundred forty-six*
> *The Indians did in ambus lay*
> *Some valient men to slay*
> *'Twas nigh unto Sam Dickinson's mill,*
> *The Indians there five men did kill*
> *The names of whom I'll not leave out*
> *Samuel Allen like a hero fout*
> *And though he was so brave and bold*
> *His face no more shall we behold*
> *Eunice Allen see the Indians comeing*
> *And hoped to save herself by running*
> *And had not her petticoats stopt her*
> *The awful creatures had not cotched her . . .*

Kidnapped from Africa as a child, hadn't Terry's people—indigenous Africans—fought to defend their world as the Massachusett, Wampanoag, Pequot, and other indigenous Americans were fighting for theirs? Couldn't she see her plight reflected in theirs? An important record of a historic event, her poem also begs a historic question: How many gifted slaves went unheralded because they were less adept at singing their songs tuned to the slavemaster's key?

Thursday, August 25, 1746

Massachusetts                    USA

---

Events/Literature                    Messages

*T*o many, a fetish is negatively associated with magic. Because the African roots of the concept were foreign to Euro-American interpreters, the word conjures meanings superstitious rather than religious, supernatural rather than spiritual, folkloric rather than philosophic. Yet in the sculpted and sainted icons of Europe is kinship to the sculpted and decorated fetishes of Africa. People everywhere, awed by our common world, attempt to decipher its mysteries.

And so it is that a visit to Glidji, a village in Togo, brings us to the door of a sanctuary containing the fetish of Mama Kole. Handpainted on the whitewashed circular wall is the date Mama Kole's fetish arrived from Ghana: August 26, 1680. Inside her space, the faithful undergo treatments for a variety of ills, the spiritual manifested physically or vice versa. Others live here for months, initiates to their religious community. Outside her walls and her realm are skeptics—those who will say that the Ghana and Togo of three hundred years ago knew nothing of dates and history. They will question the power of Mama Kole to heal.

The people themselves know a different message, passed from ancestor to elder by priests and griots. It tells the story of how strangers came to their doors long ago, forcing the people from their land; how their children were dragged to the sea, swallowed by monsters; how only their spirits returned to tell how it was that they were eaten, their lives and futures consumed by a monstrous thing; how their religion, their "ticket" home, was all they could carry with them; how it was held and sustained on the plantations of the Americas; how it returned to their mothers' land transformed, an old soul with a new name—voodoo. What a powerful "book" the fetishes have been born to oversee. History is just one of the names by which we call the stories we must tell.

Monday, August 26, 1680

Togo/Ghana

---

**Religion**                                                                 **Continuity**

*B*ack-to-Africa. For centuries, that had been the quest. In 1811, Paul Cuffe, black America's first international entrepreneur, sailed aboard his *Traveller* with its all-black crew, making the first official return. Then, in the 1820s, thousands of symbolic travelers—men, women, and children—headed "home," founding Liberia. On August 27, 1827, they issued a call to free Africans in America:

> The first consideration which caused our voluntary removal to this country . . . is liberty. . . . We did not enjoy that freedom in our native country. . . . We are proprietors of the soil we live on, and possess the rights of freeholders. . . . Our laws are altogether our own: they grow out of our circumstances; are framed for our exclusive benefit; and administered [by] officers of our own appointment. . . . Forming a community of our own, in the land of our forefathers; having the commerce, and soil, and resources, of the country at our disposal; we know nothing of that debasing inferiority with which our very colour stamped us in America: there is nothing . . . to cherish the feeling of superiority in the minds of foreigners who visit us. . . . The burden is gone from our shoulders: we now breathe and move freely; and know not . . . the empty name of liberty, which you endeavour to content yourselves with, in a country that is not yours. . . .

Telling in its tone, Liberia had been founded with the sponsorhip of slaveowners and sympathizers via the ominously named American Colonization Society—*why would people who had just fought off colonization forty years earlier find colonizing others desirable?* ACS's true mission was to disperse "a dangerous and useless part of the community"—free blacks, slavery's most relentless opponents. To those who took ACS's offer, remaining oppressed in America or finding sustenance in the devil's food of colonization was not choice, it was pragmatism.

Monday, August 27, 1827

Liberia

---

**Pan-African World**                                    **Pragmatism**

*I*t is often remarked how few women were publicly featured at the March on Washington of August 28, 1963.

Of all the featured speakers that day, none were women. But, there on the steps of the Lincoln Memorial, we were well represented. Lena Horne headlined the Hollywood contingent; Josephine Baker, arriving from Europe, briefly flashed her French Legion of Honor medals before the crowd; Marian Anderson returned to the scene where she had lifted her voice and the race in 1939 (see April 9); an army of unnamed warrior-women had fried the chicken and raised the cash to bring in busloads from across the nation; Mahalia Jackson (see September 26), Martin Luther King's favorite singer, graced the mood just before his historic ascent with the spiritual "I Been 'Buked and I Been Scorned"; and when King's voice rang out "I have a dream this day," the person most responsible for getting people out to hear him was a woman—Anna Arnold Hedgeman (see December 31). In a feat of organizing, she personally recruited the participation of forty thousand white clergy for an event that attracted 250,000 marchers, one-third of whom were white.

As the historic day rallied to a close, King looked to the future and concluded on this note: "When we allow freedom to ring, when we let it ring from every village and every hamlet, from every state and every city, we will be able to speed up that day when all God's children, black men and white men, Jews and gentiles, Protestants and Catholics, will be able to join hands and sing in the words of the old Negro spiritual: *'Free at last! Free at last! Thank God Almighty, we are free at last!'*" Thanks to the work of Anna Arnold Hedgeman and her fellow organizers, every group King mentioned was well represented that day.

Wednesday, August 28, 1963

National (Washington, D.C.)          USA

---

*F*ound among the plantation papers of Joseph Allred — thirty-seven documents related to a North Carolina land deal and matters of his estate — is a letter from a female slave formerly owned by the Pattersons, members of the Allred family. Whether the letter was written in her own hand or was written for her is unknown. Sold five times since she was forced from the Patterson home, Vilet Lester was eager for knowledge of her daughter. Now enslaved on a Bullock County plantation, on August 29, 1857, she wrote to "My Loving Miss Patty," her former mistress:

> I wish to [k]now what has Ever become of my Presus little girl. I left her in goldsborough with Mr. Walker and I have not herd from her Since . . . and Boss Says he wishes to [k]now whether he will Sell her . . . as I wis him to buy her an my Boss being a man of Reason and fealing wishes to grant my trubled breast that mutch gratification and wishes to [k]now whether he will Sell her now. So I must come to a close by Escribing my Self you long loved and well wishing play mate as a Servant until death. My Bosses Name is James B Lester and if you Should think a nuff of me to right me which I do beg the favor of you. . . . Pleas to right me So fare you well in love.

Bartered and sold, dragged from one place to another as one would a piece of furniture, amazingly, Miss Vilet is so self-possessed that she reminds the woman who thought to own her that they do, indeed, have a human kinship. However the woman may think of her, this African American woman was once her "play mate." Whether Miss Vilet and her daughter were reunited we do not know. But, one hundred and forty years after it was written, this letter remains among her former owner's treasures, their lives inextricably entwined for posterity. Something tells us that Patsey Patterson *got the message.*

Saturday, August 29, 1857

Virginia                    USA

---

**Slavery**                              **Self-affirmation**

*W*hat a stunning climb it had been from the day she arrived in Denver, broke but not broken, from Delta, Louisiana, in 1905 (see July 22), to the incorporation of her own company in 1911, to being one of the nation's wealthiest women, to this day. On August 30 and 31, 1917, more than two hundred delegates gathered at Union Baptist Church in Philadelphia for the first annual convention of the Madam C. J. Walker Manufacturing Company. And what a triumph it was for this multitude of beautiful, self-empowered women who had taken Madam's challenge, "Look Your Best for Success," to heart—and achieved both.

In an organizational strategy familiar today but revolutionary then, Walker agents were in business for themselves. Organized into a network of business and social clubs, agents shared sales and service strategies, trained at the school named for Madam's daughter A'Lelia Walker. For these entrepreneurs, as one 1913 ad proclaimed, "A diploma from Lelia College of Hair Culture is a Passport to Prosperity." When a southern domestic earned $2 per week and her northern sister earned $10, the average Walker agent earned $23. With Walker's profit-sharing plans, agents reaped greater financial rewards for themselves, their families, and their communities than most of their white male peers. "Perseverance is my motto," Sarah "Mme. C. J." Breedlove Walker told her followers. "I got my start by giving myself a start. I believe in push and we must push ourselves."

"Hit hard and hit often," she rallied. "Strike with all your might." And that was just the sales pitch in her speech, "Women's Duty to Women," delivered within weeks of the terrible wave of anti-black violence that inspired Walker Company's involvement in the Negro Silent Protest Parade (see July 28). "I want to show that Walker agents are doing more than making money for themselves," she urged.

Thursday, August 30, 1917

Pennsylvania　　　　　　　　USA

---

**Business**　　　　　　　　　　　　　　　　**Purpose**

On August 31, 1978, a photographer documented the scene at Monsieur Hassan's temple in Haiti where tourists had paid to see a woman bite off the head of a chicken and watch the blood drip from her mouth. They called it voodoo. Practitioners of the religion known as Vaudun called it a show. Marie Laveau would have called it a shame.

In 1830s Louisiana, Marie Laveau began her fifty-year reign as the "Voodoo Queen of New Orleans." A free woman, Laveau married Jacques Paris in 1819 and then left him for another man. At a time when divorce was taboo in the Catholic city, she pragmatically called herself the Widow Paris while he was very much alive and sufficiently aware of her powers not to object. Living with her lover from Santo Domingo, she then had fifteen children. Haiti's revolt, a few miles offshore, was still a recent memory then, and its success further enhanced the Haitian-based religion's credibility. With authentic insight from her lover and intimate knowledge of human nature from her work as a hairdresser and cook for the city jail, Laveau worked magic. She was one of the most powerful women of her day; fleeing slaves consulted her for safe passage, the powerful sought her amulets to make them more so. She was a healer and a wheeler-dealer.

How appropriate that Laveau is buried in New Orleans' fabled St. Louis Cemetery, where winding streets of stone catafalques and mini-castles form a city of the dead. Once, in 1789, when a high water table flooded the burial ground, coffins freed their hold and floated away. Such is the need for restraint here. In the city where Laveau lived and her soul might or might not be still at work, the dead have been permanently banished from the subterranean world. Each June 23, St. John's Eve, Laveau's faithful come to worship at her grave.

Thursday, August 31, 1978

Haiti

---

# September

*The Landsmark girls* (September 11, 1937). Photographer unknown.
Reprinted courtesy of Muriel Landsmark Tuitt.
For more information, see September 22.

*O*n September 1, 1802, a story in the *Richmond Recorder* titled "The President Again" and written by James T. Callender explained why so many red-haired children of dusky skin tones were regularly seen running about Monticello, the plantation owned by the then-President of the United States, Thomas Jefferson:

> It is well known that the man, whom it delighteth the people to honor, keeps, and for many years past has kept, as his concubine, one of his own slaves. Her name is SALLY. The name of her eldest son is TOM. His slaves are said to bear a striking although sable resemblance to the president himself.

Published in an election year, it was a clear attempt to smear the man who had vowed to his dying wife that he would never remarry. But only the racism of that day to this would find controversy in the wrong end of the story. Thomas Jefferson and Sally Hemings, a woman with whom he lived openly in Paris and under cover of slavery in Virginia, were lovers and the parents of five children. Further thickening the stew, Hemings was the youngest daughter of Jefferson's slaveowner father-in-law, his wife's half sister. In 1787, as minister to France, he brought the fourteen-year-old Sally to Paris to tend his daughter and turned her affection to him as well. There, Sally was a free woman who did not have to return to slavery in the United States. She did so, it is said, with his promise to free her and their future children. While no documentary proof exists, there are the facts of her return, their children's freedom, the memoirs of a slave, Isaac Jefferson, and of her son, Madison, and this: in 1826, when Jefferson died wealthy in legacy only, his slaves were sold to pay his debts. Jefferson's legal daughter, however, arranged freedom for Sally Hemings. Recorded in census documents as white, she then lived with a son until her death in 1835 at age sixty-two.

Wednesday, September 1, 1802

Virginia                                   USA

---

**Social History**                                   **Truth**

"*D*ear Sophronia," wrote Loney from Hazlehurst, Mississippi, on September 2, 1889, "the impression you have made upon me is so deep and powerful that I cannot forbear writing to you, in defiance of all rules of etiquette. Affection is sometimes of slow growth, and sometimes, too, it springs up in a moment."

Loney Butler was young, smitten, "burdened" of heart, and unsure of the object of his affection. "If you have a previous engagement, or if your affection is occupied otherwise . . ." he pondered aloud, afraid that he might be outdone by the competition that would certainly line up for Sophronia Collins, "the sweetest girl on the globe." He had hoped to see her the day before, but she had "disappeared secretly" before he could find her. He tried to send her a letter via a friend, then, thwarted, sent a second letter to be delivered in another's care. He remembered a time when he could count on her "precious notes." Now, was his misfortune in missing her a sign of her true feelings? "Believe me, dearest," he concluded with the hint of a prayer, "I am your sincere lover." Theirs was a love awakened in the era of Victorian propriety, a time when wordly passion spewed forth like geysers—repressed little gurgles just below the surface, percolating in wait for a chance to gush. It was a time when love took the time to blossom and be fulfilled. Corresponding throughout her years as a Rust College student, as faithful as they were to each other, the fates were not always on their side. They went without hearing from each other for months. A letter came back to Sophronia unclaimed from the post office, addressee unknown. Finally, he tried to reach her again.

"Dear Pet," Sophronia responded with delight. "Darling, you spoke in your letter as if I had forsaken you. But never will I forsake such a friend. I love you more and more each day. I think of you every hour, yes, every moment." *What a love.*

Monday, September 2, 1889

Mississippi                    USA

---

**Love**                                                              **Joy**

On September 3, 1838, Frederick Douglass escaped slavery in Maryland to freedom in New York. One week later, he reunited with and married the woman who had spirited his quest for liberty and helped make it possible, Anna Murray.

A free woman of color, Murray had been born to former slaves Bambarra and Mary Murray in 1813 (her assumed birth year). Of twelve children, she was the eighth; the first born free. At seventeen, she left her family for work in Baltimore. There, she joined the East Baltimore Improvement Society and met Douglass. Through forty-four years of marriage, Anna Murray-Douglass courageously supported her husband from bondage to publisher, presidential adviser, diplomat, and "Father of the Civil Rights movement." Yet, beyond contributing part of her savings to fund his escape, little is known of her activism. Perhaps the explanation lies in this quote from Douglass's 1855 autobiography, *My Bondage and My Freedom*:

> While, therefore, it would afford me pleasure, and perhaps would materially add to the interest of my story, were I at liberty to gratify a curiosity which I know to exist in the minds of many, as to the manner of my escape, I must deprive myself of this pleasure, and the curious of the gratification. . . . I would allow myself to suffer under the greatest imputations that evilminded men might suggest, rather than . . . run the hazard of closing the slightest avenue by which a brother in suffering might clear himself of the chains and fetters of slavery. The practice of publishing every new invention by which a slave is known to have escaped from slavery, has neither wisdom nor necessity to sustain it. . . . The singularly original plan adopted by William and Ellen Craft [see December 17], perished with the first using, because every slaveholder in the land was apprised of it.

It's a refrain passed down to liberators of every age: *Don' say all ya see; don' tell all ya know.*

Monday, September 3, 1838

Maryland/New York          USA

---

**Underground Railroad**          **Respect for One's Power**

"The faces of those white women hovering behind that black girl at the Little Rock school in 1957 do not soon leave the retina of the mind."

— Toni Morrison

*I*n the escalating battle to desegregate Central High School in Little Rock, Arkansas, as an opportunistic Orval Faubus, up for reelection as governor, lit the fuse of mob rule, President Dwight D. Eisenhower called out the National Guard to surround and secure the school. Despite the veneer, in the ensuing turf war the situation was hardly under control. At first, the nine black students, the "Little Rock Nine," were to arrive at the school's perimeter separately and be escorted in by the Guard— this at the dubious insistence of school administrators, who barred parents of the Nine from accompanying their children to school. The night before their enrollment, a reporter-friend of Daisy Bates (see April 29)—state NAACP president and chief strategist for the Nine—brought news of a mob already swarming school grounds in search of prey. "This is murder," he warned. Bates corrected her course. The children would meet off-site and be escorted into school as a group by local ministers. But the lack of a phone and exhaustion on the part of all concerned deprived Elizabeth Eckford of the message.

On September 4, 1957, unaware of the change in plans and the terror awaiting her, Elizabeth walked up the steps of the school. National Guardsmen assigned to protect her turned their bayonets on her instead, allowing only white students to enter. Fleeing the scene, Elizabeth was forced to run a hell-crazed gauntlet of white parents and their children. Only the cameras and fate prevented her being lynched on the spot. She tried to duck into a doorway but was refused. When she paused at a bus stop, Benjamin Fine, a reporter, sought to interview her; the father in him lifted her head and whispered, "Don't let them see you cry."

Wednesday, September 4, 1957

Arkansas                                      USA

**School Desegregation**                      **Human Spirit**

*T*he year 1859 marks two milestones in the literature of the African diaspora. From Brazil came Maria F. dos Reis's novel, *Ursula*. And, on September 5, 1859, Harriet Adams Wilson's fictional autobiography—*Our Nig; or, Sketches from the Life of a Free Black*—made her the first African American published on U.S. soil. Poignantly, she did not think of herself as an author; she wrote from the need of a mother. "Deserted by kindred, disabled by failing health," she confessed in her preface, "I am forced to some experiment which shall aid me in maintaining myself and child without extinguishing this feeble life." Her husband deserted her while she was pregnant, and Wilson had written the book to save herself and her son. Sadly, six months after its release she lost her son to fever, and the world of letters soon lost track of the book that historian Henry Louis Gates would republish in 1983.

In the story of how Gates authenticated the book are bare threads of Wilson's life. Her son's death notice appeared in the Amherst, New Hampshire, *Farmer's Cabinet*, and a death certificate recorded his "color" as "Black." Her birth, however, is a mystery. The 1850 New Hampshire census lists a Harriet Adams born in 1827 or 1828, the 1860 Massachusetts census records her birthplace as Virginia in 1807 or 1808. But three letters of endorsement, appendices to the first edition, suggest otherwise. Whatever the facts of her life, Harriet Adams Wilson produced a work so credible that Gates has written, "Had subsequent Black authors had this text to draw upon, perhaps the Black literary tradition would have developed more quickly and resolutely than it did. It seems possible that, by challenging racism directly and unequivocally in a society that was not yet prepared to come to terms with the issue on that level, Harriet Wilson, through no fault of her own, condemned herself to obscurity and unwittingly slowed the emergence of a distinctive Black voice in American fiction."

Monday, September 5, 1859

New Hampshire                              USA

---

**Literature**                                                    **Legacies**

*B*y September 1850, so successful was the Underground Railroad, and so much of a disruption for slaveholders were its flights and rescue missions—called "slave-stealing" by proslavers—that Congress passed the draconian Fugitive Slave Act. Not only did the act mandate issuing warrants against fugitives, but marshals who failed to execute the warrants were fined $1,000. If a slave escaped custody, marshals were liable to compensate owners. With no right to argue in his or her self-defense, any black, freeborn or enslaved, could be dragged to court and "returned" on the testimony of any white. Anyone aiding an escapee was subject to fine and imprisonment.

On September 6, 1850, twelve days before the law took effect, a letter published in the *New Bedford Evening Standard* related the seizure of a woman identified only as "Mary," and foretold the havoc to come. She had fled slavery, but her former owner trailed her from Baltimore to Massachusetts and, accompanied by a sheriff, attempted to kidnap her. As she resisted being shackled into leg irons, alarmed friends rushed to her aid. In the ensuing commotion, Mary made a fast escape.

As the few rights accorded free blacks eroded, implementation of the Fugitive Slave Act rallied whites for reasons ethical and personal. Some took a moral stand that aiding a fugitive honored a "higher authority" than U.S. law. For others, capture of light-skinned biracial people able to pass for white warned of the possibility, even the probability, that whites could as easily be mistaken for blacks and seized without recourse. These factors combined to enact state nullification laws, rescue the Marys, upgrade the route to Canada, and in 1852, make of the anti-slavery tract *Uncle Tom's Cabin* (see March 20) a runaway best-seller.

Friday, September 6, 1850

Massachusetts                    USA

---

**Escape!**                                        **Messages**

*O*n September 7, 1968, the Women's Liberation movement burst into headlines with a stink bomb raid on the Miss America Pageant in Atlantic City. As demonstrators were hauled off to jail, there, to get them out, was longtime Civil Rights attorney and activist Florynce Kennedy. Summing up the event, she said, "It's the best fun I can imagine anyone wanting to have on any single day of her life."

Among the era's most "colorful characters," euphemistically stated, tall and slim, hair cropped to a medium Afro, mouth ready for any test, Flo was into her *look* and on top of her game. Done up in her colorful best—a helmet or cowboy hat, hoedown boots, swaying beads, sparkly glasses, slogan T-shirt, oversized earrings, and always, always, a shopping bag stuffed with papers—Flo would *appear*. As a matter of principle and a way of life, this was a woman who would not be not-noticed. As for the character part, she had plenty, always in evidence. In Montreal for an anti–Vietnam War rally, she watched demonstrators shout down Black Panther Party co-founder Bobby Seale for his notion of race as a factor of the war. Kennedy "went beserk," seizing the platform and shouting down the crowd. That defining moment launched her career on the talk circuit.

"My mama always told us we were precious, so we believed it," Kennedy, one of five daughters, once said. But with being "precious" came privilege and responsibility. The girls' job was to be top students; their parents did the rest. When the Ku Klux Klan tried to terrorize the family, Wiley Kennedy took to the front porch with a shotgun: "Now, the first foot that hits that step belongs to the man I shoot." When an employer accused Florynce's mother, Zella Kennedy, of stealing, outraged and affronted, Mrs. Kennedy thumbed more than her nose (see April 7). In courage and in style, Flo Kennedy was to the manner born.

Saturday, September 7, 1968

New Jersey      USA

---

*A*s students head back to school, we remember the route paved by our ancestors to get today's students up to the school door. We note, too, that for black people, education did not begin in the United States. Africa conceived and built the world's first university—the University of Sankore—in ancient Timbuktu, in what is today the nation of Mali. There, at the crossroads of ancient international trade routes, in a bustling city of one hundred thousand people, scholars from Africa north and south of the Sahara, Asia, and Europe gathered to study law, history, literature, and medicine.

Once our ancestors were in the United States, even enslaved, the pride in and quest for knowledge could not be stilled. In Louisiana, Milla Granson ran a "midnight school" from midnight until two in the morning. A slave woman whose literate mind soared free, she accepted an "apostolic" twelve students per session. Of her hundreds of students, some wrote the freedom passes that helped many escape to Canada. Little wonder slaveowners rejected putting the escape latch of literacy in the hands of their victims. But why was the non–slave labor–based North so afraid to see blacks educated?

"White Americans had to believe that the Negro was inferior and in need of restraint," answers historian Bruce Catton. "Otherwise the whole idea of slavery was morally wrong from the beginning and the Northerner who tacitly consented to it was as guilty as the Southerner who lived with it." To southerners who held slaves; to northerners who profited from slavery by manufacturing the chains and lashes of oppression, and by spinning cotton into gold, free people were dangerous people. For they had learned lessons taught by the Milla Gransons: nothing is impossible for those who truly believe.

September 1845

Louisiana                                    USA

---

**Education**                                    **Possibility**

*J*n September 1832, Sarah Harris, "a colored girl of respect-ability," approached Prudence Crandall with her dream of going to school. Moved by Sarah's pursuit of "a little more learn-ing, enough if possible to teach colored children," the Quaker headmistress welcomed her. When white students withdrew, Cran-dall devoted herself exclusively to twenty "Young Ladies and little Misses of Color." She knew that patrons and neighbors of her two-year-old Canterbury Female Boarding School would not be pleased (see May 23). What she did not know was that they would be violent. As town outrage percolated from pathetic to pathological, one student would write, "The happiness I enjoy here pays me for all. The place is delightful; all that is wanting to complete the scene is civilized men."

Then, in 1834, "about twelve o'clock, on the night of the 9th of September," as a friend, Rev. Samuel May, recalled, "Miss Cran-dall's house was assaulted. . . . I was summoned next morning to the scene of destruction and the terror-stricken family [of stu-dents]. Never before had Miss Crandall seemed to quail. . . . The front rooms of the house were hardly tenantable. . . . Never before had I felt so deeply sensible of the cruelty of the persecution which had been carried on for eighteen months, in that New Eng-land village against a family of defenceless females. Twenty harm-less, well-behaved girls, whose only offence against the peace of the community was that they had come together there to obtain useful knowledge and moral culture, were to be told that they had better go away. . . . My bosom glowed with indignation. I felt ashamed of my country, ashamed of my color. . . ."

A saga that began with such hope ended with such shame: the siege of September 9, 1834 — in the process strengthening the abo-litionist cause and immortalizing a teacher, her students, and the courage they dared.

Tuesday, September 9, 1834

Connecticut                        USA

---

**Education**                                              **Character**

There had been a certain arc to the days of Georgia Douglas Johnson, born on September 10, 1877. Her life eclipsed with her husband's death on her birthday in 1925. A notable figure into her late eighties, in constant communication with her muse, she was colorfully known around Washington, D.C., as the "old woman with the headband and the tablet around her neck." All but forgotten (deliberately, in part) was the renowned poet whose home had been a salon to luminaries of the Harlem Renaissance era, the first African American female poet of national renown in the twentieth century, the writer of these lines, published in 1928:

*I want to die while you love me,*
*    While yet you hold me fair,*
*While laughter lies upon my lips*
*    And lights are in my hair . . .*

A multitalented musician, playwright, columnist, and short story writer of near-white complexion born to multiracial parents, her thoughts were ever dominated by the intersection of color and fortune. A poet not always as appreciated as she should have been by her family, with volumes still unpublished, her papers were literally thrown out on the day of her funeral. What must have been the sibling rivalry between offspring and dreams that produced these lines, published in 1918:

*I'm folding up my little dreams*
*    Within my heart tonight,*
*And praying I may soon forget*
*    The torture of their sight.*

And so she lives on, leaving us to treasure what was left of her to give.

Monday, September 10, 1877

Washington, D.C.          USA

*A* new century had begun but hardly a new age. In September 1902, a woman, wisely anonymous, wrote this letter, published in *The Independent*:

> I have lived all my life in the South, and have often thought what a peculiar fact it is that the more ignorant . . . whites are of us the more vehement they are in their denunciation of us. They boast that they have little intercourse with us, never see us in our homes, churches or places of amusement, but still they know us thoroughly. . . . The Southerner boasts that he is our friend; he educates our children. . . . Did not the Negro by his labor for over three hundred years help to educate the white man's children? Is thirty equal to three hundred?
>
> Many colored women . . . would deny themselves some of the necessaries of life if they could take their little children and teething babies on the cars to the parks of a Sunday afternoon and sit under the trees, enjoy the cool breezes and breathe God's pure air for only two or three hours; but this is denied them. Some of the parks have signs, "No Negroes allowed on these grounds except as servants." Pitiful, pitiful customs and laws that make war on women and babes! There is no wonder that we die; the wonder is that we persist in living. . . . [But] someone will at last arise who will champion our cause and compel the world to see that we deserve justice; as other heroes compelled it to see that we deserved freedom.

Someone, that is, like the writer herself, identifying herself only as "a colored woman, wife and mother." Her message, no longer personal, took on the stature of the Everywoman who *keeps on keepin' on* in small acts of daily rebellion.

Thursday, September 11, 1902

The South       USA

**Social History**              **Self-assertion**

*W*hen the topic is school desegregation in the sixties, it is hard to believe that one means not just the 1960s, but the 1760s *and* the 1860s also.

In 1862, sixteen-year-old Maritcha Lyons became the first black student enrolled in her Providence high school only after her mother petitioned the governor of Rhode Island. The "observed of all observers" in a goldfish bowl existence, as issues go, passing the entrance exam paled in comparison to where she was seated in class. The first year, she sat alone in a double seat. The second year, she was assigned the only single-seat desk in the room until a teacher "cleverly arranged" to have a classmate invite her to share a desk. The third year, she "pre-empted" the issue at "a sunny window seat . . . the admiration and envy of my associates." As she wrote in her unpublished memoir, *Memories of Yesterdays All of Which I Saw and Part of Which I Was*, she was "a proficient pianist" and a leader of her chorus. But "the iron had entered my soul. I never forgot that I had to sue for a privilege which any but a colored girl could have without asking. . . . If any girl tried to put 'on airs' I simply found a way to inform her of my class record. As I never had less than the highest marks, to flaunt my superiority of scholarship was never hard."

Unknown to her, in another school, Charlotte Forten (see May 24), a girl as alone and burdened as she, shared her plight that term. In her diary on September 12, 1862, Charlotte asked, "How long must we continue to suffer—to endure?" Then, boosting her courage, she wrote: "It is ignoble to despair; let us labor earnestly and faithfully to acquire knowledge, to break down the barriers of prejudice and oppression. Let us take courage; never ceasing to work—hoping and believing that if not for us, for another generation there is a better, brighter day in store."

Friday, September 12, 1862

Rhode Island                    USA

---

*O*ld habits die hard; bad habits die harder. With black expectations high and white implementation slow, the nation's most segregated post–Civil War city was its capital, Washington, D.C. There, on September 13, 1865, Sojourner Truth, a woman who had given her all in the fight to end slavery, was violently denied a post-Emancipation courtesy she helped win.

Living in the capital and working with the new Freedmen's Bureau, Truth was about to board a streetcar with a white friend when the conductor pushed her, saying he would put her off if she did not leave voluntarily. Jerking her arm with such force that her shoulder was dislocated, he almost succeeded in ejecting her when her friend interceded. "Does she belong to you?" the driver demanded, speaking of the woman who had emancipated herself and then helped free others. "She does not belong to me, but she belongs to Humanity," replied the friend. Truth reported the incident to the president of City Railway and charged the conductor with assault and battery. Not only did he lose his job, but the trial impacted streetcar etiquette—even before a verdict was handed down. In short order, reported Miss Truth, conductors welcomed black women with "walk in, ladies," and "the inside of those cars looked like pepper and salt."

In a dictated letter to a friend, Sojourner Truth wrote, "It is hard for the old slave-holding spirit to die. But die it must." A relentless voice for the rights of blacks and women, her actions were as good as her words—in fact, better. Her faith in the courts would not always be warranted or sustained—especially in the waning days of Reconstruction—but her faith in herself to act for the general good never wavered. It is the fabric that binds us still, secure in her inspiration.

Wednesday, September 13, 1865

Washington, D.C.          USA

---

**Travel and Transportation**          **Empowerment**

On September 14, 1964, as A. Philip Randolph accepted the Presidential Medal of Freedom, missing from his side was the woman who had been the wind at his back throughout his career. His wife, Lucille Greene Randolph, had died just months before he convened the historic March on Washington of 1963.

Educated as a teacher at Howard University, she moved to New York City with her first husband, but was widowed young. To support herself, she opened a Walker beauty parlor in Harlem and became a friend and associate of Madam Walker (see August 30). After her marriage to Randolph, it was at a Walker party that he met his future partner, Chandler Owens, with whom he co-founded the socialist labor newspaper *The Messenger*, with financial backing from his wife and advertising by Walker. His labor activism put him at the helm of the twelve-year struggle to organize and, in 1937, achieve collective bargaining rights for the first modern black labor union, the Brotherhood of Sleeping Car Porters. When those lean and dangerous days left him threadbare and too poor to make it home, her support got him where he needed to go. There was his leadership of the National Negro Congress in 1936, the challenge to President Roosevelt in 1941 that integrated war industry jobs, and the fight to desegregate the military in 1948. Through it all, his Lucille was there.

For fifty years, the Randolphs were a team—he on the front lines getting done the work of a people, she in the background underwriting the dream. "Buddy" their letters to each other would begin, signed with "love." When the story is told of Madam Walker's success and the empowerment of thousands of black women entrepreneurs, it must also be told that the work of women like Lucille Randolph helped power the Civil Rights era and empower African America.

Monday, September 14, 1964

National/New York          USA

---

**Business/Organizing**                                **Love**

*S*o violent was the anti–Civil Rights movement offensive in Birmingham that the city was known as "Bombingham." Then the unthinkable happened.

At 10:00 A.M. on Sunday, September 15, 1963, in the scurry of excitement that was Annual Youth Day at the Sixteenth Street Baptist Church, four girls went to the basement ladies' room to fix their hair and giggle their way back upstairs in time for the service. They never made it. A Klan member known as "Dynamite Bob" drove up in his truck, detonated his cargo, and bombed the church, killing the four girls, all under the age of fourteen: Addie Mae Collins, Denise McNair, Carole Robertson, and Cynthia Wesley. And there was more. That same Sunday, Birmingham police murdered a black boy with a shotgun blast to the back. A thirteen-year-old boy riding his bicycle was killed by a white mob. For those who brandished "Christian values" as their rationale, their Sunday killing spree had targeted the church because it was headquarters to the movement and the day because that week marked the start of school desegregation.

Who could ignore Birmingham now? It was as if the day were the grande finale of a fireworks display when one last ecstatic round of explosions claims the sky. Maybe it was. That night, President John F. Kennedy stopped "playing politics" to "take sides" at last. In a live national telecast he decried the violence that had defined his era and that would seize his own life two months later. That Wednesday, eight thousand mourners attended a mass funeral for three of the girls, Carole's family having chosen a private service. "God has a way of wringing good out of evil," Dr. King eulogized. "The holy Scripture says, 'A little child shall lead them.'" From the deaths of the four girls, an epiphany of the collective spirit would lead to mass demonstrations against segregation nationwide.

Sunday, September 15, 1963

Alabama                                    USA

---

**Children and Youth**                                    **Sacrifice**

*I*n her 1961 debut at the famed Metropolitan Opera House, Leontyne Price had received an unprecedented forty-two-minute ovation. Surpassing even its own brilliance, her voice had made of its bearer a legend. Now, on September 16, 1966, Price again claimed center stage, this time for the gala opening of the century-old institution in its new home at Lincoln Center for the Performing Arts. So extraordinary was her performance in the female title role of Samuel Barber's *Antony and Cleopatra* that her recording of two scenes from the opera would take Grammy honors as the Best Vocal Soloist Performance, Classical, in 1969.

Just as the highest honor accorded an opera singer—*prima donna assoluta*—has been truncated to the pejorative *prima donna*, so too has the tribute *diva* been diminished to mean a woman with flair though not necessarily the ability or the gifts of a true star. What made Price a diva in the finest sense of the term was her impeccable preparation matched by a sense of herself and her world. Where some, given the power of racism, might have rushed at an invitation to perform at the Met, the Mississippi-born Price rejected the initial call. Determined to be the "first black diva that was going to hang on," she timed her entrance into that stage of her life as she would onto the stage of her art. As she told photographer Brian Lanker for his book, *I Dream a World: Portraits of Black Women Who Changed America*, "I never thought any institution was more important than myself. . . . You let the institution take you over and you are vulnerable, which means that when they get ready, they can discard you."

Changing the way America looked at women of color and of considerable gifts, once the stage was set, she poised herself for the moment and entered with grace.

Friday, September 16, 1966

New York                     USA

---

**Music**                                    **Self-portraiture**

*A* free woman of color and a seamstress, educated in a private Washington, D.C., school and living in Hampton, Virginia, in the 1850s, Mary Peake began teaching enslaved and free children and adults to read from her home. When Hampton was burned to the ground at the start of the Civil War in 1861, she moved, together with her husband and daughter, across the Hampton River and continued her teaching with official sanction from Union headquarters at Fort Monroe. On September 17, 1861, she relocated to Brown Cottage, where she expanded her enrollment, opened a formal school, preserved a precious legacy, and launched an educational movement that continues to this day—all in the six months of life left to her before her death from tuberculosis at age thirty-nine. Mary Peake was a doer.

The story of her expanded school actually dates back to 1839, when fifty-three mutinous captives aboard the cargo schooner *Amistad* were brought ashore in Connecticut. In a landmark case of international import, the first Civil Rights case heard by the U.S. Supreme Court, they were freed in 1841. Throughout the *Amistad* ordeal a group of abolitionists had rallied in support. After, as the American Missionary Association, they raised awareness and money to help alleviate the plight of the enslaved—funds, services, and supplies, donated in part to Mary Peake to keep her school going in 1861. "She has several classes that spell well in the book and out of it," wrote missionary-envoy Lewis Lockwood. "She surely deserves compensation, though she began without any such expectation." The AMA assistance provided Mrs. Peake laid important ground for the five hundred freedom schools it would ultimately expand or launch. From this seed would grow Hampton University. Spreading roots as deep as Hampton's fabled oak, forty of today's historically black colleges and universities trace their lineage to the AMA-funded freedom schools.

Tuesday, September 17, 1861

Virginia                                             USA

---

**Education**                                             **Roots**

*O*n September 18, 1900, in the all-black town of Eatonville, Florida, Death prowled the room of Lucy Hurston. As she lay dying, Mrs. Hurston gave her nine-year-old daughter, Zora Neale, specific instructions. Do not take the pillow from her head until it was cold, she told her daughter. Do not let her friends and neighbors cover the mirror. And by no means let anyone cover the clock in her room. "What years of agony that promise gave me!" Zora would write years later in her autobiography, *Dust Tracks on the Road*. "In the first place, I had no idea that [her death] would be soon. But that same day near sundown I was called upon to set my will against my father, the village dames, and village custom. I know now that I could not have succeeded." Unmoved by the child's protests, the swarm of villagers performed the last rites of the living. Why prolong suffering, remove the pillow from her head. Hood the clock, that it will not stop as the departing spirit looks upon its face. Shield the mirror, that the reflection of the dying may not linger, permanently imprinting itself on the looking glass to the soul. As they raised her deathbed and turned it so that she would face east, Lucy opened her mouth to speak to her child, but a halting breath was all she could extract. "She looked at me, or so I felt, to speak for her. She depended on me for a voice."

What the child could not do then, she would later do as a writer. "Jump at de sun," her mother had urged in better days. "We might not land on the sun, but at least we would get off the ground." September 18, 1937, the anniversary of Lucy's death, saw publication of Zora Neale Hurston's landmark novel, *Their Eyes Were Watching God*.

Tuesday, September 18, 1900

Florida               USA

*A*s an article in the *Denver Rocky Mountain News* of September 19, 1880, confirmed, Clara Brown could take care of business. Once enslaved, in 1859 she walked most of the way from Kentucky to Colorado as a cook for a wagon train. The territory's first African American woman, she began the area's first laundry, and later made real estate investments in a mine and several houses. A deeply religious woman, she offered her home in nearby Central City to the area's first Methodist congregation. A devoted philanthropist, she said, "I go always where Jesus calls me, honey." Answering that call, her home was "a hospital, a hotel and a general refuge for those who were sick or in poverty." Reuniting relatives after Emancipation, she brought twenty-six people from Kentucky to Denver by rail and wagon train, helped them find homes, work, and start a school.

She had done all this for others. But her heart's desire remained unmet. All her scrimping and saving to buy the husband and children from whom she had been sold away had not recovered one of them. Sold so far apart over the years, they could not be found, even after the war's end. Brown posted a $1,000 reward for news of her daughter, Eliza Jane; no news came. Nearing eighty, cheated out of her real estate holdings, poor from having helped so many, her only remaining stock was in friends. In 1882, a letter came. Her Eliza Jane was a widow named Brewer, fifty years old, and living in Iowa. With money borrowed for her fare, Clara Brown traveled to Council Bluffs, Iowa, for the reunion of a lifetime.

At the station, even heavy rain and mud couldn't keep mother and daughter from rushing into each other's arms. Slipping, they fell, still clinging together, and never again let go. Eliza Jane followed her mother to Denver, where they spent what was left of her mother's last years enjoying each other to the fullest.

Sunday, September 19, 1880

Colorado                                    USA

---

**Family**                                    **Life's Work**

*T*he more things change, the more they remain the same. In 1983, when a boy was found to have allegedly hung himself in a Westport, Connecticut, jail, the "drum" that called African American families together in that predominantly white area was the Black Women's Book Group. Little did they know that a century and a half earlier, when similarly situated black women needed to gather, they too had formed book clubs, partaking in "mental feasts" for the mind and peace of mind in tremulous times. Laying out its table, the Female Literary Association of Philadelphia held its first such banquet on September 20, 1831.

By their constitution, "as daughters of a despised race, it becomes a duty . . . to cultivate the talents entrusted to our keeping, that by so doing, we may break down the strong barrier of prejudice." Within months, the African Female Intelligence Society of Boston was founded. In 1833, a group in Providence, Rhode Island, followed. The next year, 1834, saw the rise of the Colored Ladies' Literary Society of New York and Philadelphia's Minerva Literary Association.

Significantly, in earlier years these cities had also followed Philadelphia's lead in the Free African Society movement, following Prince Hall's lead in founding chapters of the Masons. Is it any wonder that there was an ever-ready black network—abolitionist by blood and spirit—to help their enslaved "cousins" board the Freedom Train from Philadelphia to Canada, with major terminals in New York, New Haven, Providence, and Boston?

Tuesday, September 20, 1831

Pennsylvania                    USA

---

*M*aria W. Stewart had known the worst of times. Orphaned at five, she was "bound out" to a Connecticut clergyman's family. Though well tutored in piety, she was given no formal education. At fifteen, she left to make her way as a domestic and learn to read. In 1826, she married James Stewart. When she was widowed three years later, a probate court cheated her out of the estate her husband had amassed outfitting whaling and fishing vessels. Living and teaching in Boston, when she became ill a "colored gentleman (a man of influence) and a lady friend" cheated her of $270 of the $300 raised on her behalf. The pair "laughed . . . to think what a fool they had made of me," she wrote, but she "quietly went on and did the best I could."

Maria Stewart's best was quite good indeed. As her first publisher, William Lloyd Garrison, the abolitionist editor of the *Liberator*, recalled their first meeting, she was "in the flush and promise of ripening womanhood, with a graceful form and a pleasant countenance." These qualities would stand her well on September 21, 1832, as she walked to the footlights of Boston's Franklin Hall and into the glare of public debate as the first American woman to lecture in public.

Over the next year (see February 27), this former domestic raised her mantra: "O, ye daughters of Africa, awake! arise! distinguish yourselves!" "How long shall the fair daughters of Africa be compelled to bury their minds and talents beneath a load of iron pots and kettles?" she demanded. Being the first to break convention has its crown of thorns. Early criticism left her "ashamed and [I] knew not where I should hide myself." Delivering her Boston farewell one year later to the day, she found her peace and place with a message steeped in the proud history of active, outspoken women as far back as the ancients of Egypt. "What if I am a woman?" she dared. "Amen; even so be it." So be it well for us all, indeed.

Friday, September 21, 1832

Massachusetts                    USA

---

**Heroes and Sheroes**                    **Trailblazing**

O n September 22, 1991, the centennial of her father's birth, Muriel Landsmark Tuitt recalled the man born Wilhelm Alfredt Landsmark on the Caribbean isle of St. Eustatius (known as Statia) who immigrated to the United States in 1918. "My first memories of my family history are from my father," she said. "He was a great teller of stories—about his home as a child, coming to America, and other things. On Sundays, we had a regular ritual. After Sunday School he would buy some peanuts. We would roast the peanuts and he would place a big cup in front of him. And when they were all shelled into the cup, we would sit down and eat peanuts and Daddy would read us the *New York Times*. He would read a passage and tell us, 'Now, this is what they said, but the politicians really mean this. . . .' He would read another part and say, 'Now you have to read between the lines. What do you think about this part?' We'd listen to him tell us what was going on all over the world. And to this day, the only nuts I like are peanuts!" Some Sundays her father would also cook. Herewith, her recipe for "Daddy's Cod Fish Stew":

In a large soup pot, soak 2 pounds of boneless dried, salted cod fish in 4 quarts of water for 24 hours, changing the water at least four times until the water stops foaming and all trace of salting disappears. Rinse and drain. Simmer cod fish in cold water for 1-1/2 hours or until fork-flaky. Chop 2 onions, 2 celery stalks, 1 green pepper, 1 sweet red pepper, 4 garlic cloves. Sauté in olive oil in a separate sauce pan. Add 4 skinned and cubed tomatoes and simmer for 1/2 hour with 1t basil, 1/2 t thyme, 1t curry and 2 bay leaves. When the cod fish is cooked, drain, add to mixture, salt and pepper to taste. Simmer 1/4 hour. Turn off heat. Let sit until room temperature. Reheat before serving in a covered soup tureen with your favorite hot sauce. Try it, served with rice or hard-boiled eggs, it's a perfect Sunday brunch straight from the heartland of Statia!

Sunday, September 22, 1991

National                St. Eustatius

**Family**                                    **Legacies**

*D*eath had taken Nettie Harper Dorsey and, hours later, her newborn son. "I entered the Pilgrim Baptist Church and I looked down that long aisle which led to the altar where my wife and baby lay in the same casket," said blues singer-composer Thomas Andrew Dorsey Sr. "I started the walk in the procession and the aisle grew longer and longer before me. My legs got weak, my knees would not work right, my eyes became blind with a flood of tears. There Nettie lay, cold, unmoving, unspeaking." Weeks later, for Dorsey, the pain of their deaths was worse still. "We never really miss anyone until they are gone for good," he would recall years later. "I missed Nettie on every turn of the way. When I came in after a hard day, there was no one to greet me at the door. When I sat to the table to eat, there was no smiling face across the table and I had to eat alone. When I retired for the night, there was no goodnight kiss. I became so lonely I did not feel that I could go on alone. I needed help; my friends and relations had done all they could for me. I was failing and did not see how I could live." Trying to find a path to that help, a friend, Theodore Frye, got him out of the house in which his wife and baby had died and walked him to a nearby school with a piano. There, he "plunked 'round on the piano [playing] a song or two, a hymn [until] an old tune . . . that's sung to many songs" came to him. The tune was 'Must Jesus Bear the Cross Alone?' But the words were all his, autobiographical in tone." *Precious Lord, take my hand. Lead me on, let me stand. I am tired, I am weak, I am worn. Through the storm, through the night . . . Lead me home.*

Not only did the words comfort him, they would soon heal many a wound for others. Forging a new style of personal hymn, as musicologist Michael Harper has noted, Dorsey's hymn for his Nettie changed gospel music from the strictly sacred to the intimate, giving religious music its blues voice.

Friday, September 23, 1932

Illinois                                    USA

---

**Music/Prayer**                                    **Healing**

*I*n 1862, so devastating had been the 243 years since the first Africans landed in 1619 enchained, so all-powerful the slave-holder, that even the woman with the longest lineage of freedom had someone somewhere in her family held captive. Imagine then, the ecstasy that rocked one to the marrow as the first *stone rolled away from the tomb. . . .*

I, Abraham Lincoln, president of the United States of America, and commander in chief of the army and navy thereof, do hereby proclaim and declare . . . That on the first day of January in the year of our Lord one thousand eight hundred and sixty-three, all persons held as slaves within any state or designated part of a state, the people whereof shall then be in rebellion against the United States, shall be then, thenceforward, and forever free; and the executive government of the United States including the military and naval authority thereof, will recognize and maintain the freedom of such persons, and will do no act or acts to repress such persons, or any of them, in any efforts they may make for their actual freedom.

On September 24, 1862, this Emancipation Proclamation, signed by the president two days earlier, was transferred to the War Department adjutant general's office as Executive Order No. 139. But its meaning has been recorded in these lines by Frances Ellen Watkins Harper from the poem "She's Free":

*The bloodhounds have miss'd the scent of her way,*
*The hunter is rifled and foiled of his prey,*
*The cursing of men and clanking of chains*
*Make sounds of strange discord on Liberty's plains. . . .*
*Oh! poverty, danger and death she can brave,*
*For the child of her love is no longer a slave.*

Wednesday, September 24, 1862

Confederate States          USA

---

**Emancipation**                                                    **Resurrection**

*In* 1963, the birth control pill was touted by family planners and social reformers as a saving grace for women "locked in a cycle of poverty." Psychologist Robert Coles went to the source, a woman who told him how she felt. This was her statement:

> They came telling us not to have children. . . . To me, having a baby inside me is the only time I'm really alive. I know I can make something, do something, no matter what color my skin is, and what names people call me. When the baby gets born I see him, and he's full of life, or she is; and I think to myself that it doesn't make any difference what happens later, at least now we've got a chance, or the baby does. You can see the little one grow and get larger and start doing things, and you feel there must be some hope, some chance that things will get better; because there it is, right before you, a real, live, growing baby. The children and their father feel it, too, just like I do. They feel the baby is a good sign, or at least he's *some* sign. If we didn't have that, what would be the difference from death . . . ?
>
> So I turn my eyes on the little children, and keep on praying that one of them will grow up at the right second, when the schoolteachers have time to say hello and give him the lessons he needs, and when they . . . let us have a place you can breathe in and not get bitten all the time, and when the men can find work—because *they* can't have children . . . to find some happy moments, and some hope about things.

Sometimes in our search for answers, we get truth.

1963

Massachusetts                    USA

---

*O*n September 26, 1954, there was a brand-new sound in the air. As the first gospel singer to host a national broadcast, Mahalia Jackson premiered her show on CBS Radio. Joining her as regulars were pianist Mildred Falls, organist Ralph Jones, and Jack Halloran as music director conducting a white quartet.

The show was such a success that it ensured her future and widened the audience for gospel music. Two months later, her debut recording session for the radio giant's sister company, Columbia Records, catapulted her to the world stage.

Criticized, as many a legend before her and since has been, for letting success "change" her, Jackson felt the charge had merit. But it was the repertoire that had changed, not the woman. In the days when she was ascending to the pantheon where she now firmly reigned, she had rallied a following with "Move On Up a Little Higher" and Dorsey's "Precious Lord" (see September 23). Now she sang Rodgers and Hammerstein's Broadway hit "You'll Never Walk Alone." But the strength of her Columbia contract was the company's vision of her as a crossover artist—one who could move music lovers "the world over," meaning one whose sound was black but whose artistic comfort zone was white. In fact, it was Columbia Records that had dubbed her and promoted her to international stardom as "the World's Greatest Gospel Singer." Cognizant of where she had come from and where she was going, Mahala, as she had been christened, pragmatically re-solved what might have become a stand-off dilemma to the other-wise less inspired, less seasoned. Remaining true to her musical voice and identity, she developed a sort of *musicological bilingual-ism,* as Dr. Horace Clarence Boyer notes, "creating two perform-ance styles: one for the recording studio and the other for live performance."

Sunday, September 26, 1954

National                                              USA

---

**Music**                                    **Pragmatism**

*W*e dream, but how do we know we have found our destiny? On September 27, 1923, Elizabeth Johnson Harris could look at a little bound book of ruled pages with words she had penned the day before and feel fulfilled. Her narrative began:

"My Childhood Days with My Grandparents": I was born at August Ga. December 16th 1867. At the old home formerly owned by Dr. Pauline on the South Side of the Wrightsboro Road, near the Monte Sano Heights. I am the only Daughter of Isaac and Martha Johnson, in the midst of four brothers. . . . My Grandmother took me from my mother when I was eleven months old, therefore I was raised up alone by very precise rules. . . . During my infancy, my Grandmother would take me to my mother twice a week. For nourishment from the breast—while at other times I was fed with suitable nourishments for a baby. . . . At this time of my early age there was only one brother. The two eldest had died before my coming. I can well remember how well I was cared for and dearly caressed. . . . Their attention to me was for my support and comfort thro—life . . . and their ways before me, were for my—our—good and benefit then and thereafter.

In eighty-five handwritten pages from post–Civil War glory to Jim Crow defeats, her life unfolds: schooldays, marriage (see July 5), newspaper clippings of her published poems and her son's concerts. A contemporary of Madam C. J. Walker (see July 22), born seven days apart, of roots similarly rural, her story reaches neither the low of orphaned poverty nor the high of extraordinary wealth. It is the middle road walked by an Everywoman. Today, her narrative is in the permanent archives of the John Hope Franklin Collection at Duke University, nested among the works of scholars. It is because she dared to value her own life, to make her dream her destiny, that she is with us still—ours to treasure.

Thursday, September 27, 1923

Georgia                                   USA

---

**Women and Womanhood**                                   **Aspirations**

*I*n the St. Louis riot of 1917, a marauding mob tussled down the street, shooting and lynching every black in sight. As flames rose from burning houses and the skies turned red with fire and the streets red with blood, an eleven-year-old watched in a terror that would propel the rest of her days. Eight years later, for her Paris debut, Josephine Baker took the stage in a frenzy. Nude but for the fans between her legs and in her hands, she performed "*La Dance de Sauvage*" with La Revue Nigre, and left the Théatre des Champs-Elysées a star. Introducing the Black Bottom and Charleston to Europe's fancy feet, at nineteen she was the toast of Paris nightlife. She would return home to the States from time to time and try to make a go. But she gave up trying when the demand for "mammy songs" and "polite" silence in the face of her being called a "nigger wench" made her choices matters of life and death. In 1937 she became a French citizen. When other expatriates fled their adopted home as World War II took Europe, she joined the Resistance, for which she was later awarded the Legion of Honor by French war general and president Charles de Gaulle. There were high-ups when she bought a castle, adopted children from the world over, and dubbed her family the "Rainbow Tribe." There were down-lows when she was evicted from her castle in 1968, an old woman, impoverished and alone with her cat, discarded into the rain.

On September 28, 1971, she wrote her friend Henry Janes: "I had no protection at all because the police refused to give protection to me, saying that they had not police force enough. . . . The police of Sarlat completely stopped me from going into the castle, protecting the new comers, saying that I had lost the castle and the battle of my grotesque idea of Brotherhood." Writing from the Place des Moulins Monte Carlo, she had been rescued by an old friend, Princess Grace of Monaco. But then, no matter her terror and her daring, she had always been a class act.

Tuesday, September 28, 1971

France

---

**Social History**            **Rising from Defeat**

*O*n September 29, 1967, Alex Haley stood on the dock overlooking the harbor of Annapolis, Maryland, where his first known ancestor in the Americas had been dragged ashore to slavery two centuries earlier to the day, September 29, 1767.

No artist had etched the scene. No message in a centuries-old family Bible memorialized the event. Yet Haley knew where and when and how the terrible deed had been done. Having endured the unspeakable, his family would speak it again and again, knitting together their generations. In the record of his grandmother's front porch tales, heard when he was a boy, were clues that guided Haley along his *Roots* from Henning, Tennessee, to Juffure, Gambia. "Just about as the dusk was deepening into the night," he wrote, with "lightning bugs flickering on and off around the honeysuckle vines," they would recall "snatches and patches of what later I'd learn was the long, cumulative family narrative that had been passed down across the generations." Alex's griot-grandmother recalled that "the African" had been brought to a place they pronounced "Naplis," sold off the ship to a "Massa John Walker" to work his "Spotsylvania County, Virginia," plantation; that he refused the slave name of "Toby" and bore the lash for his insolence. His name was "Kin-tay," he said, a pledge of allegiance each generation passed on in his memory. Kin-tay would point to the river near the plantation and say what sounded like "Kamby Bolongo" and tell all who might remember that he had been born four suns upriver from "Kamby." That was the way grandmother taught grandson the tale. As a man, armed with her words, Haley sailed to West Africa, where the words reclaimed their meaning. Kamby became Gambia, with its Gambia River. Upriver were griots who identified "Kin-tay" as Kunte Kinte. In Virginia, old Walker plantation records held the arrival date and purchase of a slave renamed Toby whose generations had kept him alive in mind.

Friday, September 29, 1967

Maryland          USA/Gambia

---

**Family/Historiography**                    **Reclamation**

*J*n 1966, passage of the National Historic Preservation Act ordered the excavation and testing of sites of known significance before any new construction. With this mandate, archaeologists began their dig on Reade Street, the hub of colonial New York City, before groundbreaking for a new federal office tower could begin. Once known as "Republican Alley," in 1795 the area had been laid over the "Negroes Burying Ground," built a century before. In June 1991, as a backhoe gingerly removed sixteen feet and centuries of rubble, human bones were found. But the bones were thought to be a tumble of formerly disturbed remains rather than one intact burial. Then, on September 30, 1991, came the find that would forever change history's view of the early African American experience. A large ancient nail was the first clue. Then came a colonial-period coffin lid covering a complete, intact skeleton lying face up with its arms resting at its sides. With fortune, the researchers hoped, possibly fifty such burials would be unearthed. They would uncover four hundred and twenty-seven. There, in the African Burial Ground, the spirits of people whose very existence had been literally "covered up" for two hundred years arose. And what a tale they told scientists at Howard University's Cobb Laboratory, where the remains were transported for study and preservation.

For centuries American history had declared black people void of culture. Burial number 340 decreed otherwise. Her teeth had been filed. In her grave was a clay pipe. One hundred and eleven waist beads of cowrie, amber, and glass draped her hips. Blue and white beads rimmed her wrists. From her teeth and her treasures, she was likely captured and brought to the colonies as a teenager or young adult from Senegambia (modern Senegal and Gambia). From her respectful interment, in the pride of the earliest African Americans, we find the roots of our culture.

Monday, September 30, 1991

New York         USA

---

# October

*Diana Ramos performs "Kathleen I and II"* (1974). Photographer unknown.
Reprinted courtesy of Diana Ramos.

*F*or six weeks the bark *Sunbeam* sailed the high seas in search of great whales. By the voyage's end, three would have been slaughtered and boiled down for their valuable blubbery oil on board—a good trip for owner, captain, and crew. Landfall meant a good homecoming, too, for the women who had kept watch and faith, waited and prayed them home to islands of Cape Verde, off the western coast of Africa.

To every generation are born special women who understand the wiles of the sea goddess, who well know their role in the ménage. These are the women in love with men in love with the sea—men drawn for love or lust or money or all; men whose "she" is a ship, the sea goddess their muse, and the sea their tango. And so it was on October 1, 1904, that these special women, these "second wives," left their misty hilltop homes in homage. Stepping along the jagged cliffs of Brava, past donkeys heavy laden, they paused, gathering breath, along the massive stone walls that lined their winding cobbled route to the sea. Barefoot and humble, beautiful and brown, bundles piled atop their heads, they walked, gazelles, unbowed and graceful in their mission. Arriving at the door of the sea-wife, they came to thank her for returning their husbands once more. They knew that their men had not always left willingly; that the Portuguese were known to drag their black male prey off the streets and straight to the dock in these waning years of the whale trade. But there comes a time for love and lore, a time when a woman must turn away hardship and sing of romance, knock on the door and collect her man.

As it was said in Cape Verdian proverbs by wives of men who had left them for the sea and come home with a living, "I cannot get angry with the sea, because all I have the sea has given me."

Saturday, October 1, 1904

Cape Verde Islands

$\mathcal{I}$n 1932, with the Depression in full swing, Zora Neale Hurston, fresh from two breakups—her infamous split with Langston Hughes over *Mule Bone* and a divorce—was living hand-to-mouth, like most people in those days. The days of prestigious grants and fellowships were gone, dried up with the flow of cash. But she had talent, drive, and a ready arsenal of nerve.

When Hurston shared her short story "The Gilded Six-Bits" with a friend, he forwarded it to *Story* magazine, where it was accepted and published in August 1933. While the editors never confirmed her suspicions, she was fairly certain that they must have done some "missionary work among publishers" on her behalf because she soon received four queries asking if she had a book-length work they might consider. One, from J. B. Lippincott Company, struck her. She was indeed writing such a book, she responded, though "not the first word was on paper when she wrote him that letter." Swinging into action, she used the $3 she had to pay two weeks' rent on a small house with a bed and a stove, and got to work. When her money ran out, her cousin gave her fifty cents of her own $3.50 weekly earnings for groceries. Three months later, with help from family and friends, Zora finished the book. The next bend was getting it typed. A judge asked his secretary to help on a promise that if the book was accepted, she would be paid. She read the book, agreed to type it, and even provided the paper and carbons. On October 2, 1933, Hurston's precious bundle was ready. She had $1.83; the postage was $2.00. Borrowing the rest, she sent the manuscript the next day.

Two weeks later, on October 16, 1933, Zora Neale Hurston had two things in hand: an eviction notice and a wire accepting the book, her first novel, *Jonah's Gourd Vine,* and offering a $200 advance. What a life.

Monday, October 2, 1933

Florida                                      USA

---

**Literature/Work**                                      **Success**

*A*sk author Sharon Robinson (see January 24) about her first professional love—midwifery—and she'll tell you, "I love everything about it. It's beautiful to help give life. Birth, that's the true miracle." Robinson is part of a contemporary back-to-basics movement in birthing that merges the best of what a hospital offers on the side of caution with the natural, traditional, laying on of hands woman-to-woman.

From the earliest colonial days of the Americas, black women, both enslaved and free, had been prominent midwife-healers to women across the racial divide. Then the era of doctor-assisted hospital births took over for all but the least-privileged mothers. Now the trend is swinging back in favor of midwives. Like Robinson, Faye Wattleton, a trained midwife and a former president of Planned Parenthood, advocates for the restoration of women's powers—the rights and responsibilities of women over our own bodies. But the woman who might have most inspired a rebirth of the profession was Josephine Riley Matthews of South Carolina. In a profession practitioners often consider "divinely sanctioned," with her gift for life passed down from her great-grandmother, "Mama Jo" was a fourth-generation midwife.

It was in honor of her seventy-sixth birthday that she received the greatest gift ever. On October 3, 1973, four years after she had originally planned to retire, she was called to a birth. When her handiwork was done, Josephine Riley Matthews had delivered triplets. Three years later her home state named "Mama Jo" Woman of the Year and Outstanding Older American.

Wednesday, October 3, 1973

South Carolina USA

---

**Women and Womanhood** **Reclamation**

*I*n a scrapbook devoted to his baby daughter's life, George Schuyler, proud father and journalist, wrote:

Philippa! It is the evening of October 4, 1932, and you are two days over 14 months of age! You are an excellent mimic. You clap your hands, snap your fingers, drum, dance, pat your stomach and rub your head all in direct imitation of your father. You play hide and seek with him and have a most jolly time. Yesterday . . . for the first time you walked on the sidewalk with your father and ran after dead leaves which you collected and brought to him. Today your mother took you out and you walked three blocks! Last night your mother went to the theater (*Ol' Man Satan*) and you stayed home with your father who put you to bed!

When, at age three, the daughter was declared a prodigy (see July 29), her mother would attribute it to a diet of raw food. But who could deny the added benefits of the hefty heapings of love with which that food had been served!

Tuesday, October 4, 1932

New York                    USA

*T*o visit artist Elizabeth Catlett on this day in 1982 is to be ushered past romantic Mexican walls along an idyllic garden walk into what could be called no less than a *living* room, a place where two people have made a world all their own.

It is a lush, peaceful place, honed by ritual togetherness, hewn of a tenacity of spirit forested in the 1950s, when McCarthyism dominated all like the strokes of a too-broad brush on a narrow canvas. The 1950s, when leaving the States wasn't good enough, but what more could one do? Hunted for being true to her art and her people rather than being assimilated into "the mass of American artists who must say nothing socially," she was tracked and blacklisted. The fact that her husband, the son of a poor family, envisioned in art an obligation to work for the people—the Mexican railroad workers, in particular—was further cause for intimidation. In Mexico, beyond U.S. borders, Catlett was harassed for her interests and friendships of twenty years earlier. Was there no statute of limitations? By the 1980s, as with the bad times, there seemed none on the good, either.

Behind the living room, at opposite ends of the courtyard are two studies. Throughout the workday, husband and wife walk back and forth, exchanging critiques, encouragement, fruit. "We work collectively," says the now-venerated Catlett of her marriage to fellow artist Francisco Mora, known as Pancho to family and friends, a revolutionary of the brush inspired by a revolutionary of the people. In the word *collectively* is the freedom she has found in a land where one of the stories not told north of the Rio Grande about the Alamo is that the newly seized Texas wanted a slave state, and Mexico, having ended Spanish slavery, had already elected a black president. But, here in this time, *this living room,* is talk of love—of work, of art, for one's spouse, and of life.

Tuesday, October 5, 1982

Mexico City        Mexico

*A*llen and Betty Manning had an agreement. When planting time came each spring, he would lay out eight careful rows of white-and-yellow corn in a private garden just for her beside their Newby, Oklahoma, farmhouse. Her part of the bargain was her special tried-and-true fried corn and hot water corn bread. How it got special was the reason they needed to make a bargain. Without it, she'd tear up his entire field, shucking and testing ear upon more, until she found the perfect, freshest ears. Nothing was too good for her Al, at least that's what she'd tell him when his planting and her shucking got into a contest.

Her fried corn was cooked in bacon fat with a touch of sugar. The secret ingredient in her corn bread was a little cracklin'—fried pork rind diced fine. But none of that was possible without the corn itself. Into her garden she would go for the October harvest, field-testing the ears but shucking them all the way down until each shiny kernel was clear to the eye. Taking her thumbnail, she'd pierce a kernel, squirting out the milk. "If'n it won't squirt, it's too old to make good fried corn." That was her philosophy: to be the best, start with the best. And in a family where careful attention to food preparation and excellent cooks were a tradition, her fried corn was considered the very best.

Married at age twenty-seven on July 4, 1875, she and Allen had a good life. She lived to be a hundred and two—squirting and shucking and cooking her harvest corn, preparing for, getting, and giving no less than the best.

October 1913

Oklahoma                                    USA

The Black American West Museum and Heritage Center: here, separating the wheat from the chaff of fact and western lore, is the story of black frontier life; the hard-driving days of the cowboys, mail-order brides, miners, ranchers, and sod busters, often overlooked in African American history. Located in a national historic landmark–designated home, this Denver museum honors its former owner, Dr. Justina Ford, awarded her medical license on October 7, 1902.

From 1902 to 1952, as Colorado's first and Denver's only black female physician, Dr. Ford built a multiracial general practice among the city's racial and fiscal outcasts of every color. Like most female doctors of her day, her work in obstetrics and gyne-cology kept generations of families at her door—and her at theirs. Called upon for home delivery of a baby, she was known to per-form the delivery in her slip to avoid contaminating mother and baby with street germs from her outer clothes. "I tell folks I came to Denver in time to help them build Pike's Peak," she would say. It was almost true; she'd delivered seven thousand babies in fifty years, quite a legacy for one doctor. Hers was quite a home-based office and hospital. Despite her credentials and due to racism, she and her diverse clientele were denied hospital privileges at Den-ver General. She was also denied membership in local medical societies for most of her career.

After delivering one of her last babies in 1951 at age eighty-one, she said, "This one will be of a generation that will really see opportunity. I won't see the day, you very well may, and this one certainly will. Hard feelings between the races; my people will come up from the South, your people will see that come to pass. When all the fears, hate, and even some death is over, we will really be brothers as God intended us to be in this land. This I believe. For this I have worked all my life."

Tuesday, October 7, 1902

Colorado                                    USA

---

**Medicine**                                    **Healing**

*I*t was official. With Tennessee's vote to ratify the Nineteenth Amendment to the Constitution, women's suffrage had been won that August, at last. Within weeks, for the first time in history, women across the land would be eligible to vote.

On October 8, 1920, the International Congress of Women met in Memphis, heart of the state that had brought to victory a seventy-two-year battle for suffrage and self-respect begun with the Women's Rights Convention of 1848 (see July 19). With delegates in a festive mood, it was left to Palmer Institute founder Charlotte Hawkins Brown (see June 17) to put the moment in context. Millions of women of color, along with their men, would still be denied the vote in most southern states. Challenging professed Christian women to make of their faith a fact, she detailed everyday acts of sanctioned violence by whites on blacks—including the taboo, lynching.

The next year, relentless and true to her word and her challenge, she continued to fight the good fight by suing the Pullman Company. She had been forced to ride a Jim Crow car despite her first-class ticket. Her lawyer sued for $3,000; the company offered $200. They would settle for no less than $1,500, demanded Brown. Even threats by some sponsors to abandon support for the school did not sway her. To be so deterred would be to lose more than the suit. As she wrote her attorney, "I am willing to become a martyr for Negro womanhood in this instance and give up my chance of holding, as friends, people who would withdraw because of my attitude. . . . A few of us must be sacrificed perhaps in order to get a step further."

Friday, October 8, 1920

Tennessee                              USA

---

wendolyn Parker grew up in privilege born of vision, sacrifice, luck, and very hard work. Her grandmother, Beatrice Burnett Parker, launched the NAACP's first Youth Council. Her great-grandfather, Dr. Aaron McDuffie, co-founded Durham's first "colored" hospital and the business that earned the city's reputation as the "Black Wall Street," North Carolina Mutual Life Insurance. And there was more, baggage plush but hefty for a young girl to haul. Doing her best, in the fall of 1973, Parker enrolled in New York University Law School.

It had been customary for the school paper to publish the average LSAT (Legal Scholastic Aptitude Test) scores of the incoming class. That year, the paper broke out the LSAT racially: 600s for whites, 500s for blacks. Eight years into affirmative action, seeds of its destruction were being sown; the Supreme Court's *Bakke* ruling against quotas designed to give "progress" a quantifiable benchmark was five years away. The article made it clear that so-called minorities were "special admittees." Soon after it appeared, Parker was interrupted by a stranger's decree: "A lot of us are kind of mad . . . about the scores." Engaging her own LSATs (life skills aptitude tests), she asked if he felt smarter than black students. "That's what the whole thing's about," he dared. She tested him. Their undergraduate schools: he had a solid Midwest credit; she, Harvard. Their grades and scores: hers were higher on both counts. "Just between the two of us," she jabbed, "I'd say you were pretty lucky to be here, wouldn't you say?"

What does a test score really mean? At NYU that year, it meant that whites could continue to presume a superiority born of racism over every black face. Encountering Parker might not have changed her classmate's presumptions about blacks, but it changed his presumption about himself. It was a beginning.

Autumn 1973

New York                          USA

---

**Education**                                    **Assumptions**

*O*n October 10, 1935, the curtain of Broadway's Alvin Theatre ran up on George Gershwin's *Porgy and Bess*. The show's success was shared by two African American women in leading roles—Anne Brown as "Bess" and Eva Jessye behind the scenes as the show's choral director.

So arresting was the voice of Anne Wiggins Brown that the folk opera based on the novel *Porgy* made room in its Broadway title for Bess. Significantly, as culturally black as *Porgy and Bess* was, with its story of life on Catfish Row, all of the show's creative credits (contracts and royalties, too) went to whites: Du Bose and Dorothy Heyward for the novel and the show's book; George Gershwin for the musical score; his brother, Ira Gershwin, and Du Bose Heyward for the libretto. But the authenticity of the voices, sonorous and rich, came from the choral arrangements by African American composer Eva Jessye—the same Eva Jessye who was quoted as saying, "I am a woman. I am a woman of African descent. I am a black woman. And I am happy to be exactly as God made me."

The economics of Broadway was a pattern that would continue through the end of the century—even, most notably, in the musical *Dreamgirls*, ironically based on the story of the Supremes and Motown, a music industry giant with a full roster of African American composer-arrangers. There, too, whites got credit for the tunes, but does anyone doubt that it was Harold Wheeler's arrangements and Jennifer Holiday's yet-unequaled rendition of "And I Am Telling You I'm Not Going" that turned the show (box office and record sales, too) to gold?

Thursday, October 10, 1935

New York                    USA

---

**Business/Theater**                    **Cooperative Economics**

*A*s contentious Senate confirmation hearings raged on the nomination of Clarence Thomas as the second African American named to the Supreme Court, leaked FBI files alleged he had harassed a black female colleague ten years earlier. As rumor seethed into scandal, the nation was dragged into an under-tow of race and sex that cut to the marrow of history. Black man–cum–sexual predator and black woman–cum–emasculator would face off for the cameras in a high-stakes cockfight with the two as surrogates perfectly staged by the Senate, ninety-eight of whose one hundred members were white and male, the other two being white and female. By October 11, 1991, when law professor Anita Hill sat before the microphones, what had begun as a review of one man's appointment became a national referendum on sexual harassment, the Hill-Thomas Hearings.

As brutal as the hearings were on Thomas, later confirmed by a narrow margin, and as exploitive as they were of the reluctant Hill, the national debate was no match for the public drubbing both would endure in the black community. He for his politics; she for betraying a time-honored code. "I've heard people say, 'How could she?' We black women have always been supportive of black men," noted Donna Brazile, chief aide to African American Congresswoman Eleanor Holmes Norton. "Being supportive does not mean you have to support every single black man, re-gardless." But, unique among men, poet-professor-publisher Haki Madhubuti commented, "I hope that—as a result of this specta-cle—black men will be more conscientious about how they treat women in the workplace as well as in the home." Then, on Novem-ber 18, 1991, a historic statement appeared in the *New York Times*. It was signed by 1,603 black women and it supported Hill, objected to the Thomas confirmation, and condemned the Hill-Thomas spectacle. It was appropriately titled "African American Women in Defense of Ourselves."

Friday, October 11, 1991

Washington, D.C.          USA

---

**Sexual Harassment**                                        **Growth**

*L*ike a midnight comet, Florence Mills's star blazed for only a brief time and was then history. From her rise in 1921 to her death at age thirty-two in 1927, the adulation she garnered was without equal. Reigning supreme following unprecedented success on Broadway and in Europe, she came home to Harlem on October 12, 1927. Crowds flooded the streets as word of her arrival spread.

As the lead in *Shuffle Along,* the first all-black Broadway show, Mills stopped traffic. (So great was the show's success that the city rerouted traffic outside its theater!) With her signature song, "I'm Just a Blackbird Looking for a Bluebird," she took London and Paris. "The masses love Miss Mills. More, they adore her, for it is only a step from the pedestal of a heroine to the immortality of a goddess," gushed the *Inter-State Tattler* upon her return: "People always expect good gifts from divinity. That is why we address Jehovah as 'Our Heavenly Father'—because a father provides for his children. It is the duty and privilege of divinity to dispense gifts." Such was the power of the black press to evoke hero(ine) worship—and at great cost: "It is Miss Mills' duty to give the people the one great gift within her power . . . helping to establish a real Negro theater and a genuine race drama." FLO OWES US SOMETHING, the headline demanded.

But the debt was destined to accrue interest. Postponing surgery to attend to the demands of celebrity, she died of a ruptured appendix days later. If grief can be measured, note this: in the greatest mass meeting of blacks well into the 1950s, 150,000 people honored imprisoned martyr Marcus Garvey in 1926; in November 1927, that same number augmented the five thousand mourners packed inside Harlem's Mother Zion Church. As Mills's funeral cortege edged through Harlem, her signature flock of blackbirds was released from a low-flying plane.

Wednesday, October 12, 1927

New York                    USA

*October 13*

$\mathcal{H}$aving made his mark as an artist with several series on the history of the Americas—from *Toussaint L'Ouverture*, about the hero of the Haitian Revolution, to *Migrants*, about the great migration of blacks from the plantation South to the factory North—in the 1960s, Jacob Lawrence revived his interest in Harriet Tubman to produce a book for children, *Harriet and the Promised Land*. It was the kind of book he wished he had had as a child, in the days when he attended an arts and crafts program in the basement of Harlem's 135th Street Library and wandered upstairs among the book stacks to quench his increasingly insatiable thirst.

Lawrence's *Harriet* for children was a dense rendering of the story of slavery and the adventures and perils of rescuing over three hundred people. But his publisher feared the book's accuracy: a children's book must not depict bloodshed; the heroine must not carry a gun. Lawrence censored the portrayal. Yet the book that *Time* magazine later declared a "tour de force" still drew criticism for its truths. In its October 1970 issue, *School Library Journal* published letters to the editor by librarians more comfortable with the pretty-picture school of children's book illustration. Lawrence's Tubman presumed "a certain level of maturity and perception," wrote one; ". . . grotesque and ugly," wrote another. From his adopted state of Washington, Lawrence responded: "If you had walked in the fields, stopping for short periods to be replenished by underground stations; if you couldn't feel secure until you reached the Canadian border, you, too, madam, would look grotesque and ugly. Isn't it sad that the oppressed often find themselves grotesque and ugly and find the oppressor refined and beautiful?"

When called to the battlefront of racism, there are many ways to fight for the dignity of women and of a people.

Tuesday, October 13, 1970

State of Washington     USA

---

**Art/Libraries**         **Perspective**

Dear Maria Barnett Tinnin:

Your grandmother and I send you the warmest sort of welcome. We are so glad you came to join our family circle. . . .

As I think of all the little girls of our hue who come into the world, I am especially happy for you. You have been born to two parents who will love and cherish you, who will surround you not only with affection but with their brilliance of mind and infinite charm of personality.

They will guide you in paths which will make your life one of happiness and beauty and offside your grandmother and grandfather and all your other relatives will be praying that only that which is good and lovely may ever traverse your path.

Welcome again and tell your broad-shouldered Brother Freeman that we give him the special trust of looking after you.

Need we know that the grandfather who authored this letter on October 14, 1954, was Claude A. Barnett, founder of the Associated Negro Press, the first national wire service to African American newspapers? Should it matter that newborn Maria's grandmother was the singer-actor Etta Moten Barnett? Her grandfather's skillful pen had certainly given voice to the otherwise unspoken, perhaps less eloquent, millions of adoring elders of every generation, everywhere.

"With all our love," to Maria the Barnetts were as they signed themselves—in fact and in spirit—"Your Grandma and Grandpa."

Thursday, October 14, 1954

Illinois                                    USA

---

**Family**                                    **Love**

Not since 1956 had there been a gathering of writers like this one. In September of that year, expatriate African American novelist Richard Wright and Senegal's Alioune Diop, founder of the international journal *Présence Africaine*, sponsored the First Conference of Negro Artists and Writers six months before Ghana would celebrate its status as the first modern African nation to throw off the yoke of colonial rule. To the Sorbonne from the world over came such prophets of Négritude as Aimé Césaire and future president of Senegal Léopold Senghor.

In 1997, with women writers the cause for celebration, a first for the United States, from October 15 to 18, the Africana Studies Program of New York University and the Institute of Afro-American Affairs hosted "Yari Yari," from a word meaning "future" in Kuranko, a Sierra Leonan language. Among brothers and sisters in the struggle—with the powers that be of politics and the pen— the camaraderie was electric. With *Essence* magazine's Susan L. Taylor as chairperson and veteran journalist Melba Tolliver as host, awards honored poet-novelist Margaret Walker (see June 28) for lifetime achievement, and science fiction pioneer and MacArthur "Genius" Awardee Octavia Butler (see June 5). From South Africa, Lindiwe Mabuza, author-ambassador to Germany, accepted the human rights award. From Egypt, novelist-psychiatrist Nawal El Saadawi accepted honors for her commitment to women's issues. From Haiti, emigrée Edwidge Danticat, at work on a novel rooted in the 1937 massacre of forty thousand Haitians, was the celebrated new voice. And completing the circle of history, from France came Christiane Yande Diop, widow of Alioune Diop, link to the first conference, to accept honors for her contribution to Pan-African publishing. She had kept alive the journal that was the voice of African continuity and, with its founding in 1947, the first African business established in Europe since the so-called Dark Ages.

Wednesday, October 15, 1997

New York                                   USA

---

**Events**                                   **Continuity**

On October 16, 1859, Dangerfield Newby died in the line of duty. A member of John Brown's historic raid on the Federal arsenal at Harpers Ferry, he was *a soldier in the army of the Lord*, as slaves would document in the language of the spirituals. Brown's plan to seize arms and free the slaves was noble, albeit ill advised. Frederick Douglass declined to participate. Dangerfield Newby signed on. In his pocket, a letter from his wife explained his daring: "Dear Husband. I want you to buy me . . . for if you do not get me some body else will."

In April 1859, Harriet Newby had written, "Oh, Dear Dangerfield, com this fall without fail, monny or no monney. I want to see you so much." In a later letter she continued, "It is the grates Comfort I have in thinking of the promist time when you will be here." The plantation's mistress was ill, its master desperate for cash. Mrs. Newby knew she was in danger of being sold. On August 16, she wrote the letter her husband carried into battle two months later to the day. "Dear Husband you [know] not the trouble I see," she confided. "The last two years has ben like a trouble dream to me. . . . I know not what time [Master] may sell me, an then all my bright hops of the futer are blasted, for their has ben one bright hope to cheer me in all my troubles, that is to be with you, for if I thought I shoul never see you this earth would have no charms for me. Do all you can for me, witch I have no doubt you will. . . . The baby . . . can step around everything by holding on." She closed with "love, your affectionate wife."

When Harriet Newby's letter was recovered after the raid, she was sold deeper South, never to be heard from again. But when the story is told of a love that surpasses all, we remember Dangerfield and Harriet, two courageous lovers who dared to dream.

Sunday, October 16, 1859

West Virginia                    USA

---

**Love**                                          **Courage**

*E*ven as the Women's Liberation movement gathered its first huff of strength for the long uphill climb, many black women foresaw its inability to reach the heights of their acceptance—a problem due to a certain shortness of *breadth*. So steep was the obstacle of race that the common ground of gender could not be reached. On October 17, 1968, Ti-Grace Atkinson attempted to avert it instead.

Voted down on every point she raised that day as president of New York NOW, a chapter of the National Organization for Women, Atkinson—the glamorous blond national media spokeswoman—blasted the very ground from which her own family's conservative upper-class Louisiana roots had sprung. Alienating her patrimony and her sisterhood, her resignation in the press took on those who "want women to have the opportunity to be oppressors, too," over "those who want to destroy oppression itself." Albeit well-intended, Atkinson had misgauged how profoundly she had already alienated many black women with a line like this one: "The institution of marriage has the same effect as the institution of slavery had. It separates people in the same category, disperses them, keeps them from identifying as a class. The masses of slaves didn't recognize their condition, either. To say that a woman is really 'happy' with her home and kids is as irrelevant as saying that the blacks were 'happy being taken care of by Ol' Massa.'"

In a misreading of history, this otherwise-progressive voice had kept women from "identifying" across the racial divide. Not only were the "masses of slaves" ever aware of their condition, but, on par with Ol' Massa, Miss Anne held equal sway. As much as white women resented being a "Mrs.," the Mammys and Sadies were not about to give up what they had yet to receive: respect for their lives and their families, of which "Mrs." was seen as a sign.

Thursday, October 17, 1968

New York                  USA

---

*T*heatre professionals the world over well know: Mama doesn't read plays, Mama reads playwrights. Ellen Stewart is La Mama.

When she was exhausted and recuperating in Tangiers, a friend told her that one must "have one's own pushcart." Having broken barriers to become a fashion designer at Saks Fifth Avenue, Stewart could fabricate dreams from whole cloth. On October 18, 1961, Ellen Stewart rented a pushcart—a basement at 321 East Ninth Street in New York City—for $55 per month with a vision in mind: a space for playwrights and plays to grow. Nurturing her "children," and already known by the nickname "Mama," she named her playpen Café La Mama and gave birth to the Off-Off Broadway theater movement. Her labor wasn't easy. Blacks didn't support her theatre because it wasn't "black enough." Foundations shunned her for grants because she was "too international." Through the confusion of ideologies, she kept her family of artists going by working several jobs. Her sons and daughters were grateful, but often traumatized by identity problems and growing pains. Of a writer who "got to be 'minister of culture' for the black movement," she recalled, "I would see him and he wouldn't speak to me, but he'd always call me up late that night and say, 'Mama, forgive me, I couldn't speak to you in front of my friend, but you're my mama.' And he wasn't the only one. It was heavy, heavy." It was also time to lay the burden down. A doctor warned her to give up the jobs or the theater, "I gave up the money and kept the theater," said La Mama. If she was called international, that was what she would be: "I get invited to fly on my broom to all kinds of places to be with people to create, to make workshops." Like all good mothers, she also brings home healthy food for thought. Artists from Africa, Asia, Europe—everywhere—now call the La Mama Experimental Theatre Club a home away from home.

Wednesday, October 18, 1961

New York                              USA

---

**Theater**                                          **Vision**

$\mathcal{T}$he pretense of good intentions was over as the nation succumbed to Jim Crow. In February 1909, the NAACP—the first and oldest Civil Rights organization—was founded to combat the crisis. That same year, a woman who had been denied a public school teaching post for being "too black" founded a school of her own for girls as dark-complexioned as she. With eight students and funds raised solely among blacks, Nannie Burroughs opened the National Training School for Girls in Washington, D.C., on October 19, 1909. In her mission to train "head, hand, and heart," her motto was: "We specialize in the wholly impossible."

Those were the days when cash-strapped educators pragmatically straddled the line toed by the ex-slave turned educator and Tuskegee founder, Booker T. Washington in his infamous "Atlanta Compromise." Heralding racism and humiliating hopes for social justice, he spoke the ominous lines "we can be separate as the fingers on the hand." Blacks, he said, would be content to be unconcerned with intellectual pursuits in favor of the industrial and technical trades. Two generations after slavery, Burroughs's liberal arts curriculum also taught such earning power skills as barbering, bookkeeping, home economics, interior decor, nursing, printing, sewing, shoe repair, and shorthand. But in stark contrast to those schools for blacks wholly dependent on the largesse of whites, Burroughs's school had racially unencumbered purse strings that liberated her mighty voice (see July 17).

Determined to nurture informed pride, Burroughs made African American history a required course. Contests and prizes (often cash) motivated students. Instead of saying what whites *wanted* to hear, Burroughs said what blacks *needed* to hear. Her girls were educated to honor their own beauty. "No race is richer in soul quality and color than the Negro," prodded Burroughs. "Glorify yourself!"

Tuesday, October 19, 1909

Washington, D.C.                    USA

---

**Education**                    **Respect for One's Power**

*O*n October 20, 1940, Katherine Dunham—an African American woman charged and in charge—was onstage putting the final touches on a Broadway musical that would open three days later, *Cabin in the Sky*. Dancer, choreographer, anthropologist, Guggenheim Fellow, Ph.D. scholar of Haitian dance, educator, founder of the Katherine Dunham Center for the Performing Arts at Southern Illinois University, human rights activist, Kennedy Center honoree, Katherine Dunham changed the course and cultural base of modern American dance. Later, from her Children's Workshop dance studio in East St. Louis, she would also save lives, as more than one ex–gang member would publicly attest.

Founding her first dance company in 1939, Dunham brought the world to her feet, inspired by the arts of Africa and the Caribbean. At the root of her creativity was conscience. As every company founder knows, the most difficult task is to support the vision on a firm economic base—put simply, to keep the company going. Yet while touring her dance company internationally, she added the ballet *Southland*—a dance dramatizing the lynching of fourteen-year-old Emmett Till in 1955—to her repertoire. Pressured by the U.S. State Department to remove the work, she refused, risked the consequences, and kept on going.

A 1989 portrait of her by photographer Brian Lanker captures her essence in a formal sitting. Eighty, regal, enthroned before a scene of African artifacts, her head wrapped and adorned, her left leg extended, its foot turned as only a dancer can, she looks away from the camera—far away. In her work, as she told Lanker, "Dance can free people from some of their oppressions. . . . I did not separate a physical act from its cultural context, from its spiritual meaning." She remained free.

Sunday, October 20, 1940

New York                          USA

$\mathscr{A}$s drums fell silent in the temple at Alto do Gantois in Salvador da Bahia, the Brazilian nation, led by its president, paused in an official day of mourning for Cleusa Millet. Who was this priestess who had so inspired millions?

In the ten years since her mother's death had placed the legacy of the ancestors on Mother Cleusa's shoulders to carry forward, she had not made any significant changes in the rituals that had been passed to her. More, she represented continuity and cohesion, where modern-day pressures would have otherwise seen the ancient traditions lost. Because of her, the African-based rituals once persecuted by a Catholic sociopolitical hierarchy now thrived—their pantheon of *orishas* intact. Adorned in their African masks and raffia skirts, the gods and goddesses of wind, oceans, still water, metals, and fire reigned. One of her greatest strengths, it was said, was that, like every good mother, Mother Cleusa did not favor some of her children but treated them all equally—rich and poor, from president to peasant. And, in turn, they remained loyal to her. Through contributions from wealthy donors, she transformed the temple into a shrine to her mother, a museum of Candomblé. Now, as she had been when her mother, Mother Menininha died, Cleusa Millet's daughter, Monica, was the likely, but reluctant, successor. She, too, would have to come into her own time and space.

On this day, October 21, 1998, preparations were under way for a last tribute. Mother Cleusa had died on October 15; on the twenty-second, the seventh day following her transition, the faithful would gather according to tradition. In the place of honor would be the things Mother Cleusa had loved—favorite clothes, food, treasures—and the drums of the *orishas* of the spirit world would fall silent to let her pass.

Wednesday, October 21, 1998

Salvador                                                     Brazil

---

**Religion**                                              **Continuity**

"When I was growing up in Oakland, California, in the fifties and sixties, being an African American was a simple issue," wrote Bonnie Allen. "Neighborhoods were redlined. Employment was segregated. Banks discriminated. You never asked a police officer for assistance, for fear of death and dismemberment. Other than that, you were free. God bless America."

Little wonder that Huey Newton and Bobby Seale began the Black Panther Party for Self-Defense there in Oakland on the night of October 22, 1966. Writing their manifesto, "What We Want; What We Believe," that night, they would attract bright young city-wise northerners and the bright young country-wise allied with SNCC. Quiet as it was kept, for their intellect and conscience, Dr. King, "prince of peace," was among their admirers. The feeling was mutual. As Kathleen Neale Cleaver—a legal scholar-activist best known as one of the party's leading lights and wife of exiled minister of information Eldridge Cleaver—would write, "I am old enough to remember things King actually said when he was alive. . . . I can still appreciate the challenge he hurled at the racist hierarchies of power. The King I knew about was part of a generation, just like I was, that believed we could change the world. The King I am talking about was someone who transformed my life. Now, Martin Luther King may not have intended to influence me the way he did. He certainly did not encourage the version of revolt against racial oppression I chose by joining the Black Panther Party. But he persistently generated a movement that destroyed fear instilled by a hundred years of racist terror."

Said King of the Panthers, "Were I able to co-opt those minds into my cause, there is no question that victory would be swift and eternal." Such were the signs of the times, then and now.

Saturday, October 22, 1966

California        USA

---

**Temper of the Times**        **Self-affirmation**

*O*n October 23, 1948, a front-page headline in the national edition of the *Afro-American* read POLICE SEEKING BATHTUB KILLER OF YOUNG MOTHER. In bold letters below was this: "Boy, 10, Accuses Zora." In a sordid lead, charges against Zora Neale Hurston (see July 2) were smeared across black America's most widely read paper: "Novelist Arrested on Morals Charge; Reviewer of Author's Latest Book Notes Character Is 'Hungry for Love.'" Just as her first book in six years, *Seraph on the Suwanee*, was being published to strong critical reviews, that news was shouted down by the blare of scandal. And the story wasn't true.

The nightmare began in September 1948 with her arrest by New York police on allegations by the Children's Society that she had sodomized a ten-year-old boy. Hurston knew the boy, having rented a room from his mother. But no such act had taken place. Had an investigation been done prior to her arrest, no criminal charge would have ever been filed. Instead, there was a painful pretrial hearing at which the boy testified that each Saturday for more than a year, Zora had taken him to a coal bin and abused him. Hurston's denials were corroborated by her passport; she had been in Honduras for most of that time. The story had been concocted by the boy and his mother in retaliation for Hurston's suggestion—obviously correct—that the boy was emotionally disturbed and should have a psychiatric examination. The following March, the charge against her was dismissed. But by then the damage had been done; it was the beginning of the end of her career. Twelve years later, she died in obscurity and was only later resurrected by her literary sons and daughters. Notably, Alice Walker traced Hurston's burial site to the Garden of Heavenly Rest, a potter's field, in Florida. Placing a stone on the grave, Walker set the record straight: "Zora Neale Hurston 'A Genius of the South'—Novelist, Folklorist, Anthropologist."

Saturday, October 23, 1948

Maryland        USA

---

**Social History/Literature**        **Truth**

Since the 1820s, thousands of African Americans had sailed to Liberia, achieving their dream of Back-to-Africa emigration (see August 27). Among the freeborn and the self-emancipated were those set free by owners like John McDonough on condition that they leave the United States. A member of the American Colonization Society (ACS), McDonough manumitted eighty of his two hundred slaves not as their due but as his strategy. Freed slaves worked off the price of passage as indentures. Investors, like McDonough, leveraged title to their slaves for rights to the slaves' ancestral land. As literary historian Margaret Busby notes, "In a letter to the *New Orleans Commercial Bulletin* a month later, [McDonough] exposed the real motives behind his colonization plans." With his pilgrims at sea, he wrote, "My own opinion is that without separation of the races, extermination of one or other must inevitably take place." Ridding slaveowners of the greatest impediment to slavery—free blacks—was the oil that greased the ACS's financial engine. Nevertheless, those who fled to Liberia felt truly blessed. On October 24, 1849, Henrietta Fullor wrote to McDonough, her former owner:

> St Pauls River New Orleans, Liberia. We are doing pretty well in the Agricultural line growing coffee, rice, sugar . . . after the expiration of the six months . . . for the Society. . . . We are now in the strictest sense of the word Free. . . . You will please remember us to all acquaintances and especially to our colored friends and say to them that Liberia is the home of our race and as good a country as they can find. Industry and perseverance is only required to make a man happy and wealthy in this our Adopted Country, its soil yields abundant harvest to the husbandman, its climate is healthy, its laws are founded upon justice and equity here, we sit under our own vine and Palm Tree, we all enjoy the same rights and priviledges that our white brethren does in America it is our only home. . . .

Wednesday, October 24, 1849

Louisiana            USA/Liberia

---

**Freedom**                                                                 **Values**

*I*n 1995, Minister Louis Farrakhan, leader of the Nation of Islam, had led the Million Man March to Washington, D.C. A brilliant initiative, triumphant and controversial, while it eschewed female participation, more women had been invited to address the all-male event than had appeared in the historic March on Washington of 1963 (see August 28). Now, on October 25, 1997, women, *eight to eighty*, thronged Philadelphia for the Million Woman March.

A year of planning and grassroots organizing by co-chairwomen Asia Coney and Philé Chionesu had led to this day. Rain could not dampen the spirit, nor fifty-degree weather chill the climate of love. Whether the actual attendance reached the million mark or not, there was no doubt that this day's theme of devotion to "repentance, resurrection and restoration"—and to identity, family, and the joy of our Sister Days—reached deep into the hearts of millions of women of African descent the world over. Waving traditional red, black, and green liberation flags to the beat of African drums, women from Africa, the Americas, and the Caribbean marched under a banner all their own: THE MILLION WOMAN MARCH • CELEBRATING SISTERHOOD, PEACE, FREEDOM AND JUSTICE • I WAS THERE!

From a keynote address by Congresswoman Maxine Waters of California to the remarks of South Africa's Winnie Madikizela Mandela, the message was unity with a plan. A twelve-point program ranged from education to homelessness, family life, entrepreneurism, and investigating the role of the Central Intelligence Agency in destabilizing black communities. But above all, the theme was love for oneself—healing and celebrating oneself.

Saturday, October 25, 1997

Pennsylvania                    USA

---

"*M*iss Phillis," wrote the general, taking a break from the labors of war:

Your favour of the 26th of October did not reach my hands 'till the middle of December. Time enough, you will say, to have given an answer ere this. Granted . . . I thank you most sincerely for your polite notice of me, in the elegant lines you enclosed; and however undeserving I may be of such encomium and panegyrick, the style and manner exhibit a striking proof of your great poetical Talents. In honour of which, and in a tribute justly due you, I would have published the Poem, had I not been apprehensive, that, while I only meant to give the World this new instance of your genius, I might have incurred the imputation of Vanity. This and nothing else, determined me not to give it place in the public prints. If you should ever come to Cambridge, or near Head Quarters, I shall be happy to see a person so favoured by the Muses, and to whom Nature has been so liberal and beneficent in her dispensations. I am, with great Respect, etc.

Dated October 26, 1775, the poem was by the slave-child prodigy and first African American woman author, Phillis Wheatley (see May 6). The thank-you letter, dated February 28, 1776, was by George Washington, General of the Continental Army of the Thirteen Colonies. As Washington warred for political freedom, he was personally liable for holding hundreds enslaved. A decade later, referencing a lawsuit "respecting a slave . . . whom a Society of Quakers have attempted to liberate," he wrote, "none of those whose *misfortune* it is to have slaves as attendants, will visit the City if they can possibly avoid it; because by so doing they hazard their property." In Washington's response to Miss Phillis and in his view of slaveowners as slavery's "misfortunates"—a concept put forth in the first draft of the Declaration of Independence—is the base upon which two centuries of historic contradictions vis-à-vis slavery and its true victims are firmly footed.

Thursday, October 26, 1775

Massachusetts          USA/England

---

**Literature/Slavery**                                    **Perspective**

𝒫 aris in the Roaring Twenties. Life between the wars, when black was in and hot, "when people with money but no talent helped people with talent but no money," when European nobility hobnobbed with American royalty—the Kings and Dukes and Earls of jazz—and life was a "beautiful thing" for the stylishly bored, rakishly disenchanted, and blacks who had known better and lived far worse in the USA.

In this Paris, a waiter named Langston Hughes, living on the cusp of fame as a poet, helped a fellow journeyman and singer settle in. Light-skinned, freckled, and red-haired, she had been born Ada Beatrice Queen Victoria Louise Virginia Smith, but she had also been nicknamed "Bricktop" by a Harlem club owner, and the latter name stuck. At the nightclub le Grand Duc, she caught the ear of the rich and famous with her rendition of Cole Porter's "Miss Otis Regrets She's Unable to Lunch Today," which dripped with irony and infamy. In October 1926, the Prince of Wales had a question for Bricktop: he knew how to dance the Charleston, but he would like to learn the Black Bottom, could she teach him? From that fling, she opened a club called Bricktop's and reigned supreme when Duke Ellington, Paul Robeson, Josephine Baker, and the prince came to call. Three years later, the U.S. stock market crashed, ushering in the Great Depression of the 1930s. It was the moment that brought the dancing, glory days of le Paris Noir Black chic to an end. *Ahhh,* hers were the heydays. It was grand while it lasted. Before long, Hitler had invaded Poland, and Paris night life saw the light of day. Bricktop scurried on board the *SS Washington,* one of the last American ships to leave France before German occupation would shroud the city until the end of World War II. It was October 27, 1939. Arriving home, a new play by white playwright William Saroyan, *The Time of Your Life,* was the toast of New York. Paris had been that. For now it was done. *C'est la vie.*

Friday, October 27, 1939

France

---

**Social History**                                        **Zest for Life**

*O*n October 28, 1830, Charlotte and Josiah Henson and their four children reached the promised land. Learning that they were about to be sold apart, they had fled Kentucky, boarded the Underground Railroad, and walked to Canada.

They left at 9:00 P.M. on a "dark, moonless night" in mid-September; a fellow slave rowed them across the river to Indiana. For the next two weeks, they walked by night and rested by day. When food gave out, they bartered or bought what they could, then dipped back to the south to avoid suspicion. Arriving in Cincinnati, they received temporary shelter and were driven thirty miles by wagon. On the "military road" from Scioto with little food, they were so weakened that Charlotte fell over a log, blacked out, and was feared to be dying, but she soon recovered. En route to Lake Erie, they were helped by Native Americans who fed them and provided shelter for the night. A few days later, fording a stream one hundred yards wide, the skin was torn from Josiah's back as he brought the children to shore. In Sandusky, a black shoreman's help ferried them to Buffalo, where a white captain not only paid their passage but gave them a dollar. After six terrifying weeks, they touched Canadian soil. Hugging, kissing "all round, with such joy that we all laughed," there was little time for "frolic": "We were strangers in a strange land, and would now have to make our own way."

A photo at the Connecticut home of Harriet Beecher Stowe (see March 20) adds a twist to this tale. Stowe based her character Uncle Tom on Henson. While a slave, he had been entrusted to deliver his family and others to a new owner—and did! However misguided he once was, not only did his family later flee, but he made forays (and amends) to rescue 118 others. Once in Canada, he and Charlotte helped new arrivals at their Dawn Settlement in Dresden, Ontario.

Thursday, October 28, 1830

Maryland　　　　　　USA/Canada

---

**Escape!**　　　　　　　　　　　　　　　　　**Character**

*I*t was official: what she had accomplished in giving a positive face and form to African Americans via advertising was historic. Inspired by that recognition, the Smithsonian Institution opened its Caroline Robinson Jones Collection at the National Museum of American History on October 29, 1997.

From school records to business papers, the Archives Center exhibit traced the remarkable career of a pioneering woman. There was a cotillion photo from her early days as one of ten children in Benton Harbor, Michigan, and a business portrait from her "fear and fun" days of the 1960s, when she was the first African American to be hired and trained in the hundred-year history of J. Walter Thompson, the world's largest advertising agency. The "challenges and rewards" of the 1970s saw her co-found two agencies — Zebra and Mingo-Jones. On her own in the 1980s, with campaigns that "blended sophistication and soul," she changed the way the public viewed blacks in major brand ads. By the 1990s, she was advertising's Woman of the Year. In an industry that had made the plantation slave images of Uncle Ben and Aunt Jemima synonymous with rice and pancakes, Jones's courageous talent helped give print and television ads a black face that was human, not stereotypical, and at times even glamorous.

Those who have starred in her ads are a Who's Who of entertainment, politics, and sports: Harry Belafonte, Janet Jackson, Magic Johnson, B. B. King, Gladys Knight, Patti LaBelle, Ashford and Simpson, Wesley Snipes, and former mayor of New York City David Dinkins. True to her concern that "those of us who came first make a way for others to follow," when the cheering came in her name, she created scholarships. And on this, her day, a thank-you list "to everyone who has been a part of this experience (and you know who you are)" graced the program.

Wednesday, October 29, 1997

Washington, D.C. USA

---

**Business** Images

Talk as you will of woman's deep capacity for loving, of the strength of her affectional nature. I do not deny it; but will the mere possession of any human love fully satisfy all the demands of her whole being? You may paint her in poetry or fiction as a frail vine, clinging to her brother man for support and dying when deprived of it; and all this may sound well enough to please the imaginations of school-girls, or love-lorn maidens. But woman—the true woman—if you would render her happy, it needs more than the mere development of her affectional nature. Her conscience should be enlightened, her faith in the true and right established, and scope given to her Heaven-endowed and God-given faculties. The true aim of female education should be, not a development of one or two, but all the faculties of the human soul, because no perfect womanhood is developed by imperfect culture. Intense love is often akin to intense suffering, and to trust the whole wealth of a woman's nature on the frail bark of human love may often be like trusting a cargo of gold and precious gems to a bark that has never battled with the storm, or buffeted the waves. Is it any wonder, then, that so many life-barks go down, paving the ocean of time with precious hearts and wasted hopes? that so many float around us, shattered and mismasted wrecks? that so many are stranded on the shoals of existence, mournful beacons and solemn warnings for the thoughtless, to whom marriage is a careless and hasty rushing together of the affections? Alas that an institution so fraught with good for humanity should be so perverted, and that state of life, which should be filled with happiness, become so replete with misery. And this was the fate of Laura Lagrange. . . .

*T*his passage is from "The Two Offers," by Frances Ellen Watkins Harper (see March 4). The first black short story known, it was published in the *Anglo-African Magazine* in 1859.

1859

Pennsylvania                    USA

---

**Literature/Marriage**                    **Defining Ourselves**

*R*osetta Nubin debuted in her hometown of Cotton Plant, Arkansas, at age four, standing "on boxes playing a guitar only slightly smaller than herself and singing 'Jesus on the Main Line, Tell Him What You Want.'" Dr. Horace Boyer recounts the scene: "While there was no doubt that she had an extraordinary voice — bright and clear, sonorous, warm, slightly brassy — and an easy delivery, she also knew at that tender age how to sing. Her pitch was solid; she knew the melody and could even add extra notes of her own. Her rhythm was as accented, syncopated, and intricate as any of the blues singers 'in the bottoms.'" Twenty years later, on October 31, 1938, the town was New York, the box was an artist's booth at the Decca Records studios, the distinctive voice-and-guitar presence mature, the songs "less gospel and more worldly," the solo a solo album, and the former child prodigy was Sister Rosetta Tharpe, raising a fever of world renown.

But that world was not her world. Church folk were appalled at her worldly musical ways and "sinful" jazz accompaniments, and she had to pay the price of success with estrangement from her roots. Her record "Strange Things Happening Everyday" was a jukebox hit nationwide. Criticizing her criticizers, as Boyer notes, in "a line directed at the membership of the sanctified church that attempted to scandalize her name because she mixed blues and jazz with gospel," she crooned:

*Oh, we hear church people say, They are in the "Holy way,"*
*... On that last great judgment day when they drive them all away.*

Instead of a gospel quartet, for her record "congregation," her trio "sang in voices suggestive of cynicism, satire, and levity." A perfect musical choice, that backslide made her the biggest gospel star of her day and the greatest cause for ambivalence by the sanctified who loved the Lord *and* the music of Sister Rosetta Tharpe.

Monday, October 31, 1938

Arkansas    USA/International

---

**Music**        **Choices**

# November

*Come Sunday: Miss Muriel* (1945). Reprinted courtesy
of Muriel Landsmark Tuitt.

For more information, see September 22, November 2.

"When I write for children, I write about survivors," said Ann Petry. "When I write for adults, I write about the walking wounded. I write about the relationship between black and white people in the United States. . . . Like all writers, black or white, I work against odds, real or imaginary, against hostility, against indifference." In her celebrated short story "Miss Muriel"—a love story seen through the eyes of its twelve-year-old narrator—Petry writes *for the family.* . . .

When the weather is bad and we cannot work in the garden, Aunt Sophronia and I clean house. I do not like to clean house but I do like to sort out the contents of other people's bureau drawers. We started setting Aunt Sophronia's bureau in order. She showed me a picture of her graduating class from Pharmacy College. She was the only girl in a class of boys. She was colored and the boys were white. . . .

I looked at the picture and then I looked at her and said, "You are beautiful."

She put the picture back in her top drawer. She keeps her treasures in there. She has a collar made of real lace . . . and a necklace made of gold nuggets from Colorado that a friend of my mother's left to Aunt Sophronia in her will. . . .

Sometimes I forget that Aunt Sophronia is an adult and that she belongs in the enemy camp, and I make the mistake of saying what I have been thinking. . . . "You know, this picture reminds me of the night last summer when there was a female moth, one of those huge night moths, on the inside of the screen door, and all the male moths for miles around came and clung on the outside of the screen, making their wings flutter, and you know, they didn't make any sound but it was kind of scary. Weren't you . . . "

"You get a broom and a dustpan and begin to sweep in the hall," she said. . . .

Saturday, November 1, 1958

Connecticut             USA

*S* ometime in 1621, we cannot be sure exactly when, a woman known only as Isabella gave birth to the first African child born in the Americas. Her husband's name was Antoney, and their baby was later baptized William in the Church of England at the Jamestown colony in Virginia. That is all we know. And yet we know more. Recently ripped from their former lives, what horror William's parents must have seen. But in his eyes, they could see hope and promise, and for that they must have lived and dreamed their better days.

On this day, this author's daughters, Ayodele Nailah and Dara Rashida, were born in New York City in 1971. Their father, Max Roach, had come to Brooklyn as a child, his parents fleeing the Depression and the Jim Crow South. His parents had been born in a section of the historic Great Dismal Swamp of North Carolina. Their parents were among the postwar emancipated who claimed it and renamed it Newland. In its promise was their future, their all. As their mother, my father, Bertel Adams, had come to the States from St. Kitts as a child, his mother having seen both of her twins die. My mother, Muriel Landsmark (see September 22), was American-born to two immigrants, William Landsmark and Myra Carlisle, a twin herself (see August 23). When my daughters were born, a history came back to us renewed, refreshed. Pregnant with them, I carried my grandfather's ashes Back-to-Africa and delivered them to the departing sea, that he might be reunited with the home he, like his father's fathers before him, lived for the day he would be able to return to once more.

It is for my daughters, and for yours, that these and many other books have been written. Like Isabella—in spite of all that has happened to us as a people—in their eyes I see hope. How can we say to our children any less than "Thank you."

Tuesday, November 2, 1971

International        Africa/Americas/Caribbean

---

**Family**                                              **Vision**

*O*n this day, we honor those who have offered themselves as candidates and those whose sacrifices—sometimes supreme—got them elected.

On November 3, 1992, Carol Moseley-Braun became the first African American woman elected to the United States Senate. On this day, too, symbolically (November 6, 1968, was the actual date), Shirley Chisholm of New York (see July 13) was the first elected to the United States House of Representatives. And on November 2, 1987, Carrie Saxon Perry was the first elected mayor of a major city, Hartford, Connecticut.

While the Congressional Black Caucus of elected men and women is quite visible, the alliance of mayors is less well known. In 1988, thirteen members of the National Conference of Black Mayors founded the Black Women Mayors' Caucus. In 1992, their number had swelled to sixty-seven—thankfully, too many to list. But since the first woman was elected in 1968, others in this rare sisterhood have included: Unita Blackwell of Mayersville, Mississippi (see November 22); Jane Glover of New London, Connecticut; and Sharon Pratt Kelly of Washington, D.C. Wouldn't Fannie Lou Hamer (see May 7) smile? She might not have gotten there with them, but they wouldn't have gotten there without her.

Tuesday, November 3, 1992

National                                        USA

---

**Politics**                                  **Respect for One's Power**

$\mathcal{J}$n its infamous Dred Scott decision of 1857, the Supreme Court held that blacks "had no rights which the white man was bound to respect." As devastating as it remains to this day, *Dred Scott* uniquely spotlights the plight of black women.

In 1846, Dred and Harriet Scott were a "married" slave couple living in the Missouri territory. Hired out, Scott saved his share to purchase freedom for himself and his family, but was refused. He sued. When Harriet Scott was slapped by his owner, a second suit charged assault, trespass, and false imprisonment. Because Scott resided in a territory that barred slavery under the Missouri Compromise of 1820, his white attorneys (demeaned in the press as "nigger lawyers") argued for the family's freedom. When an 1847 court backlog threatened what was thought to be their imminent freedom, the Scotts were advised to agree in advance that the decision in Dred's case would determine the outcome of Harriet's. In a series of losses, victories, and judgment set-asides, the Scotts' cases became a referendum on slavery that took an ominous turn for the worse on November 4, 1856, with the election of James Buchanan as president. With a "secret letter" to sway the Court, he prodded the decision in his inaugural address. Two days later, the Court used the Dred Scott case to find the Compromise itself unconstitutional, thereby undermining the grounds for the suit, denying the couple's right to freedom and the rights of every African American, enslaved or free.

Ironically, the basis of Harriet's case was still valid, but having merged her fate with his, it was too late. More than a century later, Harriet Scott remains ignored, legally subsumed under her husband's name, doubly disfranchised by race and by gender, by law and by history. In an ironic arc of history, a great-grandson of the Scotts would practice law in the court that first rejected his parents' rights.

Tuesday, November 4, 1856

Missouri                    USA

---

**Law**                                **Perspective**

*W*ith forty albums to her credit, five of which have been certified gold, what has made Dorothy Norwood's music so powerful is her devotion to the message. In 1972, true to her belief that "if the mountain won't come to you, then you must go to the mountain," she made a landmark thirty-city tour with Mick Jagger and the Rolling Stones. Taking her message to mass stadium audiences previously off-limits to gospel artists for reasons of religious conviction and audience appeal, she sang her gospelized hymns to the wayward and the saved. Rooted in the fear that "too much education" or "socialization" can destroy traditional family ties, she delivers her sung sermon, "The Denied Mother":

A mother goes to the train station to meet her daughter, home from college. Sighting her daughter, her arms open wide—and close empty-handed as the daughter looks at her, then walks away. The rejected mother runs after her child. Why did the daughter not embrace her mother as other daughters had done? The daughter answers that she refused her touch because she was ashamed for others to see that the old woman with the scarred, burned face was her mother. *The organ murmurs low.* When the child was three months, the mother had left her inside the house while she hung up the laundry outside. She looked around and saw the house on fire. Friends said she would die if she dared enter the house; neighbors said that both she and the baby would be burned alive. Still, she went in to save her child. Bringing the daughter through the flames, she did not protect herself; she put her hands over the tiny face so that her baby would not be scarred. But that's all right, she vows. I know a Man who sits high and looks low. *With the tremulo in her voice, the organ swells.* Norwood and her singers crown the saga with the ultimate prayer for every wounded heart—Dorsey's "Precious Lord" (see September 23)—and uphold her title, "World's Greatest Storyteller."

November 1972

Georgia                                    USA

---

**Motherhood/Music**                                    **Tradition**

It is an otherwise uninspired office in the winter of 1939 or so. Five women in a row, seated, in winter coats and hats, wait their turn. Only the hands of the middle one are visible above the picture's bottom line—thick, worker's hands, folded, stretched from too-short sleeves. Above the women, a sign reads PLEASE BE COURTEOUS TO THE GIRLS THEY ARE HUMAN. LADIES WILL BE LADIES HOME OR ABROAD, counsels another. And a third: APPLICANTS MUST HAVE FULL FEES BEFORE BEING SENT TO POSITIONS. NOT HAVING FEES IS A VERY POOR REFERENCE. As the women watch and wait, each head is angled in the same direction—looking forward to an attendant, perhaps; looking forward to more than a job, for sure— an end to their Great Depression.

In the collected memory of a 1986 photography exhibit, "Blacks in America," are other photos and other signs that tell the story of the city under poverty's seige. A little girl, her hair uncombed, is helping in the family's tenement kitchen—the kind of kitchen with ceramic sink and washtub, painted baked enamel stove on slim efficient legs, and a gas meter that eats coins and gives only as good as it gets. Three- and four-room apartments with hot water and bath are posted FOR COLORED TENANTS. And picketers brandish placards outside a drugstore: DON'T BUY HERE! BUY WHERE NEGROES CAN WORK. ALL WORKERS SUPPORT THIS CAM-PAIGN.

Segregated in northern tenements, watching and waiting are only part of the tale. The other part is a campaign for dignity from which work will come. "Buy where you can work," they tell each other, a child in one hand, a picket in the other. A change is bound to come. Stark against the wall on a printed panel are words that will make a young Langston Hughes famous: I'VE KNOWN RIVERS. MY SOUL HAS GROWN DEEP LIKE THE RIVERS. These are the signs of the times.

Circa 1939

New York                    USA

---

**Labor**                                    **Courage/Vision**

On November 7, 1931, Juliette Derricotte died. That was the story told and retold by outraged millions worldwide.

Who was this woman so callously left by the side of the road? Born in Georgia in 1897, the fifth of Isaac and Laura Derricotte's nine children, she attended Talladega College, where she joined the debating team and became president of the school's Young Women's Christian Association (YWCA). Graduating in 1918, her work with the YWCA brought her to New York City for its National Student Council training program. There, she honed her leadership skills and pioneered organizing methods that transcended race. Setting aside that issue, she launched a program that had YWCA members question acts un-Christian. This cross-cultural initiative at the height of segregation would make her a member of the World's Student Christian Federation and a delegate to events in England, China, and India. Returning stateside, she earned a master's degree from Columbia University, was named a trustee of her Talladega alma mater, and became Fisk University's dean of women. It was on the trip home to Georgia to visit her mother, accompanied by three Fisk students, that a car driven by a white couple neared hers. Within moments, the cars collided. Derricotte's car spun and crashed. Unharmed, the couple climbed from their car and, with the aid of onlookers, drove the four blacks to area doctors, not the segregated local hospital.

With news of Juliette Derricotte's death came world outrage. A woman of her accomplishments had died because a nearby hospital had no "colored ward." Those who purported to know the whos of worthiness in America were met with a hefty dose of whys. As James Baldwin once noted, "If I am not who you say I am, then you are not who you think you are."

Saturday, November 7, 1931

Georgia                                    USA

---

**Social History**                                    **Collective Responsibility**

*F*rom the minutes of a meeting of the Philadelphia Female Anti-Slavery Society on November 8, 1838: "Finding our usual place of meeting closed against us, we adjourned to the school room of Sarah Douglass who informed that there had been some dispute among the members of the Phoenix Hose company about letting us have the use of their room." Birthplace of the nation's "freedom," a barometer of Philadelphia's racial climate took the nation's measure. To calibrate a woman's life on that scale, note the rise of Philadelphian Sarah Mapps Douglass.

She was a granddaughter of Cyrus Bustill, member of African America's pioneer secular organization, the Free African Society, launched in 1787, and of the family whose bequest to the future included Paul Robeson. Her businesswoman-mother was a milliner; her father, co-founder of the First African Presbyterian Church. Into this middle-class world, Sarah was born in 1806. Privately tutored, she opened a day school in the 1820s that signaled the movement to Free African Schools from segregated charity schools. Enjoying her privilege, she continued on blithely until the city proposed the forced emigration of free blacks to Liberia. A "pass law" was threatened, a preview to South African apartheid. Rioters torched her father's church and, later, the site of an integrated Female Anti-Slavery Society meeting (see June 18). In 1833, Sarah joined a society chapter co-founded by her mother, and in 1838, she aligned her school there. "One short year ago," she wrote, "how different were my feelings on the subject of slavery! I had formed a little world of my own, and cared not to move beyond its precincts. But how was the scene changed when I beheld the oppressor lurking on the border of my own peaceful home! I saw his iron hand stretched forth to seize me as his prey, and the cause of the slave became my own." To appreciate the birth of the black women's freedom movement was to behold Miss Douglass the activist!

Thursday, November 8, 1838

Pennsylvania                                    USA

---

**Turning Points**                                    **Understanding**

And forasmuch as divers freeborn English women, forgetful of their free condition, and to the disgrace of our nation, do intermarry with negro slaves . . . and a great damage doth befall the master of such negroes . . . be it enacted, That whatsoever free-born woman shall intermarry with any slave . . . shall serve the master of such slave during the life of her husband; and that all the issue of such free-born women, so married, shall be slaves as their fathers were.

*J*n 1661, when colonial Maryland enacted a law so odious, who could have predicted it would bear fruit so sweet? On November 9, 1731, Mary Banneky gave birth to one of the nation's first scientific geniuses, Benjamin Banneker—maker of the first all-American clock; astronomer noted for his almanac, surveyor of Washington, D.C.—a black man. Mary, the daughter of a white woman, Mollie Welsh, and an enslaved African prince, Bannka, had met her husband, Robert, the way her mother had met her father—by buying, freeing, and marrying him. It was a family tradition rooted in the cruelties of English law.

Found guilty of stealing milk, Mollie had been offered a devil's bargain—be shipped to indentured servitude in the colonies or be hung. After satisfying her indenture, Welsh secured a small tobacco farm. For workers, she purchased two slaves "from a ship anchored in the Bay" in 1692. Freeing both men, she married one—Bannka. Mollie was uniquely able to flaunt the 1661 law designed to end marriage as an escape route from slavery. As Bannka's former owner, being bound to her husband's former master meant being bound to herself. Certainly, this Bannka-Banneker family tradition did not endear the family to "polite society." But as women victimized by class, gender, and race, Mollie and Mary knew how rude the polite could truly be.

Friday, November 9, 1731

Maryland                                    USA

---

**Family**                                    **Creative Thinking**

*W*ith the blanks of a preprinted form filled in by hand, a receipt was issued for the life of Maria. From Richmond, Virginia, dated November 10, 1860, the receipt reads: "Received of <u>Laura Niece . . . Thirty nine Hundred</u> dollars being in full for the purchase of <u>one</u> Negro Slave named <u>Maria</u> the right and title of said Slave <u>I</u> warrant and defend against the claims of all persons whatsoever, and likewise warrant <u>her</u> sound and healthy. As witness <u>my</u> hand and seal. <u>L. Meinhard</u>." Yet comes the fact that even in the face of such unwarranted and indefensible greed and brutality, some remained more sound and healthy than others. Fisk University preserved the story Ophelia Settle Egypt told of her mother, Miss Fannie.

Many incidents in the life of Miss Fannie could be told, but this one begins when her mistress hit the wrong slave woman with a stick. Miss Fannie hit back, and the two tussled from the kitchen out into the road, where the mistress was nearly naked, her clothes torn to shreds, by the time help came. The master informed the slave that by law she would have to be whipped. Two days later, when two men arrived with a lash, she did not hide. Instead, "she swooped upon them like a hawk on chickens" until her master interceded and this time informed her that if she would not be whipped, she would have to be sold, but she could not take her baby with her. When the day came to sell her, with tears streaming her face, she held the baby upside down, its legs splayed like a wishbone and vowed she would smash the child dead before she would leave it behind. She took her child with her.

"With her ability for work," said Mrs. Egypt, "she did not make a good slave. She was too high-spirited and independent. I tell you, she was a captain." Warrior-women, like Miss Fannie, might have been bought, but they were never owned.

Saturday, November 10, 1860

Slave States                 USA

---

**Revolt!**                             **Respect for One's Power**

*W*ell after violence destroyed Prudence Crandall's school for black girls (see May 23), the "free states" of the North had yet to be liberated. In its coverage of an anti-slavery convention attended by some of the most progressive educators of the day, the November 11, 1837, edition of the *Colored American* quoted Rev. Theodore Wright. "When we hear you talk of female seminaries and of sending your daughters to them, we weep to think our daughters are deprived of such advantages," he mourned in his impassioned landmark speech. "Not a single high school or female seminary in the land is open to our daughters." A graduate of Princeton University, the nation's first black theological seminarian, he knew how education had benefited his life and wished to share the wealth.

A decade earlier, a survey by *Freedom's Journal* revealed the dire state of education for males and females. In Maine, Portland's nine hundred blacks had one Free African School. In Massachusetts, Boston's two thousand had two primaries taught by "African female teachers, and a Grammar School under a master"; Salem's four hundred lost their one school after six months. In Rhode Island, Providence's fifteen hundred people had no school at all. In Connecticut, Hartford's five hundred had none; New Haven's eight hundred had two schools that operated three months per year. Fifteen thousand New Yorkers had two schools, and in Pennsylvania, fifteen thousand Philadelphians had three schools.

From 1827 to 1837, little had changed for the better. South Carolina criminalized teaching black children, enslaved or free. Virginia barred blacks from re-entering the state after attending school. Ohio denied black public school funds. North and South, the determined evolved an underground network united by a single mission, profound in its application to this very day: *each one teach one*.

Saturday, November 11, 1837

North and South              USA

---

**Education**                                              **Initiative**

*S*ince the end of the Civil War, when the right of suffrage was granted black men to the exclusion of women, the issue of women's suffrage was not genetics, brain size, God, or poor old Eve and her "original sin"; the issue was power. Men had it; women didn't. Fifty years later, with America and Europe on the brink of the first "world war" and women eager to have a say in their fate, the fight for suffrage was more fierce than ever. In the South, the legacy of slavery was all too visible in the high ratio of blacks to whites. A divide-and-conquer strategy was offered: grant the vote to white women, not black. By any means necessary, keep the "balance of power" tipped white.

In November 1914, the *Maryland Suffrage News* published a letter to the editor from Sen. Ben "Pitchfork" Tillman of South Carolina. "Experience has taught us that negro women are much more aggressive in asserting the 'rights of the race' than the negro men are. In other words, they have always urged the negro men on in the conflicts we have had in the past between the two races for supremacy." Supremacy? Try justice. Aggressive? We can *do* aggressive for what we know to be right—like our sister-spirit Queen Hatshepsut of Ancient Egypt.

There, in the valley of the Nile in 1500 B.C., one hundred fifty years before the boy-King Tutankhamen ("Tut"), lived Hatshepsut. "I have done this with a loving heart for my father Amun," she wrote in words inscribed on her obelisk. "It is the King himself who says: I declare before the folk who shall be in the future . . . Who shall speak in discussion, Who shall look to posterity." If Egypt preferred a man's rule, she could fix that; she had the power. Declaring herself a man, she had court artisans etch her image in stone with a beard. No problem. A master architect and builder of civilization, she held the throne for thirty-three years!

Thursday, November 12, 1914

Maryland                          USA/Egypt

---

**Suffrage**                                        **Bravado**

*A* s it is said, there is *his*-story, the story of the white man, and then there is our-story—oral histories handed down across the centuries.

So it is with "The Day the Stars Fell," both tale and prophesy assumed to be rooted in the biblical telling of a trumpet that would herald the Second Coming. "On that great gittin up mornin'," our ancestors sang, a day would come when sinners would repent the evil of slavery, "fare you well." On November 13, 1833, that day was at hand. His-story relates an eclipse. Our-story, documented across the generations, was related by Ruth Veletta Jones one hundred and fifty years later:

> Grandma said the mistress called all the slaves in. They were all pray-ing. It was so dark. They never allowed them to come inside the house. They were always on the veranda or out in the yard. "You all come in! I've always been good to you. I didn't make you suffer. You had something to eat." And it was getting darker and darker. And the stars fell and the people were singing and praying and talking about Jubilee. The [slave owner] promised everyone on the place, "You gonna be free. I'm going to set you free if the Lord will just spare me to live." And so the sun came out and he immediately forgot to set them free. He said it was in [their] best interest to stay here. . . . But he was better to them.

"My Lord what a morning," enslaved historian-composers inscribed in tablets of song. "My lord what a mornin, when the stars begin to fall. No more grief and pain for me, I heard from heav'n today, My lord's gonna set me free, I heard from heav'n today." The day of reckoning would come and slavery end. But slaveowners ignored the "trumpet," preferring shooting bullets to shooting stars. And that, dear ones, is how the War for Freedom (his-story's Civil War) began.

Wednesday, November 13, 1833

South/Virginia          USA

---

**Folklore/Historiography**          **Wisdom**

On November 14, 1960, Ruby Bridges was the only child in Louisiana's William Franz Elementary School. In the battle over segregated schools in New Orleans, white parents had denied their children an education, keeping them home from school rather than have them in a class with one little six-year-old first grader. So stark, so infamous, was the scene as U.S. marshals accompanied their little charge to and from school each day that artist Norman Rockwell made it the subject of one of his most famous paintings, *The Problem We All Live With*.

For months, white adults heaped abuses upon the child. For months, she bravely walked past them, saying not a word. Then one day, she suddenly stopped in front of them and said something. She spoke for a moment, in a voice barely audible, then, just as suddenly, continued past them as before. In school, alone as usual, her white teacher, Barbara Henry (a kindred courageous spirit), asked Ruby what she had said to them. Ruby insisted that she had not spoken to them at all. Even from the window, Henry said, she could see Ruby's lips moving. She must have said something to the people. No, Ruby explained. Every morning and every afternoon, blocks away from school, she always said a prayer for the people who taunted her. That morning, she forgot. She had stopped to say her prayer:

> Please God, try to forgive those people. Because even if they say those bad things, they don't know what they're doing. So You could forgive them, just like You did those folks a long time ago when they said terrible things about You.

And, it is said, *a little child shall lead them*. . . .

Monday, November 14, 1960

Louisiana                             USA

---

**Children and Youth**                                        **Innocence**

As Ida B. Wells-Barnett related the tale, writing from Oklahoma Territory on November 15, 1892, Will Bramlette addressed a letter to "Dear Miss Minton":

> You may not remember me and you must pardon the liberty I take. But for the sake of a friend one risks much. . . . Nearly two years ago, my friend George Harris joined me [in Oklahoma City]. . . . In our lonely hours he has talked much of you and I know how dear you are to him. Since that fatal New Year's Day, (you see he has told me all,) not a drop of liquor has passed his lips. He says it lost him the only woman he ever loved and he never wants to look at it again. He thinks you have never forgiven him, and says he doesn't blame you. He has built up a fine [legal] practice in the territory by hard work, and now he is very ill with pneumonia. He has the best attention, but he does not care to get well; he has lost all hope and says nothing when he is himself but when he is out of his mind he is always calling your name. He does not know I have written this letter, but I know a word from you would do him more good than medicine. Won't you write him a word, Miss Emily, and save the best friend I have on earth?

Barely able to read the words through a fog of tears, Emily replied:

> A little bird has brought me the news that you are a very sick man and that you do not get well because you do not seem to care to live. If I tell you that I wish you to live for my sake, will you try to get well? I have always loved you, and since you would neither write to me nor ask me again to marry you, I am going to make use of my leap year prerogative and ask you to marry me. As the New Year is near at hand, and I have no gift to send, now that I know where you are, I have been wondering if you would accept me as a New Year's gift. . . . Yours, Emily

This passage is from the story "Two Christmas Days," published in the January 1894 *AME Zion Quarterly.*

Tuesday, November 15, 1892

National                                    USA

---

**Literature/Love**                                    **Initiative**

"*W*hat shall I tell my children who are black?" asked the poet and artist Margaret Burroughs in her most famous poem.

"What shall I tell my dear one, fruit of my womb, / Of how beautiful they are when everywhere they turn," she pondered, seeking answers wherever strength and sign could be found, drawing pictures, teaching to the lives that would see the beauty she could see, remaking images as they should be, as they must be, in order for a whole, fully-evolved person to be.

"I must find the truth of heritage for myself," she answered. "And pass it on to them," she vowed, strong in will and vision and resolve. She would do just that.

In November 1961, in a room of her house, with help from her husband, Charles Burroughs, she founded the Ebony Museum of African-American History to provide a base of historical and cultural information for the community. Later renamed the Du Sable Museum of African-American History and Art—in honor of Chicago's African American founder, Jean Baptiste Pointe Du Sable—the expanded collection was moved to land donated by the city, where it continues to ask the questions and *pass on* the answers that tell children and adults who are black the things we need to know.

Thursday, November 16, 1961

Illinois                                    USA

---

**Social History**                        **Responsibility to Youth**

*O*n November 17, 1997, students at Medgar Evers College, a young historically black college in the City University of New York, were privileged with a guest lecture by anthropologist Dr. Johnnetta Betsch Cole, president emeritus of Spelman College (see April 5). Hers was the first in a lecture series dedicated to the memory of Dr. Betty Shabazz, the widow of Malcolm X and a Medgar Evers faculty member, who had died tragically that summer (see June 29).

"I charge you, if you're not in the struggle, to get in the struggle, transform this nation of ours, and while you're at it to make a better world," she challenged. "To be agents of change is to do what you are doing—getting yourself a formal education. . . . There can be nothing more revolutionary," she reminded them in the spirit of Dr. Shabazz, who had returned to school as a widow with six children. To young women: "Don't walk behind any man, because the problem of walking behind a man is that you can't see where you're going." A question-and-answer period was just ending when an uneasy query revealed a rumor being circulated—flaunted, really—that an incomplete degree from an average white school would better serve them than a four-year education at a prestigious black college. Exposing the charge as a familiar tactic designed to demean and undermine black people, Dr. Cole reminded her audience that, to this day, most African American professionals are graduates of historically black colleges. But beyond the politics and statistics, there was a deeper truth she wanted to share: "Get the education that helps you make not just a living, but a life."

The right question had been asked of the right person, and the answer was right on time.

Monday, November 17, 1997

National                          USA

---

**Education**                                         **Truth**

*"Sing us 'bout de hard luck*
*Roun' our do'*
*Sing us 'bout de lonesome road*
*We must go. . . ."*

                      —from "Ma Rainey," the 1932 poem by Sterling Brown

*J*n 1900, a fourteen-year-old Gertrude Pridgett arrived onstage at the Columbus Opera House in "The Bunch of Black-
berries" talent show. From that Georgia debut, the blues would
take her down the lonesome road to stardom as Ma Rainey. The
derisive tone of the show's title told part of the story. Wallace
Thurman's line "the blacker the berry the sweeter the juice" told
the other part. From the raw, hard, turn-of-the-century times into
the high life of the 1920s, Ma Rainey took the stage and reigned
supreme as the "Mother of the Blues." She did not invent the
twelve-bar classic form; she popularized its authentic country
cadence. With the spread of her records came acclaim. In the cultural heyday of the 1920s, when Harlem's was not the only renaissance, black was in and Ma was hot. It was the Roaring Twenties
*and didn't she roar.* A white performer would have earned more, but
she did all right for herself with ninety-two records, most her own
songs. In 1935, Madame Gertrude Rainey (as she called herself
once "Ma" and her "Pa" split) retired to the Columbus, Georgia,
home at 805 Fifth Avenue she had bought for her mother in 1920.
On November 18, 1992, that home was designated a national historic landmark open to the public.

    A half-century after her death in 1939, Ma Rainey reigns. She
was inducted into the Georgia Music Hall of Fame in 1992, and
Gambia and the United States have both issued commemorative
stamps in her honor.

Wednesday, November 18, 1992

Georgia                          USA

---

**Music**                                                 **Authenticity**

*M*arried on Christmas Day 1828, Anne Hampton and Solomon Northup vowed their love would stand the test of time, but what a test and *ooohhh* what a time.

In 1841, living a simple, uneventful family life with their three children in Glens Falls, New York, Solomon—a farmer, like his father, and a violinist—was offered a job with a traveling circus. The victim of a ruse to lure him away, he was beaten, drugged, shipped to New Orleans, and auctioned into slavery. Some time later, a letter reached Anne. He was, at least, alive, but knew nothing of his whereabouts that could aid his rescue. For twelve years he tried to escape and she tried to find him, to no avail. In 1850, passage of the Fugitive Slave Act (see September 6) further lessened their chances. Then, in September 1852, Anne received a second letter. Its postmark was the clue: Marksville, Avoyelles Parish, Louisiana. Working every conceivable angle, Anne Northup made a desperate grab at her husband's freedom. "Your memorialist and her family are poor and wholly unable to pay the expenses of restoring his freedom," she wrote, petitioning the governor of the state of New York on November 19, 1852. It worked. As an official agent of the governor, Henry B. Northup came to the rescue. Years before Solomon's birth, Henry's ancestor had owned and freed Solomon's father. In January 1853, his testimony freed Solomon. Twelve years after being kidnapped, Solomon came home to Anne.

Oh, the power of love—and luck. As exceptions prove the rule, in Anne's and Solomon's happy ending, we remember the many loves torn asunder by slavery—centuries of other lovers possessed of the will who could not find the way.

Friday, November 19, 1852

New York/Louisiana        USA

**Family**                                    **Tenacity**

For three days in 1977, November 18 through 21, the National Women's Political Caucus (NWPC) met in Houston, Texas. It was a taste of what the world might be like if women had their rightful 51 percent share of the nation's political power. As the women's movement came of age, at the hub of the United Minority Caucus was California Assemblywoman and future Congresswoman Maxine Waters.

"I don't have time to be polite," Waters would say. "Too many black politicians want to be in the mainstream. They don't want to talk about affirmative action, crime or drugs. My power comes from the fact that I am ready to talk about black people." It was good that she felt that way. For despite the benefits of affirmative action to women, the topic had been excised from the NWPC action agenda due to be forwarded to President Jimmy Carter. Along with other issues critical to the Black Women's Action Plan, it would have to get back on. In a brilliant strategy, the minority caucus formed a coalition of women of color. Word went out on the floor: "Watch Maxine Waters; wherever she runs, rush the other minority plank speakers up behind her." From there, each coalition member deferred to the next in line until the voice of Coretta King was heard. By the time this First Lady of the Civil Rights movement and its heir, the women's rights movement, finished speaking in her well-tuned alto, the plank was passed by acclamation.

Among the sheroes whose activist teachings had culminated in that victory was Modjeska Simkins, a South Carolina legend nearing eighty. Born to progressive parents, she had been raised to lead. From equalizing teachers' salaries across racial lines to dismantling the all-white primary, Simkins was a bold defender of the cause. Well into her nineties, she could stare down any foe with a phrase drenched in history: "I cannot be bought and I will not be sold."

Sunday, November 20, 1977

National/Texas                   USA

---

**Organizing**                              **Empowerment**

$\mathcal{I}$t was 1984. South Africa remained under seige by apartheid. The white minority government had alienated all but two allies, Great Britain and the United States. As president, Ronald Reagan held that South Africa's problem was not apartheid but that of a "few troublemakers" opposed to the rule of law. Nelson Mandela was in prison. Winnie Madikizela Mandela had alternated years between house arrest, detention, and solitary confinement. That June the two were allowed their first touch of hands in twenty-two years. What made that possible—and what made necessary the negotiations that brought down apartheid, released Mandela, and elected him president—was a process of unrelenting international agitation, including events like one that occurred on November 21, 1984.

In a highly visible sit-in at the South African Embassy in Washington, D.C., those arrested, handcuffed, and jailed were Congressman Walter Fauntroy, TransAfrica founder-president Randall Robinson, and Dr. Mary Frances Berry—proud thorn to the Reagan-Bush administration known as "the woman the president could not fire." The first African American woman chancellor of a major research institution, the University of Colorado at Boulder, in 1977 Berry had taken a leave of absence to accept appointment by then-president Jimmy Carter as assistant secretary of the Department of Health, Education, and Welfare. For her years of personal and scholarly activism in pursuit of human rights, Carter later appointed her to the U.S. Commission on Civil Rights. Because she did her job too well, Reagan fired her. She filed suit and was reinstated.

On Thanksgiving morning, the day after the sit-in, Berry called her mother. "Mom, I'm in jail," she said. "Well, it's a good cause," came the answer. *Our roots run deep.*

Wednesday, November 21, 1984

Washington, D.C. USA

---

**Civil Rights**                    **Collective Responsibility**

*I*n 1976, Unita Blackwell began her tenure as mayor of Mayersville, Mississippi—the first African American woman elected mayor in a state where, just a decade earlier, she could not vote.

In the 1960s, as Civil Rights workers infiltrated the front lines of enemy territory, many of the farm workers they met looked like no one had told them Emancipation had come. The NAACP had been there organizing, and many, like regional director Medgar Evers, would even die in the struggle (see February 5). But in Mayersville, as Blackwell would say, "We sure hadn't seen 'em." When she saw SNCC, she volunteered to register voters. When she saw Fannie Lou Hamer, the two helped co-found the Mississippi Freedom Democratic Party and challenged the state's all-white primary and delegation to the 1964 Democratic National Convention. When Blackwell saw the NCNW, however, she was turned off by "these 'highly elites.'" To the credit of NCNW president Dorothy Height, the organization met Blackwell's challenge to take off the gloves—the white gloves of their "clubwoman" past. There, in the trenches, said Blackwell, "The people used to arrest me every day and harass me every day. They turned cars upside down, burned crosses in my yard, threw homemade bombs at us. It wasn't just a song for us, 'We Shall Overcome.' It was our strength."

How did she sustain herself through it all? From which deep well had her activism come? It came from her parents. In 1936, when she was just three, the "boss man" had demanded she work the fields. Her parents refused and moved to Memphis. Over the years, they would move on many times. When Blackwell saw the Civil Rights movement coming, not only did she sing to "overcome," she sang a different tune: "I shall not be moved. . . ."

Monday, November 22, 1976

Mississippi                         USA

---

*O*n November 23, 1997, in full-length plum-colored gowns, the Girls Choir of Harlem stepped into the spotlight, out from behind the long shadow cast by their formidable world-renowned brothers in song, the Boys Choir of Harlem, in what would be the girls' Lincoln Center debut. It was a coming-out event worthy of note; it had taken eighteen years to reach this stage—a journey begun with the choir's founding before its fifty-three current members had been born. With no tradition of girls' choirs to accompany a boys' choir history dating back to the fourteenth century, the road to the Girls Choir debut had encountered many a funding pothole. But, as sixteen-year old Lezlie Watson noted with gleeful resolve when the group's bus arrived at the stage door of Alice Tully Hall, "We are here!"

While the concept of the girls' choir was new, what a noble tradition they would uphold as young women of song. On this day in 1862, diarist-educator Charlotte Forten (see May 24) would write that the children "from across the creek came in and sang a long time for us" such favorites as—appropriately enough to this dawning day of a new tradition by the girls' choir—"Down in the Lonesome Valley" and "No Man Can Hinder Me." On November 23, 1924, the legendary Florence Mills (see October 12) opened to rave reviews in *Dixie to Broadway*. And, on November 23, 1973, a women's singing group with a sound and a legacy all their own, Sweet Honey in the Rock, would debut in concert at Howard University.

For choirs, for the female voice, how brightly the historic Girls Choir of Harlem sunrise had shone! What a joyous day for music their footsteps had followed in!

Sunday, November 23, 1862

National                                      USA

---

"*I* knew the power of a photo to change lives," said Gordon Parks, the luminary photographer. The events of November 24, 1967, certainly proved him right. On that day, his daughter, Leslie, was born and Bessie Fontenelle, a woman whose fragile condition he was chronicling for *Life* magazine, was about to be reborn.

Leslie's birth had him riding high upon life's seesaw. From that perch he had a view of the life that could have been for each of his children had he not made a change in his own life by using his own "good common sense," as his mother termed, following the lessons she and his father had taught him. "I was born to a black childhood of confusion and poverty," he would say of his early years as one of fifteen children born to Sarah and Andrew Jackson Parks in Kansas. "My mother had freed me from the curse of inferiority . . . by not allowing me to take refuge in the excuse that I was born black." Not one to blame the victim for the crime, he knew that good fortune had given the good lessons room to flourish—the benefits of which he hoped to share with Bessie Fontenelle. "Lord, I feel like jumping out that window," she had told him when, in desperate need of heat and hope, a violent cough rocked her just the day before. A week later, drunk from stalking the "jungle of hunger and uncertainty" too long, her husband pushed her son out into the cold. He beat her and she scalded him. "All this needing and wanting is just about to drive my whole family crazy," she cried.

In Parks's gift as a photographer was the power to empower others. Leslie would become a master chef and restauranteur. His photos of the Fontenelles offered a portrait of poverty so vivid that readers sent in donations and the magazine added to the fund. His photos had changed Bessie Fontenelle's life. Her husband found a job, they bought a home, the children breathed fresh air. It was a start.

Friday, November 24, 1967

New York                                    USA

---

**Women and Womanhood**                                    Images

*F*or the relatively few women of the mid-nineteenth century able to work outside domestic service, the profession of choice was teaching. From this vantage came both the privilege and the responsibility of leadership. And although teaching a slave or free person to read was often illegal in the South, it was equally scoffed at in the segregated North, where schools for blacks had been torched by riotous whites. Prudence Crandall (see May 23), a white schoolmistress in Connecticut, was jailed for enrolling black girls. In 1841, a time when all blacks were oppressed, enslaved or free, Ann Plato of the Colored Congregational Church School in Hartford, Connecticut, mused upon her mission in "A Teacher's Prayer":

> *What shall I ask, or what refrain to say?*
> *Where shall I point, or how conclude my lay?*
> *Oh, grant me active days of peace and truth,*
> *Strength to my heart, and wisdom to my youth,*
> *A sphere of usefulness—a soul to fill*
> *That sphere with duty, and perform thy will.*

Serving that will, the Association of Colored Teachers of Long Island issued a call on November 25, 1841: "Brethren come! The cause of Education calls loudly upon you to come. Hundreds of children that are now shut out from the blessings of Education, call loudly upon you to come. If there was ever a time that called for united action, it is now. If there was ever a time for colored freemen to show their love of liberty, their hatred of ignorance, and determination to be free and enlightened, it is now!" Significantly, perhaps coincidentally, the organization's acronym was ACT. To be a true teacher was to be a liberator—a mission not unlike the terms of struggle retained in the marrow of today.

Thursday, November 25, 1841

New York                              USA

---

**Education**                              **Responsibility to Youth**

*T*he fifteenth child of enslaved parents, Mary Jane McLeod had been born free in 1875. Yet the stain of slavery still coloring white attitudes provoked an incident that left an indelible mark on her as a child. One day, while Mary Jane was playing with the daughter of the woman for whom her mother worked, the white child snatched a book from her hand. Because blacks could not read, she said, the book could not be for Mary Jane. That incident was pivotal in forging an adult Mary McLeod Bethune's dream to found a school for blacks beyond the elementary grades. She had learned a key lesson early: books symbolized the differences enforced between people black and white. There was power in the word.

But how did she turn her dream to build a school into a reality? How did she get the pivotal federal appointments that empowered her and with which she helped empower others—even in a segregated world? How did she found the National Council of Negro Women (NCNW), befriend First Lady Eleanor Roosevelt, and become adviser to President Franklin D. Roosevelt? Indeed, what possessed the FBI to clear her name after she was attacked as a communist?

A master builder, Bethune had learned to keep her *eye on the prize* and another delicate art, as she explained at an NCNW meeting on November 26, 1938. "I am diplomatic about certain things," said Mrs. Bethune. "I let people infer a great many things, but I am careful about what I say because I want to do certain things." She had learned that with discretion, the better part of valor, she could open doors bearing this key to success.

Saturday, November 26, 1938

National                                             USA

---

**Leadership**                                        **Ambition**

On November 27, 1984, Whoopi Goldberg was appearing in *Direct from Broadway*. This one-woman showcase so spotlighted her incomparable talent as an actor and her insight as a writer that it made her a star. What had begun in California as *The Spook Show*, an hour-long series of four monologues filled with the "ghosts" of contemporary life, was now on Broadway, produced by Mike Nichols, the veteran stand-up performer turned director-producer. As a little black girl with a shirt on her head, swinging its sleeves and uttering the line "This is my long blond hair," Goldberg struck a nerve. As a streetwise junkie named Fontaine, visiting Nazi victim Anne Frank's house in Amsterdam, Whoopi struck a chord:

> So I went on up the stairs 'cause, you know, 'cause I wanted to see this one book. So I like pulled on the book, and when I did that the bookcase opened up. And on the other side was a whole other room. Now, wasn't nobody up there sayin' "Don't go in"—ain't nah one a dem signs. So I walked in. I happened to turn my head and see the skylight. And I say, oh my, I'm in the room where Anne Frank and the family is. And that kinda like threw me, you know. . . . So I was checking out, you know, the differences. Because, like, *here* we *knew* what was happening—things like the Civil Rights movement, but it was a little bit different over in Europe, mon. 'Cause the Jews wasn't ready. . . . They thought of themselves as Germans, or Austrians, or whatever. And [then] these people *changed* on 'em. . . . And I started examinin' my own sh——. You know, what are my day-to-day worries . . . ? Things like why can't I get an American Express Card, you know? Oh, yeah! Why can't I find a hairdresser to mess with my coif? You know, these are my big day-to-day worries, mon. But *then*, you know, you go into a *room* like this and you hold your coif and your card up against life and death, and you know the true meaning of trivial pursuit. . . .

Tuesday, November 27, 1984

New York                                  USA

---

**Theater**                                              **Echoes**

*J*n the fall of 1964, actor-singer-activist Harry Belafonte gave those who had been in the trenches for SNCC a much-needed retreat—a trip to Africa made possible by $10,000 he personally raised to cover their expenses. Upon their return, one sojourner, Fannie Lou Hamer, reflected on the trip for *Freedomways*:

> People should go there and see. It would bring tears in your eyes to make you think of all those years, the type of brainwashing that this man will use in America to keep us separated from our own people. . . . The little things that had been taught to me about the African people, that they were "heathens," "savages," and they were just downright stupid people. But when I got to Guinea, we were greeted by the Government of Guinea, which is *Black People*—and we stayed at a place that was the government building, because we were the guests of the Government. You don't know what that meant to me when I got to Guinea on the twelfth of September. The President of Guinea, Sekou Touré, came to see us on the thirteenth. Now, you know, I don't know how you can compare this by me being able to see a President of a country, when I have just been there two days; and here I have been in America, born in America, and I am forty-six years pleading with the President for the last two or three years to just give us a chance—and this President in Guinea recognized us enough to talk to us. . . . The *world* is looking at America and it is really beginning to show up for what it is really like. "Go Tell It on the Mountain." We can no longer ignore this, that America is not "the land of the free and the home of the brave."

As the president left, Hamer began to cry, seeing all she had been through in the name of freedom in the context of the evening. Said Belafonte, "I don't think that anybody who was on that trip ever saw life in quite the same way again."

Autumn, 1964

Mississippi　　　　　　　　USA

---

*I*n November 1950, *Freedom*, a monthly newspaper, premiered with sponsorship from actor-singer-activist Paul Robeson (see January 9 and July 8), putting his money where his conscience was. Among the paper's board members was Victoria Garvin, vice-president of the CIO-affiliated Distributive, Processing and Office Workers Union, who contributed a report on women and work.

As Dr. Martin Delany had said, "To know the condition of a people, one has only to know the status of its women." A century later, Garvin wrote, "If it is true . . . then Negro people have a long way to go before reaching the ultimate goal of complete freedom and equality in the United States." With most black women working outside their homes—in contrast to white families, where most women were home-based—ironically, this placed African American women in the forefront of the fight for the rights of women in the workplace. "Historically, it is the burning desire of every Negro woman to be free," Garvin continued, "to live and work in dignity, on equal terms with all other workers. Negro women are eager to undertake a greater role to give substance to freedom and democracy, to help build an America of peace and abundance." Trade unions had a responsibility to forge a progressive agenda: to maintain women in industry, provide opportunities for training and advancement, eliminate wage bias, extend coverage of social welfare legislation to industries and occupations then excluded, and promote women into positions of union leadership.

Along a continuum with labor strategies derailed by the Great Depression, during which unions lost strength to the divide-and-conquer ploys of racism and sexism, the agenda proposed by Garvin was the foundation upon which both the Civil Rights and women's movements would build in the 1960s and 1970s.

Wednesday, November 29, 1950

National                                    USA

---

*O*f her November 30, 1902, arrival in Cape Town to join her husband, the newly appointed AME bishop of South Africa, Fannie M. Jackson Coppin wrote, "After having spent thirty-seven years in the school room, laboring to give a correct start in life to the youth that came under my influence, it was indeed to me, a fortunate incident to finish my active work right in Africa, the home of the ancestors of those whose lives I had endeavored to direct." After joining the landmark Quaker-sponsored Institute for Colored Youth in Philadelphia, she was principal from 1869 to 1902. But as impressive as her career had been, it was only half the tale.

Born enslaved, her grandfather had purchased the freedom of all his children but one, Lucy, her mother—that somehow due to the fact of Fannie's birth. Think of it: an enslaved child held up for shame as the reason for her mother's continued enslavement. Think, too, of this: her mother's newly free sister worked for $6 a month to save $125 and free Fannie. Sent to live with another aunt in New Bedford, Massachusetts, Fannie was "hired out" to a white family who allowed her to go to school but not "on wash day, nor ironing day, nor cleaning day." She worked three days and spent the others in school. Difficult as it was, the wound of her grandfather's cruelty was soothed by the aid and confidence of her aunts and her own tenacity. Rewarded with a modest AME Church–sponsored scholarship, she enrolled in Oberlin College and became, in 1865, the college's second black woman to earn a bachelor of arts degree.

Who better to help minister to a people with the weight of apartheid newly upon them as laws imposed two hundred and fifty years earlier and repealed as "repugnant and unnecessary" were resurrected in full? After all, this was the woman who would "write the book" on educating children (see January 28).

Sunday, November 30, 1902

Pennsylvania   USA/South Africa

---

**Women and Womanhood**                                    **Character**

# December

*Together: Myra and Mabel* (circa 1940). Reprinted courtesy of Muriel Landsmark Tuitt.

For more information, see August 23.

$\mathcal{I}$n the history of public transportation, protests against segregated buses and streetcars had been waged for more than a century. But not until December 1, 1955, had an entire community risen in collective outrage, vowing to ride in peace or walk with pride. On that day, Rosa Parks was riding a bus home from work when the driver—coincidentally, the same driver who had forced her off a bus and kept her fare years before—insisted she give up her seat so that a newly boarded white passenger could ride in a row of seats with no blacks. Mrs. Parks refused and was arrested, fingerprinted, and jailed for her transgression. When the local NAACP president asked if she would be willing to become a test case, she said yes.

As the story has been passed into lore, Parks, a humble uneducated woman with aching feet, was too tired to move to the back of the bus. Not so. What ached was her very soul; what weighed upon her was being "pushed around" in the name of racism. Hardly uneducated and bearing no resemblance to the mammy caricature so integral to the scheme of humiliation, she was a dignified, thoughtful, soft-spoken woman—a seamstress by training and a part-time secretary. While Parks might not have planned her protest, she had prepared for it. That summer, she had attended workshops at the famed Highlander Folk School in Monteagle, Tennessee, which sought to empower the poor and disfranchised with courses in literacy, civics, labor, and race relations. A member of the NAACP, Parks knew her activism could get her into trouble. When that "trouble" came, with her were her mother, husband, and the historic black community-wide 381-day Montgomery Bus Boycott of 1956. Her landmark case found segregated intrastate transportation unconstitutional. A model of organizing, the boycott brought its young strategist, Dr. Martin Luther King, to national prominence, and Parks won acclaim as the "Mother of the Civil Rights Movement."

Thursday, December 1, 1955

Alabama                           USA

**Civil Rights**                                             **Self-respect**

*A*s a Going Home Service delivered Gertrude Ward to her rest on December 2, 1981, the Victory Baptist Church rang out a shout, "Surely, God Is Able." A "hit" that changed the way gospel was sung and where, it was the signature song of the world famous Ward Singers and "Mom" Ward's approach to life—and death.

"Mom had always been a kind of expert on funerals," said her daughter Willa. "She would go by limo, plane, train, or bus to attend one, taking it as a personal challenge to distract the Devil from claiming the soul of the deceased. She would wear her finest fur, most elaborate hat, and brightest jewels. She would cry, moan, sing, and sway. She would say, 'You ain't getting this one, Satan. Try me, do battle with me.' If Ruth and Thelma Davis, Dinah Washington, Roberta Martin, Sam Cooke, Mahalia Jackson, and others are in Heaven, perhaps they can in part thank Mom." But well before that final send-up, Gertrude Ward had paid the price of the ticket to help many a singer on the road to earthly stardom. In a career launched with a revelation heard over a "steaming tub" (see May 30), her contribution to music far exceeded her own voice and that of her daughter, the legendary Clara Ward. Mom Ward was a businesswoman. The first black female booking agent, she set a standard for the gospel circuit. She changed the manner of dress (the Ward Singers were the first to prefer evening gowns to choir robes) and upgraded travel (Cadillacs with trailers). In the 1950s, her forty-city gospel cavalcade expanded the circuit. In the 1960s, she ventured into television, college tours, Las Vegas nightclubs, and foreign tours. So admired were her skills that she published a "Do's and Don'ts" for promoters, performers, and sponsors. But not until her death was one secret "do" documented. Found in a box were ninety-seven money order stubs to radio and television ministries in amounts ranging from $50 to $500. The "do" was this: give God a hand; self-promote.

Wednesday, December 2, 1981

California                    USA

---

**Business**                                    **Initiative**

They were everywhere. Hoochie Mamas. Hangers-on hanging out, trying to get a man—the wrong way. Circling the light of professional basketball fame, they would swarm the stands, swoop down as players exited the lockers, dart across parking lots before the getaway; anything to get a glance and pass a phone number.

Seeing her son in the midst of that craziness, being the only one she knew coping with the challenge of deflecting the media spotlight and the glare of adulation, Charlotte Brandon (mother of Terrell Brandon) knew she had to do something. She founded Mothers of Professional Basketball Players, a group that prepared players' families for life in the National Basketball Association (NBA). Six months later, with the mothers of Grant Hill and Shaquille O'Neal among them, twenty-three mothers met in New York City. In 1997, they held their first convention in Las Vegas. In 1998, it was New Orleans. From twenty-three, their numbers swelled to three hundred family members—even players—of the NBA, the Women's National Basketball Association, and the Harlem Globetrotters. In their sisterhood, they burrowed beyond the veneer of celebrity, behind the glitz of sports, to reflect upon their children (some barely twenty-one) and basketball as big business. Convention speakers addressed drugs, finance, security, and the ever-present Hoochie Mamas. No less on top of their game than the players, having scored, some of the Hoochie Mamas had taken to saving and freezing used condoms to give "less fortunate" friends a shot at getting pregnant. Hardly considered a foul, their "hoop dreams" would be played out in paternity court.

With Mamas like these, a mother's work is never done. In cities across the land, players find a home-away-from-home with each member's mom—a saving grace indeed. Sisters in the cause, they are the ultimate extended family.

December 1996

National                                    USA

---

**Motherhood/Sports**          **Creative Thinking/Sisterhood**

On December 4, 1838, the American Anti-Slavery Society was formed in Philadelphia with James Mott among its leaders. Later that month Lucretia Mott, James's wife, a feminist-abolitionist in her own right (see July 19), co-founded the national Female Anti-Slavery Society, her husband's group being for men only.

This is the anti-slavery movement story historians have told, overlooking the black women who founded the original Female Anti-Slavery Society in 1832 (see February 22). Such misstatements as this are made: "[Black women] were present from the first days of the struggle, working alongside whites wherever they were welcomed." The picture projected is one of powerlessness, passivity, a lack of initiative and creativity. Nothing could be further from the truth. Notable as the white contribution to abolition was, white women pursued abolition as a matter of conscience; black women from *womb to tomb* fought slavery as a matter of life and death. In that lay all the difference and the basis for later rifts. With the noble exception of the few John Browns, white abolitionists opted for "moral suasion" as the means to an end that too long seemed to have no end in sight. In contrast, blacks forged freedom in myriad revolts—from the legendary uprisings like those led by Nat Turner and Granny Nanny to the daily acts of rebellion by women celebrated in these pages. Our Underground Railroad was begun before the first length of track was laid and turned to metaphor. It began with the first helping hand—likely, Native American and soon after that first landing in 1619. Hence the signs and secrets imbided like mother's milk. Hence the messages in code via the spirituals. "Were you there when they crucified my Lord?" we sang, passing on news of Nat Turner. "There is a balm in Gilead to heal the sin-sick soul." Little wonder John Brown's army, known as the "Band of Gileadites," was underwritten, according to oral history, by a black woman—Mary Ellen Pleasant.

Tuesday, December 4, 1838

Massachusetts                                    USA

---

**Ideals**                                    **Self-determination**

$\mathcal{S}$ ometime in 1855 or 1856, three enslaved children, the oldest of whom was seven, left a plantation on the Isle of Wight to live with their grandmother, Dolly Reed, a free woman, on the mainland in Savannah, Georgia. In granting the unusual request of the parents, Hagar Ann Reed and Raymond Baker, slaveowner Valentine Grest did not free the children, he freed the parents to work undistracted by the need to care for them. As is the way with grandmothers, Mrs. Reed went to work as soon as she had her grandchildren in hand. Even if she could not free their bodies, she could liberate their minds through literacy.

In the 1850s, especially in states where many whites were illiterate, heavy punishment befell the literate person of color, enslaved or free. The children, therefore, had to learn by stealth. Each day, the two eldest wrapped their books in paper to deter suspicion or detection by the police and white passersby. As an added precaution, the children first walked the half mile to a square, separated, then, one by one, entered the gate through the yard and into the home of Mrs. Woodhouse, a free woman of color. There, with twenty-five other children, they attended school in the kitchen. At day's end, the trip was reversed. Neighbors who noticed the children were left with the impression that they were there to learn trades, an accepted practice. What they didn't know was that their real stock in trade would soon be their ability to write liberty passes. These passes could mean liberty for a matter of hours or for life—"wings" for those heaven-bound travelers in flight with the "angels" to Canada and Mexico. When Union forces took Fort Pulaski, emancipating the slaves, among them was Mrs. Reed's granddaughter, Susie Baker King Taylor, who bequeathed her Reed-Woodhouse legacy to her fellow ex-slaves and black soldiers in camps nearby. In 1902, she published her autobiography, educating generations more (see April 1).

Circa 1855

Georgia                                    USA

---

**Literacy**                                    **Legacies**

*T*he year 1993 was quite eventful for Marion Williams—the stellar singer who rose to world renown as a member of the Clara Ward Singers and triumphed in her own solo career. In August, she was among the few individuals ever given the MacArthur Foundation's "Genius Award"—a five-year grant of $375,000 for which the only application that counts is the application of one's talent for the greater good. And so she had, as the nation would also note in a Kennedy Center Honors televised tribute and White House dinner on December 6, 1993. In one lyric line, Marion Williams could embrace a crowd and deliver the weary from pain. Dr. Horace Clarence Boyer, the esteemed gospel singer and scholar, has said it best:

> Brought up in a Pentecostal church, Williams was well grounded in singing shout songs at very fast tempos, using fill-in words at points where the melody called for a rest, repeating words and melodic motives for intensity, and singing with a volume like few other singers. Her unique and most outstanding talent, however, was her ability to soar effortlessly into the top of the soprano register with purity and volume. It was not unusual for Williams to sing eight or nine consecutive high C's and then drop to the bottom of her register and deliver a growl in the manner of sanctified preachers. . . . To give [her "ooh"] sound more of a percussive accent, Williams would place a "wh" sound in front of "ooh," thereby producing the syllable "who." This device, now known as the "high who," became a standard practice in gospel and is used when going from the end of one chorus into the beginning of another, producing a seamless sheet of sound.

With five coveted lifetime achievement awards (presented annually since 1978), other Kennedy Center honorees include Marian Anderson, Katherine Dunham, Ella Fitzgerald, Aretha Franklin, Lena Horne, Jessye Norman, and Leontyne Price.

Monday, December 6, 1993

Washington, D.C.          USA

---

**Music**                                          **Excellence**

Those that know whereof they speak say that when Lafe Coleman was found he was not a pleasant object to see. There was no bullet in him—nothing like that. It was the marks upon his neck and the horror of his blackened face.

And Victor Forrest died, as the other two had died, upon another tree.

There is a country road upon either side of which grow trees even to its very edges. Each tree has been chosen and transplanted here for a reason and the reason is that at some time each has borne upon its boughs a creaking victim. Hundreds of these trees there are, thousands of them. They form a forest—"Creaking Forest" it is called. And over this road many pass, very, very many. And they go jauntily, joyously here—even at night. They do not go as Victor Forrest went, they do not sense the things that Victor Forrest sensed. If their souls were not deaf, there would be many things for them to hear in Creaking Forest. At night the trees become an ocean dark and sinister, for it is made up of all the evil in all the hearts of all the mobs that have done to death their creaking victims. It is an ocean arrested at the very edges of the road by a strange spell. But this spell may snap at any second and with that snapping this sea of evil will move, rush, hurl itself heavily and swiftly together from the two sides of the road, engulfing, grinding, crushing, blotting out all in its way.

*T*his passage is from the story "Goldie" by Angelina Weld Grimké, published in the November-December 1920 issue of *Birth Control Review*. The daughter of a white mother and a biracial father (an ex-slave, lawyer, and diplomat), Angelina Weld Grimké upheld the century-long tradition of the esteemed activist biracial Grimké family. As a writer and playwright in the early twentieth century, she employed her art in service to the anti-lynching and human rights movements.

Tuesday, December 7, 1920

The South                    USA

*J*n 1848, Henry "Box" Brown escaped from Virginia to freedom in Philadelphia by having himself crated in a box and freighted by train. With his legendary success, others would make a similar exit. Among them, Lear Green was crated into a sailor's chest and shipped from Baltimore to Philadelphia aboard the same steamer her mother-in-law-to-be was sailing on as a passenger. Then, in the winter of 1857, a twenty-one-year-old woman was crated for delivery by a friend. But delay and standard treatment as actual cargo almost cost her life.

Boxed in Baltimore, she, too, was shipped with her destination stamped "Philadelphia." When her crate "with the living agony in it" was delayed for the night, she was upended several times before being delivered with the other crates. She was retrieved by her accomplice and a "hackman," and her box was finally delivered to the home of Mrs. Myers, "where the resurrection was to take place." When they gingerly pried open the lid, there was the young woman in the straw, unable to speak and barely able to walk. It took three days of bed rest before she regained her strength. "How she ever managed to breathe and maintain her existence . . . it was hard to comprehend," wrote UGRR stationmaster-documentarian William Still. Yet in the story of Eliza (see January 17), made light as she hopscotched a river's breaking ice to flee her pursuers and reach freedom, one sees that "Mary," too, was empowered by a mission—to save her child. Pregnant, she was determined that her baby never know slavery.

What mother among us has not been empowered to dare the impossible by the need to care for our children? Who has not reached her river Jordan and dared the other side by faith alone? In the face of our daring, let us prize our courage and give our sister-selves a moment of praise.

Winter 1857

Maryland                              USA

---

**Escape!**                                    **Self-affirmation**

*O*n December 9, 1995, Toni Cade Bambara exited this world. Friends flooded into Philadelphia to join her family in tribute. Turning her grief into action at the memorial for "TCB," as Toni Cade Bambara signed herself, Toni Morrison vowed to "TCB," *take care of bizness* — to bring Bambara's works to print. In her years as an editor-crusader leading forays of black writers through publishing land mines, Morrison had become kin to Bambara — editor-and-author, sister-friends. True to her word, Morrison edited and published *Deep Sightings and Rescue Missions* in 1996. From the essay "The Education of a Storyteller":

> Back in the days when I wore braids and just knew I knew or would soon come to know *everything* onna counna I had this grandmother who was in fact no kin to me, but we liked each other. And she had this saying designed expressly for me, it seemed, for moments when my brain ground to a halt and I couldn't seem to think my way out of a paper bag — in other words, when I would dahh you know play like I wasn't intelligent. She'd say, "What are you pretending not to know today, Sweetheart? Colored gal on planet earth? Hmph know everything there is to know, anything she/we don't know is by definition the unknown." A remark she would deliver in a wise-woman voice not unlike that of Toni Morrison's as I relisten to it. And it would encourage me to rise to quit being trifling. . . . One day, I came bounding into her kitchen on the sunny side of Morningside Park in Harlem, all puff-proud straight from the library — and I stood over her with my twelve-year-old fast self watching her shuck corn over the *Amsterdam News* and I then announced, standing hipshot, a little bony fist planted on my little bony hip and the other splayed out sophisticated like I said.
>
> "Grandma Dorothy, I know Einstein's theory of relativity."
> And she say, "Do tell. . . ."

*Ahhhh, TCB could sure TCB. . . .*

Saturday, December 9, 1995

New York USA

---

**Women and Womanhood**                                    **Coming of Age**

*I*n 1993, the Swedish Academy named Toni Morrison its Nobel Prize laureate for Literature. In the formal announcement, the academy praised her as "a literary artist of the first rank. . . . She delves into the language itself, a language she wants to liberate from the fetters of race. And she addresses us with the luster of poetry." In nearly a century of Nobel laureates, Morrison was the first African American woman so honored.

In her historic acceptance speech, Morrison mesmerized the international assembly with her telling of the ancient parable of the old blind woman, the village children, and the bird. In her cautionary tome, the bird is language. Its current dilemma has been created by those who fear its power; it is being endangered by those who would trap it and control its destiny to manipulate and misinform. What will become of this bird, because the blind woman cannot see, she will not guess; to do so could endanger the bird. Instead, she/Morrison tells us: what will become of our language—its vitality, its vulnerability—is in our hands.

When news of the prize was first announced, Morrison said she was thrilled that her mother was "still alive and can share this with me. I can claim representation in so many areas. I'm a Midwesterner, and everyone in Ohio is excited. I'm also a New Yorker, and a New Jerseyan, and an American, plus I'm an African-American, and a woman. . . . I'd like to think of the prize being distributed to these regions and nations and races." On December 10, 1993, as the prize was formally bestowed, she accepted it, "mindful of the gifts of my predecessors, the blessing of my sisters, in joyful anticipation of writers to come." Little wonder that an artist-friend left this message on Morrison's answering machine: "My dear sister," she said, "the prize that is yours is also ours and could not have been placed in better hands."

Friday, December 10, 1993

Stockholm                Sweden

ust before the holidays, an author was asked to autograph a book to a woman and her family: Terri, Kevin, Erin (the couple's toddler), and "Little Kev" (her soon-to-be-born son). The author stopped, stunned. Everything she'd been taught told her not to do it—not to name the new baby before he was born; not to claim him "just in case." With her stomach churning recipes for disaster, she looked to the other women, more experienced mothers, standing nearby. Each looked more apprehensive than the next. But afraid to cast a pall on the woman's pregnancy, the author signed the book as asked. She was glad she did. As she later learned, between the mothers, older and new, Terri had the most to teach about parenting one's children and oneself. In her inclusion of her unborn baby was her defiance of negativity. The other women had been raised to decipher life's journeys with fear; Terri approached hers with fearlessness.

Terri and her husband, gracious people, had achieved success with the same dogged, hard work all knew well. But to the mix, they added an openness to well-formed, calculated, risk-taking. Nurturing a tiny kernel of an idea from acorn to oak, they reinvested in a bank that they expanded as major shareholders. In business, their story was special. In African American business, it was unique.

Later, one of the women present at the book signing—a success in her own right and the mother of three grown children—was asked about a miscarriage and stillbirth she had suffered. Would she do what Terri had done for both babies—plan and decorate their nurseries months before birth? She thought for a while, then confided, "I do not know what it would be, but I would buy at least one thing. I would work at expecting success for my baby. And if it didn't happen this time, not happening would be the aberration; not the other way around." Terri was the teacher.

December 1995

Massachusetts                    USA

---

**Women and Womanhood**                                **Confidence**

Sunday morning two weeks before Xmas, Rev. Steele preached his second formal sermon in St. Michaels Church on "Gossip" and truly St. Michaels was in an upheaval. . . . Even if he was to render his resignation within the next twelve hours—he would have the satisfaction of knowing that he had been a p-a-s-t-o-r and not a figure head.

He got everyone to thinking and Mrs. St. Anthony wondered if "he could rightly know what had been said about him by the Ladies' Aid. . . ."

"Humph," said Mrs. Tucker, "much he cares for your opinion or any one of the rest of us, I'm thinking. . . ."

"Mrs. Coombs and her sister, Mrs. Cook, do come to church—but I declare they would be better at home," said Mrs. Ford.

"Mrs. Cook told me," said Mrs. Phillips, "she looked at the pipes of the organ so hard that she could tell every move on them and where, with her eyes shut, and it was no wonder they had fallen down on her before this. . . ."

"Well I can't see," said Mrs. St. Anthony, "why he wanted to change things. . . ."

"The whole thing in a nut-shell is he hasn't paid the attention to our marriageable daughters we thought he should," said Mrs. Tucker. . . .

"I can't get over that sermon," said Mrs. St. Anthony—hopping back to the old subject.

"Neither can I," said Mrs. Phillips.

"There goes the Reverend and the widow now!" said Marie Phillips.

"Well that caps the climax," said old Mrs. Ford. . . .

*T*his passage is from the story, "A Christmas Party That Prevented a Split in the Church," by Margaret Black, published in the *Baltimore Afro-American* of December 23 and 30, 1916. Ms. Black, an avowed feminist, edited the paper's Women's Column.

Sunday, December 12, 1915

Maryland                                            USA

---

**Literature/Humor**                                            **Roots**

*A* s the freedom train wound its way through Georgia, the Albany Movement—significant for initiating a city-by-city offensive against segregation—officially began on December 13, 1961. To pray for the release of jailed Freedom Riders, two hundred protesters marched to City Hall, where they were arrested for parading without a permit. As they were taken off, hundreds more replaced them. In the second wave was Bernice Johnson Reagon, who would "find her voice" in the Albany jail and never stop singing for freedom. An early member of SNCC, Reagon would cite its "godmother," Ella Baker, as one of her greatest influences. Ironically, the day the Albany Movement and Reagon came of political age was Ella Baker's day. Born on December 13, 1903, in Norfolk, Virginia, Baker died on December 13, 1986, in New York City. In between, she forged a mighty legacy.

In 1969, Baker concluded her speech to the historic Institute of the Black World with the parable of a man whose doctors had given him the choice of saving his sight or his memory, not both. "Save my sight," he answered. "I would rather see where I am going than remember where I have been." Said Baker:

> I am saying as you must say, too, that in order to see where we are going, we not only must remember where we've been, but *we must understand where we have been.* This calls for a great deal of analytical thinking and evaluation of methods that have been used. We have to begin to think in terms of where we do really want to go and how can we get there. Finally, I think it is also to be said that it is not a job that is going to be done by all the people simultaneously. Some will have to be in cadres, the advanced cadres, and some will have to come later. But one of the guiding principles has to be that we cannot lead a struggle that involves masses of people without identifying with the people.

Wednesday, December 13, 1961

Georgia                                    USA

---

**Social History**                                    **Understanding**

$S$ peak the words *Eternal Father* and most claim them as the navy hymn. But for a century of West Indians, these words marked a rite of passage. A prayer for loved ones at sea, it was the immigrant's hymn sung by families for those seeking to turn the tides of fate on far-off shores. In 1917, during World War I, the family of Myra Carlisle (see August 23; December's lead photo) sang "Eternal Father" as she dared troubled waters. Leaving St. Kitts in the Caribbean for New York City after the sinking of the *Lusitania,* her ship avoided disaster sailing by night and standing still by day with passengers of every class confined below deck.

*Eternal Father strong to saaave.... Whose arms hath tossed the restless waaave....* West Indian immigrants had a way of holding on to the vowels as if clinging to a last glance of home. Forty-three years of hopes and promises would mark the trail from 1917 until Myra's *homegoing* in the winter of 1960. With each step she took toward good-bye at the PanAm gate, she shed layers of her years as easily as the winter coat she removed to reveal her airy summer dress. *Oh hear us when we cry to thee. For those in peril on the sea,* sang Myra's family as her plane slid backward from the gates of Idlewild airport. Flying "plenty miles and plenty more years," she left New York a grandmother and returned to St. Kitts a girl renewed by remembered youth.

Her eyes dimmed by cataracts, the grandmother in her could barely see when she departed New York. Not so the girl in St. Kitts on December 14, 1960. Doing what she would do for the next three months—visiting with girlhood friends, bathing her sore eyes in the Caribbean Sea—by spring Myra had changed. Even as she reversed the miles and added back the years, the change could be seen. Hurrying past customs, she ran into the embrace of her gathered clan: "I see you all now plain as day."

Wednesday, December 14, 1960

New York — Basseterre             USA — St. Kitts

---

**Women and Womanhood**                    **Re-visioning**

*O*n December 15, 1939, as a full regiment of media troops stormed Atlanta for the film premiere of Margaret Mitchell's book, dear ole Dixie might have been *Gone With the Wind*, but its dear ole Mammy was here to stay. Her myth, for years so carefully fantasized, was now more real than ever. There, in Technicolor, was her too-beautiful portrayal by Hattie McDaniel. Significantly, McDaniel was racially barred from the premiere but broke the blackout on Academy Awards night in 1940, winning an Oscar for the role, the first ever awarded an African American.

Other attempts to enshrine Mammy had been made over the years. In 1912, a statue to Mammy on the Washington, D.C., Mall was proposed. And as historian Catherine Clinton has written, "Most treacherous of all, for over 100 years she has haunted kitchen shelves; even with the handkerchief removed from her head after a 1980s update, we still recognize this pernicious incarnation grinning down at us—Aunt Jemima." But who could blame McDaniel for taking on the role? As Donald Bogle has answered with the title of his aptly named film history, the only roles then open to blacks in Hollywood were *Toms, Coons, Mulattoes, Mammies and Bucks*. McDaniel certainly had a better deal than her black co-star, Butterfly McQueen. For her part in the film, McQueen got a slap from Scarlett for not knowin' "nothin' 'bout birthin' no babies." Assessing her own film history, McDaniel said caustically, "I'd rather get paid $1,500 a week to play a maid, than $15 a week to be one." Such were the options of the day. McDaniel would further recount, with equal verve and veracity, "I portray the type of Negro woman who has worked honestly and proudly to give our nation the Marian Andersons, Roland Hayeses, and Ralph Bunches"—two opera virtuosi and a Nobel Prize laureate. That she had. For all the real mammies of little choice, McDaniel made the memory of them on film one invested with dignity.

Friday, December 15, 1939

Georgia        USA

---

**Film**               **Self-portraiture**

*I*n Marseilles, Kentucky, a woman bought herself by washing and ironing at night after giving a full day's work to her slaveowner. For seven long years, sleep came only in naps until the day she was free. The woman then set her sights on buying her children. But time ran out, and her sixteen-year-old daughter went up for auction. The price for her was nine hundred dollars; the mother had only four hundred. Finally, a man agreed to buy the daughter for the mother. The mother paid him four hundred dollars as a down payment, and he held a mortgage on her daughter until the balance was paid with contributions from friends.

In Maine, a couple shared good news in *The Liberator* of December 16, 1836:

> George Potter and Rosella his wife, would take this opportunity to express their gratitude to God, and under him, to the benevolent individuals who generously contributed in aiding them to redeem their two children from Slavery. They have the unspeakable happiness of informing the generous donors that, on the 12th inst. they received their children, aged eleven and seven years, raised from the degradation of slavery to the rank of Freemen.

Not every slave could work for herself to buy freedom for herself or for her children. Some made payments on themselves only to find the deal "forgotten." With no recourse, their money and their hopes dashed, they remained trapped. Slavery was a sadistic business. Then there were the mothers from Marseilles and the Potters of Maine, who seized the opportunity they had and made the most of it. Freedom had its price. And the price was paid by any means necessary—including by giving the devil his (or her) due. As we rescue families "bound out" to this day, not everyone can be saved, not everyone can "buy," but our collective aid and praise support those who can and do.

Friday, December 16, 1836

Kentucky/Maine USA

On Christmas Day 1848, Ellen and William Craft made one of history's most ingenious escapes from slavery. Using the biases of race and gender to their advantage, Ellen, a very light-skinned woman, masqueraded as a sickly young white man traveling with his dark-skinned slave, William. Arriving safely in Philadelphia, the couple was free at last, but imperiled, and quickly left for Boston. There, they attended night school, learning to read and to write, and became active abolitionists. Then the Fugitive Slave Act of 1850 was passed by Congress. Conscripting every American to hunt and return the "property" of slaveholders, it imposed stiff penalties on friends of runaways. A warrant was issued for the capture of William and Ellen Craft. With word and funds spirited to them via the abolitionist network, the Crafts made a hasty escape on a steamer bound for England.

Given their saga, how could anyone believe that the Crafts wished to return to slavery? Yet that dubious "news" spread throughout the American mainstream press. In its December 17, 1852, issue, the abolitionist paper *The Liberator* published a letter written by Ellen Craft from her safe haven at Ockham School in Surrey, England, dated October 26, 1852: "God forbid that I should ever be so false to liberty as to prefer slavery in its stead. In fact, since my escape from slavery, I have got on much better in every respect than I could have possibly anticipated. Though, had it been to the contrary, my feelings in regard to this would have been just the same, for I had much rather starve in England, a free woman, then be slave for the best man that ever breathed upon the American continent."

Having emancipated her body and her mind, Ellen Crafts let her authentic voice speak volumes for herself and for millions of others.

Friday, December 17, 1852

Georgia          England/USA

---

Aunt Linda was so absorbed by what she was doing that she heard no sound. Gladys paused upon the threshold of the cabin, fascinated by the old woman's strange occupation. She was bending over the contents of an old hair chest, tenderly shaking out one little garment after another of a baby's wardrobe . . . tenderly murmuring, "O, my lam, my poor lil' lam," and then as if speaking to some one unseen, she would say: "No, my darlin, no your ole mother will shorely nevah break her promise to young master, but O, if you could only see how lovely your little Gladys has growed to be! Sweet innocent Gladys and her pore ole granma must not speak to or tech her, must not tell her how her own ma loved her and dat dese old hans was de fust to hold her. . . ."

For a moment, Gladys, fresh and sweet as a flower, felt only the tender sympathy of a casual observer, for what possible connection could there be between her and this old colored woman in her sordid surroundings. . . . Gladys felt the absurdity of her fears, yet in spite of herself, the words welled up from her heart to her lips, "O Aunt Linda, what is it, what have I to do with your dead?" With an hysterical laugh she added, "Do I look like someone you have loved and lost in other days?" Then the simple-hearted old woman, deceived by the kindly note in Gladys' voice, and not seeing the unspeakable horror growing in her eyes, stretched out imploring hands as to a little child . . . saying, "O, Gladys . . . you is my own sweet Alice's little chile, O, honey I's your own dear granma. . . ." The old woman was so happy to be relieved of the secret burden . . . that she had almost forgotten Gladys' presence until she saw her lost darling fainting before her very eyes. . . .

*T*his passage is from the story "After Many Days Gone: A Christmas Story," by Fannie Barrier Williams, published in the *Colored American Magazine* of December 5, 1902.

December 1902

Virginia                                    USA

---

*I*n the winter of 1818, in one of the earliest efforts to orga-nize African American women, forty Massachusetts women founded the Colored Female Religious and Moral Society of Salem. From their constitution:

> *Article I*—At the weekly meeting of the Society, when the appointed hour arrives, and a number are convened, the exercises shall begin by reading in some profitable book, till all have come in who are expected.
>
> *Article II*—A prayer shall then be made by one of the members . . . a chapter in the Bible shall be read, and religious conversation be attended to, as time will allow.
>
> *Article III*—Four quarterly days . . . beginning on the first day of every January, to be observed as days of solemn fasting and prayer.
>
> *Article IV*—We promise not to ridicule or divulge the supposed or apparent infirmities of any fellow member. . . .
>
> *Article VIII*—If any member commit any scandalous sin, or walk unruly, and after proper reproof continue manifestly impenitent, she shall be excluded from us, until she give evidence of repentance. . . .

Alas, this was Salem, where the witchcraft hysteria of 1692 had so seized the pious that when they were done, 150 stood accused as witches and imprisoned. Of the twenty executed, fourteen were women, and it is said that the tales of Tituba (see March 1), a slave woman, had literally and figuratively inflamed the panic. In so cautiously laying out the plan of each meeting, perhaps a word to the wise had been sufficient. Unlike her fellow "witches," all white, Tituba's near-death experience was averted by her owner's property rights. Her life thus saved, her soul had time to follow. As free women of color, Tituba's daughters of the society had no such social protection. 'Twas better by far to be safe than sorry.

Winter 1818

Massachusetts                  USA

---

*I*n a scathing 1904 essay, "Not Color but Character," Nannie Burroughs declared war on the self-hatred that shackled blacks to the standards of white beauty used to disfranchise us. "What does this wholesale bleaching of faces and straightening of hair indicate? It simply means that the women who practice it wish they had white faces and straight hair." Thirty years later, she had a new theme: straighten the mind, not the hair. On December 20, 1933, before a capacity crowd of two thousand Louisianans, she spoke on "What Must the Negro Do to Be Saved?" It was vintage Burroughs. "It's not the skin that needs brightening, it's the mind," she goaded. "Chloroform your 'Uncle Toms'!"

At the Young Peoples' Forum at Bethel AME Church, here was Miss Burroughs at the depth of the Great Depression, the dust bowl dirt-poor 1930s, when scapegoating and lynching were sports permitted the otherwise powerless. Risking her unbleached skin to tell the unvarnished truth, she challenged the "leeches and parasitic leaders who are absolutely eating the life out of the struggling, desiring mass of people." The quickest way to rid one-self of them, she said, was the best way. "The Negro is oppressed not because he is a Negro, but because he'll take it," she needled. "Stop apologizing for not being white and rank your race. . . . We're a race on this continent that can work out its own salvation. A race must build for nobility of character, for a conquest not on things, but on spirit. We must have a glorified womanhood that can look any man in the face . . . and tell of the nobility of charac-ter within black womanhood. Stop making slaves and servants of our women. . . . They've made possible all we have around us."

In sum: "Aspire to be, and all that we are not, God will give us credit for trying." Ever educating, ever agitating, ever affirming, ever Miss Nannie Burroughs.

Wednesday, December 20, 1933

Louisiana                                          USA

---

**Social History**                                          **Life's Work**

*I*n 1993, the publishing hit of the year poured 206 years of wisdom into one twentieth-century memoir, *Having Our Say*, by sister-authors Sarah Louise and Annie Elizabeth Delany—Sadie and Bessie, the Delany sisters, aged 104 and 102, respectively.

They were the last survivors of a prestigious family whose motto was "Your job is to help somebody." Their father was the first African American Episcopal bishop. One brother was an assistant U.S. attorney. Sadie, with a bachelor's and a master's degree from Columbia University, taught for thirty years in the New York City public school system. And in 1923, Bessie, a Columbia Medical School graduate, opened a dental practice. By the 1990s, both had been retired for over thirty years. Yet they remained active women involved in life—vivacious, bright, and funny.

"If you asked me the secret to longevity, I would tell you that you have to work at taking care of your health," said Bessie. "But a lot of it's attitude. I'm alive out of sheer determination, honey!" Sadie agreed. "People always say that they'd like to live to be one hundred, but," said Sadie, "no one really expects to, except Bessie. She always said she planned to be as old as Moses. And when Bessie says she's going to do something, she does it. Now, I think Moses lived to one hundred twenty. So I told Bessie that if she lives to a hundred and twenty, then I'll just have to live to one hundred twenty-two so I can take care of her."

Both still had an eye for a good-looking guy, but as two bold, vibrant bachelorettes with over a century of experience each, they had learned to keep such affairs of the heart in perspective. Said Bessie, "When people ask me how we lived past one hundred, I say, 'Honey, we never had husbands to worry us to death!'"

Tuesday, December 21, 1993

New York                                         USA

---

**Women and Womanhood**                           **Longevity**

It was Christmas just before the turn of the century. From Alice Moore's vantage as a public school teacher in Brooklyn, New York, the real story was one of *guilt and gilt.* For too many of her students, the "Gilded Age" was bitterly tarnished. "With the tinkle of joy-bells in the air," she wrote, "the redolence of pine and the untasted anticipation of saccharine joys to be . . . [this] is childhood's time. . . . Yet, there are many who have never come into their kingdom at all."

There is Julia: seven and unkempt. "What will Santa bring you?" asked a classmate. "Nothin' but another beatin' I guess." Matilda lives in an orphanage. "A swarthy, pretty black-eyed Hebrew. . . . She wears the uniform of an asylum not far away. Christmas? It is incomprehensible to her. . . . But Santa Klaus she understands, and the gifts that are denied her." Florence plays in the cold, icy air, poorly dressed in hand-me-downs. "When the winds nip through from river to river she seeks shelter in a tenement, dark and fetid and noisy with brawls and drunkenness." And there is little Frank, "gazing hungrily in brilliant windows."

"These little folks are not imaginary small personages created for Sunday-school literature and sentimental dissertations on so-called sociology," wrote Moore. "They are actual." They had been robbed of childhood joy. Theirs was not the comfortable, traditional Christmas tale. They were contemporary children with barely a manger. But what could one teacher do? With "The Children's Christmas," published in the *Indianapolis Freeman* on December 25, 1897, Alice Moore made the conveniently invisible visible, then cofounded an aid society, the White Rose Mission. In 1898, she married poet Paul Lawrence Dunbar, and is today remembered by her married names, Alice Dunbar-Nelson (see February 16).

December 1897

Indiana                                    USA

---

**Children and Youth**                                    **Conscience**

*T*he war was done, the soldiers home victorious; it was Christmas Day 1918. For a group of family and friends, it was their second Christmas on millionaire's row in Tarrytown, New York, where there was plenty of room at the inn Madam C. J. Walker had built—a mansion by black architect Vertner W. Tandy and named Villa Lewaro by opera virtuoso Enrico Caruso for her daughter, A'Lelia Walker Robinson. At midnight, Madam awakened each guest with her Merry Christmas wish. Her friend Hallie Queen described the scene after they returned from church to find "Madam waiting for us before a glowing fireplace":

> In that beautiful state dining room, with its wonderful furnishings and . . . all the material good that life could expect . . . there was a distinguished minister, Rev. Brooks of Baltimore, who charmed us with stories of his European travels, then Mrs. [May Howard] Jackson, the brilliant moulder of human faces; her husband, W. T. S. Jackson, the mathematician; Lieut. O. Simmons, the army officer; a wounded overseas soldier wearing a *croix de guerre*; Mr. Williams, the politician; Mr. [Lloyd] Thomas, one of Madam's secretaries; Mrs. [Agnes] Prosser, her sister-in-law; and I. . . . After dinner we went into the wonderful music room and listened to old Christmas carols or read in the library. . . . Christmas night we motored in to New York City to attend a basketball game at the Manhattan Casino. Mme's entrance was the signal for an ovation and she was at once requested to throw the ball from her box. . . . The following day was to be a great day for she had been invited by the Mayor of the City to go out on his boat and observe the return of the Atlantic Fleet. So ended [Christmas] and it was impressed upon my mind a memory of her goodness, devotion, reverence, humility and faith.

And so, African America's First Lady celebrated Christmas and her own humble birth fifty-two years earlier in Delta, Louisiana, on December 23, 1867.

Wednesday, December 25, 1918

New York                                    USA

---

*J*n 1966, Maulana Ron Karenga, then a University of California Ph.D. candidate in political science, used philosophical
concepts rooted in African civilization over thousands of years to
celebrate and inspire contemporary African American life. He
called his creation Kwanzaa, derived from the Swahili term *kwanza,*
which means "first fruits." Each of seven days, December 26
through January 1, he dedicated to one of seven principles, the
*Nguzo Saba.* On this first day of Kwanzaa we harvest those "first
fruits" that loosed the shackles of bondage. In the spirit of *Umoja,*
"unity," we dedicate ourselves "to strive for and maintain unity in
the family, community, nation, and race"; to act as one, single-
minded in service to our freedom.

On December 26, 1776, the American colonies were at war for
independence under Gen. George Washington, a slaveholder who
would become the first president of the new republic. When
troops captured one thousand British Loyalists in a dawn raid on
that day, among the African American soldiers was Robert Shurtleff, a Massachusetts free woman! For eighteen months, Deborah
Sampson had fought in disguise. How did she do it—and why?
"Bound out" after her father's untimely death, she worked and
attended school part-time. Tall and often assigned "men's work,"
she decided to live as a man. Taking advantage of the revolutionary fervor of the time, she spent twelve dollars to make herself a
suit and enlisted in the army. When she was wounded, her doctor
did not betray her secret. Having sacrificed much for freedom—
everyone's, black and white—she was discharged with honor and
a pension. With publication of her biography in the 1790s, she
stepped onstage at Boston's Federal Street Theatre and later
toured New England in a lecture adaptation of her exploits. An
"extraordinary instance of female heroism," her tombstone reads;
"Deborah Sampson Gannett, Robert Shurtleff, The Female Soldier: 1781–1783."

Thursday, December 26, 1776

New Jersey                                    USA

*D*ecember 27: Kwanzaa day two. The day of *Kujichagulia,* "self-determination." This is the day "to define ourselves, create for ourselves, and speak for ourselves."

The South, a land of secrets and codes, would prompt William Faulkner, one of its favored literary sons, to observe, "The past is never dead; it's not even past." In the 1950s, a girl come-of-age in Pine Bluff, Arkansas, had long known of her adoption, but she had more questions. Back then, adoption was a thing people heaped under layers of shame and guilt. Not knowing how to embrace the past and the future life for which the child had been chosen, the attempt was to bury a past that could never stay dead once empowered by intrigue. Understanding her daughter's need to find the link that was hers to clasp in times of joy and need, Hattie Rutherford Watson told her daughter, Marian Etoile, what she knew of life: "Don't worry so much about the immediacy of yesteryear, look into your face and see the millennium of time."

Here today, as we stand before a new millennium, we look to our yesteryears in adopted/adapted motherlands the world over and there is doubt. Yet, linked and lifted, in all we have seen and done and overcome, the future is ours to dare. We are the ones who create the legacy that will inspire generations to come. We are the ancestors who will steady the steps of tomorrow. We are the ones who will chart tomorrow's yesterday. In our faces is the wisdom of time; in our eyes the power of sight. With vision, we move on. . . .

Circa 1960

Arkansas                                    USA

*D*ecember 28: Kwanzaa day three. The day of *Ujima*, "collective work and responsibility," the day "to build and maintain our community together, to make our sisters' and brothers' problems our problems, and to solve them together."

On December 28, 1821, the "Order Book" of the Daughters of Africa noted: "Mrs. Hannah Morris please to pay to Mrs. Elissabeth Emery Five Dollars for the President [s] Chaire of the Daughter of Africa. Phoeby Lewis President, Elissabeth Matthew, Sucr [Secretary]." On March 1, 1822: "Mrs. Morris Treasure Please to Pay to Sidney Buck and Elissabeth Griffith for Ann Hacket a sick member . . . her week allowance $1 50." On April 25, the society bought paper and ink, duly noted. By May 5, Ann Hacket's child had died; the society loaned her $4 for the burial "acordian [according] to 10 article of the Constution." And, on November 15, the treasurer paid Sarah Pratte "ten dollars for the lost of hir housband."

Their spelling was imprecise, their handwriting barely legible, their signatures often X's; but their intent was clear and their legacy indelible. In 1821, two hundred working-class Philadephian women founded the Daughters of Africa Society. Valuing sisterhood and economic empowerment, they sustained family and community. Theirs was not the first such affiliation. In 1787, the Free African Society had been founded by eight male Philadelphians, with apprenticeships for children and death benefits. Six years later, the Female Benevolent Society of St. Thomas followed. Among the co-founders of the AME Zion Church in 1796 were women who, within a generation, formed "The Mother Society," parent to all the AME women's church groups. But in the detailed records of the Daughters of Africa, a wholly secular union, one gains unique insight into daily life and witnesses the birth of an African American women's movement.

Friday, December 28, 1821

Pennsylvania               USA

---

**Kwanzaa: Ujima**         **Collective Work and Responsibility**

*D*ecember 29: Kwanzaa day four. The day of *Ujamaa*, "co-operative economics." This is the day "to build and maintain our . . . businesses and to profit from them together." Sometimes the business of business is believing in each other, as the acts of three philanthropic elders demonstrate. Their extraordinary choices and gifts have empowered people other than themselves to profit for years to come.

With the death of Mary Johnston in 1982, the secret of her extreme frugality came to light. So dearly had she valued education that she had spent twenty-five years working odd jobs to complete her college degree—and share her wealth. Ninety-one at the time of her death, subsisting on $4,500 per year for her last five years, the philanthropist donated $1,000 each year to the students of Oberlin College.

Oseola McCarty was in her mid-eighties when she made one amazing gift to the future: $150,000 from her savings to the University of Southern Mississippi to endow a scholarship fund for African American students. McCarty had saved the money in her seventy-five years as a laundress, cook, and working other odd jobs. Her hands gnarled from arthritis, Ms. McCarty said, "I wish I could do more."

And in 1988, Dr. Ruth W. Hayre, a retired educator, announced to 116 Philadelphia elementary school graduates that their job was to graduate high school; hers would be to mentor and provide their full college tuition scholarships. The legacies of two grandfathers powered her "Risers," half of whom made it to the finish line—an ex-slave whose childhood zest for learning yielded the phrase "Tell them we are rising," immortalized in a poem by Whittier; and an orphaned immigrant turned banker whose Latin inscription to her in a book of his speeches read "They live forever who live for others."

1980s–1990s

National                  USA

---

*D*ecember 30: Kwanzaa day five. The day of *Nia,* "purpose": "to make as our collective vocation the building . . . of our community . . . to restore our people to their traditional greatness."

On December 30, 1935, at the depth of the Great Depression, amid the desolate frost of nature and fortune, Marian Anderson raised her "voice of the century" to build the spirits of our community. Having broken her ankle, she could not walk into place on stage that night. Wheeled on behind a closed drape, she appeared standing in the curve of the piano at the curtain's retreat, her face mystically angular in the light, as if by some unseen inner power she had magically, majestically, parted the barriers between her and her audience. That she had. Anderson could sing "Deep River my home is over Jordan" and take you there. In a career begun with being snubbed by music schools and vocal coaches in her native Philadelphia, she triumphed in Europe, gave historic testament to the power of truth with her concert on the steps of the Lincoln Memorial (see April 9), and made her 1955 Metropolitan Opera debut as the century-old opera's first African American diva. Who but the mighty Marian could have sustained such deep, fresh tones for over thirty years, transcending so many obstacles and so much time?

The daughter of John and Anna Anderson, she bore the standard for us all. In the wisdom of a people, what she had learned kept her going forward and giving back: "There is a Negro spiritual, 'I open my mouth to the Lord and I will never turn back. I *will* go. I *shall* go, to see what the end will be.' And it sums up so much of what so many people need to feel who don't find all those wonderful things around them. I will go and I shall go to see what the end will be. Why? Because I believe in what I find at the end."

Monday, December 30, 1935

New York                    USA

*D*ecember 31: Kwanzaa day six. The day of *Kuumba,* "creativity": "to do always as much as we can in whatever way we can in order to leave our community more beautiful and beneficial than when we inherited it."

On December 31, 1967, Anna Arnold Hedgeman retired as a commissioner on religion and race of the National Council of Churches. Her career there marked neither the end nor the beginning of an era, but a continuity of our history. Best known as a deft organizer of the 1963 March on Washington (see August 28), Hedgeman had long shown creativity in getting a job done. In World War II, when the military was segregated and black nurses had not been assigned to tend the black troops white hands would not touch, Hedgeman creatively engaged First Lady Eleanor Roosevelt. "I sat in the second row where she was speaking and then I made myself last in the receiving line. I had my sentence ready. 'Mrs. Roosevelt, the Negro nurse is being cheated by our government in terms of the war effort, and I need to talk with you.' She looked at me and said, 'Of course,' and invited the organizers for tea at her apartment." Within two weeks, things happened, said Hedgeman: "She knew people." Hedgeman knew people, too; how to motivate them. "I'm my father's daughter," she said. "I'm a product of 1865 as well as 1900. He had come out of the slave system. His mother and father had been slaves and they were in our household in St. Paul, Minnesota."

At this pivotal juncture — poised on the cusp of two millennia — we are all our fathers' and our mothers' daughters. Daughters, too, of a system that would deny and dismiss us, we have come from many places to this point in our story of family and sisterly pride. Look at where we have been and all we have done. All we are and have been is in our household; all we can and will be is in our hands.

Sunday, December 31, 1967

National                                          USA

---

**Kwanzaa: Kuumba**                                          **Creativity**

# Bibliography

## Archives, Libraries, and Private Collections

Aaron Douglas Papers, Manuscript, Archives and Rare Books Division, Schomburg Center for Research in Black Culture, New York Public Library

Amistad Research Center, New Orleans, Louisiana

Beinecke Manuscript Library, Yale University, New Haven, Connecticut

Black American West Museum, Denver, Colorado

Charles Drew Papers, Moorland-Spingarn Research Center, Howard University, Washington, D.C.

Claude A. Barnett Papers, Chicago Historical Society, Chicago, Illinois

Clements Library, University of Michigan, Ann Arbor, Michigan

Colorado Historical Society, Denver, Colorado

Connecticut Historical Commission, Hartford, Connecticut

Egypt, Ophelia Settle; J. Masuoka; and Charles S. Johnson, "Unwritten History of Slavery; Autobiographical Accounts . . ." Fisk University, Nashville, Tennessee

Genealogical Collection, Free Public Library, New Bedford, Massachusetts

Indiana Historical Society, Indianapolis, Indiana

John Hope Franklin Research Center, Duke University, Durham, North Carolina, on-line archival exhibit on African American women

Josephine Baker Papers, Beinecke Manuscript Library, Yale University, New Haven, Connecticut

Katonah Museum, "Revisiting American Art: Works from the Collections of the HBCUs," 1997, exhibition catalog

Lucy Chase Manuscript Collection, American Antiquarian Society, Worcester, Massachusetts

Maine Historical Preservation Commission, Augusta, Maine

Mary Church Terrell Manuscript Collection, Library of Congress, Washington, D.C.

Meta Warwick Fuller Papers, Manuscript, Archives and Rare Books Division, Schomburg Center

Metropolitan Opera Archives, New York, New York

Museum of Modern Art Film Library and Archives, New York, New York

Museum of Television and Radio, New York, New York

National Air and Space Administration, Washington, D.C.

National Historic Trust, Washington, D.C.

National Park Service, U.S. Department of the Interior, Washington, D.C.

New York Historical Society, New York New York

Nyquist, Corinne, *"On the Trail of Sojourner Truth in Ulster County, New York,"* Sojourner Truth Library, New York State University College at New Paltz

Philadelphia Historical Society, Philadelphia, Pennsylvania

Schomburg Center for Research in Black Culture, New York Public Library

Utah State Historical Society, Salt Lake City, Utah

## Books

Adams, Janus, *Freedom Days*. New York: John Wiley & Sons, 1998.

———, *Glory Days*. New York: HarperCollins, 1995.

——, *Underground Railroad: Escape to Freedom*. Wilton, Conn.: BackPax Int'l, 1987.

Angelou, Maya, *I Know Why the Caged Bird Sings*. New York: Random House, 1970.

Aptheker, Herbert, *A Documentary History of the Negro People in the United States*, 7 vols. New York: Citadel Press, 1951–1974.

Aron, Paul, *Unsolved Mysteries of American History*. New York: John Wiley & Sons, 1997.

Bailey, Pearl, *Between You and Me: A Heartfelt Memoir on Learning, Loving and Living*. New York: Doubleday, 1989.

Baker, Jean-Claude, and Chris Chase, *Josephine*. New York: Random House, 1993.

Bambara, Toni Cade, *Deep Sightings and Rescue Missions*. Ed. by Toni Morrison. New York: Pantheon, 1996.

Bates, Daisy, *Long Shadow of Little Rock*. New York: David McKay Company, Inc., 1962.

Bearden, Romare, and Harry Henderson, *A History of African-American Artists: From 1792 to the Present*. New York: Pantheon, 1993.

Bedini, Silvio A., *The Life of Benjamin Banneker*. New York: Charles Scribner's Sons, 1972.

Bennett, Katie Brown, *Soaking the Yule Log*. Decorah, Iowa: Anundsen Publishing Co., 1995.

Berlin, Ira, and Barbara Fields, et al., *Free at Last*. New York: New Press, 1992.

Blassingame, John W., ed., *Slave Testimony: Two Centuries of Letters, Speeches, Interviews & Autobiographies*. Baton Rouge, La.: Louisiana State University Press, 1977.

Bolton, Ruthie (pseudonym), with Josephine Humphreys, *Gal: A True Life*. New York: Harcourt Brace & Co., 1994.

Boyer, Horace Clarence, *How Sweet the Sound: The Golden Age of Gospel*. Washington, D.C.: Elliott & Clark Publishers, 1995.

Brooks, Gwendolyn, *Report from Part One*. Detroit, Mich.: Broadside Press, 1972.

Buckley, Gail J. Lumet, *The Hornes*. New York: Alfred Knopf, 1986.

Bundles, A'Lelia Perry, *Madam C. J. Walker: Entrepreneur*. New York: Chelsea House, 1991.

Busby, Margaret, ed., *Daughters of Africa*. New York: Ballantine Books, 1992.

Butler, Cleora, *Cleora's Kitchens & Eight Decades of Great American Food*. Tulsa, Okla.: Council Oaks Books, 1985.

Chase, Henry, ed., *In Their Footsteps*. New York: Henry Holt & Co., 1994.

Chase-Riboud, Barbara, *Sally Hemings*. New York: Viking Press/Avon, 1979.

Chesi, Gert, *Voodoo: Africa's Secret Power*. Austria: Perlinger-Verlag, 1979.

Clark, Septima, *Ready from Within*. Navarro, Calif.: Wild Trees Press, 1986.

Coffin, Levi, *Reminiscences of Levi Coffin*. Cincinnati Western Tract Society, 1876.

Cohen, Marcia, *Sisterhood: True Story of the Women Who Changed the World*. New York: Simon & Schuster, 1988.

Coles, Robert, *The Story of Ruby Bridges*. New York: Scholastic, 1995.

Collier-Thomas, Bettye, *Treasury of African-American Christmas Stories*. New York: Henry Holt & Co., 1997.

Coppin, Fannie Jackson, *Reminiscences of School Life*. Philadelphia, Pa: African Methodist Episcopal Book Concern, 1913.

Dallard, Shyrlee, *Ella Baker: A Leader Behind the Scenes*. Englewood Cliffs, N.J.: Silver Burdett, 1990.

Dance, Daryl Cumber, ed., *Honey Hush*. New York: W.W. Norton, 1998.

Douglass, Frederick, *My Bondage and My Freedom*. New York: Miller, Orton & Mulligan, 1855.

Drotning, Phillip T., *An American Traveler's Guide to Black History*. New York: Doubleday, 1968.

Du Bois, W. E. B., *Darkwater: Voices from Within the Veil*. New York: Harcourt, Brace & Howe, 1920.

——, *W. E. B. Du Bois: A Reader*. Ed. by David Levering Lewis. New York: Henry Holt & Co, 1995.

——, *Seventh Son*, vol. 2: *Thought and Writings W. E. B. Du Bois*. Ed. by Julius Lester. New York: Random House, 1971.

Ducongé, Ada Smith, and James Haskins, *Bricktop*. New York: Atheneum, 1983.

Dunbar-Nelson, Alice, *Give Us Each Day: The Diary of Alice Dunbar-Nelson*. Ed. by Gloria T. Hull. New York: Norton, 1984.

Elaw, Zilpha, *Memoirs of the Life, Religious Experience . . . of Mrs. Zilpha Elaw, an American Female of Colour . . . Written by Herself*, 1846.

Fidelman, Geoffrey Mark, *First Lady of Song: Ella Fitzgerald for the Record*. New York: Birch Lane Press/Carol Publishers, 1994.

Fitzpatrick, John C., ed., *Writings of Geo Washington from the Original Manuscript Sources 1754–1799*. Washington, 1938.

Giddings, Paula, *When and Where I Enter*. New York: William Morrow Co., 1984.

Grant, Joanne, *Ella Baker: Freedom Bound*. New York: John Wiley & Sons, 1998.

Grimké, Charlotte Forten, *The Journal of Charlotte L. Forten: A Free Negro in the Slave Era*. New York: Dryden Press, 1953.

Gurko, Miriam, *The Ladies of Seneca Falls: The Birth of the Woman's Rights Movement*. New York: Macmillan, 1974.

Hamer, Judith A., and Martin Hamer, *Centers of the Self: Short Stories by Black American Women from the 19th Century to the Present*. New York: Hill & Wang, 1994.

Hansen, Joyce, and Gary McGowan, *Breaking Ground Breaking Silence: Story of New York's African Burial Ground*. New York: Henry Holt, 1998.

Harris, Michael W., *Rise of Gospel Blues: Music of Thomas A. Dorsey in the Urban Church*. New York: Oxford, 1992.

Harris, Middleton A., et al., eds. *The Black Book*. New York: Random House, 1974.

Hayre, Ruth Wright, and Alexis Moore, *Tell Them We Are Rising*. New York: John Wiley & Sons, 1997.

Hemenway, Robert, *Zora Neale Hurston: A Literary Biography*. Champaign, Ill.: University of Illinois Press, 1977.

Henson, Josiah, *The Life of Josiah Henson*. 1849.

Hine, Darlene Clark, et al., eds., *Black Women in America: An Historical Encyclopedia*. Bloomington, Ind.: Indiana University Press, 1993.

hooks, bell, *Bone Black*. New York: Henry Holt, 1996.

Hunter-Gault, Charlayne, *In My Place*. New York: Farrar Straus Giroux, 1992.

Hunton, Addie W., and Kathryn M. Johnson, *Two Colored Women with the American Expeditionary Forces*. Brooklyn, New York: Brooklyn Eagle Press, 1920.

Hurston, Zora Neale, *Dust Tracks on a Road*. New York: Harper Perennial, 1993 (orig. ed. 1942).

Katz, William Loren, *Black Women of the Old West*. New York: Atheneum, 1995.

Knight, Gladys, *Between Each Line of Pain and Glory*. New York: Hyperion, 1997.

Lerner, Gerda, ed., *Black Women in White America: A Documentary History.* New York: Vintage Books, 1992.

Lewis, David Levering, *When Harlem Was in Vogue.* New York: Knopf, 1981.

Lightfoot, Sara Lawrence, *Balm in Gilead: Journey of a Healer.* Reading, Mass.: Addison-Wesley, 1988.

Long, Richard A., *Black Tradition in American Dance.* New York: Prion/Smith-mark, 1989.

May, Rev. Samuel J., *Some Recollections of Our Antislavery Conflict.* Boston, 1869.

Meltzer, Milton, *The Black Americans: A History in Their Own Words.* New York: T. Y. Crowell, 1964, 1984.

Parker, Gwendolyn M., *Trespassing: My Sojourn in the Halls of Privilege.* New York: Houghton Mifflin, 1997.

Parks, Gordon, *Half Past Autumn.* Boston: Little, Brown and Corcoran Gallery of Art, 1997.

———, *Voices in the Mirror.* New York: Doubleday, 1990.

Parsons, Elsie Clews, ed., *Folklore from the Cape Verde Islands.* Cambridge, Mass., and New York: American Folklore Society, 1923.

Robinson, Jontyle Theresa, curator, *Bearing Witness: Contemporary Works by African American Women Artists.* New York: Spelman College and Rizzoli International Publications, Inc., 1996.

Robinson, Sharon, *Stealing Home: An Intimate Family Portrait by the Daughter of Jackie Robinson.* New York: HarperCollins, 1996.

Rose, Phyllis, *Jazz Cleopatra.* New York: Doubleday, 1989.

Ross, Diana, *Secrets of a Sparrow.* New York: Villard Books, 1993.

Salem, Dorothy C., ed., *African American Women: A Biographical Dictionary.* New York: Garland Publishing, 1993.

*Sierra Reference Encyclopedia by Collier's* (CD-ROM), Bellevue, Wash.: Sierra On-Line, Inc., 1996.

Smith, Jessie Carney, ed., *Powerful Black Women.* Detroit, Mich.: Visible Ink Press, 1996.

*Spinner: People and Culture in Southeastern Massachusetts,* Vol. 4. New Bedford, Mass.: Spinner Publications, 1988.

Sterling, Dorothy, ed., *We Are Your Sisters: Black Women in the 19th Century.* New York: W. W. Norton, 1984.

Still, William, *The Underground Railroad.* Philadelphia: Porter & Coates, 1872.

Story, Rosalyn, *And So I Sing: African-American Divas of Opera & Concert.* New York: Amistad, 1990.

Stovall, Tyler, *Paris Noir: African Americans in the City of Light.* New York: Houghton Mifflin, 1996.

Talalay, Kathryn, *Composition in Black and White: Tragic Saga of Harlem's Biracial Prodigy.* New York: Oxford University Press, 1995.

Thompson, Era Bell, *American Daughter.* Chicago, Ill.: University of Chicago Press, 1946.

Trager, James, *The Women's Chronology.* New York: Henry Holt, 1994.

Truth, Sojourner, *Narrative of Sojourner Truth.* 1850.

Tuitt, Muriel Landsmark, "Peanuts and the Sunday News." In *Roots & Routes,* Wilton, Conn.: BackPax, 1988.

Vogel, Susan, *Baule: African Art Western Eyes.* Yale University Art Gallery, New Haven, Conn.: Yale University Press, 1997.

Wachs, Eleanor, ed., *It Wasn't in Her Lifetime, But It Was Handed Down: Four Black Oral Histories of Massachusetts.* Columbia Point, Mass.: Commonwealth Museum, 1989.

Walker, Alice, *Living by the Word: Selected Writings 1973–1987.* New York: Harcourt Brace Jovanovich, 1988.

Walls, William J., *The African Methodist Episcopal Zion Church: Reality of the Black Church.* Charlotte, N.C.: AMEZ Publications, 1974.

Ward-Royster, Willa, as told to Toni Rose, *How I Got Over: Clara Ward & the World-Famous Ward Singers.* Philadelphia, Pa.: Temple University Press, 1997.

Warren, Gwendolin Sims, *Ev'ry Time I Feel the Spirit.* New York: Henry Holt & Co., 1997.

Washington, James Melvin, Ph.D., ed., *Conversations with God: Two Centuries of Prayers by African Americans.* New York: HarperCollins, 1994.

Wedin, Carolyn, *Inheritors of the Spirit: Mary White Ovington and the Founding of the NAACP.* New York: John Wiley & Sons, 1998.

West, Dorothy, *The Wedding.* New York: Doubleday, 1995.

Wheat, Ellen, *Jacob Lawrence, American Painter.* Seattle: University of Washington Press and Seattle Art Museum, 1986.

Williams, Juan, *Eyes on the Prize.* New York: Viking, 1987.

Winfrey, Oprah, *Journey to Beloved.* New York: Hyperion, 1998.

Woods, Paula L., and Felix H. Liddell, eds., *I Hear a Symphony: African Americans Celebrate Love.* New York: Anchor/Doubleday, 1994.

Wright, Richard, *Native Son.* New York: Harper & Brothers, 1940.

## Periodicals

"A Bishop for God's People: The Ordination of Barbara Clementine Harris, Suffragan Bishop," ordination program.

Adams, Janus, "All God's Children Need Wings" (unpublished).

"Arts Alive: Ruby Dee," *Seattle Times,* November 3, 1996.

Bailey, Aisha, "A Letter from Zimbabwe," February 1998 (unpublished).

Black, Margaret, "A Christmas Party That Prevented a Split in the Church," *Baltimore Afro-American,* December 23 and 30, 1916.

Catlett, Elizabeth, "The Role of the Black Artist," address to the 1975 National Conference of Artists, reprinted in *The Black Scholar,* June 1975.

Clarke, John Henrik, *My Life in Search of Africa,* Africana Studies and Research Center, Cornell University, Monograph Series No. 8, 1994.

Cleaver, Kathleen, "A Dreadful Absurdity," dissertation, Yale University Law School, 1988.

———, "Three Ways that Martin Luther King Changed My Life," *Black Renaissance,* 1999.

Cox, Ida B., "Wild Women Don't Have the Blues," 1924.

Dunbar-Nelson, Alice Moore [Alice Moore], "The Children's Christmas," *Indianapolis Freeman,* December 25, 1897.

*Frederick Douglass' Paper,* 1859.

Grimké, Angelina Weld, "Goldie," *Birth Control Review,* November–December 1920.

Grimké, Charlotte Forten, "Life on the Sea Islands," *Atlantic Monthly,* May 1864.

Hall, L. Priscilla, "In Praise of Black Women Lawyers," *New York Law Journal,* July 1, 1998.

Harper, Frances Ellen Watkins, "The Two Offers," *Anglo-African Magazine,* 1859.

Hopkins, Pauline Elizabeth, "Bro'r Abr'm Jimson's Wedding: A Christmas Story," Boston: *The Colored American Magazine,* December 1901.

Latimer, Leah Y., "The Smallest Soldier," *Emerge,* February 1998.

Lyons, Maritcha R., *Memories of Yesterdays All of Which I Saw and Part of Which I Was* (unpublished).

Mayer, Robert A., *Blacks in America: A Photographic Record.* New York: International Museum of Photography at George Eastman House, 1986, exhibition catalog.

*Minnie Evans: Artist.* Greenville, N.C.: Wellington B. Gray Gallery, 1993, exhibition catalog.

Morrison, Toni, Nobel Laureate Speech, the Nobel Foundation, 1993.

———, "What the Black Woman Thinks About Women's Lib," *New York Times,* August 22, 1971.

Nelson, Jill, "At Home on an Island," *New York Times,* August 22, 1993.

Robeson, Eslanda Goode, "Black Paris," *Challenge,* vol. 1, no. 4, January 1936.

Sanchez, Sonia, "After Saturday Night Comes Sunday," 1971. Reprinted by permission of the author.

*The Afro-American.*

*The Chicago Defender.*

*The Crisis,* National Association for the Advancement of Colored People, 1915–1929.

*The New York Times.*

*Update,* newsletter of the African Burial Ground and Five Points Archaeological Projects, Office of Public Education and Interpretation, African Burial Ground, 1997.

Williams, Fannie Barrier, "After Many Days: A Christmas Story," Boston: *The Colored American Magazine,* December 1902.

Williamson, Lynette Williams, "To Her Own Self Be True," *Mills Quarterly,* Winter 1998.

"Women of the World: You're not fat, you're living in the wrong country," *Marie Claire,* February 1998.

# General Index

Aaron, Hank, 4/8
Abbott, Robert, 6/15
Abolitionist movement,
 1/31, 2/6, 2/22, 2/26,
 2/27, 3/14, 3/20, 3/26,
 4/12, 5/10, 5/23, 5/24,
 5/27, 6/18, 7/6, 7/19,
 9/9, 9/17, 9/20, 9/21,
 12/4, 12/17
Abzug, Bella, 7/13
Academy Awards, 12/15
Adams, Abigail, 3/31
Adams, Armacie, 5/12
Adams, Bertel, 11/2
Adams, John, 3/31
Affirmative action, 10/9
Aframerican Woman's Jour-
 nal, 2/14
Africa, Land of My Fathers
 (Thompson), 4/30
"African American Women
 in Defense of Our-
 selves" (article), 10/11
African Burial Ground,
 9/30
African Dorcas Society,
 2/22
African Female Intelli-
 gence Society, 9/20
African Free Schools, 7/6
African Journey (Robeson),
 7/8
African National Congress,
 2/12
African Union Methodist
 Church, 8/12
African Universal Church
 and Commercial
 League, 7/20
Africana Studies and
 Research Center
 (Cornell University),
 3/27
Africana Studies Program
 (New York Univer-
 sity), 10/15
Afro-American, The, 3/31,
 10/23
"After Many Days Gone:
 A Christmas Story"
 (Williams), 12/18
"After Saturday Night
 Comes Sunday"
 (Sanchez), 4/2

Aïda (Verdi), 5/15
Alabama State College,
 5/21
Alamo, 10/5
Albany Movement, 12/13
Ali, Muhammad, 4/4
All Angels Church, 8/12
All-African Women's
 Conference, 5/2
Allen, Bonnie, 10/22
Allen, Richard, 4/12, 6/20
Allen, Sarah, 6/20
Alston, Charles, 2/18
AME Church, 6/10, 6/20,
 7/1, 11/30
AME Zion Church, 2/1,
 6/20, 7/6, 12/28
AME Zion Quarterly, 11/15
American Anti-Slavery
 Society, 4/12, 5/27,
 12/4
American Association of
 University Women
 (AAUW), 5/14
American Colonization
 Society (ACS), 8/27,
 10/24
American Daughter (Thomp-
 son), 4/30
American Equal Rights
 Association, 5/10
American Gothic (Parks),
 8/19
American Missionary
 Association (AMA),
 9/17
American Negro Academy,
 4/3
Amistad (ship), 5/23, 5/27,
 9/17
Amos, Emma, 1/18
Amsterdam News, 12/9
Anderson, Daisy Graham,
 5/19
Anderson, Ivie, 1/16
Anderson, Jourdon, 8/7
Anderson, Mandy, 8/7
Anderson, Marian, 1/8, 4/9,
 6/7, 7/24, 8/28, 12/6,
 12/15, 12/30
Anderson, Robert, 5/19
Angelou, Maya (née
 Marguerite Johnson),
 4/15, 8/17

Anglo-African Magazine,
 10/30
Anti-Slavery movement,
 4/12, 5/10
Antiwar movement, 7/13,
 9/7
Antony and Cleopatra
 (Barber), 9/16
Apartheid, 6/16, 11/8,
 11/21, 11/30
Aristide, Jean-Bertrand,
 1/13
Arkansas Civil Air Patrol,
 4/29
Arkansas State Press, 4/29
Armstead, Mary D., 8/11
Armstrong, Louis, 6/27
Ashford, Nick, 4/15, 10/29
Associated Negro Press,
 10/14
Association for the Study
 of Negro Life and
 History, 2/7
Association of Colored
 Teachers (ACT) of
 Long Island, 11/25
Atkinson, Ti-Grace, 10/17
Atlanta Baptist Seminary,
 1/23
"Atlanta Compromise"
 (Washington), 4/6,
 10/19
Atlanta University, 2/18,
 7/15
Augusta Institute, 2/9
Ayers, Ida B., 5/4

Back-to-Africa movement,
 5/2, 8/27, 10/24, 11/2
Badu, Erykah, 4/20
Bagnal, William, 8/11
Bailey, Aisha, 2/13
Bailey, Harriet, 2/20
Bailey, Pearl, 5/25
Baker, Ella, 1/22, 6/9, 6/25,
 12/13
Baker, Josephine, 8/28,
 9/28, 10/27
Baldwin, James, 11/7
Ballet Russe de Monte
 Carlo, 5/15
Baltimore Afro-American,
 12/12
Bambara, Toni Cade, 12/9

Banneker, Benjamin, 11/9
Banneky, Mary, 11/9
Baptist Church. *See* individual Baptist
churches
Barnard College, 5/1
Barnett, Claude A., 10/14
Barnett, Etta Moten, 10/14
"Bars Fight" (Terry), 8/25
Basie, Count, 1/16
Bass, Charlotta, 7/7
Bates, Daisy, 4/29, 8/22,
9/4
Baumfree, Isabella, 6/1, 7/4
Bayreuth Festival, 7/24
Beal, Frances, 6/9
Beckwith, Byron de la, 2/5
*Behind the Scenes; Or, Thirty
Years a Slave and Four
Years in the White
House* (Keckley), 3/5
Belafonte, Harry, 10/29,
11/28
*Beloved* (Morrison), 3/21,
6/19, 8/18
Benjamin, Miriam E., 4/26
Bennett College, 4/5
Bennett, Katie Brown, 7/27
Bermuda, 8/6
Berry, Mary Frances, 11/21
Bethel AME Church, 6/20
Bethune, Mary McLeod,
5/5, 5/9, 5/18, 11/26
Bethune-Cookman College,
5/18
*Between You and Me* (Bailey), 5/25
Bevel, James, 2/4
Bible, 2/1, 3/1, 3/29, 5/6,
6/5, 12/19
Biko, Stephen, 6/16
*Birth Control Review,* 12/7
Black & Tan Minstrels,
3/15
Black American West
Museum and Heritage Center, 10/7
Black Bottom, 9/28, 10/27
Black, Margaret, 12/12
Black Panther Party, 9/7,
10/22
Black Swan Records, 2/15
"Black Wall Street," 10/9
"Black Woman in the
Academy: Defending
Our Name" (symposium), 1/13
Black Women Mayors'
Caucus, 11/3

Black Women's Action
Plan, 11/20
Black Women's Book
Group, 9/20
Black Women's Liberation
Committee, 6/9
*Black World,* 4/30
"Blacks in America" (photography exhibit),
11/6
Blackwell, Unita, 4/4, 11/3,
11/22
*Bloodchild* (Butler), 6/5
"Bloody Sunday" (Selma,
Ala.), 3/25
Blues, 2/15, 3/15, 3/23,
6/27, 10/31, 11/18
Bolton, Ruthie, 2/28
Bond, Julian, 2/4
*Bone Black* (Hooks), 3/17
Boone, Sarah, 4/26
*Boston Commonwealth,* 6/2
*Boston Observer,* 4/6
Bowers, Sam, 5/28
Boyer, Horace Clarence,
9/26, 10/31, 12/6
Boynton, Amelia, 3/25
Boys Choir of Harlem,
11/23
"Boy's Estimate of His
Mother's Work, A"
(Mossell), 3/6
Bradford, Perry, 7/31
Bradley, Mamie Till, 8/24
Brandeis University, 6/4
Brandon, Charlotte, 12/3
Brandon, Terrell, 12/3
Brazil, 9/5, 10/21
Brazile, Donna, 10/11
"Bricktop." *See* Smith,
Ada
Bridges, Ruby, 11/14
Bright, Mary, 4/24
*Bright Road* (Vroman), 7/12
"Bronx Slave Market, The"
(Baker and Cooke),
6/25
Brooklyn Woman's
Homeopathic Hospital and Dispensary,
8/16
Brooks, Gwendolyn, 8/8
"Bro'r Abr'm Jimson's
Wedding" (Hopkins),
3/24
Brotherhood of Sleeping
Car Porters, 9/14
Brown, Anne Wiggins,
10/10

Brown, Charlotte
Hawkins, 3/11, 6/17,
10/8
Brown, Clara, 9/19
Brown Cottage (Virginia),
9/17
Brown, Eliza Jane, 9/19
Brown, Hallie Quinn, 2/7
Brown, Henry "Box," 12/8
Brown, James, 6/14
Brown, Jill, 6/15
Brown, John, 1/29, 4/12,
10/16, 12/4
Brown, Linda, 5/17
Brown, Oliver, 5/17
Brown, Sterling, 11/18
Brown, Willa, 6/15
Brown University, 2/13
*Brown v. Board of Education*
(1954), 1/6, 4/23,
4/25, 5/17, 5/21, 6/24,
8/15
Buffalo Soldiers, 7/25
Bumbry, Grace, 7/24
Burghardt, Mary Silvina,
2/23
Burleigh, Harry T., 3/11
Burroughs, Margaret, 11/15
Burroughs, Nannie, 3/19,
3/31, 7/17, 10/19,
12/20
Busby, Margaret, 10/24
"Business of America Is
War, and It Is Time
for a Change, The"
(Chisholm), 7/13
Bustill, Cyrus, 11/8
Busy Bee Club, 6/3
Butler, Cleora, 5/4
Butler, Loney, 9/2
Butler, Octavia, 6/5, 10/15
Byrd, Harriet Elizabeth
"Liz," 1/15

*Cabin in the Sky* (play),
10/20
Caesar, Shirley, 2/2
Café La Mama, 10/18
Café Society, 1/9
*California Eagle,* 7/7
Calvin, Bernice, 6/11
Calvin, Dolores, 6/11
Camlin's Slave Pen, 7/26
Campbell, David, 1/30
Campbell, Lucie E. "Miss
Lucie," 1/10
Canada, 3/8, 3/14, 3/20,
4/19, 9/6, 10/13,
10/28, 12/24

Canterbury Female Board-
ing School, 5/23, 9/9
Cape Verde, 10/1
Caravans, 2/2
Carlisle, Mabel, 8/23
Carlisle (Landmark),
Myra Helena "Lena,"
8/23, 11/2, 12/14
*Carmen Jones* (film), 7/12
Carmichael, Stokely. *See*
Touré, Kwame
Carnegie Institute, 2/18
Caroline Robinson Jones
Collection, 10/29
Carter, Estelle, 1/5
Carter, James Earl
"Jimmy," 6/27, 11/20,
11/21
Carter, Parthenia Harris,
1/5
Carter, Rosalynn, 6/27
Cartey, Mary, 8/23
Caruso, Enrico, 12/25
Cathy, William, 7/25
Catlett, Elizabeth, 1/18,
2/18, 10/5
Catton, Bruce, 9/8
Central High School (Lit-
tle Rock, Ark.), 9/4
Central Intelligence
Agency (CIA), 10/25
Central Park (New York,
N.Y.), 7/21, 8/12
Césaire, Aimé, 10/15
Chaney, Ben, 8/4
Charleston, 9/28, 10/27
Chase-Riboud, Barbara,
1/18
Cheney, Ednah Dow, 4/27
Cheshier, Squire, 7/27
Cheyney College, 1/28
*Chicago Defender,* 4/30, 6/15,
7/31
*Chicago Globe,* 7/15
*Chicago Tribune,* 8/20
Child, Lydia Maria, 1/29
"Children's Christmas,
The" (Moore), 12/22
Children's Defense Fund,
4/5
Childress, Alice, 1/1, 2/3
Chionesu, Philé, 10/25
Chisholm, Shirley, 5/5,
7/13, 11/3
"Chit'lin Circuit," 2/15
"Christmas Party That Pre-
vented a Split in the
Church, A" (Black),
12/12

Church for the Fellowship
of All Peoples, 2/14
Church of England, 2/11,
11/2
Church of Jesus Christ of
Latter-Day Saints
(Mormons), 1/21,
4/24
Church of the Good Shep-
herd, 7/5
*City of Richmond* (ship),
8/11
City University of New
York, 11/17
Civil Rights Congress, 2/3
Civil Rights movement,
1/22, 2/12, 2/14, 3/25,
5/8, 5/28, 6/2, 6/4, 6/9,
6/10, 6/11, 6/24, 7/13,
7/28, 8/4, 8/16, 8/21,
8/22, 9/3, 9/7, 9/14,
9/15, 9/17, 10/19,
11/20, 11/22, 11/27,
11/29, 12/1
Civil War, 1/12, 1/19, 2/1,
3/2, 3/4, 4/12, 5/12,
5/19, 8/21, 11/13
Clara Ward Singers, 5/30,
12/2, 12/6
Clark, Jim, 3/25
Clark, Septima "Mother
Conscience," 1/22
Clarke, John Henrik, 3/27
Clay, Cassius. *See* Ali,
Muhammad
Cleaver, Eldridge, 10/22
Cleaver, Kathleen Neale,
6/9, 10/22
*Cleora's Kitchens: The Memoir
of a Cook and Eight
Decades of Great Ameri-
can Food* (Butler), 5/4
Cleveland, James, 1/26
Clinton, William Jefferson
"Bill," 1/13
Clopton, William H., 5/12
Club movement, 2/22, 7/30.
*See also* Societies
Coachman, Alice, 7/14
Cobb, Jewel Plummer,
6/13
Coffin, Levi, 3/20
Cole, Johnnetta Betsch,
4/5, 4/15, 11/17
Cole, Rebecca J., 8/16
Coleman, Bessie, 6/15
Coles, Robert, 9/25
Collins, Addie Mae, 9/15
Collins, Janet, 5/15

Collins, Sophronia, 9/2
*Color Purple, The* (Walker),
1/7
*Colorado Statesman,* 7/22
*Colored American Magazine,*
3/24, 4/6, 4/13, 11/11,
12/18
Colored Congregational
Church School
(Hartford, Conn.),
8/1, 11/25
Colored Cooperative Pub-
lishing Company, 4/6
Colored Female Religious
and Moral Society of
Salem (Mass.), 12/19
Colored Ladies' Literary
Society of New York,
9/20
Colored School #3 (New
York, N.Y.), 8/12
Columbia Medical School,
12/21
Columbia Presbyterian
Hospital, 7/8
Columbia Records, 2/15,
9/26
Columbia University, 5/3,
11/7, 12/21
Communist Party, 3/12,
3/19
Coney, Asia, 10/25
Congress, U.S., 3/4, 5/11,
7/13, 7/28, 9/6, 11/3
Connecticut Pharmaceuti-
cal Association, 5/16
Constitution Hall (Wash-
ington, D.C.), 4/9
Constitution, U.S., 3/4, 3/9,
5/27, 6/18, 8/15
Thirteenth Amendment,
4/26, 6/30
Fourteenth Amendment,
4/26, 6/12
Fifteenth Amendment,
8/2
Nineteenth Amendment,
8/2, 10/8
*Contending Forces* (Hop-
kins), 4/6
Contraband Relief Associa-
tion, 3/5
Cooke, Marvel, 6/25
Cookery, The, 6/27
Cooper, Anna J., 4/3
Cooper, Gary, 1/14
Cooper Union, 5/29
Coppin, Fannie M. Jack-
son, 1/28, 11/30

Corcoran Gallery of Art, 5/29
Cornell University, 3/27
Cornish, Samuel, 3/16
*Correct Thing to Do, Say, to Wear, The* (Brown), 6/17
Coston, Julia Ringwood, 5/22
Cotton Club, 1/9, 3/23
Cotton farming, 1/17, 5/7, 7/31, 8/1, 8/2, 9/8
Cowan, Polly, 8/4
Cox, Ida, 3/15
Craft, Ellen, 7/30, 9/3, 12/17
Craft, William, 9/3, 12/17
Crandall, Prudence, 5/23, 5/27, 9/9, 11/11, 11/25
"Cress Theory of Color Confrontation and Racism" (Welsing), 3/28
Crimean War, 1/25
*Crisis, The,* 1/8, 2/7, 3/3, 6/8, 6/25, 7/10, 8/2
Cuffe, Paul, 8/27
Cullen, Countée, 4/10

"Daddy's Cod Fish Stew" (recipe), 9/22
Dafora, Asadata, 3/11
Dahmer, Ellie, 5/28
Dahmer, Vernon, 5/28
"Dakota Dick," 4/30
"Dance de Sauvage, La," 9/28
Dandridge, Dorothy, 7/12
Danticat, Edwidge, 10/15
Daughters of Africa Society, 12/28
Daughters of Conference, 6/20
Daughters of the American Revolution (DAR), 1/8, 4/9
Davis, Angela, 6/4, 6/9
Davis, Clarissa, 8/11
Davis, Ossie, 2/8
Dawn Settlement (Dresden, Ont.), 10/28
Dawson, Mary Lucinda Cardwell, 5/15
Daytona Educational and Industrial Institute, 5/18
"Deadwood Dick," 4/30
Decca Records, 10/31

Declaration of Independence, 3/19, 3/31, 6/18, 10/26
"Declaration of 1776 Is Cause of Harlem Riot" (Burroughs), 3/31
Dee, Ruby, 2/8, 3/12
*Deep Sightings and Rescue Missions* (Bambara), 12/9
De Gaulle, Charles, 9/28
Delaney, Sara "Sadie," 1/3
Delany, Annie Elizabeth "Bessie," 12/21
Delany, Martin, 2/1, 7/6, 11/29
Delany, Sarah Louise "Sadie," 12/21
Democratic Party, 5/9, 5/27, 7/13, 8/22, 11/22
Denmark, 4/14
Denver General Hospital, 10/7
*Denver Rocky Mountain News,* 9/19
Depression, Great, 3/19, 3/31, 5/20, 5/30, 6/10, 6/25, 8/19, 10/2, 10/27, 11/6, 12/20
Derricotte, Juliette, 11/7
*Des Moines Sunday Register,* 4/7
Desegregation, 1/6, 4/23, 4/25, 5/14, 5/17, 5/21, 6/24, 8/22, 9/4, 9/12, 9/15
Detroit Housewives' League, 6/10
Dickens, Charles, 7/1
Diop, Alioune, 10/15
Diop, Christiane Yandé, 10/15
*Direct from Broadway* (play), 11/27
Distributive, Processing and Office Workers Union, 11/29
*Dixie to Broadway* (play), 11/23
Dorsey, Nettie Harper, 9/23
Dorsey, Thomas Andrew, 2/2, 2/15, 9/23, 9/26, 11/5
Dos Reis, Maria F., 9/5
Douglas, Aaron, 3/22
Douglass, Anna Murray, 3/2

Douglass, Frederick, 2/20, 3/2, 3/10, 5/29, 6/28, 7/6, 7/19, 9/3, 10/16
Douglass, Sarah Mapps, 11/8
"Drapetomania; or, the Disease Causing Negroes to Run Away" (Cartwright), 3/14
*Dreamgirls* (play), 10/10
*Dred Scott* decision (1857), 5/17, 7/31, 11/4
Drew, Charles, 4/9, 5/3
Drinkard Singers, 5/30
Du Bois, Nina, 4/10
Du Bois, Nina Gomer, 7/15
Du Bois, Shirley Graham, 2/3
Du Bois, W. E. B., 1/8, 2/12, 2/23, 3/3, 4/10, 6/8, 7/10, 7/15
Du Sable Museum of African-American History and Art, 11/16
Duke University, 9/27
Dunbar, Paul Lawrence, 12/22
Dunbar Savings Bank, 7/16
Dunbar-Nelson, Alice Moore, 2/16, 12/22
Dunham, Katherine, 5/15, 10/20, 12/6
*Dust Tracks on the Road* (Hurston), 9/18
"Dynamite Bob," 9/15

Earhart, Amelia, 6/15
Eatonville (Fla.), 8/18, 9/18
*Ebony,* 4/30, 7/12
Ebony Museum of African-American History, 11/16
Ebony Oil Company, 4/23
Eckford, Elizabeth, 9/4
Edelman, Marian Wright, 4/5
"Education of a Storyteller, The" (Bambara), 12/9
Eggleston, Cecelia, 8/3
Egypt, 1/3, 10/15, 11/12
Egypt, Ophelia Settle, 11/10
Eisenhower, Dwight D., 9/4
Elaw, Zilpha, 6/20, 7/1, 8/1

Ellington, Edward Kennedy "Duke," 1/16, 8/21

Emancipation, 6/19, 6/30, 7/4, 9/19, 10/24, 12/8, 12/17, 12/24

Emancipation Proclamation, 1/4, 2/12, 7/26, 9/24

England, 1/25, 6/26, 7/8, 7/11, 7/19, 8/6, 12/17

Episcopal Church, 2/11, 3/29

Epps, Mary, 3/14

Equal Rights Convention (1867), 5/10

*Essence* magazine, 4/15, 5/22, 10/15

Ethiopia, 1/2

Eubanks, Amanda Dickson, 6/12

Evans, Minnie, 1/18, 5/31

Evers, Medgar, 2/5, 5/28, 7/13, 11/22

Evers, Myrlie, 2/5, 2/12, 5/28, 6/29, 7/13

*Eye of God, The* (Evans), 5/31

*Eyes on the Prize* (TV documentary), 1/22

Fairfield, John, 2/26

Falls, Mildred, 9/26

Family History Center (Colorado Springs, Colo.), 7/27

Farm Security Administration (FSA), 8/19

Farmer, Karen, 1/8

*Farmer's Cabinet*, 9/5

Farrakhan, Louis, 10/25

Farwell Hall (Chicago, Ill.), 8/20

Faubus, Orval, 9/4

Faulkner, William, 5/28, 12/27

Fauntroy, Walter, 11/21

Fauset, Jessie, 4/13

Federal Bureau of Investigation (FBI), 3/12, 6/4, 10/11, 11/26

Federal Street Theatre (Boston, Mass.), 12/26

Fédération Aéronautique Internationale, 6/15

Female Anti-Slavery Society, 2/22, 4/12, 4/13, 6/18, 7/18, 7/19, 11/8, 12/4

Female Benevolent Society, 12/28

Female Literary Association of Philadelphia, 9/20

Fields, Mary "Stagecoach Mary," 1/14

Fifty-fourth Massachusetts Colored Regiment, 3/2

Film industry, 1/9, 3/2, 6/19, 7/12, 7/25, 12/15

*Fire!*, 5/1

First African Methodist Episcopal Church (FAME), 1/21

First African Presbyterian Church, 11/8

First Conference of Negro Artists and Writers (1956), 10/15

Fisk University, 4/21, 6/8, 11/7, 11/10

Fitzgerald, Ella, 1/16, 3/22, 12/6

Fontenelle, Bessie, 11/24

Ford, Justina, 10/7

Forten, Charlotte, 1/31, 4/28, 5/24, 9/12, 11/23

*Forum and Century, The* (Eggleston), 8/3

France, 2/7, 6/26, 7/8, 9/28, 10/15, 10/27

Frank, Anne, 11/27

Franklin, Aretha, 1/26, 12/6

Franklin Hall (Boston, Mass.), 9/21

Franklin, John Hope, 1/13

Franklin, Martha, 1/23

Free African Schools, 11/8, 11/11

Free African Society, 9/20, 11/8, 12/28

Freedmen's Bureau, 2/9, 9/13

Freedom Farm Co-op, 5/7

Freedom Rides, 2/4, 12/13

Freedom Schools, 8/4, 9/17

Freedom Summer (1964), 8/4

*Freedom's Journal*, 2/22, 3/16, 7/6, 8/10, 11/11

*Freedomways*, 11/28

Frelimo, 6/26

Friends, Society of. *See* Quakers

*From Slavery to Affluence: Memoirs of Robert Anderson, Ex-Slave* (Anderson), 5/19

Frye, Theodore, 9/23

Fugitive Slave Act (1850), 3/21, 4/12, 4/13, 4/19, 9/6, 12/17, 12/24

Fuller, Henrietta, 10/24

Fuller, Ide, 2/23

Fuller, Meta Warwick, 2/14

Gambia, 9/29

*Gamin* (sculpture), 2/29

Gandhi, Mahatma K., 2/14

Gannett, Deborah Sampson, 12/26

Gardner, Nancy, 4/14

Garner, Margaret, 3/21

Garrison, William Lloyd, 7/6, 9/21

Garvey, Marcus, 5/2, 6/10, 7/20, 10/12

Garvin, Victoria, 11/29

Gates, Henry Louis, 9/5

Geery, Margaret, 8/12

Georgetown University, 5/25

Georgia Music Hall of Fame, 11/18

Germany, 5/20, 7/24, 10/15

Ghana, 1/3, 5/2, 7/23, 8/26

Gibson, Althea, 7/11

"Gilded Six-Bits, The" (Hurston), 10/2

Gilkey, Bertha Knox, 5/11

Gillespie, Marcia, 5/22

Girl Scouts, 4/5

Girls Choir of Harlem, 11/23

*Glory* (film), 3/2

Glover, Danny, 7/25

Glover, Jane, 11/3

Goethe University, 6/4

Goldberg, Whoopi, 11/27

"Goldie" (Grimké), 12/7

Goldman, Emma, 8/9

*Gone With the Wind* (Mitchell), 12/15

Goode, Sarah, 4/26

Goodman, Andrew, 8/4

*Gospel Gazette*, 1/26

Gospel music, 9/26, 10/31, 11/5, 12/6

Grand Duc, le (nightclub), 10/27

Granny Nanny, 8/13, 12/4
Granson, Milla, 9/8
Grant, Joanne, 6/9
Great Dismal Swamp, 11/2
Green, Lear, 12/8
Greensboro, N.C., lunch
    counter sit-in, 2/4
Grice, Hezekiah, 4/12
Grigby, Elizabeth, 12/24
Grimké, Angelina Weld,
    12/7
Guggenheim Foundation,
    6/8
Guinea, 11/28

*Hagar* (Lewis), 8/20
Hair, 3/17, 4/11, 5/13,
    12/20
Haiti, 5/24, 6/9, 7/2, 8/31,
    10/13, 10/15
Haley, Alex, 6/28, 9/29
Hall, Prince, 4/14, 9/20
Hamer, Fannie Lou, 5/7,
    6/9, 7/13, 8/4, 8/22,
    11/3, 11/22, 11/28
Hamilton, Mary, 4/16
Hampton, Anne, 11/19
Hampton, Lionel, 1/16
Hampton University, 9/17
Hansberry, Lorraine, 3/12
Harlan, John Marshall,
    5/17
Harlem Renaissance, 1/27,
    4/10, 5/1, 6/8, 7/17,
    8/9, 9/10, 11/18
Harper, Frances Ellen
    Watkins, 3/4, 7/30,
    9/24, 10/30
Harper, Michael, 9/23
Harpers Ferry Raid, 4/12,
    10/16
*Harper's Weekly*, 5/19, 6/30
Harreld, Claudia White,
    2/9
*Harriet and the Promised
    Land* (Lawrence),
    10/13
Harris, Barbara Clemen-
    tine, 2/11, 7/1
Harris, Eliza, 3/20
Harris, Elizabeth Johnson,
    9/27
Harris, Rilla Simpson, 7/6
Harris, Sarah, 5/23, 9/9
Harrison, Martha, 4/21
*Hartford Intelligencer,* 5/23
Harvard University, 2/1,
    2/23, 5/5, 6/13, 10/9
Hatshepsut, 11/12

*Having Our Say* (Delany
    and Delany), 12/21
Hawkins, Tramaine, 2/2
Hayden, Robert Carter Jr.,
    1/5
Hayes, Roland, 12/15
Hayes, Rutherford B., 7/28
Hayre, Ruth W., 12/29
*Healing, The* (Jones), 2/21
Hedgeman, Anna Arnold,
    8/28, 12/31
Height, Dorothy I., 5/5,
    7/10, 7/13, 8/4, 11/22
Hemenway, Robert E., 7/2
Hemings, Sally, 9/1
Henderson, Fletcher, 6/27
*Henry Lewis* (ship), 3/21
Henson, Charlotte, 10/28
Henson, Josiah, 3/20,
    10/28
Herman, Alexis, 1/13, 5/9
Herring, James, 2/18
Higgins, Bob, 2/21
High, Freida, 1/18
Highlander Folk School
    (Tenn.), 1/22, 12/1
Hill, Anita, 10/11
Hill-Thomas Hearings,
    10/11
*History of Mary Prince, a
    West Indian Slave,
    Related by Herself, The*
    (Prince), 8/6
Holiday, Billie, 1/16
Holiday, Jennifer, 10/10
Hollingsworth Group, 5/22
Holmes, Hamilton
    "Hamp," 1/6
Holocaust, 5/20, 7/24
"Hoochie Mamas," 12/3
hooks, bell, 3/17
Hopkins, Pauline E., 4/6
Horn, Etta, 5/11
Horne, Lena, 1/9, 4/28,
    8/28, 12/6
Horton, Myles, 1/22
House of Representatives,
    U.S., 4/26, 11/3
House Un-American Activ-
    ities Committee
    (HUAC), 3/12, 7/8
Houston, Charles, 4/25
Houston, Sissy, 5/30
Houston Street Presbyter-
    ian Church, 5/27
Houston, Whitney, 5/30
Hova dynasty, 6/26
"How Bigger Was Born"
    (Wright), 3/7

Howard University, 2/18,
    3/11, 4/9, 4/23, 7/11,
    8/3, 9/14, 9/30, 11/23
Hughes, Langston, 1/7,
    3/12, 5/1, 10/2, 10/27,
    11/6
Human rights, 1/22, 3/8,
    4/3, 5/18, 6/12, 7/8,
    7/19, 9/13, 10/15,
    10/20, 11/21, 12/7
*Hungarian* (ship), 3/21
Hunt, Ida, 4/3
Hunter, Alberta, 2/15, 6/27
Hunter, Charlayne, 1/6
Hunton, Addie W., 2/7
Hurston, Zora Neale, 1/7,
    5/1, 7/2, 8/18, 9/18,
    10/2, 10/23
Hutson, Jean Blackwell,
    1/3

"I Am a Domestic" (Ward),
    6/25
"I Bury My Wife"
    (Du Bois), 7/15
*I Dream a World: Portraits
    of Black Women Who
    Changed America*
    (Lanker), 9/16
Ickes, Harold, 4/9
*Independent, The,* 9/10
India, 2/25
*Indianapolis Freeman,* 12/22
Industrial School for Col-
    ored Girls, 2/16
Ingram, Rosa Lee, 2/3, 4/3,
    5/14, 6/23
Institute for Colored Youth
    (Philadelphia, Pa.),
    1/28, 11/30
Institute of Afro-American
    Affairs, 10/15
Institute of the Black
    World, 12/13
International Congress of
    Women (1920), 10/8
International Women's
    Day, 3/8, 7/20
*Inter-State Tattler,* 10/12
Iowa Hall of Fame, 4/30
*Isaac Asimov's Science Fiction
    Magazine,* 6/5
Islam, Nation of, 10/25
Ivory Coast, 3/13

J. B. Lippincott Company,
    10/2
J. Walter Thompson Co.,
    10/29

Jackson, Carolyn Collins, 12/23
Jackson, George, 6/4
Jackson, Janet, 10/29
Jackson, Jonathan, 6/4
Jackson, Lethe, 4/18
Jackson, Lucy, 11/30
Jackson, Mahalia (née Mahala), 5/30, 8/28, 9/26, 12/2
Jacobs, Harriet, 4/27
Jagger, Mick, 11/5
Jai, Anna Madgigine, 2/17
Jamaica, 1/25, 7/20, 8/13
James, Anna L., 5/16
Jazz, 4/20, 6/26, 7/31, 10/27, 10/31
Jefferson, Isaac, 9/1
Jefferson, Thomas, 9/1
Jemison, Mae, 6/15
Jessye, Eva, 10/10
Jesus, 6/21, 7/23, 9/19
*Jet* magazine, 8/24
Jim Crow laws, 1/1, 5/26, 5/29, 6/10, 7/17, 7/28, 9/27, 10/8, 10/19
John Hope Franklin Collection, 9/27
Johns, Barbara, 4/23
Johnson, Charles S., 5/1
Johnson, Elizabeth, 7/5
Johnson, Georgia Douglas, 9/10
Johnson, Hannah, 3/2
Johnson, James Weldon, 7/28, 8/2
Johnson, Jane, 4/13, 7/18
Johnson, John H., 4/30
Johnson, Kathryn M., 2/7
Johnson, Lyndon B., 3/25, 5/11, 6/24
Johnson, Magic, 10/29
Johnson, Martha Crawford, 7/5
Johnson, Sarah, 3/16
Johnson Publishing Company, 4/30
Johnston, Mary, 12/29
*Jonah's Gourd Vine* (Hurston), 5/1, 10/2
Jones, Charles, 2/4
Jones, Elaine R., 2/12
Jones, Gayl, 2/21
Jones, Gracy, 3/16
Jones, Lois Mailou, 2/18
Jones, Ruth Veletta, 6/28, 11/13

Jones, Sissieretta "Black Patti," 6/7
Jordan, Barbara, 7/13
Joyner, Florence Griffith "FloJo," 7/14
Joyner-Kersee, Jackie, 7/14
*Jubilee* (Walker), 3/20, 6/28
Juneteenth, 6/19

Kamper, Jane, 1/12
Karenga, Maulana Ron, 12/26
*Kebra Nagast*, 1/2
Keckley, Elizabeth, 3/5
Kelly, Leontine T. C., 6/6
Kelly, Sharon Pratt, 11/3
Kennedy Center (Washington, D.C.), 10/20, 12/6
Kennedy, Florynce "Flo," 4/7, 9/7
Kennedy, John F., 9/15
Kennedy, Zella, 4/7, 9/7
Kenya, 6/22
Kidd, William "Captain," 6/26
Kincaid, Jamaica, 8/5
King, B. B., 10/29
King, Coretta Scott, 1/15, 2/14, 5/11, 6/29, 11/20
King, Gayle, 4/15
King, Martin Luther Jr., 1/13, 1/15, 1/22, 3/25, 4/4, 4/16, 5/11, 8/28, 9/15, 10/22, 12/1
Kingsley Plantation, 2/17
Knight, Gladys, 3/30, 10/29
Kofey, Laura Adorkor, 7/20
Ku Klux Klan (KKK), 3/18, 5/9, 5/28, 8/18, 9/15
Kwanzaa, 1/1, 12/26–12/31

La Mama Experimental Theatre Club, 10/18
*La Parisienne* (Walker), 5/29
LaBelle, Patti, 10/29
*Ladies Home Journal*, 7/12
Landsmark, Muriel, 9/22, 11/2
Landsmark, William, 8/3, 9/22, 11/2
Lanker, Brian, 9/16, 10/20
Larsen, Nella, 6/8
Laveau, Marie, 8/31
Lawrence, Charles, 4/22

Lawrence, Jacob, 10/13
Lawrence, Margaret Morgan, 4/22
Lawson, Jennifer, 6/9
Leach, Patsey, 1/12
Lebanon, 7/24
Lee, Jarena, 6/20, 7/1
Lee, Rebecca, 8/16
Legion of Honor, 1/25, 8/28, 9/28
Lelia College of Hair Culture, 8/30
Lester, James B., 8/29
Lester, Vilet, 8/29
"Letter from a Birmingham Jail" (King), 4/16
Lewis, Elma, 3/11
Lewis, Ida, 5/22
Lewis, John, 1/22, 2/4
Lewis, Mary Edmonia, 1/29, 8/20
*Liberator, The*, 1/29, 3/21, 7/6, 8/21, 12/16, 12/17
Liberia, 3/18, 8/27, 10/24
*Life* magazine, 1/9, 11/24
Lightfoot, Sara Lawrence, 4/22
*Like One of the Family* (Childress), 1/1
Lincoln, Abraham, 1/4, 2/12, 3/2, 3/5, 3/20, 9/24
Lincoln Center for the Performing Arts (New York), 9/16, 11/23
Lincoln, Mary Todd, 3/5
Lincoln Memorial (Washington, D.C.), 4/9, 8/28, 12/30
Lincoln University, 4/5
Lindbergh, Charles, 6/15
Little, Joanne, 6/23
Little Rock Nine, 4/29, 8/22, 9/4
London School of Economics, 7/8
Loney, Cordelia, 3/29
Long Island Medical College, 8/16
*Long Shadow of Little Rock* (Bates), 4/29
Los Angeles Airport, 8/15
L'Ouverture, Toussaint, 4/6, 5/24
Love, Nat "Deadwood Dick," 4/30
Loving, Mildred, 6/12
Loving, Richard, 6/12

Lucas, Florence, 4/23
Lucy, Autherine, 4/25
Lucy, Grazia, 4/25
Lynching, 3/9, 6/17, 7/3,
    7/28, 7/30, 8/19, 8/24,
    9/4, 10/8, 10/20, 12/7
Lyons, Maritcha, 9/12

"Ma Rainey" (Brown),
    11/18
Mabuza, Lindiwe, 10/15
MacArthur Foundation,
    3/11, 10/15, 12/6
Mack, Ted, 3/30
Madagascar, 6/26
Madam C. J. Walker Man-
    ufacturing Company,
    8/30
*Madame Butterfly* (Puccini),
    5/15
Madhubuti, Haki R., 10/11
Makeda (queen of Sheba),
    1/2
Malagasy Republic, 6/26
Malcolm X, 6/29, 7/20,
    11/17
Mali, 2/25, 9/8
Mama Kole (fetish), 8/26
Mandela, Nelson, 2/10, 6/9
Mandela, Winnie Madiki-
    zela, 2/10, 10/25,
    11/21
Mandela, Zindzi, 2/10
*Manhattan Nocturne*
    (Schuyler), 7/29
Manning, Allen, 10/6
Manning, Betty, 10/6
Marble, Alice, 7/11
March on Washington
    (1963), 8/28, 10/25,
    12/31
Marian Anderson Citizens
    Committee, 4/9
*Marie Claire* magazine, 2/25
Maroons, 8/13
Marr, Carmel Carrington,
    4/23
Marshall, Thurgood, 4/25,
    5/17, 6/24
Martin, Roberta, 12/2
Mary McLeod Bethune
    Memorial, 7/10
*Maryland Suffrage News*,
    11/12
Mason, Biddy, 1/21
Masons, 4/14, 9/20
Massachusett, 8/25
Massachusetts Institute of
    Technology (MIT),
    1/13

Matthews, Josephine Riley
    "Mama Jo," 6/5, 10/3
May, Samuel, 5/27, 9/9
Mayer, Louis B., 1/9
McCarthyism, 3/12, 6/4,
    7/8, 10/5
McCarty, Oseola, 12/29
McDaniel, Hattie, 12/15
McDowell, Calvin, 3/9
McDuffie, Aaron, 10/9
McGwire, Mark, 4/8
McNair, Denise, 9/15
McNeil, Claudia, 3/12
McQueen, Butterfly, 12/15
Medgar Evers College,
    11/17
*Memoir of Old Elizabeth, a*
    *Coloured Woman, The*,
    3/26
*Memories of Yesterdays All of*
    *Which I Saw and Part*
    *of Which I Was*
    (Lyons), 9/12
*Memphis Free Speech*, 3/9

Meriwether, Louise, 4/15
*Messenger, The*, 9/14
*Metronome* magazine, 1/16
Metropolitan Opera, 5/15,
    6/7, 9/16, 12/30
Mexico, 10/5, 12/5
MGM (Metro-Goldwyn-
    Mayer, Inc.), 1/9
*Migrants* (Lawrence),
    10/13
Millet, "Mother" Cleusa,
    10/21
Million Man March
    (1995), 10/25
Million Woman March
    (1997), 10/25
Mills College, 12/23
Mills, Florence "Flo,"
    10/12
Minerva Literary Associa-
    tion, 9/20
Miss America Pageant, 9/7
"Miss Muriel" (Petry),
    5/16, 11/1
Mississippi Freedom
    Democratic Party
    (MFDP), 5/7, 6/9,
    7/13, 8/4, 8/22, 11/22
Mississippi Plan (1890),
    7/28
Mississippi State Sover-
    eignty Commission,
    2/5, 5/28
Missouri Compromise
    (1820), 11/4

Missouri Press Association,
    7/30
Monroe Elementary
    School (Topeka,
    Kans.), 5/17
Montgomery Bus Boycott,
    5/21, 12/1
Monumental Tennis Club
    of Baltimore, 7/11
Moore, Alice, 12/22
Moore, Audley "Queen
    Mother," 5/2
Mora, Francisco "Pancho,"
    10/5
Morehouse College, 2/9
Morgan, Joe, 4/8
Morrison, Toni, 3/21, 6/19,
    8/18, 9/4, 12/9, 12/10
Morton, Ferdinand "Jelly
    Roll," 3/15
Moseley-Braun, Carol,
    4/23, 11/3
Moss, Thomas, 3/9
Mossell, Gertrude Bustill,
    3/6
*Mother and Child* (Fuller),
    2/14
Mother Society, The,
    12/28
Mother Zion Church
    (Harlem), 10/12
Mothers of Professional
    Basketball Players,
    12/3
Motley, Constance Baker,
    4/23, 4/25, 6/24
Motown Record Corpora-
    tion, 3/30, 10/10
Mott, Lucretia, 6/18, 7/19,
    12/4
Mozambique, 6/26
*Mule Bone* (Hughes and
    Hurston), 10/2
*Mules and Men* (Hurston),
    5/1
Murray-Douglass, Anna,
    9/3
Museum of the National
    Center of Afro-Amer-
    ican Artists, 3/11
Mutchmore Baptist
    Church (Philadelphia,
    Pa.), 5/30
Mwana Kupona binti
    Msham, 6/22
*My Bondage and My Freedom*
    (Douglass), 9/3
*My One Good Nerve* (Dee),
    2/7
*My Spirit* (Titus), 3/18

NAACP. *See* National Association for the Advancement of Colored People
NAACP Legal Defense Fund (LDF), 1/6, 2/12, 4/5, 4/25, 5/7, 5/17, 6/24
Nash, Diane, 2/4
National Aeronautics and Space Administration (NASA), 7/4
*National Anti-Slavery Standard*, 3/4
National Association for the Advancement of Colored People (NAACP), 1/9, 1/22, 2/3, 2/5, 2/7, 2/12, 2/23, 4/25, 4/29, 5/7, 5/17, 6/9, 6/24, 7/28, 8/22, 9/4, 10/9, 11/22, 12/1
National Association of Colored Graduate Nurses, 1/23
National Association of Colored Women (NACW), 7/30, 8/2
National Association of Colored Women's Clubs, 8/16
National Association of Negro Musicians, 5/15
National Baptist Convention, 1/10
National Conference of Black Mayors, 11/3
National Conference on the Black Family in the American Economy, 3/28
National Council of Churches, 12/31
National Council of Negro Women (NCNW), 2/14, 5/5, 5/9, 5/18, 7/10, 7/11, 8/4, 11/22, 11/26
National Council of Women, 2/20
National Federation of Afro-American Women, 7/30
National Guard, 3/25, 9/4
National League of Colored Women, 7/30
National Museum of American History, 10/29

National Museum of Art, 8/20
National Negro Business League, 6/10
National Negro Committee (NNC), 2/12
National Negro Congress, 4/12, 9/14
National Negro Opera Company, 5/15
National Organization for Women (NOW), 10/17
National Political Congress of Black Women, 7/13
National Student Council, 11/7
National Tennis Championships, 7/11
National Training School for Girls, 7/17, 10/19
National Urban League, 2/12, 5/1, 6/9
National Welfare Rights Organization, 5/11, 7/13
National Woman's Party, 2/7
National Women's Political Caucus (NWPC), 7/13, 11/20
Native Americans, 1/21, 1/29, 8/18, 8/25, 12/4
*Native Son* (Wright), 3/7
Nazis, 5/12, 5/20, 11/27
NCNW. *See* National Council of Negro Women
Negritude, 10/15
*Negro Digest*, 4/30
Negro Silent Protest Parade (New York), 7/28, 8/30
Nelson, Horatio, 1/25
Nelson, Jill, 8/14
*New Bedford Evening Standard*, 9/6
New England Conservatory of Music, 6/7
New England Female Medical College, 8/16
New England Freedmen's Aid Society, 4/27
*New Masses*, 6/25
New Negro movement, 5/1, 7/17
*New Orleans Commercial Bulletin*, 10/24

New York City Opera, 5/15
*New York Evening Post*, 3/29
*New York Freeman*, 3/6
*New York Herald Tribune*, 7/29
New York Infirmary for Women and Children, 8/16
New York Philharmonic, 7/29
*New York Times*, 1/8, 5/8, 6/12, 8/22, 9/22, 10/11
New York University (NYU), 10/9, 10/15
*New York World-Telegram*, 8/9
Newby, Dangerfield, 10/16
Newby, Harriet, 10/16
*Newsweek*, 1/9, 2/21
Newton, Huey, 10/22
Niagara Movement, 2/12
Nichols, Mike, 11/27
Nigeria, 2/25
Nightingale, Florence, 1/25
Ninth Cavalry, 7/25
Nkrumah, Kwame, 1/3, 5/2
Nobel Prize, 3/21, 6/19, 12/10, 12/15
Norman, Jessye, 12/6
North Carolina A & T, 2/4
North Carolina Mutual Life Insurance, 10/9
North Carolina State College, 2/2
*North Star*, 7/6
Northup, Anne Hampton, 11/19
Northup, Solomon, 11/19
Norton, Eleanor Holmes, 6/9, 10/11
Norwood, Dorothy, 11/5
"Not Color but Character" (Burroughs), 12/20

Oberlin College, 1/29, 4/3, 8/20, 11/30, 12/29
Off-Off Broadway (theater movement), 10/18
Okeh Records, 7/31
*Ol' Man Satan* (play), 10/4
Old Testament, 1/2, 8/20
Oliver, King, 3/15
*Oliver Twist* (Dickens), 7/1
Olmsted, Frederick Law, 8/12
Olympics, 7/14
Onassis, Jacqueline Kennedy, 1/27

135th Street Library
(Harlem), 10/13
O'Neal, Shaquille, 12/3
*Opportunity,* 5/1
"Oppressed Hair Puts a
Ceiling on the Brain"
(Walker), 4/11
Original Dixieland Band,
7/31
*Original Ted Mack Amateur
Hour,* 3/30
*Our Nig; or, Sketches from the
Life of a Free Black*
(Wilson), 9/5
Ovington, Mary White,
2/12
Owens, Chandler, 9/14
Owens, Jesse, 7/14

Pacific Design Center
(Los Angeles, Calif.),
8/15
Palmer Institute, 3/11,
6/17, 10/8
Pan-African Congresses,
2/23, 4/3
*Paradise* (Morrison), 8/18
Paramount Records, 3/15
Paris Salon (1896), 5/29
Parker, Beatrice Burnett,
10/9
Parker, Gwendolyn, 10/9
Parks, Gordon, 5/22, 8/19,
11/24
Parks, Leslie, 11/24
Parks, Rosa, 1/22, 5/11,
5/21, 12/1
*Passing* (Larsen), 6/8
Patterson, Patsey, 8/29
Paul, Alice, 2/7
Pauline Doctrine, 6/20
Peake, Mary, 9/17
Peck, Fannie B., 6/10
Pennsylvania Abolition
Society, 6/18
Pennsylvania Hall, 6/18
*People of the State of Califor-
nia v. Davis, The*
(1972), 6/4
People's Grocery Store
(Memphis, Tenn.),
3/9, 7/28
Perry, Carrie Saxon, 11/3
Petry, Ann, 5/16, 11/1
Philadelphia Library Com-
pany of Colored Per-
sons, 1/3
Philadelphia Vigilance
Committee, 3/29
Phillis Wheatley Club, 1/23

Pickett, Tydie, 7/14
Pilgrim Baptist Church
(Illinois), 9/23
Pips, Gladys Knight and
the, 3/30
Planned Parenthood, 10/3
Plato, Ann, 8/1, 11/25
Player, Willa, 4/5
Pleasant, Mary Ellen, 5/21,
12/4
*Plessy v. Ferguson* (1896),
3/9, 5/17, 5/18
*Poems of Phillis Wheatley*
(Wheatley), 4/28
*Poems on Various Subjects*
(Wheatley), 5/6
Poitier, Sidney, 3/12
Poor People's Campaign,
5/11
*Porgy and Bess* (Gershwin,
Gershwin and Hey-
ward), 10/10
Porter, James A., 2/18
Portugal, 6/26
Potter, George, 12/16
Potter, Rosella, 12/16
Powell, Colin, 7/25
*Présence Africaine* (Diop),
10/15
Presidential Medal of
Freedom, 9/14
Price, Leontyne, 6/7, 9/16,
12/6
Prince, Mary, 8/6
Prince, Nancy Gardner,
4/13, 4/14, 8/1
Prince, Nero, 4/14
Princeton University,
11/11
*Problem We All Live With,
The* (Rockwell),
11/14
Progressive Party, 7/7
Prohibition, 3/23
Prosser, Gabriel, 8/13
Providence Academy of
Music, 6/7
Providence High School
(R.I.), 9/12
Provident Hospital
(Chicago, Ill.), 1/23,
6/13
*Provincial Freeman,* 3/8
Pulitzer Prize, 1/7, 3/21,
4/11

Quakers, 3/20, 5/23, 9/9,
10/26, 11/30
Queen, Hallie, 12/25
*Quicksand* (Larsen), 6/8

R. H. Dickerson &
Brothers, 2/24
Racism, 2/3, 3/9, 4/16,
5/28, 6/12, 7/17, 7/19,
7/28, 8/22, 8/24, 9/4,
9/9, 9/15, 10/13, 11/4,
11/8, 11/9, 11/21, 12/4
Radcliffe College, 1/13
Radio, 4/9, 6/6, 7/24, 9/26
Radio City Music Hall
(New York, N.Y.),
4/20
Rainey, Madame Gertrude
"Ma," 2/15, 11/18
*Raisin in the Sun, A* (Hans-
berry), 3/12
Ranavalona III (queen of
Madagascar), 6/26
Randolph, A. Philip, 9/14
Randolph, Lucille Greene,
9/14
Ray, Charlotte E., 4/23
Reagan, Ronald, 1/15,
11/21
Reagon, Bernice Johnson,
6/9, 12/13
Reconstruction, 3/6, 5/10,
6/10, 7/17, 9/13
Reed, Dolly, 12/5
*Regents of the University of
California v. Bakke*
(1978), 10/9
Reidsville Prison, 6/16
*Reminiscences* (Henson),
3/20
*Reminiscences of My Life in
Camp: With the 33rd
United States Colored
Troops,* 4/1
*Reminiscences of School Life,
and Hints on Teaching*
(Coppin), 1/28
*Report from Part One*
(Brooks), 8/8
Republican Party, 2/16,
7/2, 7/7, 9/30
"Resurrection City," 5/11
Réunion, 6/26
Revolutionary War, 1/8,
3/4, 4/28, 7/25,
12/26
Revue Nègre, La, 9/28
Richards, Lloyd, 3/12
Richardson, Gloria, 6/2
*Richmond News Leader,* 7/16
*Richmond Recorder,* 9/1
Ringgold, Faith, 1/18
*Ringwood's Afro-American
Journal of Fashion,*
5/22

Riverside Church (New
York, N.Y.), 6/29
Roach, Ayodele Nailah,
11/2
Roach, Dara Rashida, 11/2
Roach, Max, 4/20, 11/2
"Roaring Twenties," 3/23,
7/17, 10/27, 11/18
Robbins, Lenore, 4/9, 5/3
Robertson, Carole, 9/15
Robeson, Eslanda Goode
"Essie," 7/8
Robeson, Paul, 1/9, 3/6,
6/27, 7/8, 11/8, 11/29
Robinson, A'Lelia Walker,
8/30, 12/25
Robinson, Jackie, 1/24
Robinson, Jo Ann, 5/21
Robinson, Rachel, 1/24
Robinson, Randall, 6/9,
11/21
Robinson, Sharon, 1/24,
10/3
Rock and Roll Hall of
Fame, 1/11
Rock Hill Four, 2/4
Rockefeller, John D., 1/23
Rockwell, Norman, 11/14
Roosevelt, Eleanor, 4/9,
11/26, 12/31
Roosevelt, Franklin D.,
5/9, 5/18, 7/2, 8/19,
9/14
Roots (Haley), 3/20, 6/28,
9/29
Rosemond, Connie, 1/10
Ross, Diana, 7/21
Rudolph, Wilma, 7/14
Rush Medical College,
6/13
Russell, Charley, 1/14
Russia, 4/14
Russworm, John B., 3/16
Rust College, 9/2

Saadawi, Nawal El, 10/15
Saint Eustatius ("Statia"),
9/22
Saint Kitts, 8/23, 12/14
Saint Lucia, 7/23
Saint Luke, Order of, 7/16
Saint Luke Penny Savings
Bank (Va.), 7/16
Sampson, Deborah, 12/26
Sanchez, Sonia, 4/2
Sanders, Beulah, 5/11, 7/13
Sands, Diana, 3/12
Saroyan, William, 10/27
Savage, Augusta Fells, 2/29
Savoy Ballroom, 1/9, 1/16

Sawyer, Alta, 3/22
Scapegoating, 1/12, 3/2, 3/9
Schomburg, Arturo A., 1/3
Schomburg Center for
Research in Black
Culture, 1/3, 2/29
School Library Journal, 10/13
Schuyler, George, 7/29,
10/4
Schuyler, Philippa, 7/29,
10/4
Schwerner, Michael, 8/4
SCLC. See Southern Chris-
tian Leadership Con-
ference
Scott, Dred, 11/4
Scott, Gloria Dean Randle,
4/5
Scott, Harriet, 11/4
Screen Writers Guild, 7/12
Seacole, Mary, 1/25
Seale, Bobby, 9/7, 10/22
"See How They Run" (Vro-
man), 7/12
Segregation, 2/18, 3/25,
4/6, 4/9, 4/16, 4/25,
5/8, 5/14, 5/17, 5/18,
5/21, 5/28, 6/18, 7/17,
7/24, 7/31, 8/3, 8/9,
9/13, 9/15, 11/7,
11/14, 12/1
Sellers, Cleveland, 6/2
Selma-to-Montgomery
March (1965), 3/25
Senate, U.S., 4/23, 5/7,
5/23, 10/11, 11/3
Senegal, 9/30, 10/15
Senghor, Léopold Sédar,
10/15
Seraph on the Suwanee
(Hurston), 10/23
Shabazz, Betty, 6/29, 11/17
Shadd, Mary Ann, 3/8
Sharpeville Massacre, 3/25
She Kisses (Titus), 3/18
Sherman, William T., 1/12
Sherrod, Charles, 2/4
"She's Free" (Harper), 9/24
Shorter Chapel AME
Church (Denver,
Colo.), 7/22
Shorter College, 2/7
Showboat (play), 6/27
Shuffle Along (play), 10/12
Shurtleff, Robert, 12/26
Silver Bluff Baptist Church
(S.C.), 7/16
Simkins, Modjeska, 11/20
Simmons, Althea T. L.,
2/12

Simpson, Valerie, 4/15,
10/29
Singleton, Benjamin "Pap,"
8/18
Sixteenth Street Baptist
Church (Birmingham,
Ala.), 9/15
Sklarek, Norma Merrick,
8/15
Slavery, 1/4, 1/12, 1/17,
1/30, 2/17, 2/20, 2/24,
3/4, 3/20, 3/29, 4/19,
4/26, 5/6, 5/19, 6/1,
6/14, 6/23, 7/4, 7/18,
7/23, 8/6, 8/11, 8/29,
9/1, 9/3, 9/6, 9/8, 9/24,
9/29, 10/16, 10/26,
10/28, 11/4, 11/8,
11/9, 11/19, 12/16,
12/17
Slowe, Lucy Diggs, 7/11
Small Business Administra-
tion, 7/6
Smith, Ada "Bricktop,"
10/27
Smith Barney, Inc., 6/24
Smith, Bessie, 2/15, 6/27
Smith, Ida Van, 6/15
Smith, Jane, 5/5
Smith, Mamie, 7/31
Smith, Ruby Doris, 2/4
Smithsonian Institution,
10/29
SNCC. See Student Non-
Violent Coordinating
Committee
Snipes, Wesley, 10/29
Snow, Loum, 2/6
Snow, Valaida, 5/20
Soaking the Yule Log
(Bennett), 7/27
Societies, 2/22, 3/13, 6/10,
6/20, 7/6, 7/16. See
also individual
societies
Sojourner Rover, 7/4
Solomon (King of Israel),
1/2
Some Recollections of our
Antislavery Conflict
(May), 5/27
Sorbonne, 4/3, 6/4, 10/15
"Sorrows of Yamba,
The; or, The Negro
Woman's Lamenta-
tion" (Yamba),
7/23
South Africa, Union of,
2/10, 6/9, 10/15,
11/21, 11/30

Southern Christian Leadership Conference (SCLC), 4/16, 6/9
Southern Illinois University, 10/20
Southern Workman, The, 7/17
Southland (ballet), 10/20
Spelman College, 1/23, 2/4, 4/5, 4/11, 4/15, 5/5
Spook Show, The (Goldberg), 11/27
Springfield Baptist Church (Ga.), 2/9
SS Washington, 10/27
St. Louis Riot (1917), 9/28
St. Mark's Episcopal Church (New York, N.Y.), 1/23
Stanton, Edwin M., 1/12
Stanton, Elizabeth Cady, 7/19
Stealing Home (Robinson), 1/24
Steward, Susan Smith McKinney, 8/16
Stewart, Ellen "La Mama," 10/18
Stewart, Henry, 3/9
Stewart, James, 9/21
Stewart, Maria W., 2/27, 3/8, 9/21
Still, William, 3/14, 7/18, 8/11, 12/8, 12/24
Stokes, Louise, 7/14
Story magazine, 10/2
Story of Gospel, The (TV documentary), 2/2
Stout, Juanita Kidd, 4/23
Stowe, Harriet Beecher, 10/28
Student Non-Violent Coordinating Committee (SNCC), 2/4, 3/25, 5/13, 6/2, 6/9, 10/22, 11/22, 11/28, 12/13
Sudarkasa, Niara, 4/5
Suffrage, women's, 3/3, 3/10, 8/2, 10/8, 11/12
Sumner Elementary School (Topeka, Kans.), 5/17
Sunbeam (ship), 10/1
Supreme Court, U.S., 3/9, 4/16, 4/23, 4/25, 5/17, 5/18, 5/21, 5/26, 5/27, 6/24, 7/31, 8/15, 9/17, 10/9, 10/11, 11/4. See also individual cases

Supremes, The, 10/10
Sweden, 12/10
Sweet Honey in the Rock, 6/9, 11/23
Swing, Battle of, 1/16

Talladega College, 6/13, 11/7
Tandy, Vertner W., 12/25
Tanzania, 5/2, 6/26
Taylor, Susan L., 4/15, 5/22, 10/15
Taylor, Susie Baker King, 4/1, 12/5
"Teacher's Prayer, A" (Plato), 11/25
Television, 1/22, 2/2, 10/29
Temple of My Familiar, The (Walker), 1/7
Tenth Cavalry, 7/25
Terrell, Mary Church, 2/3, 2/12, 3/9, 4/3, 5/14, 5/22, 7/28, 7/30, 8/2
Terry, Lucy, 8/25
Tharpe, Rosetta, 10/31
Théâtre des Champs-Elysées (Paris), 9/28
Their Eyes Were Watching God (Hurston), 7/2, 9/18
There Is Confusion (Fauset), 4/13
Thomas, Alma, 7/3
Thomas, Catherine, 8/12
Thomas, Clarence, 10/11
Thomas, Debi, 7/14
Thompson, Era Bell, 4/30
Thompson, Millie, 4/4
Thurman, Howard, 2/14
Thurman, Sue Bailey, 2/14
Thurman, Wallace, 11/18
Till, Emmett, 8/24, 10/20
Tillman, Ben "Pitchfork," 11/12
Tillmon, Johnnie, 5/11
Timbuktu, 9/8
Time magazine, 1/9, 7/29, 10/13
Time of Your Life, The (Saroyan), 10/27
Tinnin, Maria Barnett, 10/14
Titus, Arzu, 3/18
"To Hell with Dying" (Walker), 1/7
"To the First of August" (Plato), 8/1
Togo, 1/20, 8/26
Tolliver, Melba, 10/15

Touré, Kwame, 2/4
Touré, Sékou, 11/28
Toussaint L'Ouverture (Lawrence), 10/13
TransAfrica, Inc., 6/9, 11/21
Traveller (ship), 8/27
Trinity AME Church (Salt Lake City, Utah), 4/24
Truman, Harry S., 5/18
Truth, Sojourner, 1/1, 3/6, 5/10, 5/21, 6/1, 6/21, 7/4, 9/13
Tubman, Harriet, 1/1, 1/31, 2/1, 2/24, 3/3, 3/10, 5/26, 6/2, 7/30, 10/13
Tucker, C. DeLores, 7/13
Tucker, Sophie, 7/31
Turner, Nat, 1/30, 2/22, 2/27, 4/18, 12/4
Turner, Tina, 1/11
Tuskegee Institute, 1/3, 5/13, 7/14, 7/20, 10/19
Tutankhamen (king of Egypt), 11/12
Twain, Mark, 6/4
"Two Christmas Days" (Wells-Barnett), 11/15
Two Colored Women with the American Expeditionary Forces (Hunton and Johnson), 2/7
"Two Offers, The" (Harper), 10/30
Tyus, Wyomia, 7/14

UGRR. See Underground Railroad
Uncle Tom's Cabin (Stowe), 2/9, 3/20, 9/6
Underground Railroad (UGRR), 1/17, 2/6, 2/26, 3/8, 3/14, 3/20, 3/21, 4/19, 5/26, 6/2, 6/14, 6/28, 7/18, 7/30, 8/11, 9/6, 9/20, 10/28, 12/4, 12/5, 12/8, 12/24
Underground Railroad, The (Still), 7/18
Union Baptist Church (Philadelphia, Pa.), 8/30
United Methodist Church, 6/6
United Nations (UN), 2/3, 4/3, 5/18, 5/25

United Negro Improve-
ment Association
(UNIA), 6/10, 7/20
University of Alabama,
4/25
University of California,
1/24, 6/4, 12/23, 12/26
University of Colorado,
11/21
University of Denmark,
6/8
University of Georgia, 1/6
University of Louisiana,
3/14
University of Michigan,
4/5, 6/13
University of Sankore, 9/8
University of Southern
Mississippi, 12/29
University of Virginia, 7/23
Urban League. *See*
National Urban
League
*Ursula* (dos Reis), 9/5
U.S. Commission on Civil
Rights, 11/21
U.S. Mission to the United
Nations, 4/23

Valentine, Hannah, 1/30
Van Buren, Martin, 5/27
Van Ness Treaty (1834),
2/17
Vaudun, 8/31. *See also*
Voodoo
Victoria (queen of Great
Britain), 6/26
Victory Baptist Church,
12/2
Vietnam War, 4/4, 5/11,
7/13, 9/7
*View from the South, A*
(Cooper), 4/3
Vigilance Committee, 7/18
Voodoo, 8/26, 8/31
Voting Rights Act (1965),
3/25
Vroman, Mary Elizabeth,
7/12

Wales, Prince of, 10/27
Walker, A'Lelia, 8/30, 12/25
Walker, Alice, 1/7, 4/11,
4/17, 4/20, 10/23
Walker, Annie E. Ander-
son, 5/29
Walker, Maggie Lena, 7/16
Walker, Margaret, 3/20,
6/28, 10/15

Walker, Minnie Tallulah,
4/17
Walker, Sarah Breedlove
"Madam C. J.", 7/22,
7/28, 8/30, 9/14,
12/25
Walker, Wyatt Tee, 1/22
Waller, Fats, 6/27
Wanzer, Frank, 12/24
"War for Freedom," 5/19,
11/13. *See also* Civil
War
"War for Liberation," 1/12,
1/19, 8/12. *See also*
Civil War
Ward, Clara, 1/26, 5/30,
12/2
Ward, Gertrude, 1/26,
5/30, 12/2
Ward, Naomi, 6/25
Ward, Willa, 5/30, 12/2
Warren, Earl, 5/17, 6/12
Warwick, Dionne, 5/30
Washington, Booker T.,
4/6, 6/10, 7/20, 10/19
Washington, Dinah, 12/2
Washington, George,
10/26, 12/26
*Washington Post*, 4/3, 5/14
Waters, Emily, 3/2
Waters, Ethel, 3/23
Waters, Maxine, 10/25,
11/20
Watson, Ella, 8/19
Watson, Hattie Ruther-
ford, 12/27
Watson, Lezlie, 11/23
Watson, Marian Etoile,
12/27
Wattleton, Faye, 10/3
*Wedding, The* (West), 1/27
Welcome, Jane, 3/2
Wells-Barnett, Ida B., 2/12,
3/9, 7/28, 7/30, 11/15
Welsing, Frances Cress,
3/28
Wesley, Cynthia, 9/15
West, Dorothy, 1/27, 5/1
Wester-Faengle concentra-
tion camp, 5/20
"What Must the Negro
Do to Be Saved?"
(Burroughs), 12/20
Wheatley, Phillis, 1/31,
4/28, 5/6, 10/26
Wheeler, Harold, 10/10
White & Clark, 3/15
White, Hardenia, 6/28
White, Isabella, 2/6

White, Josephine, 2/9
White Rose Mission, 2/16,
12/22
White supremacy, 3/9,
3/28, 5/1, 6/12, 7/8,
8/3. *See also* Racism
White, Walter, 1/9, 2/16
White, William Jefferson,
2/9
Whittier, John Greenleaf,
5/24, 12/29
Wild, Edward A., 5/12
Wiley, Jean, 5/13
Wilhelmina (queen of the
Netherlands), 5/20
William Franz Elementary
School, 11/14
Williams, Camilla, 5/15
Williams, Cathy, 7/25
Williams, Daniel Hale
"Dr. Dan," 1/23, 6/13
Williams, Delores, 7/23
Williams, Fannie Barrier,
12/18
Williams, Marion, 1/26,
12/6
Williamson, Lynette
Williams, 12/23
Wilson, Harriet Adams,
9/5
Wilson, Woodrow, 7/28
Winfrey, Oprah, 1/27,
4/15, 6/19
Witchcraft, 3/1, 12/19
"With All They Getting"
(Burroughs), 7/17
Womanhood, 3/13, 3/17,
5/24
Woman's Association of
Philadelphia, 7/6
Woman's Medical College
of Pennsylvania,
8/16
Women Against Repres-
sion, 3/28
"Women in Medicine"
(Steward), 8/16
Women's movement, 2/1,
3/28, 7/19, 9/7, 10/17,
11/8, 11/20, 11/29,
12/28
Women's National Basket-
ball Association, 12/3
Women's Political Council,
5/21
Women's Rights Conven-
tions (1848 and
1851), 4/12, 5/10,
6/21, 7/19, 10/8

Wonder, Stevie, 1/15
*Wonderful Adventures of Mrs.*
    *Seacole in Many Lands*
    (Seacole), 1/25
Wood, Ann, 12/24
Woodhouse, Mrs., 12/5
Woodruff, Hale, 2/18
Woods, Anita, 5/8
Woods, Dessie, 6/16
Woodson, Carter G., 2/7
World War I, 2/7, 5/1,
    6/15, 7/17, 7/28, 8/2,
    8/23, 11/12, 12/14,
    12/25

World War II, 5/12, 5/20,
    7/2, 9/28, 10/27,
    12/31
World's Anti-Slavery
    Convention (1840),
    7/19
World's Student Christian
    Federation, 11/7
Wright, Margaret, 3/28
Wright, Orville and
    Wilbur, 6/15
Wright, Richard, 3/7,
    10/15
Wright, Theodore, 11/11

Young, Andrew, 1/22
Young Men's Christian
    Association (YMCA),
    2/4
Young Women's Christian
    Association (YWCA),
    2/7, 6/11, 11/7

Zanzibar, 6/26
Zebra (advertising
    agency), 10/29
Zimbabwe, 2/13

# Index of Subjects

Abuse, 1/27
Adventure, 7/25
Architecture, 8/15
Art, 1/18, 1/29, 2/18, 2/29,
    3/11, 5/29, 5/31, 7/3,
    8/20, 10/5, 10/13

Business, 3/16, 5/22, 5/27,
    6/10, 7/6, 7/16, 7/22,
    7/31, 8/30, 9/14,
    10/10, 10/29, 12/2

Celebrations, 1/15, 3/8,
    4/15, 6/19, 12/10,
    12/25
Children and Youth, 5/4,
    5/8, 7/29, 9/12, 9/15,
    11/14, 12/22
Cities and Towns, 8/12,
    8/18
Civil Rights, 6/2, 11/21,
    12/1
Culture, 3/1, 3/13, 9/18,
    9/30

Dance, 5/15
Drugs, 4/2

Education, 1/28, 2/9, 2/13,
    3/27, 4/5, 5/17, 5/23,
    6/17, 9/8–9/9, 9/17,
    10/9, 10/19, 11/11,
    11/17, 11/25
Emancipation, 9/24
Emigration, 3/18

Escape!, 2/26, 6/14, 9/6,
    10/28, 12/8, 12/24
Events, 1/26, 2/11, 3/3,
    3/12, 4/10, 4/25, 5/1,
    7/28, 8/25, 8/28,
    10/15, 10/25

Family, 1/19, 1/24, 1/30,
    2/10, 2/21, 6/12, 7/5,
    7/15, 7/27, 8/8, 8/23,
    9/19, 9/22, 9/29, 10/14,
    11/2, 11/9, 11/19
Film, 1/9, 6/19, 7/12, 12/15
Folklore, 11/13
Freedom, 1/4, 3/29, 4/1,
    4/27, 5/12, 7/4, 7/26,
    8/1, 10/24, 12/17

Health. *See* Medicine
Heroes and Sheroes, 1/31,
    2/1, 2/20, 3/10, 5/18,
    5/26, 6/15, 6/29, 7/10,
    8/13, 9/21, 10/20
Historiography, 1/5, 4/6,
    6/28, 9/29, 11/13
Human Rights, 5/14, 6/16
Humor, 2/19, 8/21, 12/12

Ideals, 4/17, 6/18, 7/8, 12/4

Journalism, 4/29, 5/22

Kwanzaa, 1/1, 12/26,
    12/27, 12/28, 12/29,
    12/30, 12/31

Labor, 6/25, 8/7, 10/1, 11/6,
    11/29
Law, 2/5, 3/4, 4/23, 5/23,
    6/4, 6/24, 11/4
Leadership, 1/13, 1/22, 2/4,
    5/7, 5/9, 5/11, 6/20,
    7/20, 11/26
Libraries, 1/3, 10/13
Lifestyles, 2/25, 4/14, 7/17,
    8/14, 12/23
Literacy, 4/1, 12/5
Literature, 1/27, 3/7, 3/20,
    3/24, 4/2, 4/17, 4/28,
    4/30, 5/6, 6/5, 6/8, 7/2,
    7/23, 8/5, 8/25, 9/5,
    10/2, 10/23, 10/26,
    10/30, 11/1, 11/15,
    12/7, 12/12, 12/18
Love, 2/14, 2/28, 3/22,
    4/22, 5/3, 5/19, 9/2,
    10/4, 10/16, 11/15
Lynching, 3/9, 12/7

Marriage, 10/30
Medicine, 1/5, 1/23, 1/25,
    5/16, 8/16, 10/7
Motherhood, 3/6, 4/8, 8/3,
    8/24, 9/25, 11/5, 12/3
Music, 1/10–1/11, 1/16,
    1/26, 2/2, 2/15, 3/15,
    4/20, 5/15, 5/30, 6/7,
    6/11, 6/27, 7/21, 7/24,
    9/16, 9/23, 9/26,
    10/31, 11/5, 11/18,
    11/23, 12/6

Nursing, 1/25

Organizing, 2/12, 2/22,
    3/25, 6/9, 7/20, 7/30,
    8/4, 9/14, 11/20, 12/19

Pan-African World, 6/26,
    8/27, 11/28
Photography, 8/19
Pioneers, 1/21
Politics, 7/7, 7/13, 11/3
Prayer, 3/7, 6/1, 9/23

Race, 12/18
Religion, 3/26, 6/6, 8/26,
    8/31, 10/21
Reparations, 1/12
Resistance, 3/14
Revolt!, 3/19, 3/21, 4/13,
    6/23, 11/10, 11/22

School Desegregation, 1/6,
    9/4
Science, 4/26, 6/13

Sexual Harassment, 10/11
Signs of the Times, 10/17
Sisterhood, 4/3, 7/9
Slavery, 2/24, 7/23, 8/6,
    8/29, 10/26, 12/16
Social History, 1/8, 1/14,
    2/3, 2/6, 2/7,
    2/16–2/17, 3/5, 3/31,
    4/4, 4/21, 4/24, 5/10,
    5/20, 5/24, 5/25, 7/1,
    8/9, 8/21, 9/1, 9/11,
    9/20, 9/28, 10/8,
    10/23, 10/27, 11/7,
    11/16, 12/13, 12/20
Speeches, 2/27, 6/21
Sports, 7/11, 7/14, 12/3
Strategy, 4/18
Suffrage, 8/2, 11/12

Technology, 4/26
Temper of the Times, 3/23,
    8/22, 10/22
Theater, 1/20, 2/8, 10/10,
    10/12, 10/18, 11/27

Travel and Transportation,
    5/21, 9/13
Turning Points, 4/9,
    4/11–4/12, 5/2, 5/5,
    5/28, 9/7, 11/8

Underground Railroad,
    1/17, 4/19, 7/18, 8/11,
    9/3

War, 3/2
Women and Womanhood,
    1/1–1/2, 1/7, 2/23,
    3/17, 3/28, 3/30, 4/7,
    4/16, 5/13, 6/3, 6/22,
    6/30, 7/19, 8/5, 8/10,
    8/17, 9/10, 9/27, 10/3,
    10/6, 11/1, 11/24,
    11/30, 12/9, 12/11,
    12/14, 12/21
Work, 10/2

# Index of Inspirational Themes

Ambition, 5/4, 11/26, 12/23
Ancestors, 9/30
Aspirations, 2/28, 5/29,
    7/11, 9/10, 9/27
Assumptions, 10/9
Attitude, 7/2, 8/2
Audacity, 4/7
Authenticity, 2/2, 5/31,
    7/31, 8/31, 11/18
Awakenings, 3/31, 5/13

Beginnings, 5/6, 7/13, 7/26
Better Worlds, 1/23, 2/27,
    4/14, 8/18
Bravado, 1/14, 9/7, 11/12
Building Dreams, 6/20,
    10/12

Cause and Effect, 4/12
Change, 2/11
Character, 1/11, 5/8, 8/17,
    9/9, 9/12, 10/28, 11/30
Choices, 4/2, 8/1, 8/16,
    10/31, 11/22
Collective Economics, 3/16

Collective Responsibility,
    3/2, 3/8, 3/12, 4/24,
    6/19, 7/16, 11/7,
    11/21, 12/10, 12/16
Collective Work and
    Responsibility, 12/28
Coming-of-Age, 12/9
Confidence, 3/26, 7/14,
    12/11
Conscience, 2/26, 6/18, 7/8,
    7/28, 10/8, 12/22
Continuity, 2/19, 3/20, 5/2,
    5/21, 6/7, 8/26, 10/15,
    10/21, 11/23
Cooperative Economics,
    7/6, 10/10, 12/29
Courage, 8/24, 10/16, 11/6
Creative Thinking, 4/19,
    7/20, 11/9, 12/3
Creativity, 12/31

Dedication, 3/5, 7/21
Defining Ourselves, 5/11,
    7/4, 7/10, 8/22, 10/17,
    10/30, 12/17, 12/19

Demons, 2/21, 6/4
Determination, 1/19, 5/26,
    12/24
Echoes, 2/17, 11/27
Empowerment, 1/28, 3/15,
    4/3, 4/5, 4/23, 6/1,
    7/7, 7/22, 9/13, 11/20
Enjoyment, 1/16
Enterprise, 1/25
Excellence, 1/16, 4/3, 7/29,
    10/6, 12/6
Expectations, 3/22

Faith, 1/1
Foundations, 11/29
Freedom, 1/21, 6/26

Grief, 7/15
Growth, 3/30, 10/11

Healing, 9/23, 10/7
Heritage, 5/9
Human Spirit, 1/17, 1/30,
    6/14, 6/25, 7/9, 9/4,
    9/25

Identity, 1/8, 3/13, 3/17, 3/24, 3/28, 5/14, 6/30, 8/11, 8/14, 12/18
Images, 1/9, 2/10, 4/20, 5/22, 6/29, 10/29, 11/1, 11/24
Impossibility, 6/6
Initiative, 1/13, 1/22, 11/11, 11/15, 12/2
Innocence, 11/14
Inspiration, 1/10

Joy, 1/4, 1/31, 4/10, 4/15, 6/27, 9/2

Kwanzaa, 1/1, 12/26, 12/27, 12/28, 12/29, 12/30, 12/31

Legacies, 1/5, 1/24, 2/23, 4/1, 4/26, 5/18, 7/19, 9/5, 9/18, 9/22, 10/4, 12/5
Life, 8/3, 10/1
Life's Work, 1/7, 1/26, 2/7, 4/29, 7/1, 9/19, 12/20
Longevity, 12/21
Love, 2/20, 9/14, 10/14
Love of Learning, 1/29

Memory, 4/27, 5/19, 5/28, 6/28, 8/11
Messages, 1/20, 3/1, 4/28, 8/25, 9/6
Mutual Responsibility, 8/4

Opportunity, 5/1, 5/15, 6/15, 7/12

Passion, 1/2, 4/25, 5/12, 8/5, 10/5

Perspective, 3/4, 3/19, 4/6, 5/24, 10/13, 10/26, 11/4, 11/28
Possibility, 2/18, 6/13, 9/8
Power, 8/13, 8/28
Pragmatism, 6/3, 8/21, 8/27, 9/26
Precedents, 8/9, 9/20
Priorities, 4/4, 6/22, 7/17
Purpose, 7/30, 8/30, 12/30

Racial Dignity, 2/16, 4/16, 10/20
Re-visioning, 2/15, 3/18, 7/3, 7/5, 12/14
Reclamation, 7/27, 9/29, 10/3
Redefinitions, 3/3, 3/23
Respect for One's Power, 2/4, 3/9, 3/14, 5/5, 9/3, 10/19, 11/3, 11/10
Respect for Youth, 6/11
Responsibility to Self, 4/17
Responsibility to Youth, 1/27, 2/29, 3/27, 5/17, 5/23, 11/16, 11/25
Resurrection, 9/24
Rising from Defeat, 1/6, 7/23, 8/6, 9/28
Roots, 5/16, 9/17, 12/7, 12/12

Sacrifice, 1/12, 2/9, 4/8, 9/15
Self-affirmation, 2/1, 2/8, 4/11, 4/18, 4/21, 8/29, 10/22, 12/8
Self-assertion, 2/22, 5/7, 9/11
Self-concept, 2/25, 7/24, 8/20
Self-defense, 2/3, 6/23

Self-determination, 2/24, 5/10, 6/10, 7/25, 12/4, 12/27
Self-portraiture, 9/16, 12/15
Self-respect, 12/1
Self-worth, 4/13, 8/7, 8/10
Sharing, 4/22, 5/3, 12/25
Sisterhood, 2/14, 8/23, 10/25, 12/3
Spirit, 7/18, 8/8
Stature, 6/2
Success, 10/2

Tenacity, 1/15, 2/5, 3/25, 6/17, 11/19
Tradition, 11/5
Trailblazing, 4/30, 9/21
Transcendence, 3/7, 3/10, 6/8, 6/12
Transformation, 6/5
Truth, 2/6, 5/20, 5/27, 8/19, 9/1, 10/23, 11/17

Understanding, 2/13, 5/25, 6/9, 6/24, 11/8, 12/13
Unity, 3/29, 12/26

Values, 3/6, 8/12, 8/15, 10/24
Vision, 2/12, 3/11, 6/30, 10/18, 11/2, 11/6
Voice, 1/18, 4/9, 5/30

Wisdom, 6/21, 11/13
Witness, 6/16

Zest for Learning, 1/3
Zest for Life, 3/21, 10/27